Praise for Juan Gonzalez's
*Harvest of Empire*

"A serious, significant contribution to understanding who the Hispanics of the United States are and where they come from."
—*The New York Times Book Review*

"A profound book with an equally profound message about the origins of Latino migration, domination and colonization, and historical lessons not found in many American textbooks."
—*San Antonio Express-News*

"A compelling—and enlightening—chronicle . . . offers an insider's view of the rich and varied fabric of the people soon to be the largest minority in the United States."
—*The Miami Herald*

"Anyone who finishes *Harvest of Empire* will never again see Latinos as a monolithic group, but as a diverse society of citizens and future citizens, worthy of recognition and respect."
—*Fort Worth Morning Star*

"In what would seem an impossible task, journalist Juan Gonzalez tackles the entire history of Latinos in North and Central America in a single volume . . . illuminating."
—*Dallas Morning News*

"Required reading, not simply for Latinos but for everyone."
—*The Kansas City Star*

"Gonzalez's ever-enjoyable prose grabs the reader and fills in the gaps left by a traditional American history education."
—*In These Times*

PENGUIN BOOKS

# HARVEST OF EMPIRE

Juan Gonzalez, a columnist with New York's *Daily News*, and the winner of a 1998 George Polk journalism award, was named one of the nation's one hundred most influential Hispanics by *Hispanic Business,* and has received a lifetime achievement award from the Hispanic Academy of Media Arts and Sciences. Born in Ponce, Puerto Rico, he grew up in a New York City housing project, graduated from Columbia University, and was a cofounder of the 1960s Young Lords. He lives in Manhattan.

# HARVEST
## OF EMPIRE

*A History of Latinos
in America*

## JUAN GONZALEZ

PENGUIN BOOKS

PENGUIN BOOKS
Published by the Penguin Group
Penguin Putnam Inc., 375 Hudson Street, New York, New York 10014, U.S.A.
Penguin Books Ltd, 27 Wrights Lane, London W8 5TZ, England
Penguin Books Australia Ltd, Ringwood, Victoria, Australia
Penguin Books Canada Ltd, 10 Alcorn Avenue, Toronto, Ontario, Canada M4V 3B2
Penguin Books (N.Z.) Ltd, 182–190 Wairau Road, Auckland 10, New Zealand

Penguin Books Ltd, Registered Offices:
Harmondsworth, Middlesex, England

First published in the United States of America by Viking Penguin,
a member of Penguin Putnam Inc. 2000
Published in Penguin Books 2001

9  10  8

THE LIBRARY OF CONGRESS HAS CATALOGED
THE HARDCOVER EDITION AS FOLLOWS:
Gonzalez, Juan.
Harvest of empire: a history of Latinos in America/Juan Gonzalez.
p.  cm.
Includes bibliographical references.
ISBN 0-670-86720-9 (hc.)
ISBN 0 14 02.5539 7 (pbk.)
1. Hispanic Americans—History.   2. Immigrants—United States—History.
3. United States—Emigration and immigration—History.   4. Latin America—
Emigration and immigration—History.   5. United States—Relations—
Latin America.   6. Latin America—Relations—United States.   7. United
States—Territorial expansion—History.   8. United States—Ethnic relations.
I. Title.
E184.S75G655     2000
973'.0468—dc21          99–33526

Printed in the United States of America
Set in Sabon

The scorn of our formidable neighbor who does not know us is Our America's greatest danger. And since the day of the visit is near, it is imperative that our neighbor know us, and soon, so that it will not scorn us. Through ignorance it might even come to lay hands on us. Once it does know us, it will remove its hands out of respect. One must have faith in the best of men and distrust the worst.

—*José Martí,*
*January 10, 1891*

# Contents

# Introduction

Back in the third century B.C. the first Ch'in Dynasty emperor began China's Great Wall to stem the influx of Huns from the north. It took the Chinese several centuries to complete their barrier of stone, earth, and brick, which rises twenty-five feet high, extends for fifteen hundred miles, and remains a breathtaking testament to human insecurity.

Our American imitation is not nearly as impressive.

The federal government started its construction in the early 1990s, along sections of our two-thousand-mile border with Mexico, and by 1998, some sixty-two miles had been completed. In California, where it separates the sprawling shanty slums of Tijuana from the immaculate lawns of suburban San Diego, the wall is made of corrugated steel cobbled together from troop landing platforms left over from the Vietnam and Persian Gulf wars. There, it is ten feet high and barely an inch thick, with dull spikes combing its top. At other spots, it is made of salmon-colored concrete and has been rendered user-friendly by reinforced windows that allow passersby to peer into each other's country. On the U.S. side of the San Diego wall, a small army of Border Patrol agents, aided by helicopters and the latest computer, motion-sensor, and video technology, lies in wait day and night, ready to pounce on anyone who crosses illegally.[1] Agents apprehend an astounding ten thousand people a week and perhaps that many more still get through. In some places, people burrowed holes under the wall's base years ago. Graffiti dots the Tijuana side, slogans such as "No One Can Deny Us the Legal Right to Work."

"That wall doesn't stop anything," a young, fast-talking *coyote* told me in early 1992 as he waited for darkness to guide a group of women to the U.S. side. "What kind of steel is that?" he said, laughing. "A few weeks ago a car rammed right into it and knocked part of it down."

An old Indian woman sat huddled under a blanket nearby, her shriveled skin a maze of wrinkles. It had taken her three days to make the two-thousand-mile trip to the border from Guerrero in southern Mexico. "I'm going to see my son in Escondido," she whispered. "He's been there twenty years, but he doesn't visit much anymore. I want to see him one more time before I die." She kept staring at the ground, exhausted and waiting for night, when the *coyote* would lead her across. She is part of the endless stream of mothers, wives, fathers, and sons from all over Latin America who have set out on the same long journey to El Norte, often enduring years of separation from their loved ones, unable to return home lest the border shut them out forever.

While most make the crossing only once, some dare again and again. Jorge Giovanni López, a cocky young hustler I met in the central square of San Pedro Sula, Honduras, in 1990, described to me his numerous illegal crossings to visit relatives in Phoenix. In the same square where by day Giovanni ran a brisk black-market business exchanging Honduran lempiras for U.S. dollars, a rickety old school bus filled up at two o'clock each morning with passengers heading to the Guatemalan border and then on to the United States. The Hondurans would spend several days fording rivers and hopping buses through Guatemala and up the western coast of Mexico, until they reached Tijuana.[2]

The same scene is repeated each night in towns and cities throughout the southern half of the hemisphere as thousands set out for the United States, devising ever-changing routes of entry. Some escape homelands in economic chaos. Some flee death squads and government by bayonet. Others chase visions of wealth they have watched since childhood on television.

No one really expects makeshift walls, a few thousands more border agents, or some newfangled computer technology to stop the human flood—that would take a barrier greater than ancient China's. "We'll never stop the flow, but we can manage it better," Silvestre Reyes, the thoughtful Border Patrol sector chief in McAllen, Texas, and a former Marine captain in Vietnam, told me in 1995.[3]

The fact is, the U.S.-Mexico border has become the epicenter of momentous changes in our hemisphere: by day, a constant stream of trucks heading south, carrying goods and capital like never before to newly erected factories bustling with nearly a million low-wage workers; by night, the silent unstoppable flood of people heading north in search of the U.S. wages that can spell survival for a family the migrant has left behind. Both movements—of Yankee capital to the south and of Latin American labor to the north—have created huge windfalls for tiny investor elites on both sides of the border, while leaving horrendous social conditions in their wake. The poverty and environmental destruction along the Mexican border today in some ways surpass conditions chronicled by Dickens in nineteenth-century England or Sinclair in early twentieth-century America.

But this movement of labor northward, rivaling in size the great westward trek across the North American frontier by early European settlers, has led to something else—the Latinization of the United States. Unparalleled immigration has taken place from Mexico, the Caribbean, Central and South America since World War II, especially escalating since the 1960s. Some 14.2 million newcomers were admitted legally to the country between 1981 and 1997, and millions more came here illegally. When the final figures are in, the last two decades of the twentieth century will have surpassed the previous record from 1901 to 1920, when 14.4 million Europeans arrived. More than 50 percent of the immigrants since 1960 have been from Latin America—and that's not counting an estimated 2.7 million Latinos believed to be here illegally, or the hundreds of thousands of Puerto Rican migrants the Immigration and Naturalization Service doesn't keep track of because they are already U.S. citizens.[4]

In 1995, the Hispanic-origin population of the United States was 26.6 million, or 10 percent of all residents. If you include Puerto Rico's population of 3.8 million, the total swells to 30.4 million. Overall, the number of Latinos in the country will mushroom to more than 40 million by the year 2010. By that time, Hispanics, who are reproducing at a faster rate than either the white or the black population, and who are on the average younger, will be the largest minority group in the country.[5]

Moreover, that growth has been concentrated in the nation's largest urban areas. New York City is already 28 percent Hispanic, with some 2 million Puerto Ricans, Dominicans, Colombians, and other Central Americans in the five boroughs; Los Angeles is more than 40 percent Hispanic; Miami more than 50 percent. The four most populous states—California, New York, Texas, and Florida—contain more than 60 percent of the nation's Latinos. In both California and Texas, one of every four residents is Latino.

This demographic shift is so massive it is transforming the ethnic composition of the country and challenging key aspects of its accepted national identity, language, culture, and official history, a seismic social change that caught the power structures and institutions of U.S. society unprepared. Instead of seeking to address the causes of that change, those institutions attempted in the 1990s simply to repress and reverse it.

Not too long ago, Latin America was thought of as an exotic and beckoning backyard for U.S. power and influence, a series of nondescript banana republics and semicivilized nations where Americans often ventured for adventure or for vacations or to accumulate cheap land or make huge fortunes. The region's hapless governments became perpetual prey to the intrigues of competing circles of U.S. bankers and investors and to the gunboat diplomacy of U.S. presidents. But now Latino migrants, the product of those old inequities, have invaded the North American garden, kitchen, and living room. We are overflowing its schools, its army, even its jails.

That mushrooming presence has sparked enormous insecurity among citizens of European descent, a disturbing number of whom started to believe in the 1990s that the country was under attack by modern-day Huns, hordes of Spanish-speaking "barbarians at the gate." They saw images of Mexican street gangs in Los Angeles and Phoenix, Puerto Rican unmarried mothers on welfare in New York and Boston, Colombian drug dealers in Miami, or illegal Central American laborers in Houston and San Francisco. These immigrants, they were told in countless news reports, refused to assimilate, clung to their native language and culture, and were disproportionately swelling the ranks of the country's poor.

In response, conservatives legislated for tougher immigration and English-only laws, while violence and hate crimes directed against immigrants surged. In May 1990, for instance, twenty-one-year-old Leonard Cuen and two friends were drinking beer and popping pills in Cuen's house in suburban San Diego when they decided to go out and "shoot some aliens." One of the men with Cuen, Dwight Pannel, grabbed a high-powered rifle and fired at twelve-year-old Emilio Jiménez Bejinez, who was crossing the border three hundred yards away with his uncle. The boy was killed instantly. Pannel pleaded guilty to involuntary manslaughter and was sentenced to two years in jail, proving how little a Mexican immigrant boy's life can be worth.[6]

As the size of the Latino population skyrocketed, even politically moderate Americans became troubled by the demographic changes, by what they considered a rise of ethnic nationalism in the new immigrants. And they perceived the new multicultural education movement in the public schools and universities as helping to nurture that dangerous nationalism by questioning the Eurocentered traditions of U.S. history and by fostering such radical reforms as bilingual education.

Nothing seems to inflame advocates of our nation's Anglo-Saxon traditions so much as this issue of language. Since a people's culture—its music, literature, and customs—is inevitably expressed through its language, the growth of "foreign" language use somehow implied the growth of foreign cultures. In 1990, for instance, more than 32 million Americans spoke English as a second language, a phenomenal one-third increase over 1980, and for more than half of those 32 million, Spanish was the primary tongue. Thus, Hispanics increasingly were seen, whether rightly or not, as the vanguard of a linguistic threat. From public school classrooms and voting booths, to driver's tests, bank machines, and advertising, to two competing Spanish-language television networks, the Hispanic presence was not only growing at breakneck speed, it was digging roots.

White Americans are not alone in their fear of uncontrolled Third World immigration. In Great Britain, Pakistanis, Indians, and Jamaicans have unnerved native whites. In France, a growing right-wing movement targets Algerians and Tunisians. In Germany, immigrants from Africa, Southeast Asia, and Eastern Europe have drawn the ire of native citizens.[7] Since World War II, the shrinking of the modern world through air travel and mass communications—today, the poorest slum dweller in Honduras or Jamaica has access through television to images of U.S. society and can find a way to reach it—and the ever-widening chasm between the rich, developed countries on the one hand and poverty-stricken Asia, Africa, and Latin America on the other have fueled unprecedented mass emigration to the West. Invariably, the old colonial ties mean that Third World immigrants gravitate to the metropolises of their former colonial masters.

Here at home, however, most of us have little knowledge of the colonial and economic empire our political leaders and multinational corporations created during the period of U.S. territorial expansion in the nineteenth and early twentieth century, or how that empire laid the basis for and helped to spark massive Latino immigration after World War II. Most of us are uncomfortable thinking of our nation as an empire, even if Wall Street's currency speculators and investment bankers have repeatedly shown their ability to wreck entire economies halfway around the globe in a matter of hours—a power far greater than the Roman or Ottoman empire ever wielded. Our public schools have failed miserably in this regard, for they have taught us almost nothing about the machinations that accompanied territorial expansion, or that helped bring about U.S. economic domination of the modern world. Nor have the schools taught us the important contributions and complex saga of Latin Americans within that empire.

"Why do you Hispanics insist on speaking Spanish?" I have been asked innumerable times. "You're in America now." Or "Why are there so many Puerto Ricans on welfare? You won't get anywhere until you stop depending on the government to help you." Or "Why do you prefer to be called Hispanics or Latinos or Puerto Ricans, why not just Americans?" As a newspaper columnist, I regularly receive anonymous letters and calls from some Anglo readers so openly filled with hatred and venom toward Hispanics they make you shudder at the irrationality they reveal. Many of these callers, ironically, are the descendants of European immigrants who had to endure similar intolerance. Yet they are quick to conclude that Latin Americans in this country are ungrateful newcomers who refuse to do what others have done before them.

Immigrants have existed, of course, from the beginning of civilization. And the basic reasons people move from one land to another have not changed in all that time—starvation or deteriorating conditions, political or religious persecution, a chance to improve one's lot by starting anew somewhere else. But Latin American migration and the Latino presence in this country, as I hope to show in this book, differed from that of the Europeans in several important ways.

First, the Latino migrant flows were directly connected to the growth of a U.S. empire, and they responded closely to that empire's needs, whether it was a political need to stabilize a neighboring country or to accept its refugees as a means of accomplishing a broader foreign policy objective (Cubans, Dominicans, Salvadorans, Nicaraguans), or whether it was an economic need, such as satisfying the labor demands of particular U.S. industries (Mexicans, Puerto Ricans, Panamanians).

Second, once the Latin Americans got here, they moved not from an immigrant to a mainstream status, but from an immigrant to a linguistic/racial caste status, mostly as a result of how language and race conflicts have been dealt with throughout United States and Latin America history.

Third, most Latin Americans arrived here when the United States was already the world's dominant power, as our society was entering a postindustrial period and as our gap between rich and poor was growing, which meant that the unskilled factory jobs European immigrants had utilized to rise into the middle class were no longer a major option.

But just as important as understanding the broader social forces involved in Latino immigration is comprehending the human saga of the people involved. Why did each Latino group come when it did? Why did some come and others not migrate at all? What did the pioneers of each group find when they got here? How did they interact with other Americans? How did they build their communities? Why did some retreat into ethnic enclaves and others not? How are Latinos changing the nation, and how do Anglo-Americans, white and black, feel about those changes?

This book explores answers to many of those questions by presenting an integrated historical look at both Latin America and Latinos in the United States—how both contributed to and were affected by the development of American ideals and American reality.

The book is divided into three main sections, which I have called "Roots," "Branches," and "Harvest." The first section, composed of three chapters, traces the long and tortuous relationship between Latin America and the United States. The first chapter, covering the colonial period, summarizes how Latin America and the United States developed into such radically different societies from the 1500s to independence; the second, how the United States expanded into an empire during the nineteenth century through seizing and exploiting Latin American territories; and the third, how our leaders turned the Caribbean region into a U.S. protectorate in the twentieth century. Admittedly, reviewing five hundred years of New World history in three short chapters is a daunting task, so be forewarned: I attempt to focus on key lessons and patterns that I have culled from various histories by both Anglo and Latin American authors, with an eye toward what light can be shed on our contemporary situation.

The second section, "Branches," is composed of six chapters, each devoted to one of the major Latino groups in the country. Here I combine the research of others on the modern migration saga with my own oral history interviews and investigations as a journalist. Although all Latin Americans share the same general relationship to the United States, each nation's immigration story is unique in the times it occurred, the class and type of people who came, and the way they dealt with their new environment. Our immigrant tales are as varied as those of the Swedish, Irish, Germans, Poles, and Italians who preceded us. No doubt, several books could be devoted to each Latino group, so rich are the varied experiences, but I chose to focus my individual chapters on a family or a few individuals who tend to reflect the general migration story of that group, especially its early years. I have tried to zero in on immigrants who became leaders or pioneers of the migration, and who have thus spent some time consciously digesting their own experiences. Most of the individuals are people whom I have met during more than twenty years working as a journalist here and in Mexico, Central America, and the Caribbean. They are not the usual ethnic politicians whom outsiders look for when they want a quick read on how a community feels or acts. Rather, I have focused on grassroots leaders, people who clearly have earned the respect of their fellow migrants, but who rarely get interviewed or known outside their own communities.

The final section, "Harvest," is about Latinos in America today. It is composed of five chapters on some of the most important issues the average American usually identifies with Latinos—politics, immigration, language and culture. In addition, I have added a chapter on what I believe to be a little-understood cause for Latin American migration over the past fifty years—U.S. trade policy, or what should more properly be called globalization. Finally, there is a chapter on Puerto Rico. Why a whole chapter? Well, that tiny island in the Caribbean has been a bigger source of profit for U.S. investors during the twentieth century than any other country in the world. It also happens to be the last major American colonial possession. Yet it receives very little attention commensurate with its importance in media or academic circles. During the past few years, every major political leader and faction in Puerto Rico has called on Congress to end its colonial control and authorize a genuine decolonization plebiscite, but Washington simply ignores that request. Ending colonialism in Puerto Rico is a major issue with far-reaching repercussions for this entire nation, as well as for the 6.6 million Puerto Ricans here and on the island. Until Puerto Rico is decolonized, American democracy will not be complete.

The book is aimed at the general reader who wishes to deepen his or her understanding about Hispanics as well as at the growing number of Latino professionals, students, and intellectuals, who may know a great deal about their particular ethnic group—Chicanos, Puerto Ricans, Cubans, for instance—but little else about any other Hispanics. The ignorance and prejudice between different Hispanic groups rarely get examined. I remember getting a telephone call in January 1997 from Doña Carmen Livigne, an eighty-four-year-old Puerto Rican pioneer in East Harlem. "Mr. Gonzalez, you have to do something about all these Mexicans," she pleaded. "They're taking over our church." Livigne was an elder of Holy Agony, a Catholic church that blue-collar Puerto Rican migrants built with their contributions in the early 1950s. But in the 1990s, Mexicans started moving into East Harlem in droves. Today, the

Puerto Rican elders run Holy Agony, but Mexicans are the majority of its congregation.

"And the first thing they [the Mexicans] want to do," Livigne complained, "is put the statue of the Virgen de Guadalupe in the front of the church! They think if they have her up front they can run the place. I told them, 'That's your Virgin, not ours.'" Of course, Catholics of every nationality have their own image of the Virgin Mary. For Puerto Ricans, it is the Virgen de la Providencia; for Dominicans, La Virgen de Altagracia; for Cubans, La Virgen de Cobre. But East Harlem's battle of the virgins suggests Latinos, like the Polish, Irish, and Italian immigrants of prior eras, have much to overcome among ourselves.

So who am I to undertake such an ambitious task? Well, I was born in 1947 to working-class parents in Ponce, Puerto Rico. My family brought me to New York City's El Barrio the following year and I have lived in this country ever since. As a journalist, and before that as a Puerto Rican community activist who helped to found and direct two national organizations, the Young Lords in the 1960s and the National Congress for Puerto Rican Rights in the late 1970s, I have spent decades living in, traveling to and reporting on scores of Latino communities throughout the United States and Latin America, devouring in the process every study or account of the Latino experience I could find.

Mine is the perspective of a Latino who has grown tired of having our story told, often one-sidedly, without the passion or the pain, by "experts" who have not lived it. There have been several such well-intentioned efforts for the general reader over the years—Carey McWilliams's old classic, *North from Mexico,* Gann and Duignan's *The Hispanics in the U.S.,* Thomas Weyr's *Hispanic U.S.A.,* Earl Shorris's *Latinos, Biography of a People,* Geoffrey Fox's *Hispanic Nation,* to name just a few. And the past decade or so has seen quite a few attempts, at long last, by Latino writers and journalists—Richard Rodriguez's *Hunger of Memory,* Linda Chavez's *Out of the Barrio,* Edna Acosta-Belén's *The Hispanic Experience in the United States,* Ilan Stavans's *The Hispanic Condition,* Roberto Suro's *Strangers Among Us,* and Alejandro Portes's *Immigrant America.* Almost all of them, however, fall into what I call the safari approach, geared strictly to an Anglo audience, with the author as guide and interpreter to the natives to be encountered along the way.

In our universities, meanwhile, many fine historians have broken important ground with their research into Latino life in this country, but it has usually been narrowly focused on one Latino group or area—culture or politics or a specific period of history—and because of that has not drawn the attention of a broader audience. To mention just a few whose work was invaluable to me: Carlos Castañeda, Rodolfo Acuña, David Montejano, Arnoldo de León, Patricia Nelson Limerick, David Weber, and Juan Gómez Quiñones on Mexicans; Louis A. Pérez, Jr., and María Cristina García on Cubans; Ronald Fernández, Clara Rodríguez, Virginia Sánchez Korrol, Ivonne Acosta, the Reverend Joseph Fitzpatrick, Andrés Torres, and others on Puerto Ricans; and, of course, John Storm Roberts's penetrating history of Latino music in the United States.

Few of the general or specialized histories have attempted to mark out a broad-enough canvas, to connect the past to the present, to cut across academic disciplines, while still making the entire process coherent to both Latinos and Anglos. Few, except for Stavans's fine foray into cultural analysis, have sought to delineate a vision of the future for our fast-growing and still culturally schizophrenic Latino intellectuals. Few attempt to understand our hemisphere *as one New World, north and south*. None trace the seamless bond between Anglo dominance of Latin America—two hundred years of massive and ever-increasing transfers of wealth from south to north, what Uruguayan Eduardo Galeano has called "the open veins of Latin America"—and the modern flood of the region's people to the United States. It is the view of this book that one would not exist without the other.

If Latin America had not been raped and pillaged by U.S. capital since its independence, millions of desperate workers would not now be coming here in such numbers to reclaim a share of that wealth; and if the United States is today the world's richest nation, it is in part because of the sweat and blood of the copper workers of Chile, the tin miners of Bolivia, the fruit pickers of Guatemala and Honduras, the cane cutters of Cuba, the oil workers of Venezuela and Mexico, the pharmaceutical workers of Puerto Rico, the ranch hands of Costa Rica and Argentina, the West Indians who died building the Panama Canal, and the Panamanians who maintained it.

In this country, just how white and black America cope with the mushrooming Latin American population will determine whether our nation enjoys interethnic tranquillity in the twenty-first century or is convulsed by conflicts such as those tearing apart the multiethnic states of Eastern Europe, the Soviet Union, and elsewhere.

The reader will hopefully find in these pages not facile solutions to complex problems but a frank attempt to make sense of both the Latin American and North American experience. It has not been easy to separate my head from my heart the past eight years of laboring on this proj-

ect. I have met too many Latinos throughout my life who struggled and
sacrificed far beyond the endurance of most of us to create something
better for their children, yet found no respite and little respect, only to
be, as poet Pedro Pietri once wrote, "buried without underwears." The
deeper I have delved into the two-hundred-year record of endless
shenanigans by our statesmen, businessmen, and generals in Latin
America, the angrier I have become, especially since those leaders never
seem to learn from the past. My anger, however, is not tainted by hate; it
comes from the frustration of seeing how bountiful our nation's promise
has turned out for some, how unnecessarily heartbreaking for others, and
it is tempered by the conviction that the American people still cling to a
basic sense of fairness, that once they understand the facts, they rarely
permit injustice to stand, which is in part why I have included in the book
a plethora of *facts* not commonly known about Latinos.

Hopefully, by the time you have finished the book, you will see the
Latino in America from another viewpoint. We Hispanics are not going
away. Demographics and the tide of history point only to a greater not a
lesser Latino presence throughout the new century. Ours, however, is not
some armed *reconquista* seeking to throw out Anglo occupiers from sacred lands that were once Latino. It is a search for survival, for inclusion
on an equal basis, nothing more. It is a search grounded in the belief that,
five hundred years after the experiment began, we are all Americans of
the New World, and our most dangerous enemies are not each other but
the great wall of ignorance between us.

———

A word about language usage. I believe needless time has been spent by
Latino intellectuals in this country debating whether the term "Hispanic"
or "Latino" best describes us. Neither is totally accurate but both are acceptable, and I use them interchangeably in this book. Much as blacks in
this country went from being comfortable with "colored," then Negro,
then black, then African American, so will U.S. Latin Americans pass
through our phases. I remember back in the mid-1980s attending a joint
conference in Mexico of Mexican and U.S. Hispanic journalists. The small
Indian town near where the conference was being held organized a reception for us visitors one night. The town square was decorated with a huge
banner that read: *"Bienvenidos, periodistas hispano-norteamericanos"*
("Welcome, Hispanic–North American journalists"). So, to each his own
labels.

Likewise, we all know the word "America" has been unfairly appropriated by the people of the United States to refer to this country when

it actually refers to the entire hemisphere. Latin Americans, meanwhile, refer to the United States as *norteamérica,* or North America, and U.S. citizens are known as *norteamericanos* (apologies to Canada). And in Mexican American communities here, whites commonly are called Anglos. Here, too, I have eschewed purism, using Americans, North Americans, and Anglos interchangeably.

I have used Mexican Americans or Chicanos to refer to Mexicans born and raised in the U.S., and *mexicanos, tejanos, californios* to refer to those Mexicans who lived in the country before the Treaty of Guadalupe Hidalgo made them U.S. citizens. I have italicized Spanish words whenever possible and have provided a glossary of definitions of those words at the back of the book.

That said, I ask you to travel back with me to tear down some walls and begin a new journey through the American story.

# PART I

## Roots
## (Las Raíces)

# 1

## Conquerors and Victims:
## The Image of America Forms
## (1500–1800)

> We saw cues and shrines in these cities that looked like gleaming white towers and castles: a marvelous site.
> —*Bernal Díaz del Castillo, 1568*

The arrival of European explorers to America began the most astounding and far-reaching encounter between cultures in the history of civilization. It brought together two portions of the human race that until then had known nothing of each other's existence, thus establishing the basic identity of our modern world. French writer and critic Tzvetan Todorov has called it "the discovery *self* makes of the *other*"; while Adam Smith labeled it one of "the two greatest and most important events recorded in the history of mankind."[1]

Of the Europeans who settled America, those who hailed from England and Spain had the greatest impact. Both transplanted their cultures over vast territories. Both created colonial empires from whose abundance Europe rose to dominate the world. And descendants of both eventually launched independence wars that remade the political systems of our planet.

That common history has made Latin Americans and Anglo Americans, like the Arabs and Jews of the Middle East, cousins in constant conflict, often hearing but not understanding each other. Most of us know little of the enormous differences between how the Spanish and English settled America, or how those disparities led after independence to nations with such radically divergent societies. For just as adults develop key personality traits in the first years of childhood, so it was with the new nations of America, their collective identities and outlooks, their languages and social customs, molded by centuries in the colonial womb.

This first chapter seeks to probe how both Latin American and Anglo American cultures were shaped from their colonial beginnings in the

1500s to the independence wars of the early 1800s, particularly how each culture took root in separate regions of what now makes up the United States.

What kind of people were the original English and Spanish settlers and how did the views and customs they brought with them affect the America they fashioned? What was the legacy of the settlers' religious beliefs, racial policies, and economic relationships? How did the colonial systems of their mother countries influence their political traditions? How were the rights of individuals regarded in the two groups of colonies? How did divergent views toward land, its ownership and its uses, promote or retard the development of their societies? To what degree did the various Amerindian civilizations the Europeans conquered influence the settlers' own way of life?

## WHEN WORLDS COLLIDE

The native population at the time of first contact has been much debated. Estimates vary wildly, though there seems little doubt that it equaled or surpassed that of Europe. Most likely, it was around 60 million; some scholars place it as high as 110 million.[2] The greatest number, perhaps 25 million, lived in and around the Valley of Mexico, another 6 million inhabited the Central Andes region, while the territory north of the Rio Grande was home to perhaps another 10 million.[3] A bewildering level of uneven development prevailed among these Native Americans. The Han and Capoque were still in the Stone Age, nomads foraging naked along the bayous of the North American Gulf Coast. The slave-based city-states of the Aztecs, Mayas, and Incas, on the other hand, rivaled the sophistication and splendor of Europe. The Aztec capital of Tenochtitlán was a bustling metropolis. Meticulously designed and ingeniously constructed in the middle of a lake, where it was accessible only by well-guarded causeways, it contained some 250,000 inhabitants when Hernán Cortés first entered it. (London's population at the time was a mere 50,000 and that of Seville, the greatest city in Castile, barely 40,000.) The Spaniards were awestruck. One of Cortés's captains, Bernal Díaz del Castillo, left a vivid description of what he and his fellow Spaniards beheld that first day from the top of the central Aztec temple:

> We saw a great number of canoes, some coming with provisions and others returning with cargo and merchandise; and we saw too that one could not pass from one house to another of that great city and the other cities that were built on water except over wooden draw-

bridges or by canoe. We saw . . . shrines in these cities that looked like gleaming white towers and castles: a marvelous sight.

Some of our soldiers who had been in many parts of the world, in Constantinople, in Rome, and all over Italy, said they had never seen a market so well laid out, so large, so orderly, and so full of people.[4]

But Aztec civilization could not compare in grandeur, archaeologists tell us, to its predecessor, the city-state of Teotihuacán, which flourished for several centuries before it collapsed mysteriously in A.D. 700, leaving behind soul-stirring pyramids and intricate murals and artifacts as clues to its resplendent past. Nor did the Aztecs approach the sophistication of the Mayans, America's Greeks, whose mathematicians and astronomers surpassed any in antiquity and whose scholars invented during their Classic Period (A.D. 300 to 900) the hemisphere's only known phonetic script.

Farther north, beyond the Rio Grande, hundreds of native societies existed when the Europeans arrived, all with their own languages and traditions, though only the Pueblos of New Mexico and the Iroquois Confederation in the Northeast approached the level of civilization reached by the natives of Meso- and South America. The Pueblos were descended from the even larger and more advanced Anasazi, who flourished in present-day Colorado, New Mexico, and Arizona during the twelfth and thirteenth centuries A.D. before they, too, mysteriously disappeared. By the time the first Spaniards arrived in the region in 1540, the Pueblos numbered around sixteen thousand. They were living in small cities of multilevel adobe apartments built on high plateaus, among them Acoma, Zuñi, and Hopi. A peaceful, sedentary civilization, the Pueblos survived off the ocean of barren scrubland and buttes by planting extensively in river bottoms. They practiced a complicated animist religion that revolved around their ceremonial center, the kiva, where they taught their young that "competitiveness, aggressiveness and the ambition to lead were . . . offensive to the supernatural powers."[5]

The Iroquois Confederation, formed around 1570 by the Mohawk shaman, or chief, Hiawatha, was the largest and most durable alliance of native societies in North American history. Its influence stretched from the hinterland of Lake Superior to the backwoods of Virginia. Feared by all other Indians, the Iroquois became gatekeepers to the huge fur trade and a decisive force in the competition between the English and French for its control. They lived in towns of up to several thousand residents in wooden longhouses protected by double or triple rings of stockades. Social authority in each of the five Iroquois nations was matrilineal. Women chose the men who served as each clan's delegates to the nation's council, and each nation, in turn, elected representatives to the confederation's fifty-member ruling body, the Council Fire. That council decided all issues affecting the confederation by consensus.

The Europeans who stumbled upon this kaleidoscope of Amerindian civilizations were themselves just emerging from a long period of backwardness. The Black Death had swept out of Russia in 1350, leaving 25 million dead. There followed a relentless onslaught of epidemics that so devastated the continent that its population declined by 60 to 75 percent in the span of a hundred years. So few peasants were left to work the land that feudal society disintegrated, the price of agricultural labor soared, and new classes of both rich peasants and poor nobles came into being. The sudden labor shortage spurred technical innovation as a way to increase production, and that innovation, in turn, led to the rise of factories in the cities. The social upheaval brought about a new mobility among the long-suffering peasantry, and with it a new aggressiveness. Rebellions by the starving poor against their feudal lords became more frequent. Some even assailed the all-powerful Catholic Church, whose bishops preached piety to the common man while surrounded by the privileges of the nobility.[6]

By the fifteenth century, the frequency of plagues ebbed, population rebounded, and the continent emerged into a dazzling era of artistic and scientific achievement. The first printing presses disseminated the new knowledge widely, through books written in scores of vernacular languages, ending forever the monopoly of Latin and the stranglehold of the clergy on learning. In 1492, as Columbus launched Europe's historic encounter with the Amerindians, Renaissance geniuses like Hieronymus Bosch and Leonardo da Vinci were at the apex of their fame; the German master Albrecht Dürer, was twenty-one; Niccolò Machiavelli was twenty-three; Dutchman Desiderius Erasmus was twenty-six; the Englishman Thomas More was fourteen; Copernicus was only nineteen, and Martin Luther a boy of eight.

The revolutions in production and in knowledge were reflected in politics as well. For the first time, strong monarchs ruled England and Spain, kings who were determined to create unified nations out of fiefdoms that had quarreled and warred against each other since the fall of the Roman empire.

Foremost among those monarchs were King Ferdinand of Aragón and Queen Isabella of Castile, who joined their twin kingdoms and finally ousted the Moors in 1492 from the Kingdom of Granada, the last Arab stronghold in Europe. For most of the previous eight centuries, Moors had occupied the Iberian Peninsula, where they withstood fierce but intermittent crusades by Christian Spaniards to reclaim their land. Those crusades—the Spanish call them La Reconquista—had succeeded over the centuries in slowly shunting the Moors farther south, until only Granada remained in Arab hands.

Ironically, the Moorish occupation and La Reconquista prepared Spain for its imperial role in America. The occupation turned the country and the city of Córdoba into the Western world's premier center for the study of science and philosophy, while the fighting engendered a hardened warrior ethos in the *hidalgos,* Spain's lower nobility. It was those *hidalgos* who later rushed to fill the ranks of the *conquistador* armies in the New World. The wars provided vital practice in colonization, with Spanish kings gradually adopting the practice of paying their warriors with grants from land they recovered in battle. Finally, La Reconquista reinforced a conviction among Spaniards that they were the true defenders of Catholicism.

Unlike Spain, which grew monolithic through La Reconquista, England emerged from the Middle Ages bedeviled by strife among its own people. The most bloody of those conflicts was the thirty-year Wars of the Roses, which finally drew to a close in 1485 when Henry Tudor of the House of Lancaster vanquished Richard III of the House of York. Henry VII quickly distinguished himself by creating a centralized government and reliable system of taxation, the first English monarch to do so. His success was due in no small measure to the prosperity of English farming, to the flowering of English nationalism, and to his enlightened concessions to local self-government. Henry's subjects proudly believed themselves to be better off than any people in Europe, and they were largely right, for neither the widespread class divisions nor the famine and squalor that afflicted much of the continent during the fifteenth century could be found in England. Slavery, for instance, did not exist in the kingdom, and English serfs already enjoyed greater liberties than their European counterparts.[7] The yeomanry, small farmers who comprised a large middle class between the gentry and the serfs, fostered economic stability and provided a counterweight to curb the power of the nobility. At the same time, Parliament and the traditions of English common law accorded the average citizen greater protection from either the king or his nobles than any other political system in Europe.

Such were the conditions in 1497 when Henry, fired by news of Columbus's discoveries, dispatched explorer John Cabot to America. Cabot landed in Newfoundland and laid claim to North America for the British

Crown, but he perished in a subsequent trip before establishing a colony. That failure, along with the discovery of gold and silver in Mexico and Peru a few decades later, permitted Spain to catapult to the pinnacle of sixteenth-century world power. Meanwhile, the English, bereft of colonies and increasingly consumed by religious and political strife at home, were reduced to sniping at Spanish grandeur through the exploits of their pirates.

When they finally did embark on a New World empire a century later, the English brought with them not just their tradition of local self-government but the vestiges of their domestic conflicts as well, most important of which were the religious schisms and sects that arose after Henry VIII broke with the pope in Rome and established the Church of England. Among those sects, one in particular, the Puritans, was destined to leave a vast imprint on American society.

Another "British" conflict that was to greatly influence the New World was the colonizing of Catholic Ireland and the bloody repression that accompanied it. By their callous treatment of the Irish, Anglo-Norman Protestants set the stage for the massive Irish flight that followed. English leaders justified that occupation by claiming that the Irish were a barbarian people, but in doing so, they gave birth to notions of Anglo-Saxon superiority that they would later use to justify their conquest of Native Americans.[8]

## EARLY SPANISH INFLUENCE IN THE UNITED STATES

The textbooks most of us read in grammar school have long acknowledged that Spanish *conquistadores* crisscrossed and laid claim to much of the southern and western United States nearly a century before the first English colonies were founded at Jamestown and Massachusetts Bay. But most Anglo American historians have promoted the view that the early Spanish presence rapidly disappeared and left a minor impact on U.S. culture when compared to our dominant Anglo-Saxon heritage.

Those early expeditions, however, led to permanent Spanish outposts throughout North America, to the founding of our earliest cities, Saint Augustine and Santa Fe, and to the naming of hundreds of U.S. rivers, mountains, towns, and even several states. Moreover, they led to a Spanish-speaking population—more accurately, a Latino/*mestizo* population—that has existed continuously in certain regions of the United States since that time. That heritage, and the colonial society it spawned, has been so often overlooked in contemporary debates over culture, language, and immigration that we would do well to review its salient parts.

Juan Ponce de León was the first European to touch what is now U.S. soil. His fruitless search for the Fountain of Youth led to his discovery in 1513 of La Florida. He returned eight years later but was killed in battle with the Calusa Indians before he could found a settlement.

Nearly two decades after Ponce de León's death, Francisco Vásquez de Coronado and Hernando de Soto, their imaginations fired by the treasures Cortés had seized in Mexico, each led major expeditions in search of the fabled cities of gold. Starting from central Mexico in 1539, Coronado and his men marched north into present-day Arizona, New Mexico, Texas, Oklahoma, and Kansas, planting the Spanish flag wherever they went. By the time the expedition returned in 1542, the Spaniards had discovered the Grand Canyon, crossed and named many of the continent's great rivers, but discovered no gold. The same year Coronado set out, De Soto led an expedition out of Cuba that explored much of Georgia, South Carolina, Alabama, Mississippi, Arkansas, and Louisiana, but he and half his men perished without finding any treasure.

The most extraordinary exploit of all, however, was that of Álvar Núñez Cabeza de Vaca, who arrived in Florida in 1527—fifteen years before De Soto—as second-in-command to Pánfilo de Narváez, the bungling onetime governor of Cuba whom King Charles of Spain authorized to complete the colonization of Florida. After landing on the peninsula's western coast, Narváez led a three-hundred-man expedition inland near present-day Tallahassee, then foolishly lost touch with his ships and was killed. His men, unable to withstand the constant Indian attacks, headed west along the Gulf Coast on makeshift barges.

Only four survived the ordeal, among them Cabeza de Vaca and a Spanish Moor named Estevanico. The four spent the next seven years wandering through the North American wilderness. Their six-thousand-mile trek, one of the great exploration odysseys of history, and the first crossing of North America by Europeans, is preserved in a report Cabeza de Vaca wrote for the king of Spain in 1542. At first, they were separated and enslaved by coastal tribes, where Cabeza de Vaca was beaten so often his life became unbearable. After a year in captivity, he managed to escape and took up the life of a trader between the tribes: "Wherever I went, the Indians treated me honorably and gave me food, because they liked my commodities. I became well known; those who did not know me personally knew me by reputation and sought my acquaintance."[9]

His rudimentary medical knowledge enabled him at one point to cure some sick Indians. From that point on, the tribes revered him as a medicine man. Once a year, when the various tribes gathered for the annual

picking of prickly pears, he was reunited with his fellow Spaniards, who
remained enslaved. At one such gathering in 1533, he engineered their
escape and they all fled west through present-day Texas, New Mexico,
and Arizona. As they traveled, word spread of the wondrous white medicine man and his companions, and soon thousands of Indians started to
follow in a caravan of worshipers. The four did not finally reconnect with
Spanish civilization in northern Mexico until 1534. By then, Cabeza de
Vaca had been transformed. He no longer regarded the Native American as a savage, for he now had an intimate understanding of their culture and outlook. Instead, the barbarity of his fellow Spaniards toward
the Indians now filled him with despair. His description of his trip
through an area where Spanish slave traders were hunting Indians remains a powerful revelation into the nature of the Conquest:

> With heavy hearts we looked out over the lavishly watered, fertile,
> and beautiful land, now abandoned and burned and the people thin
> and weak, scattering or hiding in fright. Not having planted, they
> were reduced to eating roots and bark; and we shared their famine
> the whole way. Those who did receive us could provide hardly any-
> thing. They themselves looked as if they would willingly die. They
> brought us blankets they had concealed from the other Christians
> and told us how the latter had come through razing the towns and
> carrying off half the men and all the women and boys.[10]

## THE TOLL OF CONQUEST

The devastation Cabeza de Vaca warned of still defies comprehension.
By the late 1500s, a mere century after the Conquest began, scarcely 2
million natives remained in the entire hemisphere. An average of more
than 1 million people perished annually for most of the sixteenth century, in what has been called "the greatest genocide in human history."[11]
On the island of Hispaniola, which was inhabited by 1 million Tainos in
1492, less than 46,000 remained twenty years later.[12] As historian Francis
Jennings has noted, "The American land was more like a widow than a
virgin. Europeans did not find a wilderness here; rather, however invol-
untarily, they made one."

Fewer natives perished in the English colonies only because the
Amerindian populations were sparser to begin with, yet the macabre
percentages were no less grisly: 90 percent of the Indian population was
gone within half a century of the Puritan landing on Plymouth Rock; the
Block Island Indians plummeted from 1,500 to 51 between 1662 and

1774; the Wampanoag tribe of Martha's Vineyard declined from 3,000 in 1642 to 313 in 1764; and the Susquehannock tribe in central Pennsylvania nearly disappeared, falling from 6,500 in 1647 to 250 by 1698.[13]

Much of this cataclysm was unavoidable. The Indians succumbed to smallpox, measles, tuberculosis, and bubonic plague, for which they had no immunity, just as Europeans had succumbed to their own epidemics in previous centuries. But an astounding number of native deaths resulted from direct massacres or enslavement. If the Spaniards exterminated more than the British or French, it is because they encountered civilizations with greater population, complexity, and wealth, societies that desperately resisted any attempt to subjugate them or seize their land and minerals.

The battle for Tenochtitlán, for instance, was rivaled in overall fatalities by few in modern history. During the eighty-day siege of the Aztec capital by Cortés and his Texcoco Indian allies, 240,000 natives perished.[14] A few Indian accounts of the battle survive today only because of Franciscan missionaries like Bernardino de Sahagún and Diego de Durán, who as early as 1524 developed a written form of the Nahuatl language, the lingua franca of central Mexico. The missionaries urged the Indians to preserve their tragic songs and reminiscences of the Conquest, and several of those accounts, such as the following section from the Codex Florentino, vividly describe what happened at Tenochtitlán:

> Once again the Spaniards started killing and a great many Indians died. The flight from the city began and with this the war came to an end. The people cried: "We have suffered enough! Let us leave the city! Let us go live on weeds!"
>
> A few of the men were separated from the others. These men were the bravest and strongest warriors. The youths who served them were also told to stand apart. The Spaniards immediately branded them with hot irons, either on the cheek or the lips.[15]

Less than a quarter century after the arrival of Columbus, the Indian genocide sparked its first protest from a Spaniard, Fray Bartolomé de las Casas, who had arrived in Santo Domingo as a landowner but opted instead to become a Franciscan missionary. The first priest ordained in America, he quickly relinquished his lands and launched a campaign against Indian enslavement that made him famous throughout Europe. As part of that campaign, he authored a series of polemics and defended the Indians in public debates against Spain's greatest philosophers. The most famous of those polemics, *A Short Account of the Destruction of the*

*Indies,* recounts scores of massacres by Spanish soldiers, including one ordered by Cuba's governor Pánfilo Narváez, which Las Casas personally observed. In that incident, according to Las Casas, a group of natives approached a Spanish settlement with food and gifts, when the Christians, "without the slightest provocation, butchered before my eyes, some three thousand souls—men, women and children, as they sat there in front of us."[16]

Las Casas's untiring efforts on behalf of the Amerindians led to Spain's adoption of "New Laws" in 1542. The codes recognized Indians as free and equal subjects of the Spanish Crown, but landowners in many regions refused to observe the codes and kept Indians in virtual slavery for generations. Despite his heroic efforts, Las Casas, who was eventually promoted to Bishop of Chiapas in Guatemala, also committed some major blunders. At one point he advocated using African slaves to replace Indian labor, though he ultimately recanted that position. While his polemics were among the most popular books in Europe and led to widespread debate over the toll of colonization, they greatly exaggerated the already grisly numbers of the Indian genocide, thus making Las Casas the unwitting source of the Spanish "Black Legend" propagated by Dutch and British Protestants.[17]

Spain, of course, had no monopoly on settler barbarism. In 1637, the Puritans of the Massachusetts Bay Colony mistakenly concluded that local Pequots had killed two white men, so they set out to punish them. Assisted by other Indian enemies of the tribe, the Englishmen attacked the Pequot village on the Mystic River while its braves were absent, and roasted or shot to death between three hundred and seven hundred women and children before burning the entire village.[18] Forty years later, during King Philip's War, colonists and their mercenaries conducted similar vicious slaughters of women and children. An estimated two thousand Indians perished in battle and another thousand were sold into slavery in the West Indies during the conflict.[19] And South Carolina's Cherokee War (1760–1761) turned so brutal that a colonist defending a fort against Indians wrote to the governor, "We have now the pleasure, Sir, to fatten our dogs with their carcasses and to display their scalps neatly ornamented on the top of our bastions."[20]

This type of savagery, often reciprocated by Indians desperate to defend their land, became a hallmark of Anglo-Indian relations far after the colonial period. A particularly gruesome example was carried out by Andrew Jackson in 1814. Settlers and land speculators from the Carolinas had started moving into the territory shortly after the War of Independence. When the settlers tried to push out the Indian inhabitants, the

Creeks resisted and the U.S. Army, led by Jackson, intervened. During the war's decisive battle at Horseshoe Bend, Alabama, on March 27, 1814, Jackson's men massacred and cut off the noses of 557 Creeks, then skinned the dead bodies to tan the Indian hides and make souvenir bridle reins.[21]

## THE ROLE OF THE CHURCH

While all European settlers justified the Indian conquest and genocide as God's will, the Spanish and English differed substantially in their methods of subjugation, and this eventually led to radically different colonial societies. English kings, for instance, ordered their agents to "conquer, occupy and possess" the lands of the "heathens and infidels," but said nothing of the people inhabiting them, while Spain, following the dictates of Pope Alexander VI, sought not only to grab the land but also to make any pagans found on it "embrace the Catholic faith and be trained in good morals." In Spain, both Crown and Church saw colonizing and conversion as a unified effort. Priests accompanied each military expedition for the purpose of Christianizing the natives. Within a month of landing in Mexico, Bernal Díaz reminds us, Cortés presided over the first Indian baptisms, of twenty women given to the Spanish soldiers by the Tabascans of the coast: "One of the Indian ladies was christened Doña Marina. She was a truly great princess, the daughter of Caciques and the mistress of vassals . . . they were the first women in New Spain to become Christians. Cortés gave one of them to each of his captains."[22]

As the Conquest proceeded, priests performed such baptisms by the thousands. Before the holy water could dry on their foreheads, the Indian women were routinely grabbed as concubines by Spanish soldiers and settlers. The priests even performed occasional marriages between Spaniards and Indians, especially among the elite of both groups, thus fostering and legitimizing a new *mestizo* race in America. For example, Peruvian historian Garcilaso de la Vega, called El Inca, was born in 1539 to a Spanish officer and an Inca princess, while the parish register of Saint Augustine, Florida, recorded twenty-six Spanish-Indian marriages in the early 1700s, at a time when only a few hundred natives resided near the town.[23] Far more important than legal marriages, however, was the extraordinary number of consensual unions. Francisco de Aguirre, among the *conquistadores* of Chile, boasted that by fathering more than fifty *mestizo* children, his service to God had been "greater than the sin incurred in doing so."[24]

The first English colonies, by contrast, began as family settlements.

They maintained strict separation from Indian communities, sometimes even bolstered by segregation laws.[25] In North America, Indians rarely served as laborers for settlers or as household servants, and unmarried sexual unions between natives and whites were rare except for captives of war.

The English, furthermore, never saw proselytizing among the Indians as important. True, the Virginia Company listed missionary work as one of its purposes when the Crown granted Jamestown its charter in 1607. And nine years later, the Crown even ordered funds raised from all parishes in the Church of England to erect a college for the natives. But the company never sent a single missionary to Virginia and the college was never built. Officials simply diverted the money for their own ends until an investigation of the fraud prompted the Crown to revoke the company's charter and take over direct administration of the colony in 1622.[26]

Likewise, the New England Puritans segregated themselves from the Indians, not even venturing out of their settlements to win converts until decades after their arrival. In 1643, sections of Harvard College were built with money raised by the New England Company among Anglicans back home. While donors were told the funds would be used for Indian education, some of the money ended up buying guns and ammunition for the colonists.[27] So minor was Puritan concern for the Indians' souls that by 1674, fifty-five years after the founding of Plymouth Colony, barely a hundred natives in all New England were practicing Christians.[28]

At one time or another, clerics Roger Williams of Rhode Island, Cotton Mather of Massachusetts Bay, and Samuel Purchas of Virginia all vilified the natives as demonic. The Reverend William Bradford, one of the original Pilgrim leaders, insisted they were "cruel, barbarous and most treacherous . . . not being content only to kill and take away a life, but delight to torment men in the most bloody manner."[29] Throughout colonial history, only Williams's Rhode Island colony and the Quakers of Pennsylvania showed themselves willing to coexist in harmony with their Indian neighbors. Despite their low view of the Indians, the English settlers did not try to bring them under heel. At first, they merely purchased or finagled choice parcels of land from some tribes and pressured others to move toward the interior.

In the Spanish colonies, however, the natives were far more numerous, and the policies of the Catholic Church far more aggressive. Church leaders did more than merely recognize Indian humanity or accommodate *mestizaje*. The Church dispatched an army of Franciscan, Dominican, and Jesuit monks, who served as the vanguard of sixteenth-century Spanish colonialism. The monks who flocked to America perceived the chaotic rise of capitalism in Europe as auguring an era of moral decay. In the Native Americans they imagined a simpler, less corrupted human being, one who could more easily be convinced to follow the word of Christ. So they abandoned Spain to set up their missions in the most remote areas of America, far from the colonial cities and *encomiendas*.

Those missions—the first was founded by Las Casas in Venezuela in 1520—became the principal frontier outposts of Spanish civilization. Many had farms and schools to Europeanize the Indians and research centers where the monks set about learning and preserving the native languages. Quite a few of the monks were inspired by Thomas More, whose widely read *Utopia* (1516) portrayed a fictional communal society of Christians located somewhere on an island in America. One of More's most ardent admirers was Vasco de Quiroga, who established a mission of thirty thousand Tarascans in central Mexico and rose to bishop of Michoacán. Quiroga, like More, talked of trying to "restore the lost purity of the primitive Church." Since Indians had no concept of land ownership or money, the missionaries easily organized cooperative tilling of the land and even communal housing, just as More espoused.

The natives proved less malleable and far less innocent than the Europeans imagined, so much so that early colonial history is filled with countless stories of monks who met hideous deaths at the hands of their flocks. Despite those tragedies, the monks kept coming, and as the years passed, some of their missions even prospered. That prosperity enraged colonial landowners, who increasingly regarded mission Indian labor as unwanted competition for the products of their plantations. In 1767, the colonial elite finally succeeded in getting the Jesuits, the most independent of the monastic orders, expelled from the New World. By then, 2,200 Jesuits were working in the colonies and more than 700,000 Indians resided in their missions.[30]

Long before those Jesuit expulsions, Spanish monks played a crucial role in colonizing major parts of the United States. Most important were the Franciscans, who founded nearly forty thriving missions in Florida, Georgia, and Alabama during the 1600s and numerous others in the Southwest. Saint Augustine was the headquarters for the Florida missions, in which as many as twenty thousand Christianized Indians lived.[31] While most of the Florida missions eventually were abandoned, several in the Southwest later turned into thriving towns, with Spanish monks today recognized as the founders of San Antonio, El Paso, Santa Fe, Tucson, San Diego, Los Angeles, Monterey, and San Francisco.

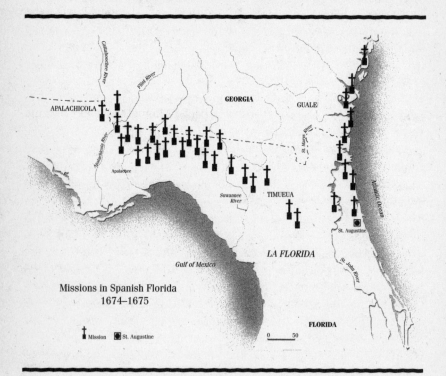

Missions in Spanish Florida
1674–1675

✝ Mission    ◉ St. Augustine

0    50

The Florida missions and settlements left a greater imprint on frontier American culture than we might believe. That influence was not always a direct one. Rather, it came by way of the Indians and Africans who remained after the missionaries were gone and who carried on some of the customs they learned from the Spanish settlers. Indians who traded with Europeans at Pensacola in 1822 were "better acquainted with the Spanish language than either the French or English," notes historian David Weber, and Englishmen who settled in Virginia, Carolina, and Georgia encountered Indians who were already cultivating peach trees the Spanish had introduced from Europe. Weber notes that the missionaries of Florida and New Mexico "taught native converts to husband European domestic animals—horses, cattle, sheep, goats, pigs, and chickens; cultivate European crops, from watermelon to wheat; raise fruit trees, from peaches to pomegranates; use such iron tools as wheels, saws, chisels, planes, nails, and spikes; and practice those arts and crafts that Spaniards regarded as essential for civilization as they knew it."

The knowledge the missionaries imparted to the Indians, whether in agriculture, language, customs, or technology, did not disappear when the last monk departed. Rather, it remained part of Indian experience so that by the time Anglos began settling in the Southeast, they discovered the "civilized tribes," among them the Creeks, the Cherokees, and the Choctaws. Even some of the most nomadic and fierce of the Southwest nations, the Apaches, Comanches, and Kiowas partially assimilated into Spanish society. In one unusual case, Apache Manuel González became mayor of San Jose, California.[32]

Apart from the missions, the Church reached into every corner of colonial life. It functioned side by side with Spanish civil government, sometimes even above it. In every town, the church was the dominant structure adjacent to which was erected the central plaza, the *cabildo,* and *la casa real.* While the Crown collected its royal fifth from the elite, the Church collected its 10 percent tithe from everyone, rich and poor, white and colored, as well as tribute from the Indians. Parish priests were the main moneylenders, and bishops held unparalleled power over the social life of colonists and natives alike. While the Church served as a buffer for the Indians against the worst abuses of Spanish civil society, it also discouraged independence or self-sufficiency and it demanded obedience from the natives it protected.

Even Europeans who dared question Church authority or doctrine were liable to be called before the all-powerful Inquisition, which could threaten anyone up to the governor with excommunication or prison, and which routinely prohibited the circulation of thousands of books and works of art it deemed sacrilegious. Its demand for blind faith toward Church doctrine impeded for centuries the spread of tolerance, ingenuity, or creativity in Latin American thought.

No English colonial Church enjoyed a monopoly power approaching that of the Catholic Church in the Spanish territories. The proliferation of sects among Protestants meant each denomination, even when its leaders wished to set up a theocratic colony, could do so only within a circumscribed area, as the Puritans did in Massachusetts and Connecticut. The Puritan witch trials of the late 1680s in Salem and surrounding Essex County rivaled the worst atrocities of the Inquisition. Twenty men and women were executed and more than 150 imprisoned, but the fanatics proved incapable of controlling everyone. Long before the witch trials, Roger Williams rebelled and founded the Rhode Island colony, where he permitted all manner of worship, and other colonies followed similar liberal policies. Catholic Maryland enacted a religious tolerance law and Quaker William Penn set up his Pennsylvania colony, which, likewise, welcomed all believers. New York City turned into such a hodgepodge of religious groups that its English governor reported in 1687: "Here, bee not many of the Church of England, [and] few Roman Catholicks, [but] abundance of Quakers—preachers, men and women, especially—singing Quakers, ranting Quakers, Sabbatarians, Anti-sabbatarians, some Anabaptists, some Independants, some Jews: in short, of all sorts of opinions there are some, and the most part of none at all."[33]

After Parliament declared religious freedom in the colonies with the Toleration Act of 1689, the emigration of sects from Europe soared. Thousands of Germans, among them Lutherans, Moravians, Mennonites, and Amish, settled in the Middle Colonies and the hinterlands of the South, as did Scotch-Irish Presbyterians in the South.

## THE ROLE OF RACE

Beyond their religious practices, the English and Spanish colonial worlds diverged substantially in their attitudes toward slavery and race. The long period of Arab domination left an indelible legacy of racial and cultural mixing that the Spanish immigrants carried to the New World. Moorish occupiers of the Iberian Peninsula had invariably taken Spanish wives, setting off an era of miscegenation so extensive that "by the fifteenth century there were dark-skinned Christians, light-haired Moors, hybrids of every shape and complexion in Castile," according to one historian. Some Muslims, called Mudejars, continued to live under Christian rule, while some Christians, called Mozarabs, learned to speak Arabic and adopted Muslim habits. The dress, foods, and traditions of Moors and Spaniards permeated each other's societies. In architecture, for instance, the horseshoe arches, tiled floors and walls, and open interior courtyards so commonly associated with Spanish design in America, all drew from Arabic inspiration.[34]

This tradition of racial mixing made it more acceptable for Spanish settlers to engage in sexual unions with both Amerindians and Africans. This was especially true for settlers from Andalusia in southern Spain, the province that endured the longest period of Moorish occupation, and which supplied nearly 40 percent of the early settlers to America.[35] At the beginning of the Conquest, Seville, Andalusia's main port, was Spain's most cosmopolitan city and the nexus for commerce with Africa. It quickly turned into the bustling crossroads for transatlantic trade as well. By the middle of the sixteenth century, the city counted nearly

100,000 inhabitants from all parts of Europe and the Mediterranean, including 6,000 African slaves.[36]

But racial mixing did not mean racial equality. As the Indian population of America gradually rebounded, and as black slave labor assumed a greater role in colonial plantation production, the Spanish and Creole upper classes became increasingly fearful of revolt—so fearful that after the Haitian revolution, the Council of the Indies, the Crown's administrative body for colonies, banned all marriages between whites and free blacks or *mulatos*. Despite the ban, the practice of mixed racial marriages continued, with dispensations often granted in cases where the honor of the woman was at stake. Upon denying one such request in 1855, the civil governor of Oriente Province in Cuba remarked, "There is little doubt that the dissemination of ideas of equality of the white class with the coloured race puts in jeopardy the tranquillity of the Island, the largest proportion of whose population consists of the said race."[37]

Apart from the ban on white-colored unions, the institution of marriage itself played a distinctive role in Spanish society. It was one of the many avenues the Church utilized to mitigate the worst aspects of slavery that were so evident in the English colonies. The Church would not permit slave owners, for instance, to separate married couples, and it sanctioned marriage between slaves and free persons. Historian Herbert Klein reports that in selected parishes of Havana between 1825 and 1829, more than a third of all marriages were between slaves, and nearly a fifth were between a slave and a free person. In many parts of Cuba, the marriage rate among slaves was equal to or higher than among whites.[38]

Perhaps even more important than formal marriage, however, was the social impact of consensual unions. No European society before the nineteenth century witnessed the level of free unions found in Latin America. Illegitimate births among free persons of all classes were close to 50 percent. Among the white upper classes, they were higher than among any other European elite.[39] Those unions, which were invariably between white men and nonwhite women, were preferable to official marriage because they did not subvert the class structure.

The prevalence of both consensual unions and miscegenation, along with the strong influence of the Catholic Church, led to major differences between how the English and Spanish regarded the rights of slaves, especially toward the end of the eighteenth century. Until then, all colonial powers had allowed masters to free their slaves. But after the Haitian revolution, the British, French, and Dutch started to restrict manumission, while the Portuguese and Spanish colonies promoted and codified the practice.

As a result, only in the Portuguese and Spanish colonies did giant classes of free blacks develop, and with them the *mulato* group (in some countries they were called *pardos* or *morenos*) that so distinguished Latin America's rainbow racial spectrum from North America's stark black-white system of racial classification. In the United States, for instance, the first federal census in 1790 reported that "free coloreds" were less than 2 percent of the population, while black slaves were 33 percent.[40] The same proportion of free blacks to slaves was roughly true in the British, Dutch, and French Caribbean colonies. But the opposite trend prevailed in the Spanish and Portuguese colonies, where free blacks or coloreds outnumbered slaves, with perhaps 40 to 60 percent of free blacks able to purchase their emancipation outright.[41] The viceroyalty of New Grenada, which included Colombia, Venezuela, and Ecuador, had 80,000 slaves and 420,000 free coloreds in 1789.[42] Cuba had 199,000 slaves and 114,000 free coloreds in 1817.[43] By 1872, free coloreds composed 43 percent of Brazil's population, outnumbering both pure whites and black slaves.

Color and status so deeply demarcated the English colonies, however, that the free colored class was considered an abnormality only barely tolerated.[44] A drop of black blood made you black in Anglo-Saxon society, while in the Portuguese and Spanish world, *mestizos* and *mulatos,* no matter how dark, were invariably regarded as part of white society, although admittedly second-class members.

Racism obviously persisted in both groups of colonies, but in the Iberian ones it assumed a muted form, its operation rendered more complex by the presence of a huge mixed-race population. The quest for white purity in Latin America became confined to a tiny upper class, while dispensations for lower-class whites to marry outside their race were routinely granted. The reasons were simple. For rich whites, marriage was first and foremost a question of securing inheritance lines. Racial mixing was not allowed to subvert the class structure, though on occasion even some of the elite officially "recognized" their mixed-race children, ushering them partially into white society. The arcane types of mixed-race offspring that developed in Latin America were astounding. Beyond *mestizos* and *mulatos,* there were *zambos* (Indian and black), *coyotes* (*mestizo* and Indian), *salta-atrás* (those with Negroid features born of white parents), *chinos* (offspring of Indian and *salta-atrás*), *cuarterones* (quadroons), and even more exotic distinctions.

For the Anglo-Saxon colonies, on the other hand, interracial marriage was taboo, by any class of whites. Even after independence and emancipation, it remained banned, and while rape or unsanctioned unions obviously occurred, Anglo-Saxons almost never recognized their mixed-race children, no matter how light-skinned the offspring or how poor the father.

## LAND AND POLITICS IN THE TWO SOCIETIES

Beyond religion and race, the Spanish and English colonies diverged radically in the way they managed their economic and political systems. Spain's colonies were royal affairs from the start. *Conquistadores* functioned as direct agents of the Crown. And Spain's main object, at least for the first century, was gold and silver; by 1600, its colonies had already produced more than 2 billion pesos' worth, three times the total European supply before Columbus's first voyage.[45] (The total surpassed 6 billion pesos, mostly in silver, by 1800.) The flood of silver coin, however, only led to massive inflation at home. Domestic industry and agriculture stagnated as more than 200,000 Spaniards left for the New World during the first century of colonization. Countless others abandoned the Spanish countryside and flocked to Seville and Cádiz to engage in mercantile trade.[46] The Crown's expulsion of the Moors and Jews only exacerbated the economic crisis, since those two groups had provided much of the country's professional and commercial vitality. Jewish merchants fled with their wealth to the financial centers of London, Amsterdam, and Genoa.[47] With Spain forced to resort to huge loans from foreign banks to meet the spiraling costs of administering its vast empire, much of the production from the mines of Mexico and Peru passed into the coffers of Dutch and English bankers and went to pay for manufactured goods to supply the colonies.

When they finally started their own American colonies nearly a century after Spain, the English and the Dutch rejected Spain's state-sponsored approach. They relied instead on rich nobles financing individual colonies and on a new type of business venture—the joint stock company. The London Company, the Plymouth Company, the Virginia Company, and the Dutch West Indies Company all secured charters from their monarchs to populate the new territories.

While the Pilgrims and other colonists indeed fled religious persecution, the same cannot be said of the companies that transported them. Utopia for these new capitalist concerns was far less spiritual in nature. It meant the chase for enormous profit: from trading for furs with the Indians; from wood and iron and other raw materials that could be shipped to England; and from charging hefty rates for relocating England's malcontents and dissidents to the New World. In 1627, for instance, the London Company declared one of its objectives to be: "The removing of the surcharge of necessitous people, the matter or fuel of dangerous insurrections, and thereby leaving the greater plenty to sustain those remaining with the Land."[48]

The mass exodus from England and Europe, however, was not simply a spontaneous emigration of the continent's persecuted and destitute, as immigrant myth would have us believe. More than half the population of the thirteen colonies before 1776 was composed of indentured servants. Among these were fifty thousand convicts who were released from English jails during the seventeenth century to populate the Maryland and Virginia colonies, and a considerable number of children who had been kidnapped and sold into servitude.[49]

Land speculators who worked in tandem with merchants orchestrated and engineered much of the exodus. Labor agents scoured the British Isles and the Rhineland for recruits to work the huge tracts of American land the speculators owned, enticing farm families to sell their property and seek instant wealth in the New World.[50] William Penn, for example, employed recruiting agents in London, Dublin, Edinburgh, and Rotterdam. Penn's merchant friend in Rotterdam, Benjamin Furly, was so successful advertising the colony in the Rhine Valley that he turned Pennsylvania into the center for German immigrants to the colonies.[51]

At first, England left colonial administration in the hands of the companies, since the Crown was preoccupied with its own domestic strife and religious battles. But by the end of the 1600s, Parliament assumed direct administration through its Board of Trade, the counterpart to Spain's Council of the Indies. Even then, however, England kept its New World bureaucracy rather tiny.

The Spanish empire, on the other hand, spawned such a huge colonial bureaucracy that 1.1 million people held religious office of some kind in the Spanish colonies by the seventeenth century, and nearly half a million held government jobs.[52] Like most bureaucracies, the colonial Church and civil government slowed the pace of decision making, buried innovation under mountains of reports and edicts, and stifled all manner of dissent. In fairness to Spain, its empire was the largest the world had ever seen. From Oregon all the way to Patagonia, it stretched over some of the world's most impassable mountains, longest rivers, most forbidding deserts and impenetrable jungles. The population of its colonies, ten times that of the mother country, required far more effort to control than the more compact and less densely populated English colonies east of the Allegheny Mountains.

Latin America's great size and mineral wealth required an enormous supply of laborers. Indians and *mestizos* mined the empire's gold and silver, built its cities and churches, tended its herds, and grew its food. And once mining declined in importance, African slaves harvested the new gold, sugar, as well as tobacco, cocoa, and indigo. For a Spaniard in America to engage in hard labor was almost unheard-of.

In the English colonies, on the other hand, Amerindians never formed part of the labor force. The colonial economy depended on three groups of workers: free white farmers, propertyless whites (both indentured and free), and African slaves. Nearly 70 percent of all white immigration to the colonies until the Revolution was made up of indentured servants. Those servants, having completed their required years of work, became free artisans in the cities or moved to the frontier to start their own farms. By the time of the Revolution, the majority of the white population was comprised of independent yeomen, small farmers, and fishermen.[53] That agrarian group—simple, unassuming, skeptical of far-off government control, and determined to create a new life out of an immense and fertile wilderness—would form the cultural core of the new North American society, or at least of its white majority.

Radically different land policies further demarcated English and Spanish colonial society. Frenzied speculation in land was ubiquitous in the English territories.[54] "Every farmer with an extra acre of land became a land speculator—every town proprietor, every scrambling tradesman who could scrape together a modest sum for investment," says one historian.[55] Both the English colonial administrators and, later, the state and federal governments fostered speculation. Time and again, those in charge of government created overnight fortunes for their friends and themselves through corrupt schemes aimed at amassing huge holdings. By 1697, for example, four Hudson Valley families, the Van Cortlandts, Philipses, Livingstons, and Van Rensselaers, had amassed for themselves 1.6 million acres spanning six present-day counties in mid–New York State, creating that state's new landed aristocracy.[56]

Where the English had their tradition of land speculation, the Spaniards had the opposite, the *mayorazgo,* in which a family's rural and urban holdings were made legally indivisible, handed down from generation to generation through the eldest son. Other family members could be assigned portions of the family estate to administer and profit from, but they could never own and, most importantly, could not sell that portion.

The biggest *mayorazgos* went to the original *conquistadores.* More modest allotments were assigned to their lower-ranking soldiers, and even smaller grants to civilian settlers. As the generations passed, intermarriage within the elite created labyrinthine mergers of old estates. Merchants, miners, and later immigrants often tried to purchase titles or marry into the established *mayorazgos.* The giant estates only got bigger, never smaller, and individual buying and selling of land for quick profit was rare.[57] The *mayorazgos,* together with the labor system of the *encomiendas,* thus became the basis for Latin America's *latifundio* system, in which a tiny portion of the white population owned most of the land and all others were reduced to laborers.

In contrast to both the English and Spanish, Native Americans invariably saw land as a resource to be used by all and owned by none. Even in the most stratified Indian societies, land was owned ultimately in common. Among the Aztecs, for instance, the *calpulli,* or extended clan, apportioned land to each member. The members, in turn, remitted a portion of their crops to clan leaders, who used that portion to pay the emperor's tribute.[58] No matter how many treaties the Indian nations may have signed to placate white settlers, they invariably saw themselves as ceding *use of the land,* not perpetual ownership.

Finally, and perhaps most importantly, the English and Spanish settlers brought with them vastly different political traditions. When each group attempted to transplant those traditions in the New World, they found themselves deeply influenced by the Amerindians who had preceded them. In Mexico, for instance, the Aztec ruler, chosen from within the royal family by a council of nobles, stood atop a highly differentiated class society. He exacted tribute from his own people and from conquered or dependent city-states like Tacuba, Texcoco, Tlaxcala, and Tarasca. The Spaniards did not dismember those centralized structures of power; instead, they appropriated them from above, erecting the scaffolding of their colonial organization, from viceroys to middle-level *corregidores,* over an already autocratic Indian foundation. And they astutely relinquished control of the *cabildos* (town councils) outside of the major cities to the Indian majority, turning the traditional chiefs into political mediators and into suppliers of Indian labor to the *encomiendas.*

The Aztecs, as we have seen, were far different from the Iroquois with whom English settlers alternately fought and allied for 150 years before independence. Lewis Henry Morgan, the founder of American anthropology and the first to systematically study the Iroquois, wrote in 1851, "Their whole civil policy was averse to concentration of power in the hands of any single individual, but inclined to the opposite principle of division among a number of equals."[59]

The Iroquois constitution, preserved over the years in oral tradition and recorded on wampum belts, led to a unique brand of democracy, which was based on consensus decision making by elected representatives. Their Confederation, according to Morgan, contained "the germ of modern parliament, congress, and legislature." Since Morgan, numerous scholars have documented how the Iroquois influenced the democratic ideas of our own Founding Fathers.[60] This country's fierce devotion to individual rights, insists historian Felix Cohen, has its roots in Iroquois thought, as does "universal suffrage for women . . . the pattern of states within a state we call federalism, the habit of treating chiefs as servants of the people instead of as masters."[61]

Some go even further. "Egalitarian democracy and liberty as we know them today in the United States owe little to Europe," argues anthropologist Jack Weatherford. Rather, "they entered modern western thought as American Indian notions translated into European language and culture."[62] Several of the Founding Fathers were influenced by the Iroquois system of checks and balances. Benjamin Franklin published the first Indian treaty accounts in 1736, and he studied native societies extensively while serving as Indian commissioner for Pennsylvania in the 1750s. During one Anglo-Indian conference in 1744, he was so moved by the oratory of Iroquois shaman Canassatego, who urged the colonies to form their own federation, that he began advocating such a system for the colonies.[63] Thomas Jefferson frequently delved into the traditions of Iroquois, and he praised their morality and oratory in his *Notes on the State of Virginia*. And Charles Thompson, secretary to the Continental Convention, admiringly described the Iroquois government as "a kind of patriarchal confederacy."[64]

Other Iroquois principles that have found their way into American democracy are the separation of military and civilian power (the code of Hiawatha required Iroquois sachems and war chiefs to be elected separately) and the impeachment of elected leaders. In some ways, the five tribes were far ahead of the Founding Fathers, for they prohibited slavery and they recognized the voting rights of women. Settlers who came to know the simplicity of Iroquois society were invariably impressed with its ability to blend individual liberty and the moral authority of the clan to restrain antisocial behavior. Crime, for instance, was almost unknown among them.

England founded colonies throughout the world, but only in North America did the traditions of English common law, local control, and parliamentary representation flourish, and a good part of that is due to the influence of Iroquois traditions on the settlers. By comparison, other former British colonies, India, Jamaica, or South Africa, for example, failed to produce the unique combination of strong and stable representative government with individual liberty found in the United States. In Latin America, meanwhile, each effort by former Spanish colonies such as Mexico, Gran Colombia, and Brazil to replicate our democratic model met with failure.

   Thus, by the early nineteenth century, three hundred years of colonialism had divided the New World into two huge contending cultural groups, the Anglo-Saxon and the Spanish-Latin, with smaller groups of Portuguese, Dutch, French, and Caribbean English colonies. The colonists of the two dominant societies had inexorably undergone a transformation. They were no longer Englishmen or Spaniards. They were now Anglo Americans and Latin Americans. They had adapted their religion, political and economic views, their speech, their music, and their food to the new land. They had built an uneasy intertwined identity with the natives they conquered and the Africans they brought as slaves. Latin America became a land of social inclusion and political exclusion. English America welcomed all political and religious views but remained deeply intolerant in its social and racial attitudes. Latin America, subsumed by the force of its Indian and African majority, became a land of spirit, song, and suffering among its masses, its elite living a parasitic existence on immense estates. North America's white settlers, segregated from the races over which they held sway, developed a dual and contradictory identity and worldview: on the one hand, a spirit of will, work, and unwavering optimism among its small farmer masses, on the other, a predilection among its elite for cutthroat enterprise, land speculation, and domination of the weak and of non-Europeans.

   The conquest of America profoundly challenged and transformed the beliefs of settlers, natives, and slaves alike, while it raised troubling questions for Europeans back home: Were all men God's children? What was savagery and what was civilization? Would the New World's racial mixing create a new cosmic race of men and women? Was Church, king, or state the ultimate arbiter of society, or were individuals free to create their own destiny? The answers they chose—and the conflicts between those answers—molded the two main New World cultures that arose. Why the Spanish colonies, so rich in resources at the dawn of their nineteenth-century independence, stagnated and declined while the young North American republic flourished, is the subject of our next chapter.

# 2

## *The Spanish Borderlands and the Making of an Empire (1810–1898)*

> However our present interests may restrain us within our limits,
> it is impossible not to look forward to distant times, when our
> rapid multiplication will expand beyond those limits, and cover
> the whole northern if not the southern continent.
>
> —*Thomas Jefferson, 1801*

When they embarked on the road to independence in 1810, Spain's American colonies were far richer in resources, territory, and population than the infant United States. Over the next few decades, however, the four Spanish viceroyalties—New Spain, New Granada, Peru, and Río Plata—fragmented into more than a dozen separate nations, most of them crippled by internal strife, by economic stagnation, by foreign debt, and by outside domination. The United States, on the other hand, expanded dramatically in territory and population, fashioned a stable and prosperous democracy, and warded off foreign control.

Why such a staggering difference in development? Historians in this country usually attribute it to the legacies of English and Spanish colonialism. The austere Protestant democracy of Anglo-Saxon farmers and merchants, they say, was ideally suited for carving prosperity from a virgin frontier in a way that the Catholic, tyrannical societies of Latin America were not.[1]

That view, however, ignores the discordant and unequal relationship that emerged between the United States and Latin America from the first days of independence. It masks how a good deal of nineteenth-century U.S. growth flowed directly from the Anglo conquest of Spanish-speaking America. That conquest, how it unfolded and how it set the basis for the modern Latino presence in the United States, is the subject of this chapter.

Our nation's territorial expansion during the 1800s is well documented, but less attention has been given to how that expansion weakened and deformed the young republics to the south, especially those closest to the ever-changing U.S. borders. Annexation of the Spanish-speaking borderlands evolved in three distinct phases: Florida and the Southeast by 1820; Texas, California, and the Southwest by 1855; and, finally, Central America and the Caribbean during the second half of the century, a phase that culminated with the Spanish-American War of 1898. Those annexations transformed an isolated yeoman's democracy into a major world empire. In the process, Mexico lost half of its territory and three-quarters of its mineral resources, the Caribbean Basin was reduced to a permanent target for Yankee exploitation and intervention, and Latin Americans were made into a steady source of cheap labor for the first U.S. multinational corporations.

Popular history depicts that nineteenth-century movement as a heroic epic of humble farmers heading west in covered wagons to fight off savage Indians and tame a virgin land. Rarely do those accounts examine the movement's other face—the relentless incursions of Anglo settlers into Latin American territory.

Ahead of the settlers came the traders and merchants—men like Charles Stillman, Mifflin Kenedy, and Richard King in Texas; Cornelius Vanderbilt, George Law, and Minor Keith in Central America; William Safford, H. O. Havemeyer, and John Leamy in the Antilles; and John Craig in Venezuela—all of whom amassed huge fortunes in Latin American lands and products. The merchants were joined by adventurers and mercenaries like General John McIntosh (Florida), Davy Crockett (Texas), and William Walker (Nicaragua), who swore allegiance to inexperienced or weak Latin American governments, then forcibly overthrew them in the name of freedom.

Most U.S. presidents backed the taking of Latin America's land. Jefferson, Jackson, and Teddy Roosevelt all regarded our country's domination of the region as ordained by nature. The main proponents and beneficiaries of empire building, however, were speculators, plantation owners, bankers, and merchants.[2] They fostered popular support for it by promising cheap land to the waves of European immigrants who kept arriving on our shores, and they bankrolled an endless string of armed rebellions in those Spanish-speaking lands by white settlers. To justify it all, our leaders popularized such pivotal notions as "America for the Americans" and "Manifest Destiny," the latter term emerging as the nineteenth-century code-phrase for racial supremacy.

NEW AMERICAN STATES
IN 1825

CANADA
(BRITISH)

UNITED STATES
1776

MEXICO
1821

*Atlantic
Ocean*

BAHAMAS (Br.)
CUBA (Sp.)
HAITI
(1804)
BRITISH
HONDURAS
(Sp.)
SANTO DOMINGO (1821)
JAMAICA (Br.)
PUERTO RICO (Sp.)

CENTRAL
AMERICA
1821

*Pacific Ocean*

VENEZUELA
1811
GUIANAS
Br.
Du. Fr.

COLOMBIA
1819

ECUADOR
1822

BRAZIL
1822

PERU
1824

BOLIVIA
1825

CHILE
1824
PARAGUAY
1811

ARGENTINA
1816
URUGUAY
1825

☐ Independent nations
▨ European colonial
possessions

But along with the conquered lands came unwanted peoples: Native Americans, who were pushed farther west, then herded onto reservations, and several million Mexicans, Cubans, Filipinos, and Puerto Ricans, who were placed under U.S. sovereignty. Even when Congress officially

declared some of the conquered peoples U.S. citizens, the newly arrived
Anglo settlers routinely seized their properties, and those seizures were
then upheld by the English-speaking courts the settlers installed. The
Mexican Americans of the Southwest became a foreign minority in the
land of their birth. Spanish-speaking, Catholic, and largely *mestizo,* they
were rapidly relegated to a lower-caste status alongside Indians and blacks.
Cubans and Filipinos eventually won their independence but found their
nations under the thumb of Washington for decades afterward, while
Puerto Rico remains to this day a colony of second-class citizens.

## THE REVOLUTIONARY YEARS: FROM INSPIRATION TO BETRAYAL

At the beginning of the 1800s, few Latin Americans could have foretold
how the United States would treat them. The U.S. War of Independence,
after all, was an enormous inspiration to intellectuals throughout the
Spanish colonies. Some Latin Americans even fought alongside George
Washington's rebel army. Bernardo de Gálvez, the Spanish governor of
Louisiana, opened a second front against the English when he invaded
British-controlled West Florida, defeated the garrison there, and reclaimed the peninsula as a Spanish colony. Merchants in Havana, meanwhile, supplied critical loans and supplies to Washington.

After the Revolution triumphed, Latin American patriots emulated
the Founding Fathers. Fray Servando de Mier, a leading propagandist of
Mexican independence, traveled to Philadelphia during Jefferson's presidency and often quoted Thomas Paine in his own polemics against
monarchy.[3] In 1794, Antonio Nariño, a wealthy Bogotá intellectual and
admirer of Benjamin Franklin, translated and secretly published the
French Assembly's Declaration of the Rights of Man. José Antonio Rojas, the prominent Chilean revolutionary, met Franklin in Europe and
later shipped numerous crates of Raynal's writings about the North
American revolution to Chile. In 1776, Rojas penned his own list of
Chilean grievances against the Spanish monarchy. Simón Bolívar, the
great Liberator of South America, traveled throughout the United
States in 1806. Inspired by its accomplishments, he launched Venezuela's
independence uprising a few years later.[4]

Perhaps the best example of the close ties between revolutionaries of
the north and south was Francisco de Miranda, the "Morning Star" of
Latin American independence. Born in 1750 into a prosperous merchant
family in Caracas, Miranda joined the Spanish army at seventeen. He
later traveled to North America, where he served first with Gálvez's

Spanish troops in Florida, then with French general Comte de Rocham-
beau's troops. Handsome, erudite, and charismatic, Miranda was be-
friended by several U.S. leaders, including Alexander Hamilton and
Robert Morris, and he met with President Washington. After a long personal odyssey through Europe, where he served as both a decorated general in Napoleon's army and a lover of Russia's Catherine the Great,
Miranda returned to the United States and sought to win our government's backing for a campaign to liberate the Spanish colonies.[5]

Like all the well-known patriots of Latin America, however, Miranda
was a *criollo* from the upper class. That limited his ability to win a mass
following for independence among his own countrymen, for the *criollos*,
unlike the Anglo-American revolutionaries, were a distinct minority
within their own society. Of 13.5 million people living in the Spanish
colonies in 1800, less than 3 million were white, and only 200,000 of those
were *peninsulares*, born in Spain. Latin American rebels lived in constant
fear of the 80 percent of the population that was Indian, black, and
mixed-race, and that apprehension intensified during the final years of
the U.S. Revolutionary War, when several major uprisings broke out
among the Indians of South America.[6]

The specter of those uprisings made the *criollos* content at first to demand from Spain simply better treatment, not full-blown independence.
They railed against high taxation, for more autonomy, and against the restrictions the Crown imposed on trade outside the empire. They condemned Spain's discrimination against them, how the Crown granted
only *peninsulares* a monopoly on overseas trade, how it excluded *criollos*
from top posts in the colonial government, and how it confined them
only to mining and agriculture.[7] But no matter how much they might
complain, the *criollos* dared not risk open rebellion for fear of unleash-
ing revolt from the multitudes they had always oppressed.

In the end, the spark for Latin America's revolution came not from
within the colonies but from Europe.[8] In 1808, Napoleon invaded Spain
and installed his brother Joseph as king, setting off a chain of events that
would lead to the breakup of the entire Spanish colonial empire. The
Spanish people rejected the French invaders, formed local resistance
juntas throughout the country, and launched a guerrilla war to return
their imprisoned king to the throne. When they heard of the events in
Europe, *criollo* leaders in the colonies followed the lead of the Spanish
resistance. They formed juntas of their own in all the major American
cities and assumed control of their local affairs in the name of the king.

The rebel juntas in Spain soon convened a new Cortes, and that Cortes
promulgated a liberal constitution, one that granted full citizenship to

colonial subjects in the American colonies for the first time. But the Cortes stopped short of full equality when it refused to permit the colonies, whose population far outnumbered Spain's, a proportionate share of delegates. That refusal angered the most radical *criollo* leaders, who decided to break with the new Spanish government and declare their independence.

From then on, the Latin American revolution charted its own course. Even Napoleon's defeat at Waterloo and the ouster of the French from Spain a few years later failed to bring the shattered empire back together. King Ferdinand, who was restored to the throne after Napoleon's defeat, refused to accept the loss of his colonies and sent his army to subdue the upstart Latin Americans. A series of wars ensued throughout the continent between loyalists and rebels, and in several regions between the patriotic leaders themselves. The conflicts differed from country to country, yet everywhere the human toll was immense. The mammoth size of the colonies made for an epic, disordered, and bloody canvas. Mexico's independence wars, for instance, began in 1810 after parish priest Miguel Hidalgo led an uprising of thousands of Indian peasants and miners in the town of Dolores in the rich Bajió region northwest of Mexico City, using a statue of the Indian Virgen de Guadalupe to rally his followers. By the time the wars ended in 1821, more than 600,000 were dead, 10 percent of the country's population.[9] Venezuela had lost half of its nearly 1 million inhabitants.[10] Overall, the Latin American wars lasted much longer and proved far more destructive to the region's inhabitants than the U.S. War of Independence, which claimed only 25,000 lives.

Despite their turbulent and debilitating fight for independence, the Latin American patriots always looked to the United States for their example. Several of the new nations modeled their constitutions on ours. During their wars, they pleaded for military aid from us, and after their victory, they sought friendship and assistance for their postwar reconstruction.[11]

Most U.S. leaders, however, coveted the Spanish colonies as targets for the nation's own expansion and held little regard for the abilities of the Latin American patriots. "However our present interests may restrain us within our limits," Jefferson wrote to James Monroe in 1801, "it is impossible not to look forward to distant times, when our rapid multiplication will expand beyond those limits, and cover the whole northern if not the southern continent."[12] Democracy no better suited Spanish America, John Adams said, than "the birds, beasts or fishes."

Miranda was the first to be surprised by the U.S. attitude. In 1806, after securing £12,000 from the British government for an expedition to liberate Venezuela, he rushed to the United States in expectation of further help, but President Jefferson and Secretary of State Madison rebuffed his appeals. Despite their refusal, Miranda managed to put together a rebel force from Anglo volunteers he recuited along the Eastern Seaboard. Once the expedition landed in Venezuela, however, Miranda's countrymen mistook it for a contingent of British soldiers. Instead of heeding his call for a revolt, the Venezuelans sided with the Spanish army, which quickly routed the rebels. Miranda barely managed to avoid capture and flee the country.

A decade later, with independence fever sweeping South America and the liberation armies battling fiercely against a powerful Spanish force, the United States rebuffed Bolívar as strongly it had Miranda. Monroe, first as Madison's secretary of state and then as president, insisted on neutrality toward the South American wars. Like Jefferson before him, Monroe hoped to keep Spain friendly enough so it would eventually sell its Cuba and Florida colonies to the United States, a feeling shared by most of our nation's leaders. "We have no concern with South America," Edward Everett, editor of the influential *North American Review,* wrote at the time. "We can have no well-founded political sympathy with them. We are sprung from different stocks."[13]

Latin American freedom, however, did have support among many ordinary Americans, even a few in high places, who opposed our neutrality. Among those was Henry Marie Brackenridge, whom Monroe sent to the region to assess the situation in 1817 as part of a U.S. commission. "The patriots . . . complain that our government is cold towards them, as if ashamed to own them," Brackenridge reported back.[14] By then, the Latin Americans were becoming increasingly suspicious of U.S. intentions. That suspicion turned to bitterness after an incident that year involving two merchant ships, the *Tiger* and the *Liberty.* Soldiers from Bolívar's Republic of Gran Colombia seized the ships near the Orinoco River in Venezuela after discovering that their hulls were filled with military supplies for the Spanish army. The White House demanded that Colombia release the ships and indemnify their owners. Bolívar responded by condemning the two-faced U.S. policy. In a series of angry diplomatic letters, he reminded the White House that the U.S. Navy had intercepted and captured several merchant ships, even British ships, ladened with supplies for his revolutionary army. So why were North Americans now supplying his enemy?[15]

Unknown to Bolívar, this peculiar brand of neutrality was about to pay off handsomely. The Adams-Onís Treaty of 1819 ceded Florida to the United States, but as part of those negotiations Monroe promised Spain

that our country would continue denying aid to the Latin American patriots.[16] The Latin American leaders, unaware of the secret agreement,
could not believe how the United States kept turning its back on them.
Bolívar, who had once praised our country as a "model of political
virtues and moral enlightenment unique in the history of mankind,"
turned increasingly antagonistic to it by 1819. That year, he remarked:
"In ten years of struggle and travail that beggar description, in ten years
of suffering almost beyond human endurance, we have witnessed the in-
difference with which all Europe and even our brothers of the north
have remained but passive spectators of our anguish."[17]

But there were deeper reasons behind the U.S. reluctance to see the
Latin Americans succeed. Always foremost in the minds of southern
planters and their congressional delegates was the issue of slavery. The
planters watched with alarm as Latin America's independence wars
dragged on, how Creole leaders like Bolívar were enlisting thousands of
*pardos, mestizos,* Indians, and slaves in their armies, repaying the castes
with greater social mobility and the slaves with their freedom.

Our slave owners were well aware that after Bolívar's second defeat
by the Spanish army, Haiti's president, Alexandre Pétion, had helped finance his return to South America in 1815, outfitting seven ships and six
thousand men with weapons and ammunition on condition that Bolívar
emancipate Venezuela's slaves.[18] The Liberator's subsequent public con-
demnations of slavery enraged planters in this country. "Slavery is the
negation of all law, and any law which should perpetuate it would be a
sacrilege," he proclaimed at the founding congress of Bolivia in 1826.[19]
Clearly, plantation owners here feared that emancipation fervor would
spread from Latin America into the United States—by 1850, all the former Spanish colonies that had won their independence had abolished
slavery—and that fear turned them into implacable foes of Latin American liberation.[20]

Abandoned by the U.S. government from their inception, reviled by
the conservative monarchies of Europe, the Latin American republics
concluded that their only reliable ally was England. Some six thousand
English, Scotch, and Irish, most of them unemployed veterans from the
British wars against Napoleon, signed up for Bolívar's army in 1817–
1819. Among those volunteers was Daniel O'Leary, who went on to
serve as Bolívar's top secretary.[21] That British aid, together with the daring battlefield strategies of Bolívar, San Martín, Bernardo O'Higgins,
Santander, and the other great generals, succeeded by 1826 in routing the
last of the Spanish armies on the continent.

All of Spain's vast empire except Cuba and Puerto Rico was now free. That year, Bolívar convened the first Pan American Congress, where he elaborated his dream for a hemispheric confederation. His plan for uniting the revolutionary nations so worried U.S. leaders that Congress delayed sending representatives until the gathering had adjourned, and afterward, our government made clear to Bolívar that it was adamantly opposed to any expedition to liberate Cuba and Puerto Rico.

## FREEDOM, FILIBUSTERS, AND MANIFEST DESTINY

If the South American liberators found policy makers in Washington aloof, Latinos living near the U.S. borderlands found their Anglo neighbors downright hostile. The gobbling up of chunks of Florida between 1810 and 1819 set the pattern for U.S. expansion across the Spanish borderlands. Jefferson's Lousiana Purchase in 1803 had brought the first group of Spanish-speaking people under the U.S. flag. But our nation did not "purchase" Florida in the same way it purchased Louisiana. The Adams-Onís Treaty was more akin to a street corner holdup. It culminated two decades of unceasing pressure on Spain by southern speculators to give up the territory, an area which was then much larger in size than the current state since it stretched along the Gulf Coast all the way to the towns of Natchez and Baton Rouge.

The few thousand Spaniards inhabiting Florida's fortified Gulf Coast towns had made great strides, since the Franciscan missions of the sixteenth century, in building ties with the Indians of the Southeast. For nearly two centuries, the Creek, Choctaws, Cherokees, and Chickasaws had formed a buffer between Spanish Florida and Anglo settlers in Georgia and Kentucky. Known as the "civilized tribes" because they readily adopted European dress, tools, and farming methods, they numbered about forty-five thousand in the year 1800. The Florida colony, however, was an irritant to the Anglos, since it provided refuge both to Indians on the warpath and to escaped slaves from the southern plantations.[22] Moreover, the plantation owners regarded with horror the racial mixing between fugitive slaves and Indians that was commonplace among the Seminoles.

By the early 1800s, so many Anglo settlers were moving into Florida that Spanish soldiers in its thinly populated garrison towns could no longer control the territory. In a gamble aimed at reasserting that control, Spain agreed to legalize the newcomers, but in return the settlers had to pledge loyalty to the Crown, raise their children as Catholics, and

refrain from land speculation or political assembly.[23] The policy back-
fired, since it made it easier for settlers to immigrate and only postponed
Spain's loss of the colony.[24]

In 1810, a group of settlers in West Florida launched a direct challenge
to that authority. They resorted to a form of rebellion that eventually
turned into a hallmark of Anglo adventurers and buccaneers throughout
the Spanish borderlands: a band of newcomers or mercenaries simply
captured a town or territory and proclaimed their own republic. The
Spanish called them *filibusteros* (freebooters), and the uprisings were
known as filibusters. In one of the earliest attempts, a group of Anglo settlers captured the Spanish garrison at Baton Rouge on September 23,
1810, and declared their independence. The rebellion prompted President Madison to send in federal troops to occupy the surrounding territory, and Congress later incorporated the area into the new state of
Louisiana.[25] The rest of West Florida fell into U.S. hands during the War
of 1812, after General James Wilkinson, head of the U.S. Army and a
master at filibustering, captured the Spanish garrison at Mobile in 1813
and Andrew Jackson captured Pensacola in 1814. Spain's government,
still paralyzed by the Napoleonic wars, was in no condition to resist any
of the incursions.

Other filibuster revolts soon spread to East Florida (see table 1). Most
of the revolts garnered backing from political leaders in the South who
were anxious to expand slave territories and to speculate in Florida land.
One of those leaders, Andrew Jackson, had engaged in repeated speculation throughout his life. In 1796, for instance, Jackson bought a half-
interest in five thousand acres of the Chickasaw Bluffs in Mississippi for
$100. He immediately sold a portion for a sizable profit. Twenty years
later, as a U.S. Army commander, Jackson forced the Chickasaws to negotiate a treaty opening the territory to white settlers. He promptly sold
the remaining part of his investment for $5,000.[26] But the parcel of land
that always fired Old Hickory's imagination most was Florida. Several
times, his soldiers invaded East Florida on the pretext of hunting down
Seminole bands. Thanks to Jackson's repeated forays and to the filibuster
revolts of Anglo settlers there, Spain gradually concluded that the U.S.
thirst for Florida would never be quenched; the Adams-Onís Treaty was
the result. In it, Spain ceded to the United States an area larger than Bel-
gium, Denmark, the Netherlands, and Switzerland for a mere $5 million.
Spain hoped that by giving up Florida it would salvage the remainder of
its tottering empire, especially the province of Tejas, which had already
been the scene of four separate filibuster revolts by bands of Anglos between 1801 and 1819.[27] As its only concession in the treaty, Washington

officially renounced all other claims on Spanish lands and accepted the Sabine River as its border with Spain's Texas colony.

Such was the situation in 1822, when President Monroe, who for years had refused to aid the Latin American revolution, suddenly did an about-face and became the first world leader to recognize Mexico's independence. Monroe followed that up the next year with an even more audacious act. He declared the Americas off-limits to any new European colonization with his famous Monroe Doctrine. Actually, Monroe issued the warning quite reluctantly, and only after much British prodding. The British pressure was brought on by the defeat of Napoleon and the subsequent decision of Europe's Holy Alliance to back an attempt by Ferdinand VII to recover Spain's Latin American colonies. England was already ensconced as Latin America's biggest trading partner, and British foreign minister George Canning feared that any recolonization of the region would close off that commerce. So Canning urged Monroe to join him in warning the European powers to stay out of America. Canning, however, wanted reciprocity for his alliance. He wanted Monroe to renounce any plans to colonize Texas or Cuba, something Monroe would not do.[28]

---

### TABLE 1
## THE FILIBUSTERING RECORD

*(Invasions by U.S. Citizens into Spain's Colonies or the Latin American Republics during the 1800s)*

1801—Philip Nolan crosses into Texas with a band of armed men; he is captured and shot by Spanish soldiers.

1809—General James Wilkinson's "volunteers" occupy parts of West Florida.

1810—Anglo settlers declare a republic in Baton Rouge, West Florida. Federal troops occupy the area and Congress annexes it into Louisiana.

1812—Former general John McIntosh captures Amelia Island and Fernadina, declaring the Republic of Fernadina. Spanish troops defeat him.

1812—Former U.S. lieutenant Augustus Magee, Mexican Bernardo Gutiérrez, and a group of Americans invade East Texas and are routed.

1813—General James Wilkinson captures Mobile in West Florida.

1817—Henry Perry invades Texas and marches on La Bahía.

1819—Mississippi merchant James Long invades Texas but fails to establish the Republic of Texas.

1826—Hayden and Benjamin Edwards seize Nacogdoches and proclaim the Republic of Fredonia. Mexican soldiers defeat them with help from Stephen Austin.

1835—General Ignacio Mejía and two hundred Americans raid Río Panuco in Tamaulipas. His defeat prompts Mexico to ban American immigration.

1836—Sam Houston and Texas rebels, along with a small number of Tejano federalists, revolt against General Santa Anna's rule. They defeat Santa Anna at San Jacinto and proclaim the Republic of Texas.

1839—Antonio Canales, a Mexican federalist, S. W. Jordan, and five hundred Americans declare the Republic of the Rio Grande. They become divided and are defeated by Mexican troops.

1848—Former Spanish army officer Narciso López, backed by publisher William O'Sullivan, invades Cuba with Anglo rebels. His uprising fails.

1849—López returns and invades at Cárdenas, but is routed once again. Of his six hundred men, all but five are North American.

1851—López invades a third time, this time at Bahía Honda. Once again, North Americans are a majority of his four hundred volunteers. Spanish troops capture and execute him.

1853—William Walker invades Mexico and declares the Republic of Sonora. Mexican troops chase him back across the border.

1855—Walker arrives in Nicaragua, seizes power and rules as dictator for two years until he is routed by the combined armies of Central America and Cornelius Vanderbilt.

1858—Walker invades Nicaragua again and is routed a second time.

1860—Walker invades Honduras, is captured, tried, and executed.

---

Seeking to maneuver between the geopolitical schemes of England and the Holy Alliance, Monroe chose instead to act alone. After years of refusing support to the Latin American revolution, he suddenly reversed course. On December 2, during his annual address to Congress, he issued the most important policy statement in hemispheric history, announcing that the Latin American countries were "henceforth not to be considered as subjects for future colonization by any European powers . . . it is impossible that the allied powers should extend their political system to any portion of [the continent] without endangering our peace and happiness."[29]

The new policy was hailed at first by Latin American leaders. At last, they thought, U.S. neutrality toward their struggle would end. "An act worthy of the classic land of liberty," said Colombia's president Santander. The European monarchies, of course, were more worried about the guns of the powerful British navy than the threats of the upstart North American republic. Nonetheless, with England and the United States as nominal protectors of Latin American independence, the new countries of the region at least managed to avert the catastrophes that befell much of Africa and Asia when the European powers divided those areas between them during the great colonial partitions of the late nineteenth century.

Notwithstanding the Monroe Doctrine's strong language, European governments successfully pursued more than a dozen major interventions into Latin America during the rest of the century, and numerous minor ones, with only occasional U.S. opposition.[30] Worse than the many U.S. failures to honor its own policy was how subsequent presidents turned the doctrine into its opposite. Latin America, especially the Caribbean Basin, was turned into a virtual U.S. sphere of influence. Bolívar, weary of the growing arrogance from North Americans, declared before his death that the United States seemed "destined by Providence to plague America with torments in the name of freedom."[31] During the twentieth century, a succession of presidents used Monroe's words to justify repeated military occupations of Latin American nations. This duel interpretation of the doctrine's provisions continues to this day. It underscores an unresolved contradiction of U.S. history—between our ideals of freedom and our predilection for conquest.

The earliest example of that contradiction came during the next phase of borderlands expansion, the repeated annexations of Mexican territory between 1836 and 1853. Prior to those annexations, the United States of Mexico, as the new country called itself, and the United States of America were eerily similar in territory and population. In 1824, Mexico comprised 1.7 million square miles and contained 6 million people, while the United States stretched for 1.8 million square miles and had 9.6 million people. That equivalence was radically transformed over the next three decades as Anglo settlers poured onto Mexican land.

The settlements began with Moses and Stephen Austin and the town of San Felipe de Austin. Moses, who had lived in Missouri when Spain controlled the Louisiana territory, secured permission from the Spanish crown in 1820 to found a town of Anglo families in the province of Tejas.

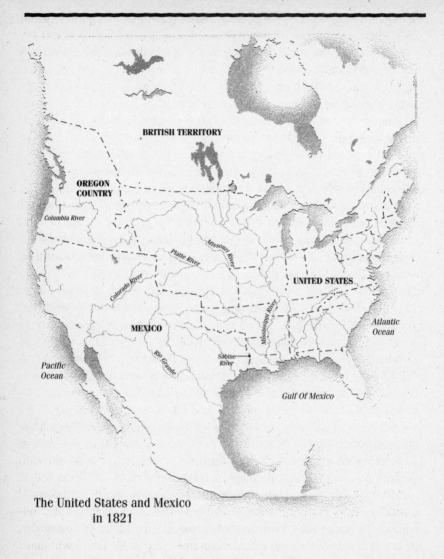

The United States and Mexico
in 1821

Within a year, Austin died and Mexico won its independence, but his son
Stephen chose to carry out his father's plan. The new Mexican government honored Spain's grant so long as Austin's settlers took an oath of
allegiance to Mexico and converted to Catholicism. San Felipe was so
successful that dozens of other Anglo colonies in Texas soon followed.[32]
Farther south, at the mouth of the Rio Grande, Connecticut merchant

Francis Stillman landed by ship near Matamoros with a cargo of hay and oats in 1825. Impressed by the demand for his goods, Stillman sent his son Charles to the area to set up a branch of the family business.[33] Charles, or Don Carlos as the Mexicans referred to him, proved to be a wizard at trade. Before long, he was the biggest merchant and landowner in the region. By 1832, three hundred foreigners were living in Matamoros, most of them North Americans.[34] Among them was James Power, who married Dolores de la Portilla, an heiress of the rich De la Garza landowning family. Power thus initiated a form of land acquisition that hundreds of Anglo adventurers in the Southwest copied—he married into the Mexican elite and thereby acquired a *mayorazgo*.[35] Across the river from Matamoros, Don Carlos Stillman founded the town of Brownsville, where his son James Stillman was born in 1850. That son would grow up to be a titan of American finance as the president of First National City Bank and as the notorious ally of robber barons John D. Rockefeller and J. P. Morgan.

Far to the north of the Rio Grande, Anglo settlers had started moving into East Texas in the 1820s. Many were illegal squatters drawn by fraudulent sales of land at 1 to 10 cents an acre from speculators who had no legal title.[36] Some of those squatters soon took to filibustering.[37] The Hayden Edwards revolt, in particular, prompted the Mexican government to bar further immigration by U.S. citizens. It even abolished slavery in 1829 in hopes of cutting off economic incentives for southerners to emigrate.

But it was too late. By then, Anglo settlers far outnumbered the Mexicans in Tejas. "Where others send invading armies," warned Mexican secretary of state Lucas Alaman, in an eerie precursor to our modern immigration debate, "[the Americans] send their colonists. . . . Texas will be lost for this Republic if adequate measures to save it are not taken."[38] Local Mexican authorities, unlike the government in Mexico City, welcomed the economic boom that accompanied the influx of foreigners, just as today Anglo businessmen routinely welcome Mexicans who have crossed illegally into the country and are willing to work for low wages.

When General Santa Anna seized power in Mexico City in 1833, one of his first acts was to abolish the exemptions from taxes and antislavery laws that prior Mexican governments had granted the Texans, giving them the excuse they needed to break from Mexico City's "tyranny."

Few incidents in U.S. history so directly confront our cultural identity as does the Texas War of Independence and its legendary Battle of the Alamo. For more than a century and a half, the fort's siege has been a part of American mythology. Its 187 martyred defenders, among them

William Barret Travis, Jim Bowie, and Davy Crockett, have been immortalized as American heroes despite the fact that they openly defended slavery, that they were usurping the land of others, and that they were not even American citizens. Technically, they were Mexican citizens rebelling to found the Republic of Texas.

Most of the Anglo settlers had been in the province less than two years. Many were adventurers, vagabonds, and land speculators.[39] Travis had abandoned his family and escaped to Texas after killing a man in the United States. Bowie, a slave trader, had wandered into the Mexican province looking to make a fortune in mining. Sam Houston, commander of the victorious rebels, and Crockett were both veterans of Andrew Jackson's grisly victory over the Creeks at Horseshoe Bend, and they shared Old Hickory's racist and expansionist views toward Latin America.

Houston, a onetime governor of Tennessee, was part of Jackson's White House kitchen cabinet before moving to Texas in 1832. While Houston plotted the rebellion, Jackson offered unsuccessfully to purchase Texas outright from Mexico. The two men were so close that Jackson's enemies, among them former president John Quincy Adams, accused Houston of being Jackson's secret agent in Texas. Although historians have found no documentary proof of this, Jackson certainly was aware of his disciple's plans for the Mexican province.[40]

After the Alamo defeat, Houston's rebel army won the war's decisive battle at the Battle of San Jacinto, captured Santa Anna, and forced him to sign a treaty recognizing Texas independence in exchange for his freedom. But the Mexican government refused to sanction the treaty, and the precise boundaries of Texas remained in dispute for some time. The territory remained nominally independent until its annexation in 1845 only because northern congressmen kept blocking its admission to the union as a slave state. While the debate raged, cotton farming took hold in the Texas Republic and its leaders allowed the territory to be turned into a major transit point for smuggling slaves from Cuba into the southern states.[41]

Texas annexation touched off a fever for even more westward expansion. The slogan of the Monroe Doctrine, "America for the Americans," was barely two decades old when a new battle cry suddenly replaced it in the popular imagination—"Manifest Destiny." John O'Sullivan coined the term in July 1845 in his *United States Magazine and Democratic Review*. O'Sullivan, a publicist for the Democratic Party and friend of several presidents, counted Poe, Longfellow, and Whittier among the contributors to his influential magazine and was a steadfast advocate of expansion into Latin America, especially Cuba, where he personally financed several filibuster expeditions.

Proponents of Manifest Destiny saw Latin Americans as inferior in cultural makeup and bereft of democratic institutions. Our country's Calvinist beliefs reinforced those territorial ambitions perfectly. Americans could point to the nation's prosperity, to its amazing new networks of canals, steamboats, and railroads, as proof of their God-given destiny to conquer the frontier. Newspapers and magazines of the day were replete with articles by noted phrenologists like Dr. George Caldwell and Dr. Josiah C. Nott, who propounded the superiority of white Europeans over Indians, blacks, and Mexicans.

"To the Caucasian race is the world indebted for all the great and important discoveries, inventions, and improvements, that have been made in science and the arts," Caldwell wrote in his influential *Thoughts on the Original Unity of the Human Race*. Nott, one of the South's best-known surgeons, took Caldwell's views one step further. He urged the need for eugenics to keep the white race pure. "Wherever in the history of the world the inferior races have been conquered and mixed in with the Caucasian, the latter have sunk into barbarism," Nott proclaimed in a speech in 1844.

The phrenologists were not some marginal intellectual sect. By 1850, their ideas were part of mainstream thought in this country. Proponents traveled from town to town, carrying casts of skulls and detailed charts of the brain, giving speeches and distributing free books, and charging money to read heads. World-famous scholars such as Samuel George Morton, the Philadelphia ethnologist who possessed the largest collection of human skulls on earth, buttressed their conclusions with "scientific" studies on the relative size, capacity, and composition of the brains of different races. Morton, according to Nott, "has established the fact, that the capacity of the crania of the Mongol, Indian, and Negro, and all dark-skinned races, is smaller than that of the pure white man." Nott even extended those differences to single out other Caucasians or "mixed-breeds." Contrasting whites in the United States "with the dark-skinned Spaniards," he wrote, "It is clear that the dark-skinned Celts are fading away before the superior race, and that they must eventually be absorbed."[42]

With southern planters pressing to increase their proslavery votes in Congress, and many northerners captivated by the racialist theories of Manifest Destiny, the national outcry to annex more Mexican land became overwhelming. To no one's surprise, the entry of Texas into the union precipitated war with Mexico. It was a conflict that even the last president of the Texas Republic, Anson James, regarded as shameful. James blasted President Polk and war hero General Zachary Taylor for their attempts "to induce me to aid them in their unholy and execrable design of manufacturing a war with Mexico."[43] More than 100,000 U.S. soldiers served in the war, and nearly 14,000 perished, the highest mortality rate of any war in our history.[44] Their advance into Mexico produced horrifying incidents of brutality and racism by U.S. troops. A few even drew the public condemnation of generals Grant and Meade. Grant later admitted the war was "one of the most unjust ever waged by a stronger against a weaker nation."[45]

As the army advanced toward Mexico City, however, those same theories of Mexican inferiority sparked a national debate over how much of Mexico the United States should claim. By taking too much land, some argued, the country would be absorbing millions of racially mixed Mexicans, which in the long run might threaten the Anglo-Saxon majority. The Treaty of Guadalupe Hidalgo finally forced Mexico to relinquish that half of its territory that was the least densely populated and that included the present-day states of New Mexico, California, Nevada, parts of Arizona, Utah, and the disputed sections of present-day Texas. Five years later, the United States added an additional strip of land in Sonora, the Gadsden Purchase.[46]

Also included in the 1848 treaty was the crucial 150-mile-wide Nueces Strip, between the Rio Grande and Nueces rivers. The U.S. negotiators demanded its inclusion as part of Texas despite the fact that Spain, and later Mexico, considered the strip part of Coahuila province. The Nueces, which is equal in size to present-day Massachusetts, Connecticut, and New Jersey combined, was especially important because it included the fertile Lower Rio Grande Valley and because the plains north of that valley were teeming with wild horses and cattle. The herds, introduced by Spanish settlers in the early 1700s, numbered more than 3 million head by 1830.[47] Securing control of those herds, and of the original Spanish land grants in the region, soon produced vast fortunes for early Anglo settlers like Charles Stillman, Richard King, and Mifflin Kenedy.

Out of those Mexican lands, the U.S. cattle industry was born, even though the majority of ranch hands in the industry's early decades were anything but Anglo. The *vaqueros,* or cowboys, were generally *mestizos* or *mulatos*, sometimes even blacks or Indians. Certainly this was true on the famous King Ranch below Corpus Christi, which eventually grew to nearly 1 million acres. So dominant was the Mexican *vaquero* in the industry that Anglo cowboys copied virtually all the culture of the range

from them. As historian Carey McWilliams has noted, the cowboy got
from the *vaquero:*

> his lasso or lariat, cinch, halter, *mecate* or horsehair rope, "chaps" or
> *chaparejos,* "taps" or stirrup tips *(lapaderas),* the chin strap for his
> hat *(barboquejo),* the feedbag for his horse *(morral)* and his rope
> halter or *bosal.* Even his famous "ten gallon hat" comes from a mis-
> translation of a phrase in a Spanish-Mexican *corrido "su sombrero
> galoneado"* which referred to a festooned or "gallooned" sombrero.

The Nueces Strip and the northern part of New Mexico were the only
regions where the original Mexican inhabitants remained a clear majority over the Anglos even after annexation. Because of that, the language
of the range, even that used by Anglo Americans, is derived mostly from
Spanish words, among them bronco, buckaroo, burro, mesa, canyon,
rodeo, corral, loco, lariat. Yet the cowboy myth in popular folklore, the
one Hollywood has propagated around the world, is of a lone white Anglo sitting tall in the saddle, with Mexicans of the Old West invariably
portrayed either as bandits or doltish peasants riding donkeys.[48]

Texas, however, was not the richest prize of the war with Mexico—
California was. From the early 1800s, New England sea captains who
reached the Pacific sent back glowing reports of that far-off Spanish
colony. Despite those reports, few Anglos had settled in the Far West before the Mexican War because of the long and difficult overland passage
through Indian country necessary to get there. Then, two weeks before
the Treaty of Guadalupe Hidalgo was signed, gold was discovered at Sutter's Mill on the American River. The news touched off an overnight
stampede. Prospectors streamed into the territory from the East, Mexico, and South America, even from Hawaii and Australia. Within a year,
California's non-Indian population rocketed from 20,000 to 100,000,
overwhelming the original Mexican inhabitants, who numbered only
about 13,000, and the territory's several hundred thousand Indians.

The first Mexican and South American prospectors to reach the California fields had a distinct advantage, for they drew on a tradition of gold
and silver mining that dated back to the *conquistadores.* Not surprisingly,
they had more initial success than the inexperienced Anglos from back
East. That success frustrated the white prospectors and soon led to physical attacks, even lynchings, of Mexicans. In 1850, the state imposed a foreign miners tax to give Anglos a better edge.

Even though the gold fields petered out within a few years, the California discoveries provided immediate dividends to the entire country, just as Aztec gold and silver had for sixteenth-century Spain. The mines turned out more than a quarter billion dollars in ore during their first four years. Their revenues spawned a generation of new bankers who rapidly turned to financing myriad other ventures throughout the West. Eventually, the Anglo immigrants shifted their attention to the state's more enduring wealth, its soil. Thousands seized or squatted on the large estates of the native *californios*. Within two decades of the Sutter's Mill discovery, most Mexicans in the state had been driven off their land.

Just as Texas became the country's cotton and cattle center after the war, and California and Nevada its source for gold and silver mining, Arizona and New Mexico gave birth to two other critical U.S. industries—copper and wool.

New Mexico had served as a nexus for sheep raising from early colonial times, the first herds arriving with *conquistador* Juan de Oñate in 1598. By then, Spain already boasted the oldest and most advanced sheep culture in Europe. Its herdsmen introduced the *churro* and *merino* breeds to North America. The *churro*, a small, scrubby animal ideally suited to the arid Southwest, made possible the existence of many far-flung and remote Spanish outposts in the region. Sheep provided not only food and clothing to settlers and soldiers but also were a main source of cash. Over the centuries, New Mexicans evolved an intricate tradition of sheep raising, with formally defined rights, ranks, privileges, even organizations among the sheepherding workforce. As cattle did for South Texas, sheep raising defined much of the culture of New Mexico, Colorado, and parts of California. But the sheep did more than provide culture; they created enormous wealth. Two years after New Mexico became a U.S. territory, southwestern herders were clipping a mere 32,000 pounds of wool annually. By 1880, the number of pounds had zoomed to 4 million.[49]

What sheepherding was for New Mexico, copper became for Arizona. The Spaniards opened their first silver and copper mine, the Santa Rita, in western New Mexico in the early 1800s. That was followed by the Heintzelman mine in Tubac, Arizona, which employed eight hundred men by 1859. Then came the famous Clifton and Bisbee mines in the 1870s. Between 1838 and 1940, Arizona mines produced $3 billion in metal, most of it copper. Workers in the mines were overwhelmingly Mexicans, either natives to the territory or migrants recruited from across the border by labor contractors. "By the mid-1880s," writes Chicano historian Rudy Acuña, "Chihuahuan farmers, after planting their crops, traveled to eastern Arizona and local mines, working for day wages, returning home at harvest time."[50]

But the Mexican contribution to American prosperity didn't stop there. Before the coming of the railroads, Mexican workers provided the main teamster workforce in the Southwest, moving goods across the territory in long mule caravans. And after the railroads arrived, they were the section hands and laborers who maintained them. While the Mexican population of the ceded territories was only 116,000 in 1848, it grew steadily after the war as hundreds of thousands more came and went between Mexico and the United States as migrant laborers, which meant that Mexican influence on the region was far greater than the early population figures might suggest.

The combination of mineral and animal wealth the Anglos found on the annexed Mexican lands, plus the Mexican laborers Anglo businessmen recruited to extract it, provided the underpinnings of twentieth-century western prosperity. That combination made possible the vast expansion of our country's electrical, cattle, sheep, mining, and railroad industries.[51] Yet this historic Mexican contribution has been virtually obliterated from popular frontier history, replaced by the enduring myth of the lazy, shiftless Mexican.

## ANGLO SETTLERS HEAD SOUTH OF THE BORDER

The Mexican annexations of 1836 to 1848, however, were not sufficient to satisfy the expansionist schemes of Manifest Destiny proponents. Some called for seizing more of Mexico's mineral-laden northern territory. Southern planters especially coveted the tropical Central America isthmus, where a half-dozen fledgling republics seemed ripe for conquest.

Perhaps the foremost representative of those expansionists was William Walker. A Tennessee-born lawyer and journalist, Walker hardly fit the image of the swashbuckling mercenary dictator he would become. Originally trained as a doctor, he was soft-spoken, a mere five feet, five inches tall, and weighed a paltry 120 pounds. After a stint as a reporter in San Francisco, Walker appeared in November 1853 in Baja California with a small band of armed followers. From there, he launched an uprising in Mexico's Sonora province, proclaimed the Republic of Sonora, and named himself its president. Within a few weeks, Mexican troops chased him and his ragtag followers back to the United States, where federal agents arrested him for violating U.S. neutrality laws. His audacious uprising made him an instant folk hero of the expansionist press, and all the newspapers reported extensively on his trial and eventual acquittal.

After the trial, Walker shifted his attention farther south, to the little-known isthmus of Central America that had broken away from Mexico in 1823 and formed a loose confederation called the United Provinces of Central America. A few British and North American businessmen, fired by dreams of building a canal across the isthmus to link the Atlantic and Pacific oceans, had started visiting the region shortly after its independence.[52] In 1838, the confederation splintered into five independent countries, and the leaders of those countries were soon locked in intermittent shooting wars with each other. By then, the U.S. government, already concerned about a future canal, reached agreement with Colombia on the need to build that waterway through Panama, which was then a Colombian province. That agreement, cemented in a treaty in 1846, stipulated that the United States would guarantee the neutrality of any future canal.[53]

The California Gold Rush, however, created an instant demand for a faster route to the Pacific Coast. The only sea route at the time, from New York to San Francisco around Cape Horn, took four months, and the narrow Central American isthmus offered the best bet for cutting that time dramatically.

Two competing New York merchant groups had recently secured contracts from Congress to carry mail between California and the East Coast by steamship lines and then overland through Panama. The U.S. Mail Steamship Company, operated by George Law and Marshall O. Roberts, had the Atlantic portion of the route, while William H. Aspinwall's Pacific Mail Steamship Company had the western portion. Using a generous $900,000 annual subsidy Congress allotted them for the mail, the companies decided to transport people as well. Unfortunately, the part of the trip that involved an arduous fifty-mile trek by mule train across Panama's jungle was too forbidding for the average person heading for California. So Aspinwall negotiated a deal with the Colombian government to build a railroad across the isthmus. His Panama Railroad took six years and $2 million to build, and it claimed four thousand lives, most of them West Indian and Chinese laborers whom Aspinwall imported. Once completed, however, the line paid for itself three times over within the first few years of operation.[54]

While Aspinwall was building his line in Panama, Cornelius Vanderbilt, perhaps the most ruthless baron of his age, moved to carve out a quicker competing route through Nicaragua. Vanderbilt and Joseph L.

White, a former congressman, founded the Nicaragua Accessory Transit Company, a combination steamship and railroad line that began operation sooner than Aspinwall's railroad. The Nicaragua company grossed $5 million the first year, with profits of between 20 and 40 per cent.[55]

Aspinwall's railroad and Vanderbilt's steamship line, however, were inadequate for U.S. merchants who wanted a canal through which their goods could travel on ships. Most engineers and politicians in the country favored a canal route through Nicaragua. While a Panama route was shorter, Nicaragua's was easier to build, they argued, since it could incorporate the natural waterways of the San Juan River and giant Lake Managua.

As a result, Nicaragua started to draw increasing attention from both Washington politicians and Anglo fortune hunters. In 1853, U.S. sailors went ashore to defend Vanderbilt's company in a dispute with the local government, and in 1854, the navy bombarded and destroyed the town of San Juan/Greytown over another financial dispute between a U.S. company and local authorities.[56]

Colonel Henry L. Kinney, a land speculator and founder of the Texas Rangers, arrived in 1854. Kinney immediately purchased 22 million acres of Nicaraguan land from trader Samuel H. Shepherd, who claimed he had been "granted" the land in 1839 by the Miskito king. The Nicaraguan government, as might be expected, refused to recognize Kinney's claim to 70 percent of its territory. Shareholders in Kinney's Central American Land and Mint Company included U.S. attorney general Caleb Cushing and Warren Faben, President Pierce's commercial agent in San Juan/Greytown.[57]

A *New York Times* correspondent who lauded Kinney's colonization scheme back then wrote, "Central America is destined to occupy an influential position in the family of nations, if her advantages of location, climate and soil are availed of by a race of 'Northmen' who shall supplant the tainted, mongrel and decaying race which now curses it so fearfully."[58]

To enforce his dubious claim, Kinney armed some followers and launched a revolt against the government, but he was forced to flee after Vanderbilt, anxious that the land dispute not affect his own investments, pressured the British and U.S. governments to oppose his claims.

Despite Kinney's setback, Yankee influence in Nicaragua kept growing. More than six hundred North Americans were living in the country by 1855.[59] By then, England, still the most powerful nation in the world, made clear that it would challenge any U.S. plans to dominate a transoceanic canal project. That year, the two nations negotiated the Clayton-Bulwer

Treaty, in which they agreed to jointly guarantee the neutrality of any future canal, and to refrain from occupying or controlling any of the Central American countries. Neither nation, of course, bothered to consult any of the governments in the region affected by the treaty.

But politicians and merchants weren't the only ones suddenly eyeing Nicaragua. Walker, undaunted by his Mexican fiasco, set sail from San Francisco in 1855 with a band of fifty-six mercenaries he had recruited, supposedly to fight for a faction in Nicaragua's continuing civil war. Shortly after arriving, Walker rebelled against the faction that employed him, seized control of the country, and, in one of the most bizarre episodes of Latin American history, declared himself president.

During his time in office, Walker reinstituted slavery, declared English a coequal language with Spanish, and ordered all lands to be registered. The latter decree facilitated passing many land titles into the hands of Anglo American settlers.[60] Both Walker and the Nicaraguans, however, were actually pawns in a nefarious high-stakes contest for control of the region's commerce by competing groups of U.S. investors. A group of Transit Company officials who had temporarily wrested control of the shipping line from Vanderbilt helped finance Walker's army, while George Law, owner of the U.S. steamship line in Panama and Vanderbilt's chief competitor, supplied Walker with guns. In order to defeat his economic rivals, Vanderbilt bankrolled the allied armies of Costa Rica, Salvador, and Honduras, which defeated and routed Walker in 1857.

Some have attempted to dismiss the Walker adventure as a minor footnote of American history. But during his two years of psychotic and racist rule, more than eleven thousand North Americans settled in Nicaragua, equal to one-third of the total white population in that country at the time.[61] Most of those immigrants were Walker supporters and anywhere from three thousand to five thousand joined his occupying army. In this country, thousands rallied in the major cities to cheer Walker as a hero. A Broadway musical based on his exploits became an overnight hit; the Pierce administration sanctioned his outright aggression by recognizing his government; and the Democratic Party convention of 1856, influenced by Walker's actions, nominated James Buchanan, a more rabid proponent of Manifest Destiny, over his opponent Pierce. As president, Buchanan proceeded to welcome Walker to the White House after his expulsion from Nicaragua. By then, a thousand U.S. citizens had been killed in Walker's War—a death toll far greater than the Spanish-American or Persian Gulf wars.[62] Walker made two more unsuccessful attempts to return to power in Nicaragua. On his final try in

1860, he landed in Honduras, where local soldiers promptly captured and executed him.

By then, Manifest Destiny and the fervor for expansion were being rapidly eclipsed by the conflict over slavery and the war between the North and South. Following the end of the Civil War, the triumphant northern industrialists turned their attention to buying up the western frontier and building a railroad system to connect that frontier to the rest of the country. While a few U.S. policy makers still dreamed of a Central American canal route, the Central American leaders, bitter over the Walker episode, refused to consider the project for decades. The memory of Walker assured that Colombia and Nicaragua would balk at any project that involved American control over their territory.

So Central America turned to Europe instead. In 1880, Frenchman Ferdinand de Lesseps, seeking to replicate his triumph in building the Suez Canal, secured Colombia's permission to begin work on a Panama waterway. Like Vanderbilt's line through Nicaragua and the Panama railroad, the De Lesseps project opted to use West Indian blacks as imported laborers. The French transported fifty thousand blacks to work on the project, but De Lesseps's company collapsed in 1889, engulfing Europe in the biggest financial scandal in history. When all work on the half-finished canal abruptly ended, the West Indian workers were left stranded. As a result, West Indian colonies suddenly sprouted in the towns of Colón and Panama City.[63]

De Lesseps's failure left the U.S.-owned Panama Railroad as the only means of transportation across Central America. Throughout the nineteenth century, the railroad remained the single largest U.S. investment in Latin America and the Colombian government's prime source of revenue. The trip by ocean steamer and the Panama Railroad continued to be the fastest means of transport between the two American coasts until 1869, when the first transcontinental railroad began operating. The Panama line also became a constant source of conflict, as U.S. troops intervened more than a dozen times before 1900 to enforce American control or to protect the line from warring Colombian factions.[64]

For the rest of the nineteenth century, railroads and banana growing became the prime interest of the Anglo merchants who settled on the isthmus. In 1870, Charles Frank, a steward on the Pacific Mail Steamship Line, began growing bananas on land the Panama Railroad owned. During the same decade, Santo Oteri and the Machecca brothers, Italian immigrants from New Orleans, set up banana plantations along the coast of Honduras and Guatemala. Their firm eventually became the Standard

Fruit Company.[65] In 1871, Costa Rica's president granted tycoon Henry Meiggs Keith the contract to build a railroad from the capital of San José to the country's undeveloped Atlantic Coast. Keith, like others before him, imported thousands of West Indian and Chinese laborers for construction. He and his nephew, Minor Keith, eventually branched out into fruit growing. By 1886, their Tropical Trading and Transport Company was shipping twenty thousand tons of bananas annually to the United States.[66]

Far more important than Central America, however, was Mexico. The reign of dictator Porfirio Díaz (1876–1911) turned the country into a paradise for foreign investors. By the time Díaz was overthrown, U.S. investment in Mexico totaled $2 billion. Led by the Rockefellers, Guggenheim, E. H. Harriman, and J. P. Morgan, North Americans ended up controlling all the country's oil, 76 percent of its corporations, and 96 percent of its agriculture. The Hearst family, whose newspapers and magazines routinely lauded Díaz, owned a ranch with a million cattle in Chihuahua. U.S. trade with Mexico, which amounted to only $7 million in 1860, jumped tenfold by 1908. By then, the United States was consuming 80 percent of Mexico's exports and supplying 66 percent of its imports.[67]

## THE LURE OF THE GREATER ANTILLES

The same quest for trade, commerce, and conquest that propelled Americans into Mexico and Central America brought them to the Greater Antilles. As early as 1809, Thomas Jefferson had been eyeing Cuba.[68] "The annexation of Cuba to our federal republic will be indispensable to the continuance and integrity of the Union itself," wrote John Quincy Adams in 1823.[69] But U.S. leaders were unwilling to risk a war with the British navy over the island. They preferred allowing a weak Spain to keep control of Cuba rather see it independent or under the sovereignty of another nation.[70] As Martin Van Buren expressed it, "No attempt should be made in that island to throw off the yoke of Spanish independence, the first effect of which would be the sudden emancipation of a numerous slave population, the result of which could not be very sensibly felt upon the adjacent shores of the United States."[71]

Spain, after all, permitted North Americans to invest in Cuban property, and that was the most important matter. By 1823, as many as fifty North Americans owned plantations valued at $3 million just in the province of Matanzas.[72] Those planters soon joined with Cuban *criollos* and Spanish landlords to seek annexation to the United States. Planter D. B. Woodbury and merchant William F. Safford founded the city of

Cárdenas in 1828 as a port to export sugar. So many U.S. citizens moved
there that sections became virtual North American enclaves. "Our language is more common there than in any other Cuban city," wrote a visitor to Matanzas in 1859.[73] As early as 1848, President Polk offered Spain
$100 million outright for the island. Four years later, President Pierce
upped the offer to $130 million, without success.

While U.S. presidents sought to buy Cuba, American adventurers
sought to capture it with guns, just as they did with Florida, Texas, and
Nicaragua. Between 1848 and 1851, three filibustering expeditions attacked the island. Each was led by Narciso López, a rich former Spanish
army officer who favored annexation to the United States, and in all
three attempts, North Americans made up most of the combatants. Of
six hundred who attacked Cárdenas in 1849, for instance, only five were
Cuban.[74]

Railroad construction in the late 1850s brought thousands of Anglo
engineers and mechanics to the island.[75] This flow of immigrant labor
from the North did not slow until the early 1870s, when the first Cuban
War of Independence, known as the Ten Years' War, forced thousands of
native Cubans and Yankee settlers to flee.

The North Americans returned as soon as the war ended, however.
They rapidly dominated sugar production and established beachheads in
other island industries. Bethlehem and Pennsylvania Steel started iron,
manganese, and nickel subsidiaries, and U.S. investments grew to more
than $50 million by 1890. By then, 94 percent of Cuba's sugar exports
were going to the United States.[76] Among the new arrivals was Lorenzo
Dow Baker, a Massachusetts captain who had initiated a steady trade of
bananas from Jamaica to the United States. Baker joined Boston shipping agent Andrew Preston in 1885 to form a new company, the Boston
Fruit Company. Their firm was importing 16 million bunches of bananas
annually before the turn of the century.[77]

So important did Cuba become to the United States that by the 1880s
it already accounted for nearly one-fourth of our nation's world commerce.[78] On the eve of the Spanish-American War, the island was a
Spanish colony in name only.

A similar pattern developed in the Dominican Republic. After Haiti's
independence in 1804, Haitian armies invaded the eastern end of Hispaniola and freed the Dominican slaves, but they also oppressed the local elite. The occupation eventually sparked a popular rebellion that
drove out the Haitians and led to the founding of the Dominican Republic in 1844. The first emissary from Washington, John Hogan, arrived
the following year. Hogan immediately fixed his sights on the military

potential of spectacular Samana Bay in the northeast. Samana, he reported back home, is "capable of providing protection to all the navies of the world."[79] Dominican president Pedro Santana negotiated an initial deal to provide the bay as a coal refueling station to the U.S. Navy. Santana even broached the idea of the U.S. annexing his country, but opposition in both nations quickly scuttled the scheme.

Next to arrive was William L. Cazneau, who had been involved in Texas secession and later backed Walker in Nicaragua. Cazneau, a fervent expansionist, resurrected the annexation scheme. He won over William Seward, the secretary of state for both Andrew Johnson and Ulysses S. Grant.[80] At Seward's suggestion, Grant publicly announced he favored it, and the white Dominican elite, who were desperate to safeguard against another Haitian invasion, welcomed his offer.

The rest of the Caribbean, however, was too alive with revolutionary ferment to accept annexation quietly. Puerto Rican and Cuban patriots were locked in battle against Spanish rule, while popular movements were in open rebellion against conservative oligarchies in Haiti and the Dominican Republic. When the Haitian rebels triumphed in 1869, they offered their capital of Port-au-Prince as a safe haven to all Caribbean democrats. Among those who accepted the offer were Puerto Rico's Ramón Emeterio Betances and Dominican generals Gregorio Luperon and José Cabral.[81]

In the midst of all this ferment, Grant signed his annexation treaty with Dominican dictator Buenaventura Báez. Grant's idea was to turn the Caribbean country into a colonizing venture for any American blacks who were dissatisfied with the post–Civil War South. The treaty outraged patriots throughout the Antilles, who saw it as the beginning of direct American control of their islands.[82] When he learned of it, Luperon prepared to invade his homeland from Haiti to overthrow Báez. The dictator appealed for U.S. help and Grant ordered the navy to "to resist any effort to invade Dominican territory by land or sea."[83] Grant's navy may have been all-powerful in the Caribbean, but the president had overestimated his strength at home. The Senate, still dominated by post–Civil War Reconstruction radicals, did not share his dreams for a Caribbean empire. Led by Massachusetts abolitionist Charles Sumner, chair of the Foreign Relations Committee, it defeated Grant's treaty in 1870.[84]

The treaty's failure, however, did not deter American planters, who had suddenly discovered another weak, underdeveloped Latin American country that was ripe for exploiting. Before 1850, the bulk of Dominican trade had been with Europe, largely exports of tobacco, cocoa, and coffee.[85] That changed rapidly after three thousand Cuban and Spanish planters relocated to the country during the first Cuban War of Independence. The newcomers, with their advanced steam-driven mill technology, turned sugar into the leading Dominican crop almost overnight. Not far behind the transplanted Cuban planters were British, Italian, and North American planters. Americans Alexander Bass and his son William first acquired the Consuelo Mill in San Pedro de Macorís in the late 1880s. Then, in 1893, the family established the Central Romana, which would become one of the largest plantations in the Western Hemisphere.[86] As the sugar crop expanded, so did the importance of the American market. By 1882, less than forty years after independence, half of all Dominican trade was with the United States. The arriving Americans found a ready benefactor and ally in General Ulises Heureaux, the country's dictator from 1886 until 1899, when he was assassinated by Liberal Party rebels. During his reign, Heureaux reduced tariffs for U.S. imports, concluded numerous secret deals that benefited U.S. sugar growers, borrowed heavily abroad, first from Dutch financiers and later from Wall Street bankers, and filled his jails with anyone who opposed his policies.[87] By the time of his death, his nation had become another economic possession of the United States.

The pattern in U.S.–Latin American relations by now was unmistakable. During the first seventy-five years of their independence, Latin America's leaders had watched incredulously as their northern neighbor annexed first the Floridas, then Texas, then another huge chunk of Mexico. They followed with consternation the exploits of Walker in Nicaragua, of López and his mercenaries in Cuba; they were aghast at the arrogant way North American leaders treated them in diplomatic circles, at the racist labels those leaders used to describe Latin Americans in the U.S. popular press; they watched fearfully as annexation schemes gave way to massive economic penetration, so that by century's end, the Dominican Republic, Mexico, Spain's Cuban and Puerto Rican colonies, and much of Central America had become economic satellites of an expanding U.S. empire.

Anglo Americans, on the other hand, saw a radically different and more benign canvas. Their view of the country's growth was perhaps best captured by historian Frederick Jackson Turner, who saw in the conquest of the frontier the essence of North American democracy, individualism, and progress. "American social development," Turner said in a famous speech in 1893, "has been continually beginning over again on the frontier." That frontier was for Turner the "meeting point between savagery and civilization." He believed that "this fluidity of American life, this expansion westward with its new opportunities, its continuous touch with the simplicity of primitive society, furnish the forces dominating American character." Turner, however, focused exclusively on how European settlers confronted Native Americans and a virgin land. His analysis mentioned nothing of Mexicans and other Latin Americans encountered on the frontier, either as settlers or immigrant laborers, or of their contribution to shaping our national character.

Moreover, this view of the frontier as a democratizing element obscures how western expansion permitted violence to flourish against outsiders as a solution to political problems. Whenever a politician such as Sam Houston or Davy Crockett found his rise barred by opponents at home, he simply packed his bags, conquered some new territory, and created a state where he and his allies could dominate. The frontier thus became an outlet for violence and corruption, for those within American society who wanted the fewest rules and least control.

U.S. territorial expansion did not climax with the closing of the western frontier; rather, it reached its culmination with the Spanish-American War of 1898. The mysterious explosion of the USS *Maine,* together with the prowar fever created by Hearst and other expansionist publishers, convinced President McKinley to seek a declaration of war from Congress. But McKinley balked at recognizing the Cuban rebel army's provisional government as a partner in that war. "Such recognition," McKinley told Congress, "is not necessary in order to enable the United States to intervene and pacify the Island."[88]

Cuban patriots, who were on the verge of victory after thirty years of proindependence struggle, had other ideas. "If intervention shall take place on that basis, and the United States shall land an armed force on Cuban soil," warned Horatio S. Rubens, a lawyer for the Cuban resistance, "we shall treat that force as an enemy to be opposed."[89]

Aware that the Cubans had a combat-hardened army of thirty thousand, Congress rebuffed McKinley and opposed any intervention that did not recognize Cuba's right to independence. Led by Senator Henry M. Teller of Colorado, Congress adopted a final joint war declaration that renounced any U.S. "intention to exercise sovereignty, jurisdiction, or control over said island except for the pacification there of."[90] Thanks to the Teller Amendment, the Cuban rebels welcomed the U.S. invasion and provided critical support to General William R. Shafter's U.S. troops. But once on Cuban soil, Shafter and his solders, mostly southern white volunteers, treated the black Cuban soldiers with utter contempt. "Those people are no more fit for self-government than gunpowder is for hell," Shafter would say.[91] After the capture of Santiago in the key battle of the war, Shafter barred Cuban soldiers from the city, re-fused to allow their general, Calixto García, to attend the Spanish sur-render, and permitted the old Spanish colonial authorities to remain in charge of civilian government.[92]

A long line of historians, beginning with Julius W. Pratt in his 1934 study, *American Business and the Spanish American War,* have since in-sisted that McKinley and the U.S. business establishment were dragged unwillingly into the war and into a colonial empire by Hearst and by pro-expansion intellectuals like Roosevelt, Henry Cabot Lodge, Alfred T. Mahan, and Henry Adams. In *The Rise of Modern America,* Arthur M. Schlesinger asserts that Wall Street actually favored peace with Spain over war. Those historians somehow divorce the war from the entire story of nineteenth-century U.S. expansionism in Latin America. Others, such as Martin Sklar, Walter La Feber, and Philip Foner, offer less ideal-ized accounts. They demonstrate that key sections of American business were demanding rapid expansion into the markets of Asia and Latin America. Foner, in particular, points to how corporate titans Astor, Rockefeller, and Morgan all turned avidly prowar in the months preced-ing Congress's declaration.[93] Spain, a teetering, stagnant power, was never a match for the rising United States. Its defeat finally achieved what Jefferson, John Quincy Adams, and the other Founding Fathers had long sought: plopping Cuba, the juiciest plum of the Caribbean, into U.S. palms, and securing Anglo-American domination over Latin America for the next century. The Treaty of Paris that formally ended the war gave the United States direct control not only of Cuba but also over Puerto Rico, Guam, and the Philippines.

The end of the war brought a new wave of Yankee companies. On March 30, 1899, banana merchants Baker and Preston merged their Boston Fruit Company with Minor Keith's Central American holdings. They called the combined firm the United Fruit Company. At its incep-tion, United Fruit owned more than 230,000 acres throughout the region and 112 miles of railroad.[94] More than any other U.S. company, United Fruit became the twentieth-century symbol of U.S. imperialism. It would evolve into a corporate octopus, controlling the livelihood of hundreds of thousands and toppling governments at will.

The Spanish borderlands had been brought to their knees. The next century would reveal the price of that conquest.

# 3

# Banana Republics and Bonds: Taming the Empire's Backyard (1898–1950)

Laborers are wanted in Hawaii to work in the sugar fields, and in Cuba for the iron mines. Good wages are offered, and many are persuaded to emigrate.

—*Charles Allen, governor of Puerto Rico, 1900–1901*

Victory in the Spanish-American War and the sudden acquisition of overseas colonies made the nation uneasy at first. True, Frederick Jackson Turner and others were espousing the view that territorial expansion and Anglo-American freedom were inseparable, and most Americans believed that, but occupying foreign lands and lording over their peoples seemed to contradict the very liberties for which the nation had fought its own revolution. Not surprisingly, the war with Spain led to our first anti-imperialist movement—against suppression of the Filipino independence movement.

On the whole, outright territorial annexations ceased after 1898. Wars of conquest, the sanctioning of armed invasions by filibuster groups, the purchase of territories, gave way to gunboat diplomacy and to a more disguised yet far more extensive system of financial domination. Economic conquest replaced outright political annexation, as the region evolved into the incubator for the multinational American corporation. By 1924, Latin America accounted for nearly half of all foreign U.S. investment, according one U.S. Department of Commerce estimate (see table 2).

How that gunboat diplomacy and economic penetration deformed the Caribbean region's economy and paved the way for the huge influx of Latino immigrants during the second half of the twentieth century is the subject of this chapter.

### TABLE 2
### U.S. DIRECT INVESTMENT[1]
### 1924

|                          | (*Millions*) |
| ------------------------ | ------------ |
| Europe                   | $1,000       |
| Asia and Oceania         | 690          |
| Latin America            | 4,040        |
| Canada and Newfoundland  | 2,460        |

As we shall see, a series of military occupations early in the century—sometimes brief, sometimes lasting decades, but always for the most spurious of reasons—allowed U.S. banks and corporations to gain control over key industries in every country. Latin American ventures sprang up on Wall Street overnight as sugar, fruit, railroad, mining, gas, and electric company executives raced south on the heels of the marines. Thanks to the aid of pliant local elites and of U.S. diplomats or military commanders who often ended up as partners or managers of the new firms, the newcomers quickly corralled lucrative concessions while the host countries fell deeper into debt and dependence.

Whenever conflict erupted with a recalcitrant nationalist leader, the foreign companies simply called on Washington to intervene. The pretext was usually saving U.S. citizens or preventing anarchy near our borders. To justify those interventions, our diplomats told people back home the Latin Americans were incapable of responsible government. Journalists, novelists, and film producers reinforced that message. They fashioned and perpetuated the image of El Jefe, the swarthy, ruthless dictator with slick black hair, scarcely literate broken-English accent, dark sunglasses and sadistic personality, who ruled by fiat over a corrupt banana republic. Yet even as they propagated that image, our bankers and politicians kept peddling unsound loans at usurious rates to those very dictators.

Critical details of how the dictators rose to power and terrorized their people with Washington's help, or how their regimes provided a "friendly" business climate for North American firms, remained hidden deep in diplomatic correspondences. As U.S.-owned plantations spread rapidly into Mexico, Cuba, Puerto Rico, the Dominican Republic, Honduras, and Guatemala, millions of peasants were forced from their lands.

Some were even displaced from their native countries when some of those same firms initiated cross-border labor recruitment efforts to meet the shifting labor needs of their far-flung subsidiaries. At first, the migratory labor streams flowed largely *between* the subject countries. West Indians, for instance, were recruited to build the Panama Canal, Haitians to cut sugar in the Dominican Republic, Puerto Ricans for the cane fields of Hawaii. But beginning with World War II, which shut down the supply of European labor, North American industrialists initiated massive contracting of Latin Americans for the domestic labor front. Thus began a migration process whose long-term results would transform twentieth-century America.

## PUERTO RICO

Nowhere did the new U.S. policy leave such a profound legacy as in Puerto Rico. When General Nelson Miles landed in the town of Guánica on July 25, 1898, in the midst of the Spanish-American War, most Puerto Ricans greeted his arrival and rejoiced at his promise to end Spanish colonialism. "Our purpose is not to interfere with the existing laws and customs which are beneficial for your people," Miles declared in a proclamation.[2] Few imagined then that the island would remain a U.S. possession for the entire twentieth century, or that it would become the most important colony in our own country's history. Two years after the occupation started, Congress passed the Foraker Act, which declared the island a U.S. territory and authorized the president to appoint its civilian governor and top administrators. The new law permitted islanders their own House of Delegates, but it reserved for Congress the right to annul any laws those delegates passed. It assigned trade, treaty, postal, sanitary, and military powers to the federal government and it gave the island only one nonvoting delegate in Congress.[3] In many ways, the Foraker Act gave Puerto Ricans less self-government than they had enjoyed under Spain. Throughout most of the nineteenth century, after all, Puerto Ricans had been citizens of Spain and island voters had sent as many as sixteen voting delegates to the Spanish Cortes. And, in 1897, Spain had promulgated a new Charter of Autonomy, which gave the island virtual sovereignty.[4]

The Foraker Act, though, went beyond disenfranchising Puerto Ricans. It forbade the island from making commercial treaties with other countries and it replaced the Puerto Rican peso with the American dollar, while devaluing the peso.[5] This made it easier for U.S. sugar companies to gobble up Puerto Rican–owned lands. As a result, thousands of former independent coffee farmers joined the ranks of the mushrooming agricultural proletariat.

Legal challenges to the new law quickly led to several precedent-setting cases before the Supreme Court. Known as the "Insular Cases," they were all decided by a narrow one-vote margin, yet they have provided the principal legal backing for this country's holding of colonies to the present day. They are the equivalent for Puerto Ricans of the Dred Scott Decision for African Americans. Ironically, the same group of justices ruled in Dred Scott and the Insular Cases. The pivotal decision was *Downes v. Bidwell* in 1901. In that case, the Court ruled that "the Island of Porto Rico is a territory appurtenant and belonging to the United States, but not a part of the United States within the revenue clauses of the Constitution."[6] Since the island was not an incorporated territory of the United States, as the frontier territories had been, the Court ruled that the Constitution did not automatically apply in Puerto Rico unless Congress specifically granted Puerto Ricans citizenship.[7] In his dissent, Justice John Marshall Harlan issued a most eloquent rebuttal to the horrendous implications of the decision: "The idea that this country may acquire territories anywhere upon the earth, by conquest or treaty, and hold them as mere colonies or provinces, the people inhabiting them to enjoy only such rights as Congress chooses to accord to them, is wholly inconsistent with the spirit and genius as well as with the words of the Constitution."[8]

Despite the Foraker Act and the Insular Cases, many Puerto Ricans continued to back the U.S. occupation. Labor leaders who had suffered persecution under Spain, and big landowners who saw statehood as opening the U.S. market to their products, especially welcomed it. Trade union leaders never forgot that General Miles's soldiers freed from a Spanish jail the island's legendary labor figure, Santiago Iglesias. Iglesias and his Socialist Party turned into relentless advocates for statehood.[9] So was Luisa Capetillo, the feminist and anarchist popularly known as the first woman in Puerto Rico to wear pants in public. Capetillo blasted those who called for independence as "egotists, exploiters and aristocrats" who were trying to divide Puerto Rican and American workers.[10]

After the Foraker Act's passage, U.S. sugar growers flocked to the island. They not only set up plantations, but they also began recruiting Puerto Rican cane cutters to work in their overseas subsidiaries. Charles Allen, island governor from 1900 to 1901, noted that Anglo emigration agents penetrated the rural districts and offered golden inducements to these simple folk to travel and see foreign lands. Laborers are wanted in Hawaii to work in the sugar fields and in Cuba for the iron mines. Good wages are offered, and many are persuaded to emigrate. They crowd the seaport towns of Ponce, Mayaguez and Guanica. Very few embark at San Juan. . . . Most of them have gone to Honolulu, some thousands have gone to Cuba, and a few to Santo Domingo."[11]

Between 1900 and 1901, more than five thousand Puerto Ricans were transported to Hawaii in a dozen shiploads under contract to the Hawaii Sugar Planters Association.[12] It was a traumatic odyssey, first by ship to New Orleans, then by train to San Francisco, then by ship again to Honolulu, and scores escaped along the way from the harsh treatment they received.[13] The bulk of the migrants eventually settled on Oahu, where they founded the first major Puerto Rican community outside their homeland.

Back in Washington, Congress repeatedly turned down petitions by Puerto Rican leaders for full self-rule and eventual statehood for the island. Its refusal angered even the most avidly pro-annexation leaders, like Dr. Julio Henna and José Celso Barbosa. By 1914, the full Puerto Rican House of Delegates, frustrated by the U.S. intransigence, asked Washington to cede the island its independence. Congress responded instead with the Jones Act in 1917, imposing U.S. citizenship on all Puerto Ricans over the unanimous objection of their House of Delegates.

"The Congress of the United States," declared Minnesota representative Clarence Miller, "says to the people of Porto Rico, once and for all, that they are part of the United States domain and will always remain there; that the legislation for independence in Porto Rico must come to a decided and permanent end."[14]

For the next thirty years, the island remained a direct colony, its Anglo governors appointed by the president, its population virtually ignored by Congress, and U.S. policy toward it controlled by a handful of American sugar companies. The companies so exploited their workers that in the 1930s and 1940s, Puerto Rico became notorious as the poorhouse of the Caribbean and as a hotbed for strikes and anti-American violence. Not until 1948, in response to a growing nationalist movement and to pressure from the United Nations to end colonialism, did Congress allow Puerto Ricans to elect their own governor. Four years later, the United States approved a form of limited self-rule, the Commonwealth of Puerto Rico, which exists to this day.

In fashioning this new political relationship, the Roosevelt and Truman administrations found an able ally in Luis Muñoz Marín, perhaps the most influential figure in the island's modern history. A socialist and *independentista* as a young man, Muñoz became an admirer of Roosevelt and founded the Popular Democratic Party as a New Deal vehicle for the island. Once he gained control of the island's legislature, he pioneered a rapid industrialization program, Operation Bootstrap, which he turned into an economic development model for Third World countries. He lured foreign investment to the island, invariably U.S. companies, by offering them low wages, a tax-free environment to set up their factories, and duty-free export to the mainland.

Flushed by his early economic success, Muñoz deserted the proindependence majority within his own party and opted instead for a form of local autonomy that would keep the island tied to the U.S. economy. That autonomy, Muñoz promised, would only be a transition stage to independence, and in the meantime, Puerto Ricans would retain their own language and culture. The voters, buoyed by the island's postwar prosperity, approved his commonwealth model in 1952. His opponents blasted the referendum as a fraud, since it offered an option only between the existing colony or commonwealth, and neither independence nor statehood was on the ballot.

After the commonwealth vote, Washington began proudly pointing to Puerto Rico in international circles as a "showcase of the Caribbean," both politically and economically. True, by the 1950s the island was boasting one of the highest average incomes in Latin America, but the glowing statistics masked another reality. Every year, the number of people abandoning the countryside for Puerto Rico's cities far outnumbered the new jobs the economy was creating. To prevent renewed unrest, Muñoz and officials in Washington started to encourage emigration north. By the early 1950s, their policy was sparking the largest flight of Latin Americans to the United States that the hemisphere had ever seen (see chapter 4).

## CUBA

The U.S. occupation of Cuba followed a far different path. Much richer in resources than Puerto Rico, with a developed native landowning class and a battle-tested independence army, Cuba was not easily subdued. During the initial occupation, U.S. officials turned the island into a protectorate by forcing the Platt Amendment into the Cuban constitution.

The first occupation government improved roads and health care and opened many new schools. It also presided over a rush of foreign investment. Cuban landowners, crushed by the debt and property destruction of the independence war, became prey to American fortune hunters. "Nowhere else in the world are there such chances . . . for the man of moderate means, as well as for the capitalist as Cuba offers today . . ."[15] an investor of the period boasted. "A poor man's paradise and the rich man's Mecca," said the *Commercial and Financial World* in describing the island. Percival Farquhar, for example, arrived in 1898 and soon controlled an electrification project and a railroad from Havana to Santiago. Minor Keith's United Fruit Company acquired 200,000 acres for a pittance.[16] By 1902, the new Tobacco Trust in the United States controlled 90 percent of the export trade in Havana cigars. All told, U.S. investments nearly doubled, to $100 million, between 1895 and 1902.[17]

The Cuban elite, led by Tomás Estrada Palma, a naturalized U.S. citizen whom the U.S. installed as the country's first president, welcomed the Americans at first, in return for a slice of the growing economic pie. Estrada Palma, like many well-to-do Cubans, favored eventual U.S. annexation. His reelection bid in 1905, however, was marred by widespread voter fraud that provoked violent protests. U.S. troops returned in 1906, installed a provisional government, and stayed for three years.

This second occupation, headed by General Charles E. Magoon, ended up looting the country. When Magoon arrived, Cuba's national treasury had a $13 million surplus; when he left, it had a $12 million deficit. Public works projects he ordered routinely turned into boondoggles that lined the pockets of U.S. contractors. The plum of those concessions went to Frank Steinhart, who had arrived in Cuba as an army sergeant during the first occupation government and was appointed the American consul general in Havana after the troops left. Steinhart then lobbied Washington for the second military occupation and provided valuable intelligence to the U.S. troops. To reward him, General Magoon gave Steinhart the lucrative concession for expanding the Havana Electric Railway, Light and Power Company. Magoon also permitted him, as financial representative for Wall Street's Speyer and Company, to broker a $16.5 million loan to Cuba in 1909 for Havana sewage construction. By 1921, Havana Electric was reporting profits of $5 million a year and the public was calling Steinhart Cuba's Rockefeller.[18]

U.S. soldiers returned for a third time in 1912 to put down a racially charged revolt by black sugar workers. By then, nearly ten thousand Americans were living on the island: they ran the railroads, public utilities, mining and manufacturing companies, sugar and tobacco plantations, shipping and banking concerns, and held much of the government's debt.[19] More than three-fourths of the land was owned by foreigners.[20] Government employment and managerial jobs with foreign companies became the main source of income for the native upper class, and public corruption its primary source of wealth.[21] In 1917, President Wilson dispatched troops for a fourth time to help put down a rebellion against Conservative leader Mario García Menocal, the U.S.-backed candidate who had been reelected president in yet another fraud-tainted vote.

Soaring unemployment in the early 1920s forced many Cuban workers to follow in the tracks of their countrymen who had migrated to the United States during the nineteenth century. The new wave of immigrants settled in New Orleans, New York, Key West, and especially in Tampa, where Spanish, Cuban, and Italian cigar makers had established a thriving industry.[22] At home, the crisis led to frequent labor strikes, and out of that unrest emerged Gerardo Machado, the country's first modern dictator. President Machado made Cuba hospitable for uneasy foreign investors by crushing or coopting the rebellious labor movement. He enjoyed strong support from the directors of National City Bank, J. P. Morgan and Company, and Chase, who showered his government with loans. With each new loan, however, the bankers exacted more control over his government's spending. As the years passed and Machado's reign of terror grew, so did popular resistance.

After one such uprising paralyzed the country in 1933, President Roosevelt concluded that Machado had to go. Roosevelt sent veteran emissary Sumner Welles to head off the unrest by forcing the dictator's resignation. But Welles arrived too late. A nationwide general strike toppled both Machado and a U.S.-backed transitional government and brought to power a provisional revolutionary government, one that Welles could not control. The new government, led by Ramón Grau San Martín, embarked on a radical transformation of the country. It abolished the Platt Amendment, gave women the right to vote, and decreed a minimum wage and an eight-hour day. The liberal revolution Grau launched lasted a mere one hundred days.

Welles was horrified by the Grau government's threat to U.S. interests. Although he considered himself a liberal, Welles, like most U.S. emissaries to Latin America, insisted on local leaders following his wishes. When the Grau government refused to listen, Welles urged Fulgencio Batista, the new commander of the Cuban army, to stage a coup. In January 1934, Batista, whom Welles would laud as an "extraordinarily brilliant and able figure," did just that.[23] Batista's soldiers unleashed a bloody repression that crushed the Grau movement, killing or jailing most of its leaders and scattering the rest into exile abroad. From 1934 to 1944, whether as army strongman or president, Batista became Cuba's unquestioned ruler. To the United States, he offered welcome stability for foreign investors. To the Cuban people, he offered social reforms aimed at improving conditions among the poor. He accomplished the latter by cleverly coopting the program of the Grau movement he had just destroyed. Batista even legalized the Communist Party in exchange for its guaranteeing him the support of Cuba's trade unions. And, in 1940, he oversaw the writing of the most democratic and progressive constitution in Cuba's history. Those reforms were made easier by temporary economic prosperity that bolstered Batista's standing, a prosperity brought about by World War II, and by the increased demand for Cuban agricultural products in the United States. Despite that prosperity, Grau San Martín, who still had a big popular following, won the presidential elections in 1944, and his party stayed in power for the next eight years. Grau's Auténtico Party, however, proved to be the most corrupt in Cuban history. So many officials robbed the treasury that Batista staged another coup in 1952 and easily returned to power. His second period as maximum leader (1952–1958) was even more ruthless than the first. Once again, he jailed or simply eliminated his opponents, but this time, he failed to produce any economic miracles. This time, Cuba's economy, by now a total appendage of the U.S. market, started unraveling. Unemployment skyrocketed, incomes dropped, prostitution and corruption became rampant, and Batista increasingly depended for his power on a bizarre alliance of Wall Street investors, mobsters, and the Cuban managers of U.S. corporations.[24] The Batista dictatorship finally collapsed when the guerrillas of Fidel Castro's twenty-sixth of July Movement marched into Havana on January 1, 1959.

## PANAMA

After Cuba and Puerto Rico, the single largest U.S. expansion into Latin America was the Panama Canal, a project so ambitious, so grandiose, and so critical to the U.S. quest for economic power in the world that President Teddy Roosevelt devised a whole new nation just to house it. As mentioned earlier, commercial groups in the United States had been calling for a Central American canal since the 1850s, with rival groups backing either a project through the mosquito-infested jungle of Colombia's Darién province, or the route along Vanderbilt's old steamship and stagecoach line in Nicaragua. Nicaragua had the widest initial support among most engineers who had studied the project. But Ohio senator Mark Hanna, the powerful chairman of the national Republican Party, had other ideas. Hanna's close friend, New York lawyer William Nelson Cromwell, was an investor in the Panama route. A $60,000 donation by Cromwell to the Republicans in the midst of the debate seems to have strengthened Hanna's resolve and enabled him to secure a congressional majority for the Panama route.[25]

Colombia's president at the time was José Manuel Marroquín. As luck would have it, Marroquín had just come through a costly three-year civil war and was seeking a quick infusion of cash to bolster his exhausted treasury. So he offered President Teddy Roosevelt precisely what Nicaragua's president at the time, José Santos Zelaya, was refusing to give the United States—sovereignty over a ten-kilometer zone on both sides of the canal route. The result was the Hay-Herrán Treaty of 1903. But the treaty hit a snag at the last moment when Marroquín's opponents in the Colombian congress rejected the ten-kilometer provision as a violation of national sovereignty.

Their rejection enraged Roosevelt, who was not about to permit some petty feud among inferior Latin Americans to stop the greatest engineering project in U.S. history. Roosevelt countered by backing a plan for the province's armed secession. With the president's backing, Cromwell, along with Frenchman Philippe Bunau-Varilla and Panamanian Manuel Amador, both investors in the Panama project, prepared a blueprint for the uprising during a series of meetings in a New York hotel. On November 2, 1903, Bunau-Varilla and Amador led a rebel band that captured the port towns of Panama City and Colón. While U.S. sailors dispatched by Roosevelt assured the revolt's success by blocking the entry of Colombian troops into Colón harbor, Amador proclaimed Panama's independence. The new Panamanian government promptly named Bunau-Varilla its new ambassador to the United States, and he lost no time in signing the now renamed Hay–Bunau-Varilla Treaty. So embarrassing was the "independence" revolt that Congress was forced to hold hearings in which Roosevelt's role as the Panamanian godfather was revealed.[26]

It took ten long years (1904 to 1914) and 35,000 workers for the U.S. Panama Canal Company to complete the project. Most of the workers were English-speaking West Indians recruited by the company. If you include the families of those workers, more than 150,000 West Indians migrated to Panama during construction. This enormous migration, which equaled more than a third of Panama's Spanish and Indian population of 400,000, transformed every aspect of the new country's life.[27]

While press accounts praised the marvelous North American engineering feat through some of the world's thickest jungle, they rarely mentioned the critical role immigrant black workers played, or their disproportionate sacrifice. During the first ten months of 1906, for instance, the death rate for white canal employees was seventeen per thousand, while among West Indians, it was fifty-nine per thousand.[28]

The canal's opening led to enormous expansion of transoceanic trade for the United States, and the waterway became an invaluable military resource for the country during both World War I and World War II. The Canal Zone itself soon evolved into a miniature separate country within Panama, with several U.S. military bases and thousands of troops permanently assigned to guard it. Many of the West Indian laborers could not afford to return home when the main construction was complete, so they stayed on as maintenance workers. Canal Zone administrators and military commanders, many of them white southerners, soon replicated the same racial apartheid system that had existed for centuries in the American South. They established separate "gold" payrolls for American citizens and much lower "silver" ones for the noncitizen West Indians. Native Panamanians, meanwhile, were excluded from any jobs in the Zone. Blacks lived in squalid segregated company towns, while the whites resided in more opulent Zone communities, where everything from housing to health care to vacations were subsidized by the federal government.[29] For decades afterward, West Indians and Panamanians clashed with each other and with the Zone's Anglo American minority over the discriminatory conditions (see chapter 9).

But the checkered story of U.S. control in Panama, Puerto Rico, and Cuba pales beside the bloody sagas of the Dominican Republic and Nicaragua, where long U.S. military occupations provoked costly guerrilla wars.

## THE DOMINICAN REPUBLIC

The U.S. presence in the Dominican Republic, as we have noted, began with nineteenth century dictator Ulises Heureaux, who saddled his country with massive foreign debt. To stave off bankruptcy, he hatched a refinancing plan in 1892 with the country's Dutch creditors and some New York investors. As part of the scheme, the Dutch sold their debt to a newly formed U.S. firm, the Santo Domingo Improvement Company, one of whose officers was a member of President Benjamin Harrison's cabinet. The new firm paid off the Dutch bonds and secretly gave Heureaux millions of dollars in new loans. Heureaux, in turn, gave the firm control of the national bank and one of the country's two railroads.

Only after Heureaux's assassination in 1896 did the new Dominican government discover that the former president had racked up $34 million in debt, the bulk of it to foreign creditors. The country's annual customs revenues, its main source of income at the time, was a mere $2 million. A good portion of the debt, it turned out, had been fraudulently marketed by the Improvement Company to unsuspecting Catholic farmers in Europe who thought they were lending money to the Dominican religious order, not the Dominican Republic![30]

When a financial crisis hit in 1905, and customs revenues plummeted, the new government suspended debt payments, which prompted several European powers to threaten intervention to collect their money. President Roosevelt, worried that sea lanes to his unfinished Panama Canal might be imperiled by a European occupation, stepped in and offered to consolidate the Dominican debt with a new loan from a New York bank. Roosevelt insisted, however, that the Dominicans turn over all customs revenues to a U.S.-appointed agent and earmark the lion's share of it for debt service. No longer would they be able to raise government spending or increase taxes without U.S. consent.

From that point on, the country was effectively a financial protectorate. Once Roosevelt's overseers arrived, they jump-started additional legal reforms to benefit foreign investors. In 1906, for instance, they pressured the government to grant tax exemptions to all sugar produced for export. In 1911, they convinced it to permit the division of communally owned lands, making it easier for sugar growers to enlarge their holdings. Each time Dominican officials balked at some new demand from Washington, Yankee warships appeared offshore to force their submission.

Defenders of the protectorate justified it by pointing to the country's history of political violence and instability—in the first seventy-two years of independence, Dominicans had experienced twenty-nine coups and forty-eight presidents. Some of the very people who ridiculed Dominican instability, however, conveniently overlooked that foreigners had financed much of the fighting. By 1915, a decade after Washington's protectorate commenced, political violence had not diminished. Rather than question its methods, Washington chose to tighten its hold on the country's purse strings.

By then, war was looming in Europe, and President Woodrow Wilson had a new worry, that a major faction in Dominican politics might try to ally their country with Germany. To avert that possibility, he demanded from the president, Juan Isidro Jiménez, the right to appoint U.S. citizens to key posts in the Dominican government and to replace the country's army with a new U.S.-trained National Guard. For a nation that had fought so long against Spanish, Haitian, and French occupation, these new conditions were unacceptable. Even Jiménez, who had been installed by the United States, rejected them. Wilson retaliated by freezing the government's customs revenues. Still, the population refused to back down; thousands of government employees rallied behind their leaders and worked for months without pay.

In May 1916, Wilson sent in the marines, dissolved the legislature, imposed martial law and press censorship, and jailed hundreds of opponents. The occupation would last eight long years. It prompted widespread protests against the United States throughout Latin America, created deep bitterness in the Dominican population, and radically altered every sphere of Dominican society.

Supporters of the occupation point to the many improvements the marines brought about—supervising construction of the Caribbean's most modern highway system, reforming government financing, building hundreds of public schools, and carrying out successful public health campaigns against malaria, and venereal and intestinal diseases. But the building program was financed with more foreign borrowing and by new taxes on property, alcohol, and other domestic manufacturing. And much of the early prosperity the country enjoyed was due to the war in Europe, which drove up the demand for sugar, tobacco, and other Dominican agricultural products. And no matter how the economy fared, Dominicans chafed under successive martial law governors who ruled them arrogantly in their own country. Even the elite in the cities refused to cooperate with the occupation army.

In the eastern part of the country, around the sugar plantation region of San Pedro de Macorís and Romana, a half-dozen peasant bands mounted sporadic guerrilla resistance. The guerrillas, led by Martín Peguero, Ramón Natera, and Vicente Evangelista, proved adept at frustrating the Americans. Marines dispatched to the area committed so many atrocities against the local population that they drove most civilians to the side of the guerrillas.[31]

The infrastructure and health improvements the marines ushered in did not compare to the profound economic and military changes they set in motion. Those changes left the country irreversibly dependent on the United States. In 1919, for instance, a customs law opened the country to imports by declaring 245 U.S. products duty-free, while it sharply lowered tariffs on 700 others. The surge of imports that ensued drove many local Dominican producers out of business.

New property tax and land registration acts followed. The land law, in particular, created tremendous upheaval. Like all former Spanish colonies, the Dominican Republic's land tenure system had revolved for centuries around family-owned *mayorazgos*. The holdings of individuals were rarely demarcated from the rest of the family; informal agreements on land use predominated. The first land speculators and planters from the United States found the system an obstacle to the quick buying and selling of property. So, just as in Texas, California, and other former Spanish territories, they quickly set about rewriting the land laws. The sugar companies made the first try in 1911, but Dominicans were slow to implement the changes, and massive forging of titles and poor records doomed the effort. But the occupation government was more efficient. The marines ordered the immediate registration, surveying, and division of all communal lands and created a new land court to arbitrate disputes and administer the law.

As might be expected, the sugar companies hired the best lawyers and quickly bamboozled or bested thousands of illiterate peasants in the new land courts. Take the case of the New York–based Barahona Company, which was organized in 1916, the year of the invasion. By 1925, it had amassed 49,400 acres, largely from buying communal holdings, and was the second-largest plantation in the country. The Central Romana mushroomed in size from 3,000 acres in 1912 to 155,000 acres in 1925.[32] By 1924, twenty-one sugar companies controlled 438,000 acres—a quarter of the country's arable land. More than 80 percent of it belonged to twelve U.S. companies.[33] As land for subsistence farming diminished, staples had to be imported from the United States and the prices of food skyrocketed.[34]

But the sugar boom did not lead to higher wages. Instead of increasing what they paid their Spanish-speaking workers, the growers shifted to bringing in English-speaking blacks from Jamaica, the Virgin Islands, Turks and Caicos, whom they regarded as more docile and better suited to their needs than the Dominicans, Cubans, or Puerto Ricans. At some Dominican sugar mills, the entire workforce became English-speaking. Many of those migrants settled in the country after the harvest season, and their descendants inhabit areas around the old mills to this day. Local residents, angry at how the immigrant blacks siphoned jobs away from natives, took to labeling them *cocolos,* a racial pejorative that still persists in the Caribbean.[35] Finally, the American planters at Central Romana and other giant mills turned to Haitian laborers. Nearly half of 22,000 contract workers officially imported in 1920 were Haitians, but some estimates put the number of legal and illegal Haitians during the harvest season as high as 100,000.

Appalled by the greed of the sugar companies, military governor Harry S. Knapp protested to the secretary of the navy in 1917: "I would greatly prefer to see the Dominican people, and especially the poorer classes, brought to the point where they can work a small plot of land on their own account and leaving the fruits of their labors in Santo Domingo, than to see great companies come here and exploit the country, taking out of it immense sums in the form of their profits."[36] Knapp's complaints were ignored.

The occupation's other lasting legacy was the national police. As soon as they landed, the marines set about building a modern force that could control the population permanently. Unfortunately, once the marines left, that force copied the same arbitrary methods of the occupation army. One of the early recruits to the new police force was a former security guard for one of the sugar companies, Rafael Leónidas Trujillo. American commanders, impressed with the young man's intelligence and leadership ability, promoted him rapidly through the ranks.

In 1920, Republican Warren Harding captured the White House, and the new president dispatched Sumner Welles, the same diplomat who would later engineer Batista's coup, to arrange a U.S. withdrawal from Santo Domingo. Welles antagonized most Dominican leaders with his heavy-handed meddling in their plans for a postevacuation government while he was simultaneously lobbying for business contracts for his friends in the United States. Those contracts saddled the country with even greater debt than before the occupation.[37] It was not until 1924 that Welles finally arranged the withdrawal of the marines. Once they were gone, Trujillo, who was notorious for his corruption and ruthlessness, rose rapidly to commander of the rechristened national army, then was elected president in 1930 during a campaign in which his soldiers terrorized all opponents. At first, Washington was cold to him, but American diplomats eventually decided his stern methods were preferable to continued instability.

For the next thirty years, either as president or through handpicked successors, Trujillo perfected the most notorious dictatorship in the hemisphere, running the country as a private fiefdom for his family and friends. Known throughout the country as El Jefe, or The Boss, his atrocities became legendary. He routinely kidnapped and raped Dominican women, even the wives and daughters of his subordinates.[38] He tortured,

jailed, or executed thousands, including eighteen thousand Haitians massacred by his army in October 1937. His spies even tracked down and
murdered his opponents in exile. His psychotic cruelty was immortalized
in Gabriel García Márquez's haunting novel, *The Autumn of the Patri-
arch*. Only when he tried to assassinate the president of Venezuela in
1960 did the U.S. government, hoping to prevent a repeat of Batista's
overthrow in Cuba, begin to work for El Jefe's ouster. In May 1961, a
group of his own officers assassinated him with the support of the CIA
(see chapter 7).

## NICARAGUA

Nicaraguans, meanwhile, were living through their own reign of the
*jefes*. In their case, it was the rule of Anastasio Somoza García and his
family. The Somozas' reign, like Trujillo's and Batista's, had its origins
in an American occupation. Despite the debacle of the Walker wars,
Nicaragua was a stable and prosperous country at the dawn of the twentieth century, thanks to José Santos Zelaya, a popular Liberal who served
as president from 1893 to 1909. On the surface, Zelaya provided the kind
of forward-looking, well-managed government other Latin American
nations lacked. He even welcomed outside investment and paid the foreign debt on time. But he was also a nationalist, one who handed out lucrative commercial monopolies to favored Nicaraguans while refusing
special treatment for foreigners. That brought him into conflict with the
handful of U.S. executives who owned extensive banana, mahogany, and
mining concessions in the country.

The concessions, all unregulated and untaxed, had been granted by
Miskito leaders in the English-speaking Bluefields section along the Atlantic Coast before Zelaya came to power. The foreign managers often
quarreled with the central government over new taxes, and in both 1894
and 1899 they fomented unsuccessful anti-Zelaya revolts. Each time, the
U.S. Navy intervened to protect their properties from confiscation.[39]

Zelaya's dispute with the Bluefields companies was just the beginning
of his troubles. As we have seen, he lost the transoceanic canal project at
the turn of the century because he would not give the United States sovereignty over the transitway. Then, in 1907, war broke out between
Nicaragua and a coalition of Honduras, Guatemala, and El Salvador. Zelaya's army won several quick victories and occupied Honduras. With
Nicaraguan troops advancing rapidly, the North American banana companies there convinced President Roosevelt to dispatch marines to protect their plantations. U.S. troops were on the verge of confronting

Zelaya's army when secretary of state Elihu Root and Mexican president Porfirio Díaz convinced the Nicaraguan leader to withdraw. Their
peace talks ended with the establishment of a Central American Court
of Justice to arbitrate future conflicts.[40] The war, however, had raised
Zelaya's stature considerably. He was now an unquestioned regional
power—much to the discomfort of U.S. officials.

After William Howard Taft succeeded Roosevelt, Taft's secretary of
state Philander Chase Knox fashioned a new policy for the Caribbean.
Historians dubbed it "dollar diplomacy." Knox, one of the best corporate
lawyers of his day, was no stranger to Latin America. He had spent time
in Panama and Cuba, and his former law firm represented the Fletcher
family of Pittsburgh, which owned two major Nicaraguan firms, the
United States and Nicaragua Company, and La Luz and Los Angeles
Mining Company.

Knox's idea of financial reform was to set up customs receiverships in
the region, and to replace European investment bankers, who held most
of Central America's debt, with U.S. companies. To accomplish those
ends, Knox did not scoff at calling in the marines.[41] He immediately decided Zelaya was an obstacle. After losing the canal project, Zelaya had
embarked on his own vision for a transit route across Nicaragua—a railroad that would unite the west coast to the isolated Atlantic region. He
cut a deal with a German firm to build the railway and secured a $1.2
million loan from a British-French syndicate. Such financial independence irked not only Knox but also the banking houses of Brown Brothers, J. W. Seligman, and J. P. Morgan and Company, all of which were
seeking a slice of the Central American loan business. In 1909, Juan
Estrada, a Liberal Nicaraguan army officer, and Conservative Emiliano
Chamorro rebelled against Zelaya. By then, sensational American newspaper accounts had begun vilifying the charismatic president as a
butcher and tyrant, creating the first El Jefe stereotype among the American public.[42]

The Estrada rebellion against Zelaya, like that of Amador and Bunau-
Varilla in Panama, was hardly homegrown. It was planned in New Orleans and financed by U.S. companies through Alfonso Díaz, an
executive of the Fletchers' Los Angeles Mining Company.[43] Scores of
Anglo soldiers of fortune joined the rebels as advisers, in a throwback to
the old filibuster revolts of the nineteenth century. Among the mercenaries were Godfrey Fowler, an active-duty captain in the Texas National
Guard; Leonard Groce. who had been mining in Central America for
years; and Virginia-born businessman Lee Roy Canon. Shortly after the

rebellion started, Nicaraguan troops captured Canon and Groce as they were trying to dynamite a troop boat. Zelaya had them court-martialed and sentenced to death. That was all the excuse Taft needed to break diplomatic relations and launch a campaign for Zelaya's ouster. The U.S. pressure quickly forced his resignation, but the crisis ended only when Estrada and Díaz, Washington's choices, gained power in 1910.

The new leaders dutifully carried out all the "reforms" Knox wanted. They refinanced Zelaya's old English-French debt through Brown Brothers and Seligman, they installed a U.S. overseer to collect customs duties, and they invited American troops into the country. In the process, they also looted the treasury.[44] By the middle of 1912, the two Wall Street firms controlled the new National Bank of Nicaragua (chartered in Connecticut), and the Pacific Railroad (incorporated in Maine). Zelaya's own dream of uniting eastern and western Nicaragua by rail line died with his ouster.[45] For the next thirteen years, a small force of marines remained in the country as Washington and Wall Street dictated the country's financial affairs.

The marines left in 1925 but were forced to return the following year when a new civil war erupted. This time, General Chamorro was trying to reinstall Díaz to power over Liberal Juan Sacasa, who had won the previous year's election. The marines claimed neutrality but threw their support to Díaz after peasants in the countryside took up arms to bring the popular Sacasa back to power.[46] The peasant revolt lasted seven years, and it turned rebel leader Augusto César Sandino into a legend. Hundreds of volunteers from other countries joined Sandino's army, as it repeatedly eluded both government forces and the six thousand marines sent by Washington. When those soldiers bombed and machine-gunned to death some three hundred unarmed men, women, and children in a massacre at Ocotal in July 1927, public sentiment in the United States turned against the war occupation.[47] The marines hung on on until the Nicaraguans elected Sacasa president once again in 1932, whereupon public protests forced their withdrawal.

Sandino then rode triumphantly into Managua and embraced Sacasa at the presidential palace. It was the first time the United States had faced defeat in Latin America, and our leaders would not forget it. Before departing, the marines managed to train a new National Guard and install its English-speaking commander, Anastasio Somoza García. Somoza's soldiers ambushed and executed Sandino two years later. The assassination, according to several historians, had the secret backing of Ambassador Arthur Bliss Lane.[48] Somoza wasted little time in ousting

Sacasa and turning Nicaragua into his personal fiefdom. After Somoza, his two sons succeeded him as the country's strongmen, assuring Somoza family control right up to the Sandinista revolution in 1979.

———

What propelled our government to assume this role of regional police-man throughout the Caribbean and Central America in the early twenti-eth century? Some historians argue that prior to World War I, our leaders genuinely feared that the Germans or other Europeans would establish beachheads near U.S. shores. But even after World War I ended and left the United States the unquestioned power in the Caribbean, the interventions continued.

Others point to the crush of U.S. bankers and businessmen who loaned money to Latin American governments, much of it on unsound ventures. National City Bank opened the first Latin American branch of a U.S. bank in Argentina in November 1914; five years later, it had established forty-two branches.[49] U.S. firms floated some $2 billion in Latin Ameri-can government bonds during the 1920s, most of it in Mexico, Central America, and the Caribbean. Once those loans were made, the bankers expected the marines to protect their investment.[50] But then came the Wall Street Crash. Beginning with Bolivia in 1931, every Latin American country except Haiti defaulted on its loans. U.S. investors retreated from the region throughout the Depression years.

Whatever the reason for those early interventions, Franklin D. Roo-sevelt's election to the presidency brought a new approach to Latin America. Overt bullying from Washington and military occupations largely ended. Instead, American diplomats in the region sought to con-trol events through pliant pro-U.S. dictators who were expected to main-tain order. The mid-1930s and the 1940s thus became the heyday of *los jefes*. Except for a few, their names are almost unknown to the U.S. public. But to their countrymen, they represent lost decades so filled with horror and darkness that some nations are only now recovering.[51] Such was the period not only of Trujillo, Batista, and the Somozas, but of Guatemala's Jorge Ubico Castañeda, El Salvador's Maximiliano Hernández Martínez, and Honduras's Tiburcio Carías Andino. What seemed to unite them all was their ability to curry favor with Uncle Sam, first as allies against fascism during World War II, then as dependable anti-Communists in the late 1940s and 1950s.

Following the war, North American companies that resumed invest-ment in the region invariably saw the *jefes* as dependable strongmen who offered welcome stability after decades of unrest. Direct U.S. investments tripled in Latin America between 1955 and 1969, mostly from mining, petroleum, and manufacturing, and profit margins skyrocketed.[52] Between 1950 and 1967, for instance, new U.S. investment in Latin America totaled less than $4 billion, but profits were nearly $13 billion.[53]

The soaring commerce and the rise of a Communist bloc in Europe and Asia brought with it a renewed determination by Washington to control its Latin American backyard. Wherever social democratic or radical leftist regimes came to power and threatened the business climate for U.S. companies, Washington responded by backing right-wing opponents to overthrow them. In 1954, the CIA helped oust the liberal reform government of Jacobo Arbenz in Guatemala.[54] In 1961, the agency organized the failed Bay of Pigs invasion of Cuba. Four years later, the marines invaded the Dominican Republic again, just as rebels loyal to the democratically elected president Juan Bosch were about to defeat a group of generals who had ousted Bosch in a coup two years before. Similar scenarios emerged in Chile under Salvador Allende, in Peru under Juan Velasco Alvarado in the 1970s, and in Nicaragua under Sandinista leader Daniel Ortega in the 1980s. When all else failed, our leaders resorted to direct invasion, as with Grenada in 1983 and Panama in 1989.

But as U.S. capital increasingly penetrated Latin America during the century, something else began to happen: Latin American labor headed north. More than a million people, one-tenth of Mexico's population, migrated to the Southwest between 1900 and 1930.[55] Some fled the chaos and repression of the 1910 revolution, but many were recruited as cheap labor for the railroads, mines, and cotton and fruit farms out West.

The Santa Fe and Southern Pacific, for instance, enlisted sixteen thousand Mexicans in 1908 for their lines. Henry Ford brought several hundred Mexicans in 1918 as student-workers to Detroit, so that by 1928, there were fifteen thousand Mexicans living in the Motor City.[56] In 1923, Bethlehem Steel contracted a thousand Mexicans to work in its Pennsylvania mill. That same year, National Tube Company brought thirteen hundred migrants from Texas to work in its plant at Lorain, Ohio.[57] Great Western Sugar Beet Company brought more than thirty thousand Mexicans to the Colorado beet fields in the 1920s and 1930s. The Minnesota Sugar Company offered transportation, housing, and credit to Mexicans to migrate to that state. By 1912, there was a Mexican *colonia* in Saint Paul.[58] Similar contracting occurred in Michigan and Kansas.

After World War II, the trickle of migrants became a torrent, beginning with the Puerto Ricans in the 1950s, and followed by the Cubans and Dominicans in the 1960s, the Colombians in the 1970s, and the Central Americans in the 1980s. The migrations came from the same Caribbean countries our soldiers and businessmen had already penetrated, cowed, and transformed. But each country's diaspora, as we shall see, was markedly different. Different in class makeup. Different in customs. Different in where and how they settled, and in how America responded to them. Their separate odysseys were as rich in experience and as varied as those of the English, Irish, Italians, and Poles who came before them. Yet, they shared one bond that other waves of immigrants had not—a common language.

Toward the end of the twentieth century, those Latin American newcomers started to transform this country in ways no one had expected. Anglo conquest had boomeranged back to U.S. shores.

# PART II

# *Branches*
# (Las Ramas)

# 4

# *Puerto Ricans: Citizens Yet Foreigners*

> Marcantonio lost the election. They're jumping every Spic they
> can find.
>
> —*New York City cop,*
> *1950*

U ntil World War II, Mexican farmworkers were the most familiar
Latin Americans in this country. True, a Latino might occasionally
turn up in a Hollywood film role, or leading a band in a New York
nightclub, or as the fancy fielder of some professional baseball team,
but outside the Southwest, Anglo Americans rarely saw Hispanics in
everyday life and knew almost nothing about them.

Then the Puerto Ricans came.

More than 40,000 migrated from the Caribbean to New York City in
1946 alone. Actually, a small Puerto Rican enclave had existed in that
city since World War I, and that *colonia* grew to 135,000 by the end of
World War II, but the year 1946 saw an astonishing explosion in Puerto
Rican arrivals, one that continued without letup for the next fifteen
years. By 1960, more than 1 million were in the country, part of what one
sociologist dubbed "the greatest airborne migration in history."[1] Today,
almost as many Puerto Ricans live in the fifty states, 2.8 million, as on the
island, 3.8 million.

My family was part of that 1946 wave. My parents, Juan and Florinda
Gonzalez, arrived on one of the first regular Pan American Airline flights
from San Juan. Along with the Mexican *braceros* out West, they were pioneers of the modern Latino diaspora.

Puerto Ricans were uniquely suited for a pioneer role. To this day, only
we among all Latin Americans arrive here as U.S. citizens, without the
need of a visa or resident alien card. But this unique advantage, a direct
result of Puerto Rico's colonial status, has also led to unexpected obstacles. Despite our de jure citizenship, the average North American,
whether white or black, continues to regard Puerto Ricans as de facto
foreigners. Even the Supreme Court, as we have seen, has had difficulty

explaining the Puerto Rican condition. The contradiction of being at once citizens and foreigners, when joined with the reality that ours was a racially mixed population, has made the Puerto Rican migrant experience in America profoundly schizophrenic, more similar in some ways to that of African Americans or Native Americans than to any other Latino group.

To comprehend that schizophrenia, we would do well to examine the forces that shaped the Puerto Rican worldview: Why did the migrants leave their homeland in such numbers? What happened when they arrived here? How did others regard them? How did they cope with and survive in their new conditions? Why did so many get stuck in poverty, unable to climb the immigrant ladder? Hopefully, my family's story, one very typical of that early migration, will provide some insight.

## WHY WE CAME

One morning in May 1932, road workers found chief engineer Teofilo González, my grandfather, feverish and delirious at their work camp on Puerto Rico's southwest coast. He died a few days later of pneumonia, and his death immediately plunged his young wife, María González Toledo, and their six children into abject poverty.[2]

My grandmother had married Teofilo in 1914 in the mountain town of Lares. She was sixteen at the time, an orphan, illiterate, and desperate to escape from her Spanish-born godmother, who had raised her as a virtual servant. Her new husband was thirty-four, well educated, and the eldest son of a prosperous coffee grower whose own parents had migrated to Lares from the Spanish island of Majorca in the late 1850s.

Puerto Rican *criollos* resented the Majorcan *peninsulares* who quickly bought up most of the businesses in Lares and rarely employed the town's native-born residents.[3] The Majorcans were loyal to the Spanish Crown, while Lares was a hotbed of separatist and abolitionist sentiment. On September 23, 1868, El Grito de Lares erupted. It was the most significant independence revolt in island history. My grandfather's parents, Teofilo González, Sr., and Aurelia Levi, were only teenagers then, but they cheered the Spanish soldiers who quickly crushed the rebellion. To quell further unrest, Spain's Cortes abolished slavery on the island in 1873, but my great-grandparents, like many of the small coffee farmers in the region, circumvented the emancipation decree and illegally kept a few black laborers on their farm as semislaves. This infuriated their youngest son, Onofre, who soon turned into a political dissident opposed to Spanish rule.

According to family legend, my great-grandparents scoffed at Onofre and called him a crazed idealist. They were still ridiculing him when the Spanish-American War erupted and U.S. soldiers landed at Guánica. Soon after, Onofre stole several of his father's horses and rode south to volunteer his services to the Yankee invaders. He returned after a few weeks, proudly galloping into Lares as the lead scout for a column of U.S. soldiers.[4]

That early military occupation, as we have seen, quickly disillusioned even its Puerto Rican supporters. It wrecked the small coffee and tobacco growers who were the backbone of the island's economy. U.S. sugar companies gobbled up the land and created a vast agricultural proletariat whose members only worked a few months of the year. For the multitudes of poor, life became unbearable. "I have stopped at farm after farm, where lean, underfed women and sickly men repeated again and again the same story—little food and no opportunity to get more,"[5] Theodore Roosevelt, Jr., governor of the island for a time, wrote in 1929.

During those desperate years, María and Teofilo González lost five of their eleven children to disease. Still, they were in better shape than most, thanks to his job building roads for the government. After her husband's death in 1932, though, the family's fortunes plummeted. María sold the big house they owned in the southern coastal city of Ponce and moved to a squalid shack in El Ligao, the worst section of the Mayor Cantera slum high in the hills of town. She found work as an aide in Ponce's Tricoche Hospital and occasionally as a coffee bean picker in the fields near Lares.

But the odd jobs could not provide enough money to support a large family, so she reluctantly gave several of her children away to friends in hopes of saving them from starvation. Her oldest daughter, my aunt Graciela, she placed with neighbors who owned a local store, and there the girl worked behind the counter in return for food and board. She sent another girl, my aunt Ana, to live with a neighbor as a housekeeper. She dispatched one son, my uncle Sergio, to live with a childless schoolteacher.

But her two youngest, my aunt Pura and my father, Pepe, were too young to be useful to anyone, so she placed six-year-old Pepe in an orphanage. The day she left him with the nuns at the orphanage, his terrified wails almost crushed her heart. Her guilt was so great that after a few years, she reclaimed him from the nuns and sent him to live with another childless teacher. But the teacher sexually abused Pepe for years, turning him into a sullen and explosive alcoholic. Throughout the rest of his life there was such aimless rage buried inside him that whenever he drank heavily, he would always recite the story of how his mother had abandoned him.

Pura, the only one left at home, became her mother's constant companion—the other children were permitted to visit their mother only a few Sundays a month. María dragged the little girl with her everywhere. She hid her under the sink in the hospital whenever the supervisors appeared; in the fields, she would tie a can around Pura's neck and show her how to pluck the coffee beans with her tiny fingers. The psychological scars left in all of them by their long childhood separation were so deep that decades later, after they'd all been reunited and the family had moved to New York City, the González brothers and sisters never spoke openly of those times.

The 1930s were the most turbulent in Puerto Rico's modern history, and Ponce, where my family had settled, was the center of the storm. The Depression turned the island into a social inferno even more wretched than Haiti today. As one visitor described it:

> Slow, and sometimes rapid, starvation was found everywhere. If one drove a car over the country roads, one was delayed again and again by sorrowing funeral processions carrying the caskets of dead infants.
>
> Most of the cities were infested by "wolf gangs" of children ranging in ages from six to sixteen, many of whom had no idea who their parents were. They pilfered and robbed; they "protected" parked automobiles, and if the drivers didn't want to pay for such protection, they siphoned gasoline out of tanks, stole hub caps, slashed tires. They slept where they could—in parks, in hallways, in alleys.[6]

Ponce's hilltop El Ligao was notorious for its violence and crime. Neighbors often feuded and brutal killings in machete or knife fights were commonplace. One day, Pura González watched in horror as a young resident named Saro, who sold ice in a small pushcart, was dragged bleeding through the dirt street in front of her house by four men who brazenly hanged him from a tree, stabbed and castrated him. Saro, she discovered, was a numbers runner. An important town official had placed a bet with him, but when the number hit and the official came to collect his money, he discovered Saro had blown it all on liquor. As a lesson to El Ligao, the official ordered Saro's public execution.

Ponce was, at the same time, Puerto Rico's most prosperous and cultured city. It was the center of the island's Nationalist movement, whose president was Pedro Albizu Campos. Albizu graduated from Harvard in 1916, served in the U.S. Navy, and spent years traveling throughout Latin America. In 1932, he returned to his homeland and assumed the party's leadership. A charismatic speaker and devout Catholic, Albizu wasted no time tapping into the country's long-felt frustration over U.S. control, and soon took to propagating an almost mystical brand of anti-Yankee, anti-Protestant nationalism.

By the time of Albizu's return from abroad, the greed of the U.S. sugar plantations had created a social tinderbox. Wages for cane cutters, which had been 63 cents for a twelve-hour day in 1917, were down to 50 cents by 1932. Forty percent of the workforce was unemployed, yet company profits remained high.[7] During the last six months of 1933 alone, eighty-five strikes and protests erupted, several of them directed against the colonial government. In one of those strikes, thousands of sugar workers demanding an eight-hour day rebuffed their own ineffectual leaders and called on Albizu Campos and the Nationalists for help. For the first time, the Nationalists and the labor movement were becoming united. In other parts of the country, picket line violence during walkouts by needleworkers in Lares and Mayagüez left two dead and seventy injured.[8]

To stem the anti-Yankee violence, federal agents arrested Campos and several of the party's leaders on sedition charges in 1936. While they were in jail, the youth brigade of the party, the Cadets, scheduled a peaceful march in Ponce to press for their release. Governor Blanton Winship refused at the last moment to issue them a permit, but the Nationalists decided to march anyway.

The day was Palm Sunday, March 21, 1937. My aunt Graciela was sixteen and caught up in the Nationalist fervor at the time. Luckily, she decided to skip the march that day and go on a picnic with her sisters, Ana and Pura. They all trekked up to El Vigía, the magnificent hilltop estate of the Serralles family, owners of the Don Q rum distillery. From the rolling castle grounds you can look down on all of Ponce. Pura, who was child at the time, recalls that shortly after the Nationalists gathered, the church bells began to ring, and when she looked down the mountain toward the plaza she saw people scattering in all directions. A young woman they knew ran up to them, screaming, "There's a massacre in town. The Nationalists and the soldiers are fighting. The hospital is full of wounded." When the smoke had cleared, 21 people were dead and 150 were wounded. A human rights commission would later report that all had been gunned down by police. It was the biggest massacre in Puerto Rican history.[9]

After the Palm Sunday Massacre, hysteria and near civil war swept the island. Nationalists were hunted and arrested on sight. Some headed for exile in New York City or Havana. Graciela, our family's only Nationalist Party member, decided that nothing could be won by fighting the Americans. With Albizu Campos in jail and the Nationalist ranks decimated, she abandoned the party.

By the early 1940s, my grandmother María managed to reunite the family. Her children were grown up by then, and the outbreak of World War II had made jobs more plentiful. My father, Pepe, enlisted in the all–Puerto Rican sixty-fifth Infantry and served with the regiment in North Africa, France, and Germany. His brothers, Sergio and Tomás, were drafted a year later.

The Puerto Ricans of the sixty-fifth were segregated from the other American soldiers throughout the war and assigned largely to support work for combat units. Because they spoke no English, they found themselves frequently ridiculed by their fellow GIs. Beyond the prejudice they faced, they were deeply shaken by the devastated countryside of southern France and Germany, which reminded them of the lush green hills of Puerto Rico. Displaced French farmers became haunting reminders of their own destitute *jíbaro* countrymen. The war transformed not only the González brothers, but also every Puerto Rican who participated in it. For the first time, a large group of Puerto Ricans had left home and traveled the world. Many of them were exposed to ethnic prejudice for the first time. And for the first time they had fought in defense of a country they knew nothing about. Nonetheless, the veterans returned home, like their Mexican American counterparts, believing they had earned a place at the American table; for the first time, they felt like citizens.

While María González's three sons were away at war, their army paychecks pulled the family out of poverty. But the returning González brothers found the island nearly as poor as they'd left it. As soon as he got back, Pepe married my mother, Florinda, an orphan whose own mother had died giving birth to her, and whose father had gone off one day to work in the sugar plantations of the Dominican Republic and never returned, leaving her and her older brothers to be raised by their grandmother.

The postwar period, however, brought rapid change. In 1946, President Truman appointed the first Puerto Rican governor of the island, Jesús Piñero. Soon afterward, on December 15, 1947, Pedro Albizu Campos returned home after serving ten years in federal custody for his sedition conviction. Thousands of Nationalists greeted him at the airport as a returning hero. "The hour of decision has arrived," Albizu Campos warned his followers.[10] As the Nationalist Party and the U.S. government hurtled toward a final bloody confrontation, the González family and thousands of others packed their bags and headed for New York.

## EARLY LIFE IN NEW YORK CITY'S EL BARRIO

They settled in the tenements of El Barrio in northern Manhattan, and there they encountered both helping hands and hostility. My uncle Tomás was the first to arrive in 1946. A fellow migrant found him a job serving coffee at the Copacabana, the most famous nightclub in New York at the time. Tomás immediately sent for his brothers, Sergio and Pepe, and landed them jobs at the Copa as dishwashers. Even though mobster Frank Costello ran the place then, politicians and police inspectors, high-priced lawyers, and professional ballplayers all flocked to the club to listen to performances by the era's biggest entertainers. The Filipino waiters and Puerto Rican kitchen workers reveled in the club's glamour and intrigue and enjoyed boasting about the famous people they routinely served.

My parents settled in a cold-water tenement flat on East 112th Street, near First Avenue. The block was part of East Harlem's Italian section. The neighborhood's Sicilian elders would gather each day inside unmarked storefront social clubs. At night, the men, most of them garment workers and many of them members of the anarchist or social movements, would play dominoes outdoors while they debated the future of the union movement. By the late 1940s, many of the Italian immigrants' sons were joining neighborhood street gangs. The gang members, who were determined to keep their tidy ghetto off-limits to outsiders, would patrol the big city-owned Jefferson Pool and the string of bars along First and Second Avenues, chasing off any blacks or Puerto Ricans who wandered into the neighborhood.

Ethnic tensions stayed under control as long as Vito Marcantonio was the local congressman. Marcantonio, an old-style socialist, managed to fashion a unique coalition of East Harlem's ethnic and racial groups, one that had kept him in the House of Representatives from 1934 to 1950. Marcantonio could always be found advocating for the poor, whether it was unemployed workers being evicted from their homes or families with no food to eat. For years, he was the lone critic in Washington of U.S. rule in Puerto Rico. In 1937, he helped elect this country's first Puerto Rican to political office. His protégé, Oscar García Rivera, won an assembly seat that year as the candidate of both the Republican and American Labor parties.[11] The city's political establishment, on the other hand, abhorred Marcantonio and his radical notions. In 1950, his enemies finally beat him in an election and ousted him from Congress, but even then it took an unprecedented alliance of the Republican, Democratic, and Liberal Party bosses to unite behind one candidate.

With Marcantonio gone, East Harlem lost its main voice for working-class unity. Racial tensions flared up immediately, with some Italians blaming Puerto Ricans for his defeat. The elders of our family still recall the terrible election night in November 1950 when the ethnic war began. That night, Eugenio Morales, a onetime neighbor from Ponce's El Ligao, was visiting my grandmother, María, and her grown daughters, Graciela and Pura. A handsome, dark-skinned, humorous man, Morales delighted the women with a stream of hilarious reminiscences about life in Puerto Rico. Around 10:00 P.M., as Morales got up to leave, Pura heard the radio blaring the news about Marcantonio's losing his election, but no one was paying much attention.

"Be careful out on those streets," my grandmother told him. "The Italians on this block know us, but you're a stranger—" She didn't say what she was thinking, that the González family was so light-skinned most of us could easily pass for Italian, but not Eugenio with his chocolate complexion.

"Don't worry, Doña María," he said with a shrug and a smile. "I can take care of myself." Then he walked out. A few minutes later, there was a loud banging at the door. Graciela rushed to open it and Eugenio collapsed at the entrance, blood spurting from his head, mouth, and chest. The bones on one side of his face had collapsed and fragments were piercing the skin. An ambulance rushed him to Metropolitan Hospital, where a few minutes later medics wheeled in a bloodied man named Casanova, a Puerto Rican amateur boxer. Casanova, Eugenio later learned, had been beaten and stabbed by Italians. Half an hour later, another battered Puerto Rican was admitted. Eugenio overheard a young Irish cop whisper to one of the nurses in the emergency room, "Marcantonio lost the election. They're jumping every Spic they can find."[12] Eugenio Morales never visited our family in East Harlem again, nor did any other of our dark-skinned relatives or friends. To keep from being run out of the neighborhood by the racist attacks, Puerto Ricans started organizing their own street gangs, groups like the Viceroys and Dragons, and soon the city's major newspapers were depicting a city terrorized by Puerto Rican and black gangs. As the years passed, however, the new migrants became too numerous to frighten off and the street gangs faded in importance.

Despite that bitter 1950s gang war era, common work experiences and the bond of the Catholic religion gradually drew Puerto Ricans, Italians, and Irish together—as neighbors, as friends, sometimes even as family. My aunt Pura, for instance, married Bing Morrone, whose parents owned the only grocery store on our block, and their children, my cousins Anthony, María, and Julie, all grew up as both Puerto Rican and Italian.

This was still the era when working with your hands was considered the most honorable of professions, when downtown white-collar office workers were few in number. It was the era before the welfare system turned into an economic crutch, chaining countless Puerto Rican families into dependence on government. Jobs were still plentiful, mostly the kind that threatened to puncture or amputate your limbs with needles, presses, or blades, those mechanical contraptions of some entrepreneur who'd already made your dream of wealth his reality, but those jobs in postwar America, the chance to provide something better for your kids with enough ten- and twelve-hour sweat-filled days, made it possible to endure everything else.

My mother and aunts had their pick of employers when they arrived. Aunt Graciela, who had been a skilled seamstress in garment plants in Puerto Rico, could command a salary as high as $30 a week, a tidy sum in those days. "Sometimes we would go out and in one day try out three or four different factories until we found one that we liked," she recalled.

The González brothers moved on from the Copa to better-paying union jobs in the meatpacking, restaurant, and taxi industries. By the mid-1950s, our family, along with many other Puerto Ricans, started moving into public housing projects the federal government was building all over the city for the working poor. As we left East Harlem, however, we said good-bye to that close-knit network of Puerto Rican pioneers.

Meanwhile, new Puerto Rican communities were cropping up in Chicago, Philadelphia, and sections of Ohio, as both the U.S. and Puerto Rican governments encouraged emigration as a safety valve to prevent further social unrest on the island.[13] Labor recruiters wound through the poorest neighborhoods, loudspeakers mounted atop their cars, offering jobs in the United States and the travel fare to get there. In Lorain, Ohio, for instance, the National Tube Company, a U.S. Steel subsidiary booming with military contracts, recruited 500 Puerto Ricans from the island to work in the company's steel mill in 1947–1948. Carnegie-Illinois Steel of Gary, Indiana, recruited 500 to work in its mill in 1948. And, in 1951, the Ohio Employment Service brought 1,524 Puerto Ricans to Youngstown and Cleveland.

Much of the hiring was contracted to the Philadelphia-based H. G.
Friedman Labor Agency. (The president of the agency was the son of a
Spanish-American War veteran who settled in Puerto Rico and organized the island's police department.) Once the migrants arrived in the
mills, they sent for their families, while others came on their own after
hearing stories about all the jobs in the steel, rubber, and auto industries
of the Midwest.[14]

More than a million Puerto Ricans were living in the United States by
the mid-1960s, most of them in New York City. But they were still largely
invisible to Anglo society. They quietly pushed carts in the city's garment
center, cleaned bedpans in the hospitals, washed dishes in hotels and
restaurants, performed maintenance for the big apartment buildings, or
they worked on factory assembly lines, or drove gypsy cabs, or operated
*bodegas.* By then, however, the migration had spilled all over the Northeast and Midwest. Farms in Connecticut, eastern Pennsylvania, Upstate
New York, Ohio, and South Jersey recruited Puerto Ricans to pick the
crops. When the harvest ended, the migrants settled in nearby towns, and
thus sprouted the Puerto Rican *barrios* of Haverstraw, New York;
Vineland, New Jersey; Hartford, Connecticut; and Kennett Square,
Pennsylvania.

## THE SECOND GENERATION

As the children of those migrants started attending public schools in
the 1950s, they—I should say, we—entered a society accustomed to thinking only in black and white. It didn't take long for the white English-
speaking majority to start casting uneasy glances at the growing number
of brown-skinned, Spanish-speaking teenagers who didn't seem to fit
into any established racial group. New York tabloids took to portraying
young Puerto Rican criminals as savages. The most notorious of them
were Salvador "Cape Man" Agron and Frank Santana.[15] Despite the
clear working-class character of the Puerto Rican migration, Hollywood
created the enduring image of Puerto Ricans as knife wielders, prone to
violence and addicted to drugs in such films as *Cry Tough* (1959), *The
Young Savages* (1961), and *West Side Story* (1961).[16]

Most of us became products of a sink-or-swim public school philosophy, immersed in English-language instruction from our first day in
class and actively discouraged from retaining our native tongue. "Your
name isn't Juan," the young teacher told me in first grade at P.S. 87
in East Harlem. "In this country it's John. Shall I call you John?" Con-
fused and afraid, but sensing this as some fateful decision, I timidly

said no. But most children could not summon the courage, so school officials routinely anglicized their names. Though I had spoken only Spanish before I entered kindergarten, the teachers were amazed at how quickly I mastered English. From then on, each time a new child from Puerto Rico was placed in any of my classes, the teachers would sit him beside me so I could interpret the lessons. Bewildered, terrified, and ashamed, the new kids grappled with my clumsy attempts to decipher the teacher's strange words. Inevitably, when the school year ended, they were forced to repeat the grade, sometimes more than once, all because they hadn't mastered English. Even now, forty years later, the faces of those children are still fresh in my mind. They make today's debates on bilingual education so much more poignant, and the current push toward total English immersion so much more frightening (see chapter 12).

Our parents' generation rarely protested the way we were treated in school, which is understandable. After the terrible poverty they'd faced in Puerto Rico, they believed that an education—any education—was their children's only hope for progress. And if that meant putting up with a few psychological scars from Americanization, then so be it. My grandmother, who was illiterate, drove that into my father, who was barely literate himself, and he pushed my sister, Elena, and me to study with a frenzy that bordered on cruelty. It was not unusual for him to beat us mercilessly with a leather strap for bringing home a poor report card. These days, he'd probably be thrown in jail for child abuse.

As time passed, the González family became a melting-pot success story by anyone's measure. One by one, each of us completed high school and joined the first college-educated generation in the family's history. My uncle Sergio and aunt Catin produced a college instructor in Greek and Latin, another son who rose to be an official in the Nixon and Reagan administrations, and a South Bronx social worker. I went to Ivy League Columbia College and eventually on to a career in journalism; my sister became a public school and later a college instructor; another cousin became a doctor; another a psychiatric social worker; another a police detective.

But we in that second generation—smart, urban, English-dominant— remained acutely aware that the broader Anglo society still regarded Puerto Ricans as less than full Americans. We studied the history and culture of Europe in our classes, but nothing about Puerto Rico or Latin America, not even an inkling that our tiny homeland possessed any history and culture worthy of study. After the Vatican II reforms ushered in vernacular Catholic Masses, even the Church relegated Puerto Ricans and Latinos to the basements of most parishes, despite our being its fastest-growing membership.

The country's ingrained racial traditions meant that black or dark-skinned Puerto Ricans faced even greater prejudice. The lighter-skinned among us tended to settle in more stable Italian or Irish neighborhoods, and to pass for white. The darker-skinned ones, unable to find housing in the white neighborhoods, formed all–Puerto Rican enclaves or moved into black neighborhoods. In many cities, our communities emerged as buffer zones between blacks and whites. In Philadelphia, for instance, the Puerto Rican community evolved into a narrow north–south corridor on either side of Fifth Street, which ran almost the entire length of the city, separating the white eastern neighborhoods of town from the black western ones.

While de facto segregation has been a pernicious part of this society since the end of slavery, in our case, it became an unbearable assault on our family bonds. *"¿Y tu abuela, dónde está?"* ("And your grandmother, where is she?") is a familiar Puerto Rican refrain and the title of a popular poem by Fortunato Vizcarrondo. The phrase reminds us that black blood runs through all Puerto Rican families. Puerto Ricans resisted the sharp racial demarcations so prevalent in this country, and their implicit diminishment of our human worth. But gradually, almost imperceptibly, I watched my aunts and uncles begin to adopt antiblack attitudes, as if this were some rite of passage to becoming authentic Americans. "A hostile posture toward resident blacks must be struck at the American-izing door before it will open," is how writer Toni Morrison so aptly de-scribes it.[17]

The social imperative to *choose a racial identity,* and then only in purely black-and-white terms, impelled those of us in the second gener-ation at first to jettison our native language and culture, to assimilate into either the white or the black world. My uncle Sergio and aunt Catin were my family's exception. They were the only ones who never left East Harlem. There, they fiercely clung to the culture of the island. In their home, *aguinaldos,* the music of Puerto Rican *jíbaros,* could always be heard, a dominoes hand was always in the offing, weekend family *fiestas* were routine, and the neighbors, whether Puerto Rican or Anglo, black or white, were always welcome.

Not surprisingly, one of the first expressions of community organiza-tion in the 1950s was an event that celebrated cultural pride—the annual Puerto Rican Day Parade. As the Puerto Rican population grew, the pa-rade became the largest of the city's many ethnic celebrations. By the 1990s, more than a million people attended it.

In the midst of the high tide of Puerto Rican migration, something else happened—African Americans rose up against racial segregation, unmasking the chasm that still existed between black and white society. We Puerto Ricans found ourselves having common ground with both sides, yet fitting in with neither. We simply had not been a part of the congenital birth defect of this country, the Anglo-Saxon slave system and its Jim Crow aftermath.

In 1964, the Reverend Milton Galamison, Malcolm X, and other black leaders led a boycott of New York City public school parents against racial discrimination. A handful of Puerto Rican community leaders from the prewar migrant generation joined the boycott. Among them were Frank Espada, Evelina Antonetty, and Gilberto Gerena Valentín. Espada, a community organizer before joining Republican mayor John Lindsay's administration, would later develop a career as a brilliant photographer chronicling the Puerto Rican diaspora. Antonetty went on to found United Bronx Parents, the seminal parent advocacy group for Puerto Ricans in education. And Gerena Valentín, a nationalist, one-time Communist Party member, and labor union organizer, would later create an influential federation of Puerto Rican hometown clubs. Those clubs formed the political base with which he captured a city council seat in the 1970s. They, and others like them, comprised the first postwar leadership of the emerging Puerto Rican community in New York.

That wave of leaders, however, was soon eclipsed by an even more radical group. The assassinations of Malcolm X (1965) and Martin Luther King (1968) sparked mass urban riots among blacks and polarized the civil rights movement, and many of us who were influenced by those events found greater affinity to the black power movement than to the integration movement. That identification intensified as thousands of Puerto Ricans went off to fight in the Vietnam War, only to return, like the veterans of World War II, to a country that still misunderstood and mistrusted them as foreigners.

As we came of age, we responded to that mistrust and misunderstanding with open rebellion. A slew of new nationalist and left-wing organizations sprang up among Puerto Ricans. Some were inspired by the old Nationalist Party in Puerto Rico or by the Black Panther Party here. The most influential was the Young Lords, an organization I helped to found in 1969. During its apogee (1969–1972), the Lords galvanized thousands of young Latinos into radical politics, and an amazing portion of the group's members later became influential leaders of the community (see chapter 10).[18]

Fueled by that political awakening, a cultural renaissance emerged among Puerto Rican artists. Writers Piri Thomas and Nicolasa Mohr, poets Pedro Pietri and José Angel Figueroa, playwrights Miguel Piñeiro and Miguel Algarin caught the public's attention as vibrant voices of the Puerto Rican migrant experience. Even Latin music experienced a resurgence as Eddie and Charlie Palmieri, Ray Barretto, and Willie Colon began producing politically charged lyrics that celebrated the new sense of emerging Puerto Rican power.[19]

The essence of that new movement was a sudden realization of who we were, economic refugees from the last major colony of the United States. That realization caused us to reject the path of our immigrant predecessors from Europe: the first generation accepting decades of second-class status while it established a foothold, the second securing an education and assimilating quietly, and the third emerging as 100 percent melting-pot American.

Puerto Ricans, we concluded, were in a different position from Italians or Swedes or Poles. Our homeland was invaded and permanently occupied, its wealth exploited, its patriots persecuted and jailed, by the very country to which we had migrated. Our experience was closer to Algerians in France before independence, or to Irish Catholics in England today.[20] For decades, textbooks made in the United States had taught island schoolchildren our homeland was incapable of self-government and would perish economically without Uncle Sam. But in the early 1970s a new generation of independent Puerto Rican scholars arose to challenge that premise. They confirmed for the second generation that Puerto Rico was as capable of being a prosperous independent nation as Israel or Taiwan or Switzerland, but that its history had been consciously distorted to encourage a sense of dependence.

Our parents instinctively sympathized with this new awakening. Unlike white America, where New Left activism divided father and son, mother and daughter, the new nationalism brought the two Puerto Rican generations closer together. It inspired the young to reclaim and study our language. It helped us understand the suffering our parents had endured. And it transformed our psychological outlook. Never again would a Puerto Rican quietly accept an Anglo's barking, "Speak English, you're in America now!" or the rote admonition, "If you don't like it here, go back where you came from."

By the mid-1970s, however, economic recession struck, and new groups of Latinos began arriving in the nation's cities. Competition soared for a diminishing number of unskilled jobs, and the class nature of the Puerto Rican migration radically changed. Many college graduates and professionals from the island, unable to find jobs there, relocated to the United States, as did many of the poorest and least skilled urban slum dwellers. At the same time, the first generation of migrants, the former factory workers and *bodega* owners, having accumulated substantial savings, started returning to the island to retire or to fill jobs in the booming tourist industry, where a good command of English was required. So many Puerto Ricans left this country that the decade witnessed net migration back to the island.

Thus, the Puerto Rican migrant community became dominated during the 1980s by two very different social classes, both highly dependent on government. At the top was a small but growing number of intelligentsia and white-collar professionals, many employed in social programs or the educational system, and at the bottom a large and fast-growing caste of low-paid, unskilled workers, alongside an underclass of long-term unemployed and welfare recipients. Missing in any significant numbers were two critical groups: the private business class whose members provide any ethnic group's capital formation and self-reliant outlook, and the skilled technical workers who provide stability and role models for those on the bottom to emulate.

Meanwhile, life in America's inner cities by the early 1980s was verging on chaos. A dwindling tax base, brought about by the flight of industry and skilled white workers to the suburbs, massive disinvestment by government in public schools and infrastructure, and the epidemics of drug and alcohol abuse, all tore at the quality of city life. As might be expected, the chaos took its heaviest toll on the African American and Puerto Rican migrant communities of the inner cities.

The third generation of Puerto Ricans, those who came of age in the late 1980s and early 1990s, found themselves crippled by inferior schools, a lack of jobs, and underfunded social services. They found their neighborhoods inundated with drugs and violence. They grew up devoid, for the most part, of self-image, national identity, or cultural awareness. They became the lost generation.

But the schism over identity and the quandary over language and heritage soon turned into problems not just for the Puerto Ricans. As Latin American immigration exploded, many Anglos started to worry that America's social fabric was disintegrating. The biggest source of that worry, as we shall see, was the nation's growing Mexican population.

# Mexicans: Pioneers of a Different Type

> The whole race of Mexicans here is becoming a useless com-
> modity, becoming cheap, dog cheap. Eleven Mexicans, it is
> stated, have been found along the Nueces in a *hung up* condi-
> tion.
>
> —*Galveston Weekly News,*
> *1855*

The Mexican diaspora is at the core of our country's Latino heritage. Not only are two of every three Latinos in the United States of Mexican origin, but only Mexicans can claim to be both early set-tlers on U.S. soil *and* the largest group of new arrivals. So many Mexicans have come since 1820 that they are now the second-largest immigrant nationality in our history. No Hispanic group has contributed more to the nation's prosperity than Mexicans, yet none makes white America more uneasy about the future.

Most troubling are the descendants of the Mexican pioneers, for once you admit Mexicans' long history on U.S. soil, you must necessarily ac-cept Hispanic culture and the Spanish language as integral components of our own national saga.

Mexicans, in fact, have lived "here" since before there was a Mexico or a United States. And they have been immigrating to this country almost from its inception. Since 1820, when the federal government started keeping immigration records, only one other country, Germany, has sent more immigrants to our shores.

Whether or not Mexican immigration continues to surpass all others, as it has in recent decades, depends largely on what happens *below* the Rio Grande. We often forget that Mexico is the most populous Spanish-speaking country in the world. It has 95 million residents, a high birth rate, and desperate poverty. A disturbing portion of its national wealth flows outside its borders each day and into the pockets of Wall Street shareholders. So much of that wealth has been siphoned off in recent years that the Mexican economy finds it increasingly difficult to feed and clothe its population. If these conditions do not change, Mexico will remain an inexhaustible source of migrants to the United States, which is why Americans need to pay more attention to our southern neighbor than to what is happening in, say, Israel or Palestine, in Ireland or in the Balkans.

### TABLE 3
### TOP SOURCES OF LEGAL IMMIGRATION TO THE UNITED STATES BY COUNTRY FISCAL YEARS 1820–1996[1]

| | |
|---|---|
| All Countries | 63,140,227 |
| Germany | 7,142,393 |
| Mexico | 5,542,625 |
| Italy | 5,427,298 |
| United Kingdom | 5,225,701 |
| Ireland | 4,778,159 |
| Canada | 4,423,066 |
| Austria-Hungary | 4,360,723 |

Mexican Americans, meanwhile, face a frustrating identity problem similar to that of Puerto Ricans. They are both native-born and immigrants, pioneers and aliens, patriots and rebels; no matter how far back some may trace their ancestry on our soil, they are still battling to emerge from the obscure margins of official U.S. history, still clamoring to be fully recognized and understood, as we will see in the following story of one pioneer Mexican American family, the Canales clan of South Texas.

José Francisco Canales came to the New World in the 1640s from Reus, Spain. He settled in the isolated northeastern town of Monterrey, in what is now northeastern Mexico, and by 1660 he owned one of six stores in the town. His grandson, Blas Canales, was born in 1675 in Cerralvo, just north of Monterrey. Both towns had been founded by Christianized Jews trying to escape the Spanish Inquisition and had become flourishing mining centers on the northern frontier.[2]

In the late 1740s, the viceroy of New Spain authorized José de Escandon, a young army captain from Querétaro, to explore and colonize the

region above Tampico all the way up to the Nueces River. The territory
was then home to the Lipan Apaches in the west, Comanches in the
north, the Coahuiltecans along the Río Bravo, and the Karankawas
along the Gulf Coast.[3]

After some initial exploration, Escandon set out in 1749 with several
hundred *criollo, mestizo,* and Indian families from central Mexico, all
drawn by promises of free land. He quickly established a string of settlements stretching up the Rio Grande, and along the river itself he
founded the present-day cities of Camargo and Reynosa.[4] One of Escandon's chief aides was Captain Blas de la Garza Falcon, a Canales family member by marriage.[5]

Over the next few years, Escandon returned to start several more settlements, the last of which was the town of Laredo in 1755, thus capping
one of the most successful colonizing ventures in the New World.[6] Altogether, the young captain is credited with establishing twenty towns and
eighteen missions in less than ten years, all but one of which still exist.
The missions he founded logged three thousand Indian converts in their
first few years, far more than the Puritans accomplished in their first
fifty.

Escandon called his colony Nuevo Santander. Tightly linked through
the family connections of its original land-grant settlers, and isolated
from the rest of the colonial Spanish world by barren scrub plains and
hostile Indians on either side of the valley, Nuevo Santander became a
uniquely self-sufficient and self-contained pastoral community. The
colony's life and the commerce of its towns revolved around and were
unified by the river. The settlers used the fertile lands closest to the river
for crops, and those at the edges of the river valley for livestock.[7] North
of the Rio Grande, an immense dry plain stretched to the Nueces River
150 miles away. Thick grass grew year-round on that plain, and the countryside was dotted with chaparral and mesquite, ebony and huisache
trees. The settlers' herds multiplied so rapidly that within two years the
one hundred families in the towns of Camargo and Reynosa owned
thirty-six thousand head of cattle, horses, and sheep.[8]

Several Canales family members traveled with Escandon's colonizing
expedition. They settled first in Mier, on the southern side of the Río
Bravo, but by the early 1800s, one of them, José Antonio Canales Salinas,
secured a royal land grant on the northern banks of the river, in present-
day Starr County, Texas. His land, which covered about ten thousand
acres, was called the Sacatosa Grant and, later, the Buenavista Ranch.
Like most of the original land grantees, the Canales family prospered
and became members of the region's nineteenth-century elite. José An-

tonio Tiburcio Canales, for example, was one of the original signers of Mexico's declaration of independence.[9]

By the 1820s, however, immigrants from the United States, Ireland, and Germany began settling in the region, especially farther to the north, and the Mexicans along the Río Bravo felt increasingly threatened as the Anglos started to dispute their ownership of the grazing land south of the Nueces. It was over the Nueces Strip, in fact, that President Polk engineered the Mexican War. In early 1846, after Texas had joined the union, General Zachary Taylor's army crossed into the disputed territory, provoking a Mexican army attack.

One Canales descendant, General José Antonio Rosillo Canales, emerged a hero of the war, adopting guerrilla tactics against General Taylor's army with devastating results. During February 1847, his band inflicted more than 150 casualties on the Americans, who soon dubbed him the "Chaparral Fox." By the war's conclusion, Canales had become so famous he was elected governor of Tamaulipas.[10]

Once the Treaty of Guadalupe Hidalgo relinquished the Nueces Strip to the United States, however, the inhabitants of Nuevo Santander were shocked to see the very river that had bound them together for a hundred years suddenly turned into its opposite—a dividing line between two hostile nations. The Anglos even changed the river's name, from Río Bravo to Rio Grande. Those Canales family members who lived below the river in Mier were now under different sovereignty than those living on the Buenavista Ranch and other small properties on the U.S. side. With the new sovereignty came a host of new laws, especially for land registration, tax, and inheritance. The new codes were promulgated and administered in English—a language the *mexicano* majority did not understand—and by lawyers, sheriffs, and judges who could always count on the U.S. Army to enforce an Anglo's interpretation whenever a dispute arose.

Mifflin Kenedy, a Florida riverboat captain, arrived in the area in the summer of 1846. The army had recruited him to operate a fleet of boats up the Rio Grande. Kenedy sent for his longtime pilot, New York–born Richard King, and after the war the two men purchased some of the boats at army auction, so they could transport the swarms of prospectors passing through on their way to the California gold fields.[11] To secure a monopoly of the river transport, Kenedy and King decided to form an alliance with Charles Stillman. The cartel they created was blessed with the friendly assistance of Brevet Major W. W. Chapman, the local army commander, who arranged lucrative army supply contracts for them.[12]

Meanwhile, farther to the north, another Anglo rancher had discovered his own way of cashing in on the fighting. H. L. Kinney, a notorious smuggler south of the Nueces, secured an appointment as a colonel and quartermaster for General Winfield Scott's troops and turned his ranch into a boomtown of two thousand people. After the war, Kinney founded the city of Corpus Christi on the site of his ranch.[13]

From the start, the Anglo settlers saw the Mexicans in South Texas as an obstacle to progress, and routinely cheated them out of their land. Often it was seized at sheriffs' sales and auctioned for pennies an acre for failure to pay taxes.

"Many [Mexicans] didn't know how to read or write," said Santos Molina, a Canales family descendant who lives in Brownsville. "They didn't understand their rights and those of their grandparents. Anybody could tell them, 'your grandfather lost his land, sold it,' and they couldn't prove otherwise."[14]

Violence against Mexicans became commonplace. "The whole race of Mexicans here is becoming a useless commodity, becoming cheap, dog cheap," wrote the Corpus Christi correspondent for the *Galveston Weekly News* in 1855. "Eleven Mexicans, it is stated, have been found along the Nueces, in a *hung up* condition. Better so than to be left on the ground for the howling lobos to tear in pieces, and then howl the more for the red peppers that burn his insides raw." [15] Lynching of Mexicans continued into the early 1900s, with Canales family members witnessing one as late as 1917.[16]

Whole communities were driven from the towns of Austin, Seguin, and Uvalde. A scant six years after Texas independence, thirteen Anglos had gobbled up 1.3 million acres in "legal" sales from 358 Mexican landowners.[17] Among them was Scottish immigrant John Young, who opened a general store in Brownsville after the war and married Salome Balli, member of a prominent Mexican land-grant family, thus gaining control of her family's estate. Edinburg, seat of Texas's Hidalgo County, is named after Young's native city in Scotland. After Young died in 1859, his widow married his clerk, John McAllen. By the 1890s, the McAllen and Young ranches measured 160,000 acres, and the onetime clerk, following in the footsteps of his old boss, had his own town, McAllen.[18]

Merchants Stillman, King, and Kenedy soon joined the land rush as well. Stillman gained control of the giant Espiritu Santo Land Grant by buying up fraudulent squatters' titles and outlasting the real Mexican owners in the courts. He founded Brownsville on part of the estate and turned it into the gambling, saloon, and prostitution center of the region.[19] While Stillman concentrated on the land around Brownsville, his steamboat partners King and Kenedy turned their attention to cobbling together cattle empires in the northern countryside. Stephen Powers, the sharpest land lawyer in the region, was their able assistant in that effort. Like Young and McAllen, Kenedy got his start by marrying a wealthy Mexican. In his case, her name was Petra Vela de Vidal.[20] The Kenedy Ranch, "La Para," eventually stretched to 325,000 acres and employed three hundred ranch hands, virtually all of them Mexican.[21] As for King, by the time he died in 1885, his ranch encompassed 500,000 acres, employed more than five hundred people, and even contained its own town, Santa Gertrudis.

"The Santa Gertrudis ranch house," recalled former Texas Ranger George Durham, in a chilling insight into life on the Nueces Strip, "was more like an army arsenal inside. In one big room there were eighty stands of Henry repeating rifles and maybe a hundred boxes of shells. Two men stood in the lookout tower day and night, and there was always a man at the ready for each of those rifles."[22]

That arsenal was there for a reason. Many of the new land barons rustled cattle from one another and from the herds of the *tejanos*. Richard King, an infamous cattle thief, was said to have turned the Texas Rangers into his own private security force. "His neighbors mysteriously vanish whilst his territory extends over entire counties," wrote a newspaper correspondent for the *Corpus Christi World* about King in 1878. "Fifty cents a head is paid to Mexicans for branding cattle on the plains with the King monogram, and somehow no one's herds can be induced to increase but those of the future cattle king."[23]

Mexicans who dared challenge the Anglo encroachment were often branded as bandits and outlaws. The most famous "bandit" of them all, Juan "Cheno" Cortina, was another Canales ancestor.

In July 1859, Cortina, whose mother owned the Rancho del Carmen, shot a Brownsville marshal after witnessing him whip a drunken Mexican. He then rode into town with fifty followers, raised the Mexican flag, and shot to death the local jailer and four other whites who had been terrorizing Mexicans. The town's whites dispatched a militia and a company of Texas Rangers to capture him, but Cortina raised an army of twelve hundred Mexicans and routed them. He then declared a war against the Anglo settler minority.

For the next two decades, Cortina's band launched sporadic guerrilla raids into Texas from safe havens on the Mexican side. Neither the Rangers nor a contingent of federal troops dispatched to the territory, and commanded by Colonel Robert E. Lee, was able to capture him. Accused of cattle rustling and indicted for treason, Cortina became the most feared Mexican American in Texas. Mere rumors that he was in the vicinity panicked whole towns.[24] The only respite from his attacks occurred between 1862 and 1867, when Cortina declared a truce with the United States and turned his guns on the French army, after it occupied Mexico and installed the Austrian archduke Maximilian as emperor. One of Cortina's top officers during the resistance to France was Servando Canales, a veteran of the Mexican-American war and son of General José Antonio Canales. Like his father, Servando Canales went on to serve as governor of Tamaulipas. Cortina, however, remained the most powerful politician in the region until he was arrested in 1875 by President Porfirio Díaz at the request of the United States and thrown into jail in Mexico City.

The Cortina wars slowed but did not stop the Anglo expropriation of Mexican wealth. In 1850, property in Texas had been pretty evenly divided between the two groups. That year, according to the U.S. Census, *tejanos* comprised 32.4 percent of the workers in the state and owned 33 percent of its wealth. Over the next twenty years, however, things changed drastically. By 1870, *tejanos* were 47.6 percent of the workforce but possessed only 10.6 percent of the wealth.[25]

In South Texas, where Mexicans remained the overwhelming majority, one-third of the ranches and all the large estates were in Anglo hands by 1900. Only the smaller *tejano* farmers clung to their titles. Among the diehards was Luciano Canales, who ran the family's Buenavista Ranch. Because of Luciano's determination, Fiacro Salazaar, his great-grandson, still retains title to two hundred acres of the old ranch. "They had to protect it with guns," Salazaar, a San Antonio army engineer, recalled in a 1992 interview. "Any poor fellow who didn't, lost it."[26] Even as thousands lost their land, though, other Mexicans kept migrating into the Southwest. More than a million arrived in the region between 1900 and 1930.[27]

———

By the 1920s, the Rio Grande Valley was as segregated as apartheid South Africa. Mexicans comprised more than 90 percent of its population, but the white minority controlled most of the land and all the political power. Imelda Garza, a retired public school teacher who was born in the town of Benavides in 1923 to Gervasio and Manuelita Canales, never met an Anglo until she was thirteen. "Not too many whites, either, just a few workers, pure rednecks," Imelda said. "I met a black person for the first time when I moved to Kingsville to teach at Herrel Elementary School."

Her brother-in-law, Santos Molina, admits to "having seen Anglos around" during his childhood in Brownsville, "but I only got to meet them when I went to Oiltown high school." [28]

The first organized attempt to break down that segregation came in 1929, when seven Mexican organizations met in Corpus Christi to found the League of United Latin American Citizens. LULAC's goal from its inception was the complete assimilation of Mexicans and their acceptance as equal citizens by Anglo society. To accomplish that, LULAC made its chief goal teaching Mexicans to master English.[29]

Once the Great Depression hit and unemployment surged among whites, though, not even Mexicans who spoke fluent English escaped the anti-immigrant hysteria. More than 500,000 were forcibly deported during the 1930s, among them many who were U.S. citizens. One of the few areas of the country spared the hysteria was the Rio Grande Valley, where Mexicans were able to find safety in numbers.

"There were no jobs, but the land took good care of us," recalled Canales family member Santos Molina, now a San Antonio high school teacher. "We planted corn and grain and watermelons, calabazos and beans. We had four or five milk cows. We hunted rabbits and deer. Goats would cost you about a dollar then, so we had plenty to eat."[30]

The onset of World War II brought yet another reversal in U.S. policy toward Mexican immigrants. Three months after President Roosevelt declared war on the Axis powers, the United States and Mexico reached agreement on a new program to import Mexican workers. As many as 100,000 Mexicans a year were soon being contracted to work here. It was called the *bracero* program, and it would last in one form or another until 1965. While it did, it brought millions of migrants into the country for seasonal work, and each year after the harvest a good portion of them found a way to stay in the country illegally. Not that most Americans cared. Until the 1960s, few paid attention to the human traffic along the border, least of all the inhabitants of the area, for whom the international demarcation line was more a fantasy of the politicians in Washington than an everyday reality.[31]

But World War II did something else. It transformed the thinking of a whole generation of Mexican American men who served in it, just as it did to Puerto Ricans. More than 375,000 Mexican Americans saw active duty in the U.S. armed forces, many in critical combat roles. From Texas alone, five *mexicanos* were awarded the Congressional Medal of Honor. In the Battle of Bataan, as many as a quarter of the wounded were Mexican American.[32]

Santos Molina and Manuel Garza were two Canales family members who served in combat, in the same army so many of their ancestors had fought against. Molina enlisted in 1940 and was assigned to an airborne unit of the Seventh Infantry Division, where he led a squad onto Normandy beach on the second day of the Allied invasion of France. Nearly all his men were killed or wounded that day, and while Molina survived unscathed, he was severely wounded by machine gun fire later in Germany.

When the war ended, the Mexican American veterans returned home to much of the same discrimination and racism they had left behind, only this time they refused to accept it.

Manuel Garza, who served in a field artillery unit with the Special Forces in Europe, returned home to Kingsville, the nerve center of the King family ranch and one of the most racist towns in South Texas. "In town, the White Kitchens chain had cooks and busboys who were Mexicans, but they wouldn't let the Mexicans come in to eat," Garza recalled. "One day a bunch of us in uniform just walked in and forced them to serve us. The same thing with Kings Inn. It was in a neighborhood of pure Germans. Those people never let us in there. When we came out of the army, we started making a whole lot of noise and they let us eat. Today, they have more Mexican customers in Kings Inn than anything else."

Similar protests erupted throughout the Southwest. When Brownsville's Congressional Medal of Honor winner, Sergeant José Mendoza López, was denied service at a local restaurant, it touched off a furor among *mexicanos*. Middle-class organizations like LULAC, and the newly formed American GI Forum, pointed with pride to the war records of their members and demanded equal treatment.[33]

For the first time, the Mexicans even dared to challenge the Anglo minority's monopoly of political power. While working as a Kingsville truant officer in the 1950s, Nerio Garza, Manuel Garza's brother, became so angry at the Anglos' racism he decided to run for office. He roused the town's Mexican population against the lack of paved streets and lights and sewers on their side of town, and handily won his first race for town commissioner, where he remained for most of the next thirty years.

Despite Garza's victory in Kingsville, and a few others in Los Angeles and San Antonio, the cry for equality and respect from the generation of World War II went largely unheard, and segregationist policies against Mexicans persisted into the 1960s.

"The first time I was made to sit on the sidewalk for speaking Spanish I was six years old," recalled Sandra Garza, the daughter of Imelda and Manuel Garza. "I got caught because I was speaking to the janitor. He was *mexicano* and my next-door neighbor."[34]

By the 1960s, the majority of students at nearby Texas A&M were

Mexican Americans. For the first time, they ran a slate that won control of the student government. They began calling themselves Chicanos, turning the slang word that had always been used among the poor in the Southwest to describe those born north of the Rio Grande into a badge of pride. The moniker became a way for young people to connect culturally with the Mexican homeland, in much the same way that the change from "Negro" to "black" had affected the civil rights movement in the South.

Some Chicanos even started referring to the Southwest as Aztlán, the name Aztec historians in the Codex Ramírez (1583–1587) gave to the area north of Mexico from which their ancestors had come. Reacting to the decades of Anglo racism, they now quixotically saw Aztlán as a historic homeland in which Mexicans would eventually become the majority again, recovering their land from the white settlers.

South Texas was emerging as the center of Chicano unrest. When a slate of five working-class Mexican Americans won control of the Crystal City council in the Rio Grande Valley in 1963, the victory electrified Chicanos throughout the Southwest. Shortly afterward, a strike at La Casita Farms by Cesar Chavez's United Farm Workers union stirred young Chicanos with visions of recapturing majority rule—at least in South Texas.

One of the most influential groups to arise during the period was the Mexican American Youth Organization (MAYO), founded in San Antonio by Willie Velázquez, a young community organizer for the Catholic Bishop's Committee on the Spanish Speaking, and Crystal City's José Angel Gutiérrez. Gutiérrez and Velásquez, both sons of Mexican immigrants, would end up symbolizing two trends within the new movement. Gutiérrez, whose father fought with Pancho Villa in the Mexican revolution, was a charismatic college-educated radical. He proselytized throughout the Southwest for an independent political party of Chicanos to counter the Democratic and Republican parties, both of which he saw as racist.

Willie Velázquez, whose family also fled Mexico during the revolution, was more pragmatic. His parents had grown up in the Chicano *barrio* on the West Side of San Antonio, where his father became a meatpacking worker after returning from World War II.[35] One of Willie's classmates at St. Mary's College in San Antonio was a tall, gangly Chicano named Henry Cisneros. Velásquez was never comfortable with the more revolutionary ideas of Gutiérrez. This may have been due in part to his Catholic education or to the influence of Congressman Henry Gonzáles, the local hero who paved the road to power for Mexican Americans through mainstream electoral politics, or to his longtime friendship with Cisneros. Whatever the reason, Gutiérrez and Velásquez eventually parted ways. Gutiérrez went on to found the militant Raza Unida Party, while Velásquez started the far less confrontational Southwest Voter Registration and Education Project, and turned into the foremost advocate of Hispanic voting rights in the country.

Gutiérrez's new group, however, caught fire much more with the young Chicanos. It won a series of election victories in 1969 in a bunch of small Texas towns, including Crystal City and Kingsville. In Kingsville, a Raza Unida slate led by the party's state chairman, Carlos Guerra, and aided by Chicano students from Texas A&M, sought to capture control of the city council. Their slate challenged both the white ranchers and the older generation of established *tejanos,* among them Nerio Garza. Many of the militants regarded Garza as too accommodating to the white establishment. Their attack against him divided entire families, including the Canales, and the bitterness those battles engendered remain to this day. Sandra Garza joined the militants against her uncle Nerio, while Nerio's daughter, Diane Garza, defended him.[36]

"We had shitheads like that Guerra," recalled Diane Garza, a longtime administrator in the Brownsville public schools, during an interview decades later. "Those sons of bitches were instilling 'Burn the *gringo,* hate the *gringo,*' but yet in turn their girlfriends were all *gringas.* They came here and instilled all this drop out of school bit, but their radical ways were not in the best interests of the town."[37]

The conflict even turned violent.

"I was teaching here in Brownsville," recalled Diane Garza, "and I received a phone call that they were planning on lynching my dad. I still remember the night vividly. I call them 'La Raza Sumida.' They had gasoline cans in their hands. We had to call not only the highway patrol but the Texas Rangers. They couldn't even begin to break the crowd of idiots. We had locked my dad in the house. They were saying things like 'Nerio is a coconut.' But at gut level everyone knew who Nerio Garza was. He stood up to the ranch, to the big guys and the little ones, it didn't make any difference."

Carlos Guerra's group, some of its supporters conceded years later, pitted Mexicans against one another unnecessarily. "They thought my uncle was a *vendido,*" recalled Sandra Garza. "But it was just the old blood not understanding the new. If you look at it now, they could have worked well together."

After the Kingsville election, Sandra Garza, who never forgot her parents' accounts of the Canales family legacy, or their stories of the land the *gringos* had taken from them, threw herself into the Chicano *movimiento.* For the next decade, she moved from town to town in the

West and Southwest, as a teacher and community organizer, trying to reclaim those lost lands and that cultural tradition. She worked in Colorado with Corky González's Crusade for Justice, in northern New Mexico with Reies López Tijerina's Alianza Federal de Pueblos Libres (Federal Alliance of Free Towns), then in California and Texas with labor unions organizing Latino workers. When I first interviewed her in 1992, Garza was a staff organizer in El Paso, Texas, with the Union of Industrial Needle Trade Employees (UNITE).

The Canales story has been repeated over and over in the Southwest by other Chicano families. It is sometimes difficult for white Americans to understand how deep the roots of Mexican Americans are in that part of the country. Most whites who live in the region, after all, only arrived there during the last fifty years. At best, their migration story goes back a few generations, hardly comparable to that of the old Mexicans. Farmworker leader Cesar Chavez's family, for instance, moved to Arizona in 1880, long before it was a state. The family owned land there until the Great Depression bankrupted them and forced them to move to California as migrant laborers. López Tijerina, who was born in Texas in 1926, often recounted the story of how his great-grandfather was killed by Anglos who stole the family's land.

Even many recently arrived Mexican immigrants can usually point to long historical ties to the Southwest. In a study of the old Mexican neighborhood of Lemon Grove in San Diego, for instance, ethnographer Robert Alvarez documents nearly two hundred years of a migratory circuit between Mexico's Baja California and our own state of California by the same extended families of miners and farmers. Family members would travel back and forth between the two territories in response to economic conditions. The two Californias, Alvarez maintains, have historically been one in geography, economics and culture. Only in the last fifty years did the border become a barrier to those ties. Furthermore, Mexican family networks and solidarity were actually strengthened through the migratory circuit as individual family members relied increasingly on the remittances of distant relatives for survival.[38]

Mexican labor. The Mexican market. Mexican music and food. Mexican television and radio. Mexican names of cities, states, rivers, and mountains. Anglo America continues to deny how much the social, cultural, political, and economic reality of the West and Southwest has been shaped by Mexicans. They have been part of its creation and they will form an even bigger part of its future. That undenied Mexican heritage will haunt the rest of us until we accept it as our own.

# 6

# *Cubans: Special Refugees*

Few immigrant groups have commenced their economic adaptation to American life from a position of such relative advantage.

—*Alejandro Portes*[1]

During the summer of 1994, thousands of Cubans appeared off the Florida coast in a flotilla of wooden rowboats, makeshift rafts, and automobile tires lashed together with rope. Each day that summer, the U.S. Coast Guard reported astonishing jumps in the number of Cuban *balseros* trying to reach our shores. The exodus quickly overwhelmed Florida's immigration centers, which were already straining to cope with a stream of desperate Haitian boat people, and it fueled a growing national debate over immigration.

President Clinton reacted by doing what no U.S. president had ever done—he ordered a halt to the special treatment of Cuban refugees. For more than thirty years, a succession of presidents had dispensed unprecedented financial aid to those fleeing Cuba. During that time, Congress had financed numerous efforts by the refugees to topple Fidel Castro's Communist regime and the CIA had employed many of them as trusty Cold War foot soldiers. Neither Dominicans fleeing the civil war of 1965, nor Haitians fleeing the terror of Papa Doc Duvalier and a string of Haitian military juntas, got comparable treatment. Washington routinely rejected asylum requests from Haitians picked up at sea while it invariably granted asylum to the far smaller numbers of Cuban *balseros*. Under Clinton, many Haitians were even forcibly returned to their country.

But in 1994 the Cuban red carpet was pulled. By then, American fixation with the Cold War was over. Fear of immigrant hordes was replacing dread of Communist guerrillas. Henceforth, Clinton said, Cubans trying to reach the U.S. illegally would be detained and denied automatic entry just like any other immigrants. By the time he made his announcement, more than 1 million Cubans were living in the United States.

The *balseros* of 1994 were actually the fifth major wave of Cubans to land on our shores since thousands of tobacco workers migrated here during Cuba's independence wars in the nineteenth century. While middle-class Cubans continued to visit the United States throughout the first half of the twentieth century, few took up permanent residence until after the 1959 revolution of Fidel Castro reignited massive emigration. In the forty years since then, four major waves of Cubans have left. Each has been so distinctive in its social composition and political outlook that the Cuban diaspora is perhaps the most complex of all Latino immigrant sagas.

The refugees of the 1960s and 1970s were largely from the upper and middle classes and brought with them enormous technical skills. Those advantages, together with the massive aid the federal government dispensed to them, turned Cubans into this country's most prosperous Hispanic immigrants. Beginning with the Mariel boat wave in 1980, however, the Cubans who came were generally poorer and darker-skinned. *Los marielitos,* as they were called, confronted a nativist backlash among white Americans and burgeoning class and racial conflicts within their own refugee community, making their experience more comparable to that of other Latino immigrants.

Because of the tremendous disparities in class, education, and race among the various waves, there is no typical Cuban refugee, and some observers even question whether the terms "refugees" and "exiles" remain appropriate descriptions for today's Cuban immigrant community. I have chosen to focus on the experience of one Cuban family, the Del Rosarios of Miami, who seem to me representative of a significant but understudied segment of the community. Some of the family members arrived in 1994 with the *balseros,* while others have been in this country much longer. Luis Del Rosario, the family's most articulate spokesman, arrived here in 1979. Quiet, razor-thin, nearly bald, and in his mid-forties, Luis was a former political prisoner in Cuba who, after settling in Miami, became active with Brothers to the Rescue, a militant exile group known for flying small planes over the Florida Straits to assist *balseros.*

I met him in the summer of 1994, while I was reporting on the *balseros.* Luis had just learned that one of his brothers, his sister-in-law, and their children had left Cuba on a raft and were lost somewhere at sea. Over the next few weeks, finding them became his personal obsession. The more we talked during those frantic days, the more I realized that the Del Rosario family could help illuminate aspects of the Cuban diaspora.

## THE EARLY MIGRANTS

The first Cuban migration to the United States is nearly forgotten these days. It occurred during the late nineteenth century, when more than 100,000 people, 10 percent of Cuba's population, fled abroad to escape the upheavals of the independence wars. The majority were unemployed tobacco workers who sought jobs in the new cigar factories that Spanish and Cuban manufacturers were setting up in Key West, Tampa, New Orleans, and New York City.

In 1885, Vicente Martínez Ybor and Ignacio Haya purchased forty acres of swamp near Tampa, drained the land, and set about building a company town. That town would become known as Ybor City. Martínez Ybor promptly set up a steamship line between Havana, Key West, and Tampa, assuring himself a steady supply of workers and turning his new town into the cigar capital of the country. By 1900, there were 129 cigar factories in the town and fifteen thousand residents.

The steam line and the flourishing cigar industry created flesh-and-blood ties between Cuba and the United States. By the early twentieth century, as many as 50,000 to 100,000 people traveled annually between Havana, Key West, and Tampa—so many that Cubans typically did not have to pass through customs or immigration.[2] While Cuba's millions of poor suffered under the turbulent regimes of Machado and then Batista, the small Cuban elite tied to U.S. companies basked in luxury. Its members invested their money on Wall Street. They sent their children to U.S. colleges. They went for treatment at U.S. hospitals. They vacationed in Saratoga Springs and other society resorts. Many even became U.S. citizens.

The 1959 revolution, however, sparked immediate flight. Some 215,000 left for the United States in the first four years. Thousands more went to Spain and Latin America.[3] That first wave was composed of the most wealthy: managers of U.S. corporations, the officers of dictator Batista's army and police, doctors, lawyers, scientists, and their families.[4] Metropolitan Miami's Hispanic population skyrocketed from a mere 50,000 in 1960 to more than 580,000 in 1980.[5]

"Few immigrant groups have commenced their economic adaptation to American life from a position of such relative advantage," wrote sociologist Alejandro Portes in a study of Cubans and Miami. The U.S. government provided a shelf full of government assistance programs under the 1966 Cuban Adjustment Act, programs that Mexicans, Puerto Ricans, and other Latinos never received. The refugees became instantly eligible for public assistance, Medicaid, food stamps, free English courses, scholarships, and low-interest college loans. They could secure immediate business credit and start-up loans. The state of Florida went even further—it provided direct cash allotments for Cuban families. Dade County opened civil service lists to noncitizens. The University of Miami Medical School even started special programs to help Cubans meet licensing requirements.[6]

Many of the refugees found additional assistance from covert programs of the Central Intelligence Agency. In those early days, both President John Kennedy and the exiles were confident Castro's revolution would be quickly overthrown. Their view was not dampened by the defeat of the CIA-sponsored Bay of Pigs invasion in 1961, and the capture of thousands of exiles from the expeditionary force, known as Brigada 2506. By 1962, the CIA station at the University of Miami was the biggest in the world next to the agency's Virginia headquarters. The agency had so many Cubans on payroll that it became one of Miami's largest employers.[7] Those CIA paychecks provided many of the exiles a standard of living far beyond the imagination of any immigrants before them.

The refugees, in addition, brought with them extensive technical skills and perhaps the highest educational levels of any Hispanic immigrant group in U.S. history. At a time when only 4 percent of Cubans on the island had reached the twelfth grade, more than 36 percent of the refugees had college degrees, or at least some college education.[8]

Thanks to the unique combination of their own skills and federal largesse, the early exiles set about creating the Cuban miracle in Miami. Within a few short years, the sleepy resort along Biscayne Bay was transformed into a commercial boomtown and a nexus for international trade. Cuban entrepreneurs who started their new life in this country with a small grocery or jewelry store quickly moved into banking, construction, and garment manufacturing. Some went to work for major U.S. firms and launched those firms into the Latin American market. Others served as real estate or banking agents in the United States for rich South Americans.[9]

At the same time, the refugees developed an intensely loyal internal market among their own. More than any other Hispanic immigrants, Cubans hired workers and purchased goods from within their own community.[10] Those who managed to get loan officer positions at small Miami banks made sure to lend start-up funds to fellow refugees who could not secure credit from Anglo lenders. They did so by pioneering the "character loan." An exile who didn't have collateral or credit could get a business loan based on his background or standing in Cuba. The borrowers proved to be impeccable risks and the loan policy turned many Cuban bank officers into millionaires.

Exiles who were barred from joining unions by the racist father-and-son policies of the building trades turned instead to pickup construction jobs among their own people. As the community grew, so did the mom-and-pop building partnerships. By 1979, half of the major construction companies in Dade County were Cuban-owned.

At the same time, New York factory owners who felt their profits being squeezed by that city's garment unions jumped at the opportunity in the 1960s to abandon the North and set up production in Miami. In the decade before 1973, those relocations tripled the number of garment jobs in South Florida to 24,000. The new factories provided work for Cuban refugee women, many of whom ended up as contractors to the owners.[11] By 1987, there were 61,000 Hispanic-owned firms in Miami with gross receipts of $3.8 billion, the largest by far of any city in the United States.[12]

The Cuban refugees were warmly welcomed during the 1960s and 1970s by a nation caught up in the fever of the Cold War. But that welcome changed almost overnight in 1980, as television news started to broadcast pictures of the Mariel boat people. More than 125,000 Cubans entered the country during the four months of the Mariel flight. The new refugees, America realized, were no longer from the island's elite. They were largely poor, black, unskilled, and in some cases mentally ill or dangerous felons. Fidel Castro, according to some reports, took the opportunity to rid himself not just of dissidents but of criminals as well.

For the first time, Cuban arrivals found a hostile reception and were dispersed to more than a dozen army bases scattered about the country. Racial attitudes combined with economic fears—the sight of so many new refugees entering the country at a time of high unemployment angered many Americans. That anger grew when the refugees, frustrated with the cold treatment they were receiving, mounted noisy protests at several detention centers.

I recall visiting one refugee-processing center as a newspaper reporter that year and finding my own image of Cubans radically challenged. That image had been shaped by years of interaction on the streets of New York with the 1960s wave of refugees. Because of that experience, I had grown up believing that Cubans were usually white, well educated, and somewhat arrogant toward Puerto Ricans. Over the years, a certain enmity had developed between the two communities. We Puerto Ricans were resentful that many *barrio* businesses and the better-paying jobs in Spanish-language media had been gobbled up by the new Cuban arrivals

both here and in our homeland—more than sixty thousand Cubans settled in Puerto Rico during the 1960s. So you can imagine my surprise
when I encountered, behind the barbed wire of Fort Indiantown Gap,
Pennsylvania, several thousand Cubans, almost all of them black, all
speaking in the same rapid-fire colloquial Spanish and with the same un-
affected humility I had known among Puerto Ricans in East Harlem.

Mariel had repercussions far beyond the Cuban or Puerto Rican community. It came only months before a national election in which Republican candidate Ronald Reagan made an election issue out of President
Carter's failure to control immigration, an issue that helped Reagan capture the White House. Similarly, the little-known governor of Arkansas
at the time, Bill Clinton, attributed his defeat in a reelection effort that
year to the voters' anger over his accepting so many Mariel refugees into
Arkansas's Fort Chaffee. As we shall see later, Mariel marked the beginning of a major shift in how Americans regarded immigration (see chapter 11).

## THE DEL ROSARIOS AND LIFE
## UNDER THE REVOLUTION

Luis Del Rosario arrived in this country in the summer of 1979, a year before Mariel, as a pardoned political prisoner. His family is originally from
a rice-growing area in Camagüey Province in the center of the island. His
grandparents migrated there from the Canary Islands in the 1890s, when
Spain, desperate to counter the growing independence sentiment among
*criollos,* encouraged *peninsulares* to settle on the island. His parents
were poor farmers—they rented land from a more prosperous relative—
so they did not suffer the extreme misery that dogged Cuba's masses: the
plantation workers, sharecroppers, and urban poor who formed the base
of support for Castro's revolution.

Several Del Rosarios, in fact, had minor jobs with the Batista government. Luis's uncle, Chilo, served as a railroad policeman in Havana. Another uncle, Antolin, was a cop in Matanzas. The immediate family was a
big one, seven boys and three girls. In the years before the revolution triumphed, Luis recalls, guerrilla leader Camilo Cienfuegos commanded a
detachment of fighters from Fidel's Twenty-sixth of July Movement in
their province. Cienfuegos's band arrived at their farm one day and
asked permission to camp on the land, and Luis's father, though he was
a Batista supporter, dared not refuse.

Luis was only ten when Castro's guerrilla army marched into Havana
in January 1959. His parents sought at first to live in peace with the new

regime. They even prospered from some of its early reforms. The government, for instance, built new houses for everyone in the region. All of the houses had cement floors, plywood walls, and zinc roofs—a step up from the dirt-floor hovels that were commonplace.[13] The new Del Rosario house had three bedrooms. The seven boys slept in one room, the girls in the second, and their parents in the third.

The government also built new schools and it launched extensive baseball and soccer programs for the region's youth. "The baseball uniforms were really important to us," Luis recalls. "We had gloves and bats and competed against other towns. I played for years, both in school and in the Little Leagues. Because of that kind of thing, I'd say ninety percent of the people supported Fidel at first." Numerous foreign studies of Cuban attitudes in the early days of the revolution confirm that view.[14]

But by the mid-1960s, euphoria for the revolution had waned. Young people started to quit their government-assigned jobs and move to Havana in search of better work. Luis heard the first real antigovernment sentiment around that time. After the death of his father in 1964, he moved to the capital and joined his brothers in a house in upper Havana, and together they started a small foundry in the back of the house. They would take old motors and discarded metal parts, then melt and recycle them into copper, bronze, or iron for the government. Nearly all of the dozen or so employees were family members. Luis tended the single antiquated oven and his brother Wenceslao served as the plant's main molder. Family foundries like theirs became critical to Cuba's survival after the U.S. embargo cut off access to spare parts for the many American-made cars and industrial machines in the country.

"It was a rustic operation," Luis recalls. "We had no technology and we used to burn ourselves a lot. Molten metal would spill pretty often and set off explosions. But we worked hard and the foundry made us a good living. If we had been allowed to grow, the country would be free today."

That never happened. In 1968, the government began nationalizing even small enterprises. "Some officials came and told us our foundry would become the property of the people," Luis recalled. "I got so angry I busted up our machines before we left."

Despite the bitter experience with the foundry, Luis still dreamed of prospering under socialism. He went to work as a postal clerk and later as a truck driver transporting food to the state-owned stores that dispensed all consumer goods under the country's system of rationing. It was during his daily trips around the Cuban countryside that Luis began to see firsthand how conditions were unraveling.

"Everything was going backward. If I tried to defend the revolution, others would tell me, 'How can you say that? Fidel only throws dirt at us.'" One day, a notice arrived from the government ordering him to report for military service, but he simply moved and decided to dodge the draft. Things were so disorganized in Cuba by then the government never prosecuted him. Two of his other brothers did enlist, however, and one, Augusto, earned a rapid promotion to sergeant.

Luis passed the next few years managing several state stores in Havana. The stores were routinely bedeviled by long lines and shortages of goods and they invariably turned into centers for both public discontent and private corruption. Since some products always remained in abundance after ration cards were redeemed, store managers took to bartering or selling their surplus—five pounds of rice, say, for five pounds of meat.

"Many of us lived practically from robbing the government," Luis said. "The rationing system just didn't work."

By the early 1970s, Luis had come to hate the revolution. He and several brothers joined a clandestine group, the National Liberation Movement of October 10th. They were just amateur conspirators, he admitted, who would meet to plan grandiose sabotage operations but never carry them out. Eventually, an informant alerted the army, and soldiers arrested two of Luis's brothers, Gustavo and Wenceslao, outside an airport in Camagüey Province, as they were preparing to hijack a plane to the United States. A few months later, police arrested Luis for subversion. Convicted in a quick trial, he was sentenced to twelve years in jail but ended up serving only six and a half.

Unknown to Luis, a new group of anti-Castro Cuban Americans who were intent on normalizing U.S.-Cuba relations had traveled to Havana to meet with Fidel Castro. The group called itself the Committee of Seventy-five. It was immediately condemned by old-line anti-Castro groups in Miami as a front for Communist sympathizers. But the committee managed to convince Castro to pardon more than a thousand political prisoners on condition that all the prisoners left Cuba immediately.[15] Among those freed was Luis Del Rosario. On June 6, 1979, more than twenty years after Fidel marched out of the Sierra Maestra, Del Rosario, his wife, and two children boarded a Boeing 727 at José Martí Airport in Havana and flew to Miami. The rest of their relatives remained behind.

———

Luis quickly found work in a construction firm owned by another refugee, availed himself of all the federal programs, put a down payment on a house, and enrolled his children in Catholic schools. Several years later, after allowing his son Ismael to join the civil air patrol, he developed an interest in flying, obtained his own pilot's license, and started flying air charters out of the Miami area. Meanwhile, he kept finding ways to get the rest of his family out of Cuba.

In the early 1990s, he joined Brothers to the Rescue, a group with historical links to the CIA, and through the organization he came into contact with the aging chiefs of Miami's refugee community, a cadre of political bosses obsessed with returning to power in Cuba, who have made a lifelong, in some cases lucrative, career of stoking anti-Castro passions among their countrymen and the general U.S. population.

"They are a bunch of old men who just want Fidel out so that they can replace him," Del Rosario said of those leaders. Many of the working-class refugees who arrived in recent years share his view, he said, but few voice it publicly, for they fear ostracism as Communist sympathizers or physical attack by the anti-Castro underground. These most recent immigrants are the moderate side of the Cuban immigrant community most Americans never see. They oppose Castro's revolution, while at the same time not disputing that its early years brought much actual progress to Cuba's poor majority. They agree that many of the Batista backers who fled in the early days of the revolution to Miami were indeed criminals and exploiters of the nation. They do not seek to recover confiscated estates and fortunes they never possessed. They long for a Cuba free of violence, terror, and one-party rule, but they wish the unrelenting U.S. embargo against Cuba would end so they can freely visit the island and assist those relatives still there.

Two years after the boat exodus, I talked with Del Rosario again. His brother and family had been picked up at sea by the Coast Guard, kept in Guantánamo for more than a year, then quietly paroled into the United States. With new national elections approaching, President Clinton's policy of closing the doors to Cuban boat people had been just as quietly shelved. "This country doesn't care about Cubans," Rosario told me. "We're just pawns of politics."

# 7

## Dominicans: From the Duarte to the George Washington Bridge

No man could know whether his neighbor, or his lifelong
friends, or even his brother or son or wife, might inform against
him. . . . Everyone feared. No one trusted anyone.

—*John Bartlow Martin,*
*former ambassador to the*
*Dominican Republic*

During the weekend of July 4, 1992, hundreds of Dominican immigrants rioted in the Washington Heights area of New York City after rumors spread that a white policeman had fatally shot a young Dominican in the back. For several days, neighborhood youths torched cars, looted Korean- and white-owned businesses, and hurled rocks and bottles at police. City officials, fearing a repeat of the Los Angeles riot that had broken out two months earlier, rushed to calm residents with promises of an investigation. Although a Manhattan grand jury later concluded that the policeman had acted in self-defense against a known drug dealer, and that the alleged witnesses to the shooting had fabricated their stories, the first Dominican riot on U.S. soil had suddenly thrust a national spotlight on a new Latino immigrant group.

Between 1961 and 1986 more than 400,000 people legally immigrated to the United States from the Dominican Republic, and another 44,000 moved to Puerto Rico, while thousands more entered both places illegally. More than 300,000 Dominicans lived in New York City by 1990, and the total was expected to reach 700,000 early in the millennium, making Dominican migration one of the largest to this country of the past forty years.[1]

Much like the Puerto Ricans of the 1950s, Dominicans went largely unnoticed at first. New Yorkers tended to mistake them for blacks who happened to speak Spanish. By the 1990s, however, they had become the second-largest Hispanic group in the Northeast. As mainstream newspaper accounts of Dominicans involved in violent crime or drug trafficking became commonplace, some whites started to react with anger and blamed the new immigrants for the city's decline.

Rarely did the postriot news reports, however, seek to explain why so many Dominicans came to the United States in the first place. Few explored the new immigrants' enormous success in neighborhood commerce or their high enrollment in the public university system. And none of the reports clarified what was distinct about the Dominican diaspora from that of earlier European or even from other Latino immigrants.

---

The Dominican exodus, unlike that of Puerto Ricans and Mexicans, began largely as a refugee flight in the mid-1960s. Much of it followed a popular uprising in April 1965 that sought to restore to power the country's first democratically elected president, Juan Bosch. President Lyndon Johnson, fearing the revolt would lead to a Castro-style revolution, dispatched 26,000 troops to invade the country, and those soldiers sided with the Dominican army in its efforts to crush the revolt. The U.S. occupation then paved the way for Joaquín Balaguer, a longtime aide of assassinated dictator Trujillo, to capture power during elections that followed in 1966. Those elections, despite supervision by U.S. and international observers, were plagued by right-wing violence against Bosch supporters. To diffuse the postelection crisis, U.S. officials hastily facilitated the mass exodus to the United States of the very revolutionaries our government had helped crush.[2]

For the next thirty years, Dominican political life was dominated by the same personalities and unresolved conflicts of the April 1965 revolution. Bloody political repression against Bosch's followers lasted for more than a decade. More than three thousand were killed between 1966 and 1974 alone. Thousands of others suffered imprisonment and torture.[3] Because of that right-wing repression, those who fled the country in the late 1960s and the 1970s were typically from the political left. Washington, however, refused to classify the Dominicans as refugees, as it did the Cubans who were fleeing Fidel Castro at the same time, so Dominicans received no federal assistance on arrival. Not until the 1980s, after the reign of terror ended back home, did Dominican immigration assume more an economic than a political character.

Those Dominicans who came here, whether in the early or later waves, were generally better educated, more urbanized, and more politically active than the average Mexican or Puerto Rican migrant. They also proved more adept at business enterprise, launching thousands of *bode-*

*gas,* supermarkets, and consumer goods stores in New York City, just as Cubans were doing in Miami. Manhattan's Washington Heights became their El Barrio and their Little Havana. The newcomers, though, were largely *mulato* and black, and they quickly encountered racial discrimination even from other Hispanics.

Estela Vázquez was one of those Dominican pioneers. She arrived here as a teenager in August 1965, accompanied by her mother, her younger brother, and her sister. Her family's experiences typify those of the Dominican diaspora. They provide some insight into the obstacles the early immigrants faced, the organizations and networks they formed, and the unique identity they created.

## THE LUCIANOS—THE EARLY YEARS

For Estela Vázquez Luciano, as for most Dominicans, modern existence began on May 30, 1961, when El Jefe, General Rafael Leónidas Trujillo, was assassinated by fellow officers after thirty-one years of wielding absolute power. President Kennedy and the CIA, the world would later learn, had decided to oust Trujillo even though previous U.S. governments had groomed and backed him.[4] Four turbulent years followed Trujillo's death. During that time, the country staged its first democratic election for president and Juan Bosch, a populist reformer and intellectual, won the vote in a landslide. But Bosch's attempts at land reform and his refusal to repress the country's Communist movement placed him in immediate conflict with the sugar growers and the U.S. government. Only seven months after his inauguration, he was overthrown by the army and forced into exile in Puerto Rico.

Bosch remained popular even in exile, however, and two years after his ouster, on April 24, 1965, a charismatic young follower of his, Colonel Francisco Caamaño, led a revolt of young army officers to restore him to power. From the moment the revolt began, the people of Santo Domingo poured into the streets to reclaim their democracy from the generals. Estela Vázquez, who was seventeen at the time, immediately bolted from her grandmother's house and followed the giant crowds toward the Duarte Bridge in the middle of downtown to confront the soldiers who had overthrown Bosch.

That she ran from the house that day seemed somehow fated for Estela, descended as she is from a line of poor but fiercely independent women. Her grandmother, Ramona Luciano, was a peasant from Baní, near the country's western border with Haiti. As a young woman, Ramona Luciano had fallen in love with Juan Mejías, a rich local landowner who kept her as one of his many *queridas* for years. Their long relationship produced seven children, one of them being Ana María Luciano, Estela's mother, who was born in 1920.[5]

Ramona left Baní in the 1930s and moved with her children to Santo Domingo, where she enrolled her daughter Ana María in one of the many seamstress schools dictator Trujillo had created for women. By 1938, Ana María had married Alcibiades Vilchez, the owner of a small *pulpería* (grocery store), with whom she had three children. The eldest, Estela, was born in 1948. The family was relatively privileged, thanks to minor connections they had to Trujillo officials. One of Ana María's many brothers, Joaquín Mejías, who was also fathered out of wedlock by the same rich Baní landowner, was a top assistant to Trujillo confidant Manuel Moja López. Rafael Sención, another brother, was a chauffeur to Moja López. In a country where everything was accomplished by personal ties, the lowly chauffeur, Uncle Rafael, eventually became *"padrino"* of the whole family.

When Trujillo named Moja López ambassador to Washington in 1958, Uncle Rafael moved to the United States as his driver. He thus became the first Luciano family member to leave for El Norte. Back then, a Dominican traveling abroad was unheard-of except for the very rich and famous. In early 1961, Uncle Rafael secured a passport for one of his sisters, Esperanza, to work as a servant in Washington. That same year, another sister, Consuelo, emigrated to New York. Even then, three months before Trujillo's death, acquiring passports was virtually impossible without the dictator's approval. Consuelo, for example, had to produce twenty-four photos and take one to each police precinct in the capital so the authorities could check if she was a prostitute or known political dissident.

Not all of Ana María's family avoided the Trujillo terror. Another of her brothers, Juan Mejías, once made the mistake of publicly criticizing El Jefe. He was promptly arrested and thrown naked into La Cuarenta, a notorious prison on the outskirts of the capital. There he was tortured so badly that when he finally emerged, he had been driven insane and had lost all hearing. For the rest of his life he wandered the streets of the capital, homeless, since no family member dared give him shelter.

The absolute power Trujillo wielded is almost unimaginable today. A former U.S. ambassador to the country recalled in his memoirs that "Telephones were tapped, hotel rooms were wired with microphones. Mail was opened, cables scrutinized. Worst of all, as the dictator's secret informers seeped throughout the land, no man could know whether his neighbor, or his lifelong friends, or even his brother or son or wife, might inform against him. . . . Everyone feared. No one trusted anyone."[6]

"If the police were looking for you," recalled Dr. Arnulfo Reyes, a survivor of the repression, "you dared not run away. If you did, they would come and kill all the members of your family. So people just sat in their houses and waited for the police to come."[7]

Estela was still in junior high school when Trujillo was assassinated. At first, along with everyone else in the family, she mourned the death of the only leader most Dominicans had ever known. But those feelings of loss rapidly gave way to outrage as victims of the Trujillo years returned from exile abroad, and the stories those exiles revealed about the tortures they had endured under his depraved rule, stories which were all widely disseminated in the country's revived free press, jolted Dominican society from its thirty-year slumber. Soon, students began marching by the thousands to demand democratic elections and an end to the series of caretaker juntas that kept jockeying to fill the vacuum left by Trujillo's death. Radical newspapers and books proliferated. Leaders of the leftist June Fourteenth Movement became instant folk heroes. Estela, like most young Dominicans, was swept up by the political whirlwind.

In May 1963, with the country in upheaval, with jobs scarce and with her husband too sick to work, Ana María Luciano decided to leave her children in the care of her mother and head to New York City to look for a job. She moved in with her sister Consuelo in the Bronx and landed work at a coat factory on Lower Broadway in Manhattan, which enabled her to send money back home each month to her husband and children. Soon after she arrived, she received word that her husband had died. She paid for the burial but could not afford to fly back for the funeral.

One night in June 1965, when Ana María arrived home from work, she found a telegram waiting for her: SOLDIERS ARRESTED ESTELA. SHE'S IN LA VICTORIA, the message from her mother read. Ana María grabbed the first flight back to Santo Domingo.

Most Americans still recall exactly what they were doing the day they heard the news John Kennedy had been shot. So it is with Dominicans, who recall every detail of the afternoon of April 24, 1965, the day the Dominican revolution began. Estela Vázquez was sitting in her grandmother's house listening to the radio show of velvet-voiced commentator Francisco Peña Gómez.

Every Saturday, Peña Gómez, the youth leader of Juan Bosch's Dominican Revolutionary Party (PRD), would host a weekly show. It was called *Tribuna Democrática (Democratic Tribune),* and it was especially

popular among poor, darker-skinned Dominicans who all knew that
Peña Gómez was one of the few blacks to hold a prominent political post
in the country.

Listeners who tuned in that day were startled when they heard Peña
Gómez announce that young officers in the army had launched a rebellion to bring President Bosch back to power. They were led, Peña told his
listeners, by Colonel Caamaño, son of an infamous Trujillo-era general.[8]
Estela rushed with her boyfriend and several of her cousins to Avenida
Mella, one of Santo Domingo's big commercial streets, then down to the
Duarte Bridge, the narrow span that controlled access to the heart of the
city's colonial downtown area. As day turned to night, the people built
barricades and contructed a makeshift encampment to prevent government soldiers stationed at the city's outskirts from entering town. Those
who supported the return of Bosch called themselves the "Constitutionalists"; their opponents were dubbed the "Loyalists." Few in the crowd
had any idea whether Caamaño and the pro-Bosch rebel soldiers had
managed to seize power, but still they cheered an endless string of civilian speakers proclaiming a people's victory.

On the second night of the uprising, military planes began dropping
bombs on the downtown area. In response, Bosch supporters, led by
cadres of the June Fourteenth Movement, attacked and occupied several
police stations. Estela, who was too young to participate in the precinct
assaults, carried weapons and ammunition for the rebels instead.

On the third morning of the revolt, the air force resumed all-out attacks on the Duarte Bridge. More than fifty people were killed and a
hundred wounded, but the Constitutionalists, reinforced by Caamaño
and his rebel soldiers, managed to hold the critical gateway to the city.[9]
After that victory at the bridge, civilian support for the rebels mushroomed, government soldiers began deserting their posts, and it appeared
that the generals were on the verge of surrendering. But President Johnson and his emissaries were determined not to allow it. On April 28,
Johnson sent in the marines as U.S. officials leaked exaggerated claims to
the press that Communists were in control of the rebellion and that
American lives were in danger. The White House called the intervention
"neutral," but federal documents declassified since then leave no doubt
that U.S. officials cooperated with and encouraged the ruling junta's effort to stamp out the pro-Bosch forces.[10] Caamaño's rebels, several thousand strong, retreated to the heart of the capital, where they were soon
contained inside fifty-four square blocks of the colonial city known as
Ciudad Nueva. There, cut off from the rest of the Dominican people by a
U.S.-enforced security corridor, the rebels remained in control of the

nerve center of the country—the presidential palace, the ports, the telephone company, the main post office, and the radio and television stations.

In that rebel area, Estela lived for a month until a patrol of soldiers arrested her one afternoon in May as she slipped out to visit her grandmother. The soldiers took the teenager to her grandmother's house to be identified. "Here, take this rope and hang her," her grandmother Ramona told them, an old picture of dictator Trujillo still on the wall. "I don't want any Communists in my family."

Ana María Luciano arrived in the capital in June and tried to secure her daughter's release. She appealed to every old political connection of the Lucianos, and finally secured a meeting with Colonel Benoit, head of the new military junta.

"My family have always been supporters of Trujillo," she told the busy colonel. "We are not Communists. We don't know about politics. My daughter is only a child."

"Señora Luciano, I can't release her," the soft-spoken colonel said. "You don't know your own daughter. She'll run right back to the Zona Prohibida [Prohibited Zone] and take up with those Communists again."

"Sir, I promise you, I won't allow it. She's leaving with me for New York. She won't come back."

By August, Ana María's persistence paid off. Colonel Benoit ordered Estela's release—and her immediate deportation. Soldiers escorted her from prison to the airport, where her mother, her younger sister, Doraliza, and her six-year-old brother, Rafael Leónidas, were waiting. At the age of seventeen, Estela Vázquez had become a political exile.

## BUILDING A NEW LIFE IN NEW YORK CITY

Ana María Luciano returned to her old factory on Broadway, but the supervisor refused at first to rehire her. Puerto Rican Eva Estrella, one of the factory's veteran seamstresses, was furious. "Ana María didn't go to Santo Domingo to party and dance," Eva told the boss. "She went there to save her children. If she doesn't come back to work, all of us go on strike."

The next day, Ana María was back at her machine, and as soon as she could, she found Estela a job in a small sweatshop nearby on Astor Place. Her first week on the job, Estela was stuck for hours on a New York subway when the Northeast was paralyzed by the greatest power blackout in U.S. history. In less than one year Estela had lived through a fierce revolution, three months in a dank prison cell, dislocation to a strange new country, the shock of becoming a teenage factory worker, and a blackout in a New York City subway tunnel.

The following year, she married a young Puerto Rican coworker of one of her cousins, and their marriage produced two children, Evelyn and Alejandro. For a while, they all lived with Estela's mother and younger brother and sister—seven people crammed into a two-bedroom basement apartment that never saw sunlight and seldom had heat in winter. To ward off the cold, they slept most nights in their overcoats, wearing plastic fur-lined boots Ana María brought home from the factory.

The lives of the Dominican pioneers, just as those of the Puerto Ricans before them, were dominated by the search for work and the day-to-day battle for survival. Both had come from islands where government unemployment was unknown and the acceptance of charity frowned upon. Ana María Luciano, who stayed at the same factory for twenty-one years, until it closed in 1984, always boasted even in retirement that she had never taken charity from anyone, especially the government. But those in the second generation found it harder to reconcile those old values with their new reality. Estela's husband, for instance, abandoned her in 1973 for one of his mistresses, which forced her to resort to welfare along with her two young children. She kept struggling as a single parent, though, eventually learning English, getting her high school equivalency diploma, leaving the factory, enrolling in a community college, and finally landing a job she could be proud of—as an organizer at Mount Sinai Hospital in East Harlem with Local 1199, the health care workers' union.

## THE NEW *COLONIA* IN NEW YORK

Most Dominicans who arrived in the 1960s settled near established Puerto Rican communities, the most popular being on the Upper West Side of Manhattan. Those early arrivals had expected to go home once the Balaguer terror ended, but as the years passed, the new society they'd found gradually altered their expectations and reconfigured their dreams.

The first organizations the immigrants formed were social clubs and sports associations that were meant to keep alive their sense of community. The more well-known were Club María Trinidad Sánchez, on Broadway near 104th Street, and the Thirtieth of March and the Twenty-seventh of February clubs, both named after important dates in Dominican history. The Centro Educacional Caribe, one of the first civic associations, was founded in the early 1970s by Alfredo White, a one-time leader of the sugarcane workers in San Pedro de Macorís. There, the immigrants learned English and began to study the American political system.

The new arrivals were generally better educated than either Puerto Rican migrants or Dominicans back home.[11] One 1980 study revealed that 41 percent of New York City's Dominican immigrants had completed ten years of school or better, nearly twice the average of city dwellers in the Dominican Republic.[12] On the whole, they were also more aware of politics than the average Puerto Rican or Mexican. The upheavals of the post-Trujillo era had turned Dominicans into the most radical group of Spanish-speaking immigrants in U.S. history, akin to the Russian workers who reached the United States after the failed 1905 revolution, or the Italian anarcho-syndicalist immigrants of the 1920s.

Many joined branches of political parties opposed to the Balaguer regime as soon as they arrived. By early 1970, some young Dominicans, following the example of Puerto Ricans who founded the Young Lords, started their own radical organization. It was called El Comité and it spearheaded a large tenant squatters' movement on the Upper West Side against New York's new urban renewal program, which was then gutting and demolishing low-rent tenements to make way for middle-income housing. The campaign against urban renewal failed, as the city's brash and ambitious relocation commissioner under Mayor Lindsay, Herman Badillo, systematically demolished hundreds of Upper West Side tenements and single-room-occupancy hotels and pushed the low-income Puerto Ricans up to the South Bronx and the Dominicans to northern Manhattan.

From the West Side, the community shifted at first to the area around City College, at 135th Street and Broadway, and as more immigrants arrived, it spread farther north to Washington Heights, which eventually became its center. At City College, the first organizations of Dominican students were formed in the late 1970s. Out of those groups emerged a core of teachers, doctors, and lawyers who today are the community's principal leaders. Guillermo Linares, the first Dominican-born city councilman, was a founder of one of those first groups. After graduation, he taught in the public schools and together with Fernando Lescaille, another fellow CCNY alumnus, he founded the Association of Progressive Dominicans (ACDP), the first social action group in Washington Heights. By the mid-1980s, ACDP members had won control of the local school and community boards, and those victories provided the springboard for Linares's election.

The surge in Dominican migration soon strained the traditional close ties between Dominicans and Puerto Ricans, ties that date back to the nineteenth century and early twentieth century, when many Puerto Ricans left their island to find work in the sugar plantations of the more prosperous Dominican Republic. Cultural interchange and intermarriage between the two groups were common back then. Both former Dominican president Joaquín Balaguer and his archenemy, Juan Bosch, for instance, claimed Puerto Rican ancestry on their mothers' side. And many Puerto Ricans assisted Dominican migrants in the 1960s to navigate the hostile and inscrutable Anglo world the newcomers found. But, in recent years, sharp tension has emerged between the groups, both here and in Puerto Rico.

Much of the tension has resulted from illegal Dominican immigration to Puerto Rico. In 1990 alone, the Immigration and Naturalization Service deported more than 13,200 Dominicans who entered Puerto Rico illegally.[13] Every night, smugglers launch *yolas* filled with Dominicans from eastern coastal towns and set sail across the Mona Passage to Puerto Rico. No one knows how many have drowned after paying $400 each to the *coyotes* to take them across the treacherous passage, but Puerto Rico newspapers are periodically filled with stories of dead Dominicans washing up onshore.[14]

Those who make it land near the western towns of Aguadilla, Mayagüez, and Arecibo, then travel to the San Juan area and on to New York or Miami. Since Puerto Rico is U.S. territory, it has no mandatory immigration or customs checkpoints for the scores of U.S.-bound flights that leave each day. But Dominicans, lured by the island's climate, common language, and culture, and by its greater prosperity, often decide to stay. Current estimates of the Dominican population run as high as 300,000. With island unemployment stubbornly high, an anti-immigrant backlash was inevitable. Puerto Ricans, echoing the fears of Americans here, perceive Dominicans as taking scarce jobs away from natives. At the same time, island press reports typically portray Dominicans as shiftless and prone to crime and drug trafficking. In urban neighborhoods such as Santurce's Barrio Obrero and Villa Palmeras, whose populations are now overwhelmingly Dominican, that resentment has turned increasingly racial.

Exaggerated accounts of the Dominican influx to the island are routinely passed on to Puerto Rican relatives in the United States, where competition over jobs and business opportunities has created increasing rivalry between the two immigrant communities in the Northeast, one that echoes the growing tension between Mexican Americans and the newer Central American immigrant communities in the far West.

The Puerto Rican–Dominican rivalry has moved from one *barrio* industry to another. Twenty years ago, virtually every *bodega* in New York and Boston was Puerto Rican–owned. Today, it is rare to find one not owned by a Dominican. The same is true of the livery taxi cabs that operate in the outer boroughs of New York. Thirty years ago, the industry was dominated by Puerto Ricans and African Americans. Today, it is largely Dominican and Jamaican. At Latin nightclubs and on Spanish-language radio, where Puerto Rican salsa once reigned, merengues from the Dominican Republic are more likely to be heard. Some Puerto Ricans even blame Dominicans for the 1980s epidemic of cocaine and crack trade in northeastern cities. Thus, we see some of the same immigrant conflicts developing within the Latino community as existed between early-arriving Latinos and Anglo Americans.

Yet, side by side with the poverty, drugs, and low-wage labor among Dominicans, we find many immigrant success stories. Enrollment at jammed Hostos Community College in the South Bronx, originally created out of the educational battles of the 1960s as a school for Puerto Rican adult workers, is today nearly 60 percent Dominican and nearly 90 percent female. Dominicans in the City University are now routinely elected as student government presidents and a significant U.S.-raised professional class of Dominicans has emerged.

Not only have Dominicans spawned a thriving mom-and-pop business community, they are also increasingly breaking into the medium-size food and retailing industry. Several chains of independent New York supermarkets—the Pioneer, Associated, and C-Town chains—are now dominated by Dominican owners. By the early 1990s, the National Association of Supermarkets had become the richest economic bloc of Dominicans in the country. Even banks and factories owned and operated by Dominican immigrants have sprouted in recent years.

From designer Oscar de la Renta to jazz pianist Michel Camilo, to the novelists Julia Alvarez and Junot Diaz, Dominican contributions to U.S. culture are increasingly gaining national attention. And the amazing dominance in recent years of Dominican athletes in major league baseball has been a source of enduring national pride to the immigrant community. From Sammy Sosa to Juan Samuel to George Bell, from Pedro Guerrero and Tony Fernández to Juan Guzmán, Julio Franco, and José Rijo, from Mélido Pérez to Alfredo Griffin, the list of Dominican baseball stars seems endless. Many come from the same section of the country, San Pedro de Macorís, where giant sugarcane plantations once dominated the landscape and U.S. Marines once hunted down guerrillas.

Often forgotten in the stereotypes, however, is the incredible mass poverty that drives young Dominicans to this country. The Dominican standard of living plummeted throughout the 1980s and early 1990s. A government doctor there earned the equivalent of $160 a month in 1991. A public school teacher earned about $70.[15] Overall, more than 60 percent of the population earns poverty wages. As long as a Dominican doctor can earn more money washing dishes in Manhattan than performing surgery back home, how can he be expected to resist emigration?

In the United States, the smartest child in the family aspires to be an investment banker, an Internet venture capitalist, a doctor. In the shantytowns of Santo Domingo and the Caribbean, the brightest and the best dream of reaching the United States to pull their family out of poverty. Today there is hardly an urban household in the Dominican Republic that does not have some family member living in the United States and sending occasional financial help back home.[16]

In the three decades since the Lucianos arrived, other family members have followed. All dreamed at first of returning. In 1979, Estela did go back. It was her first visit since her exile fourteen years earlier. By then, the Balaguer repression had ended and Antonio Guzmán, a member of Juan Bosch's old party, was the new president, so the New York exiles felt safe in returning. But the Guzmán government proved to be as corrupt as Balaguer's. Estela encountered a nation mired in poverty she had never imagined. The mushrooming population was straining all urban infrastructure. Electrical blackouts were commonplace. Drinking water was polluted. Shantytowns dotted the capital. Roads were in disrepair and unemployment was higher than ever.

That was when she realized she could not live back home.

Given the history of U.S. exploitation and bullying of the Dominican Republic, and the tremendous economic gap that exploitation has created, it seems unlikely that massive emigration will abate in the twenty-first century. Like Estela Vázquez, many Dominicans will continue being patriots from afar, in love with their homeland but unable to live there.

"I think if the U.S. offered more visas," she admitted one day in 1993, "everyone would leave the country. That's how bad things are."

# 8

## Central Americans: Intervention Comes Home to Roost

So many were tortured to death that if the army took you into custody and you survived, those in your circle would suspect you as a traitor. Women who were raped were too ashamed to return to their homes. Families and communities just disintegrated.

—*Mario González, Guatemalan immigrant*
*psychologist, 1998*

Although a few Salvadorans lived in San Francisco's Mission District and the Pico-Union area of Los Angeles as far back as 1970, and a tiny Guatemalan enclave took shape in Chicago's Humboldt Park area around the same time, Central Americans were a negligible presence in the United States until the final decades of the twentieth century. The U.S. Census counted 94,000 Salvadoran-born inhabitants in the entire country in 1980. That figure skyrocketed to 701,000 ten years later—an eightfold increase—and today more than 1.2 million Salvadorans reside here, nearly 20 percent of their homeland's population.[1] Similar astonishing jumps occurred in that decade for Guatemalans (from 71,642 to 226,000) and Nicaraguans (from 25,000 to 125,000).

This sudden exodus did not originate with some newfound collective desire for the material benefits of U.S. society; rather, vicious civil wars and the social chaos those wars engendered forced the region's people to flee, and in each case, the origins and spiraling intensity of those wars were a direct result of military and economic intervention by our own government.

As it had done with earlier Cuban and Dominican arrivals, Washington pursued a dual and discriminatory policy toward the new immigrants: the Immigration and Naturalization Service welcomed the Nicaraguans but intercepted and interned the Guatemalans and Salvadorans. By routinely denying refugee status to the latter two groups, our government condemned Salvadorans and Guatemalans who managed to sneak across the border to a precarious and illegal existence at the margins of Anglo society. They became the preferred gardeners, cooks, and nannies of a vast underground economy that mushroomed in the 1980s to service middle-class America.

Despite those obstacles, the new immigrants showed amazing resilience and a dogged work ethic. They rapidly established vibrant immigrant networks and self-help organizations; they mounted vigorous court challenges and lobbying campaigns to reform federal immigration policies; they emerged as a critical source of economic aid to their destitute homelands through the billions of dollars in annual remittances they sent home to relatives; and gradually, as their numbers multiplied, they transformed and reconfigured the Latino population of the United States.

———

To comprehend this new Latino wave, we must have a rudimentary sense of what the immigrants left behind. Simply put, the vast majority of Central Americans today live in perpetual misery alongside tiny elites that enjoy unparalled prosperity. The average cat in our country eats more beef than the average Central American. In Nicaragua, 54 percent of the people have no safe drinking water. In Guatemala, 44 percent are illiterate, and Indians, who constitute half the country's population, have an average life span of forty-eight years.[2] Seven out of ten Hondurans live in desperate poverty, only one rural resident in ten has electricity, and less than two in ten have access to safe drinking water.[3] Infant mortality was seventy per 1,000 births in 1990, compared to less than nine per 1,000 in the United States.

These conditions were made worse by the "lost decade" of the 1980s, when the Latin American debt crisis and the periodic devaluations of the region's currencies against the U.S. dollar drove down the real value of wages while driving up the cost of American imports. In every Central American country except Costa Rica, the per capita domestic product dropped from 1980 to 1996 (see table 4).

While the economic stagnation was region-wide, the immigration flow was not. The bulk of emigrants came from three war-torn countries. Fatalities from those wars had passed a quarter of a million by 1989—five times the U.S. death toll in Vietnam. More than 140,000 died in Guatemala, 70,000 in El Salvador, 60,000 in Nicaragua—unimaginable devastation for a region that has fewer inhabitants than the state of Texas.[4]

---

TABLE 4

## GROSS DOMESTIC PRODUCT PER CAPITA 1980–1996
### (IN 1990 U.S. DOLLARS)[5]

| Country | 1980 | 1990 | 1996 |
| --- | --- | --- | --- |
| Costa Rica | $1,986 | $1,865 | $2,016 |
| El Salvador | 1,219 | 1,026 | 1,171 |
| Guatemala | 1,044 | 857 | 915 |
| Honduras | 636 | 585 | 596 |
| Nicaragua | 979 | 645 | 637 |

---

Central America's victims perished mostly at the hands of their own soldiers or from right-wing death squads, and invariably from weapons made in the U.S.A., since in each country our government provided massive military aid to the side doing most of the killing. Even though international human rights groups repeatedly documented government-sponsored terror in the region, including several infamous assassinations of U.S. citizens and Catholic clergy, the Reagan and Bush administrations, obsessed with stopping Communism in the region, refused to assist the thousands streaming across the Mexican border to escape that terror. Between 1983 and 1990, the INS granted only 2.6 percent of political asylum requests from Salvadorans, 1.8 percent from Guatemalans, and 2.0 percent from Hondurans, yet it granted 25.2 percent of those from Nicaraguans, whose Sandinista government Washington was seeking to overthrow.[6] Even when the INS denied asylum to a Nicaraguan, the agency rarely sent that person home—of 31,000 denied between 1981 and 1989, only 750 were actually deported.[7]

Unfortunately, public knowledge about the wars in Central America was so scanty that most Americans, when asked, could not even tell what side our government was backing in which country.[8] Leaders in Washington sought to portray the region as pivotal to the worldwide battle between democracy and Communism. Such simplistic justifications obscured long-festering divisions between rich and poor in the region, and they ignored our own government's historic complicity in exacerbating those divisions.

## NICARAGUA: FROM SOMOZA TO THE SANDINISTAS

In Nicaragua, as we have seen, Washington backed the Somoza family's dictatorial rule and tolerated its pillaging of the country for more than forty years. During that time, more Nicaraguan military officers received training at the U.S. Army's School of the Americas in Panama than from any other country in Latin America.[9]

Most Nicaraguans had had enough of the Somozas by the mid-1970s. The turning point came with the massive earthquake that razed much of the capital of Managua in 1972. While their countrymen were digging out of the rubble, Somoza cronies and soldiers stole millions of dollars' worth of desperately needed international relief supplies, causing an outcry from the public. From then on, even the Catholic hierarchy and the members of the elite, many of whom had benefited from the Somoza era, turned against the regime.

A new generation of revolutionaries arose. They called themselves the Sandinista National Liberation Front, after the country's legendary martyred leader, Augusto Sandino, and the guerrilla army they formed spread rapidly through the countryside. But even as the guerrillas advanced, and public sentiment turned heavily against the Somozas, the White House and Congress continued to back the regime. By the time the Carter administration finally decided to arrange a peaceful removal of Somoza in 1979, it was too late. A nationwide popular uprising toppled the clan and brought the Sandinistas to power.

At first, the Carter White House tried to work with the Sandinista revolutionaries, but that all changed when Ronald Reagan was elected president the following year. Reagan immediately authorized the CIA to arm, train, and finance many of the former Somoza soldiers and henchmen into the infamous Contra army. For the rest of the 1980s, the Contras and their CIA directors pursued a hit-and-run war of sabotage and terror aimed at destabilizing the new government. The covert war was overseen from the Reagan White House by Lieutenant Colonel Oliver North and was conducted from bases in Honduras and Costa Rica. While the Reagan and then the Bush administrations intensified the war and sought to isolate the Sandinista government internationally, the number of Nicaraguans fleeing their country kept growing.

## EL SALVADOR—FROM *LA MATANZA*
## TO THE KILLING FIELDS

A similar pattern emerged in the Salvadoran civil war, whose origins go back to another almost-forgotten North American henchman, General Maximiliano Hernández Martínez. In 1932, shortly after seizing power in a military coup, Hernández masterminded the slaughter of some 30,000 Pipil Indians. The Pipil, impoverished peasants from the country's Izalco region, had rebelled against the local landlords and had sought help in organizing the revolt from the country's small Communist Party. Party leader Augustín Faribundo Martí was executed during the fighting, and the army's bloodletting against the peasants, known in Salvadoran history as *La Matanza,* was so widespread that it succeeded in stamping out popular opposition for the next forty years and virtually eliminated all traces of Indian culture from El Salvador.

With U.S. approval, Hernández banned all unions and ruled the country with an iron fist from 1932 to 1944, whereupon disgruntled army subordinates engineered his ouster. From then on, members of the tiny Salvadoran oligarchy, known as the fourteen families, alternated control of the government with the generals, while intermittent coups between factions of the elite became a way of life.

In the Salvadoran countryside, the coffee oligarchy gobbled up so many farms that the number of landless peasants quadrupled between 1961 and 1975, and more than 350,000 Salvadorans were forced to migrate to thinly populated Honduras to work in that country's banana plantations. The Honduran government, overwhelmed by the migrants, responded with mass deportations, a policy that only exacerbated tenions along the border, and those tensions soon escalated into a shooting war in 1969 between the two countries. The outside world derisively labeled it the Soccer War, and while the conflict lasted only one week, it destabilized the entire region by effectively terminating Honduras's role as a safety valve for Salvador's unemployed. By the time the war ended, more than 130,000 Salvadoran migrants had been forced back home, the rest fleeing to Mexico and the United States. Those who arrived in this country eventually found their way to San Francisco and Los Angeles, where they created the first Salvadoran *colonias* in the United States.

Those migrants repatriated to El Salvador posed an immediate social problem for the government. Unable to find jobs or land on which to farm, they resorted to mass demonstrations; many started squatting on properties controlled by the oligarchy. The government responded, as it had in Hernández's time, by calling out the army and allowing right-wing death squads to butcher the protesters. The most notorious of the para-military groups was ORDEN (the Democratic Nationalist Organization), which had been founded in 1968 by National Guard chief General José Antonio Medrano, who supplemented his government job by moonlighting for the CIA.

———

There was one important force in Central America, however, that had changed substantially since the days of Sandino and Faribundo Martí—the Catholic Church. The Church historically had been a bulwark of Latin America's oligarchies, but by the late 1960s it was assuming a new role. Scores of parish priests, nuns, and missionaries, responding to the social call of the Second Vatican Council, threw themselves into social action among the region's poor. They organized scores of new civic groups, turning their churches and missions into centers for democratic dissent.[10]

The grassroots awakening proved an unexpected challenge to the Salvadoran oligarchy, as it aroused thousands of peasants, urban slum dwellers, and trade union members to use the country's ballot box for the first time. So strong did the new movement become that its opposition candidates were on the verge of winning national elections twice in the 1970s. To head off those victories, the National Guard launched coups in both 1972 and 1977. The stronger the popular movement grew, the more blatantly the oligarchy rigged election results, so that after a while many Salvadorans started losing hope of any peaceful reform.

In 1979, another army coup aborted the results of a democratic election, but this time the country erupted into civil war. Over the next two years, with right-wing death squads hunting down dissidents, more than eight thousand trade union leaders were murdered, wounded, abducted, or disappeared. The ferocious repression prompted many young Salvadorans to respond in kind. By 1980, five separate opposition guerrilla groups were operating in the countryside, and they banded together to form the Faribundo Martí National Liberation Front, named after the martyred leader of the 1932 uprising.

That same year, a right-wing death squad assassinated San Salvador's archbishop Oscar Romero, a fierce critic of the Salvadoran junta, and several months later, four American Catholic nuns and lay workers were raped and killed by government soldiers. Those killings signaled to the outside world that the violence in Salvador had spiraled out of control. Instead of denouncing a government that would permit such atrocities, the Bush and Reagan administrations, believing that the country's oligarchy was the only reliable anti-Communist force, rewarded that government. Washington quickly turned El Salvador into the biggest recipient of American military aid in Latin America. Seventy percent of the record $3.7 billion the United States pumped into El Salvador from 1981 to 1989 went for weapons and war assistance.[11] As the number of weapons in the country escalated, so did the numbers of Salvadorans fleeing the devastation those weapons caused.

## GUATEMALA: BODIES FOR BANANAS

In similar fashion, the tragedy of modern Guatemala owes its origins to U.S. foreign policy. A garrison state for more than forty years, Guatemala was home to the longest and bloodiest civil war in Central American history. The roots of that war go back to an almost-forgotten CIA-sponsored coup in 1954, which overthrew a democratically elected president.

Throughout the early part of the century, Guatemalan presidents faithfully protected the interests of one landowner above all others, the United Fruit Company. President Jorge Ubico, who ruled the country from 1931 to 1944, surpassed all his predecessors in the favors he bestowed on UFCO. By the time Ubico left office, UFCO owned more than a million acres of banana fields in Central America; it had a bigger annual budget than any nation in the region; its fleet of eighty-five ships carried most of the region's outside trade; it owned fourteen hundred miles of rail, including the largest line between Mexico and Panama. In Guatemala, UFCO and its affiliate, International Railways of Central America (IRCA), were the country's two largest employers, with twenty thousand people on their payrolls.[12]

President Ubico was somewhat of a fascist sympathizer in a country whose coffee-growing elite was largely German-descended. Nonetheless, he curried favor with Washington during World War II by interning German nationals, confiscating their plantations, and opening his economy further to U.S. investors. Those policies brought Guatemala considerable prosperity while the war lasted and enabled Ubico to finance an ambitious public works program, including the best highway system in Central America. The progress came at a cost, however. Ubico forced Guatemala's huge population of landless Mayans to work on government projects in lieu of paying taxes. He made all Indians carry passbooks and used vagrancy laws to compel them to work for the big landowners.[13] As for Ubico's penchant for jailing opponents and stamping out dissent, Washington simply ignored it so long as U.S. investment in the country flourished.

Ubico, like all the region's dictators, eventually aroused the population against him. In 1944, a coalition of middle-class professionals, teachers, and junior officers, many of them inspired by Franklin D. Roosevelt's New Deal liberalism, launched a democracy movement. The movement won the backing of the country's growing trade unions and rapidly turned into a popular uprising that forced Ubico to resign.

The first democatic election in Guatemalan history followed in 1945, and voters chose as president Juan José Arévalo, a university philosophy professor and author who had been living in exile in Argentina. Tall, handsome, and heavily built, Arévalo was a spellbinding orator. From the moment he returned home to launch his campaign, he became an almost messianic figure to Guatemala's impoverished masses.

Arévalo promised his countrymen a peaceful revolution, one that would take as its inspiration neither the mechanical materialism of the Communists nor the rapacious capitalism of Ubico and the old guard. He called it spiritual socialism, and once in office, he pressed forward with an ambitious program of reform. He abolished Ubico's hated vagrancy laws, recognized labor rights, established the country's first social security and rural education programs, and offered government loans to small farmers. Quite predictably, his reforms sparked resistance from United Fruit and from the Guatemalan upper classes. In an effort to counterbalance that resistance, Arévalo, even though he was personally opposed to Communism, ended up depending on the the country's small but well-organized group of Communists and the trade unions they controlled to marshal public support for his program.[14]

After six years in office, Arévalo was succeeded by Jacobo Arbenz Guzmán, a young military officer and Arévalo disciple. Arbenz swept to victory in the 1951 elections and vowed to take Arévalo's peaceful revolution a step farther by redistributing all idle lands to the peasants. Arévalo knew that in a country with no industry to speak of, with more than 70 percent of the population illiterate, and with 80 percent barely eking out survival in the countryside, ownership and control of land was Guatemala's fundamental economic issue. The country's soil was immensely fertile, but only 2 percent of the landholders owned 72 percent of the arable land, and only a tiny part of their holdings was under cultivation.[15]

The following year, Arbenz got the Guatemalan Congress to pass Decree 900. The new law ordered the expropriation of all property that was larger than six hundred acres and not in cultivation. The confiscated lands were to be divided up among the landless. The owners were to receive compensation based on the land's assessed tax value and they were to be paid with twenty-five-year government bonds, while the peasants would get low-interest loans from the government to buy their plots. As land reform programs go, it was by no means a radical one, since it only affected large estates. Of 341,000 landowners, only 1,700 holdings came under its provisions. But those holdings represented half the private land in the country. Most importantly, it covered the vast holdings of the United Fruit Company, which owned some 600,000 acres—most of it unused.

Arbenz shocked UFCO officials even more when he actually confiscated a huge chunk of the company's land and offered $1.2 million as compensation, a figure that was based on the tax value the company's own accountants had declared before Decree 900 was passed. United Fruit and the U.S. State Department countered with a demand for $16 million. When Arbenz refused, Secretary of State John Foster Dulles and CIA director Allen Dulles convinced President Eisenhower that Arbenz had to go. The Dulles brothers, of course, were hardly neutral parties. Both were former partners of United Fruit's main law firm in Washington. On their advice, Eisenhower authorized the CIA to organize "Operation Success," a plan for the armed overthrow of Arbenz, which took place in June 1954. The agency selected Guatemalan colonel Carlos Castillo Armas to lead the coup, it financed and trained Castillo's rebels in Somoza's Nicaragua, and it backed up the invasion with CIA-piloted planes. During and after the coup, more than nine thousand Guatemalan supporters of Arbenz were arrested.

Despite the violent and illegal manner by which Castillo's government came to power, Washington promptly recognized it and showered it with foreign aid. Castillo lost no time in repaying his sponsors. He quickly outlawed more than five hundred trade unions and returned more than 1.5 million acres to United Fruit and the country's other big landowners. Guatemala's brief experiment with democracy was over. For the next four decades, its people suffered from government terror without equal in the modern history of Latin America. As one American observer described it, "In Guatemala City, unlicensed vans full of heavily armed men pull to a stop and in broad daylight kidnap another death squad victim. Mutilated bodies are dropped from helicopters on crowded stadiums to keep the population terrified . . . those who dare ask about 'disappeared' loved ones have their tongues cut out."[16]

Within a few years of the Arbenz overthrow, most Guatemalans lost hope that peaceful change and democratic elections would return. Inspired by Fidel Castro's Cuban revolution, radical students and intellectuals took to the hills in 1960, where they formed several guerrilla groups to resist the dictatorship. To hunt them down, the government responded with scorched-earth campaigns, pacification programs, and paramilitary death squads, often with assistance from U.S. Special Forces advisers. By 1976, more than twenty thousand people had been killed. While the slaughter expanded in the countryside, a series of army strongmen wielded power in the government, and sham elections alternated with military coups as the elite disputed among themselves the best way to crush the guerrillas. One of those army strongmen was Carlos Arana Osorio, a colonel who rose to head of state in 1970. Arana earned the name "Butcher of Zacapa" for all the massacres that took place while he directed the counterinsurgency campaign in the late 1960s. "If it is necessary to turn the country into a cemetery in order to pacify it," Arana once boasted, "I will not hesitate to do so."

The dead and disappeared reached 75,000 by 1985; another 150,000, most of them Indians, had fled by then into Mexico. But Guatemala's dirty war barely raised eyebrows in Washington. Lawmakers and the press were far more concerned with El Salvador, where the murders of priests and nuns had sparked outrage among U.S. Catholics, and with Nicaragua, where the Reagan administration had drawn its line in the sand against Communism.

## THE EXODUS TO EL NORTE

By the early 1980s, Guatemala, El Salvador, and Nicaragua were all engulfed in wars for which our own government bore much responsibility. In El Salvador alone, human rights groups estimated that five hundred people a month were being massacred by the death squads. The carnage caused so many refugees to stream across the Mexican border that 500,000 Salvadorans had arrived in the United States by 1984.[17] Their presence raised an unsettling question: Why were so many people fleeing a government our country supported?

For nearly thirty years, U.S. law, as expressed in the Immigration and Nationality Act of 1952, had granted refugee status only to people escaping Communist regimes. But the Central American exodus—and the public outcry that resulted—changed all that. In the final year of the Carter administration, Congress enacted Public Law 96-210, the 1980 Refugee Act. The new law declared anyone eligible for political asylum who had suffered persecution or who had a "well-founded fear of persecution based on race, religion, nationality, membership in a particular social group, or political opinion." It no longer mattered what kind of regime was in power in the refugee's homeland.

Before the law could take effect, Ronald Reagan assumed the presidency and reasserted the fight against Central America's "Communists" as a linchpin of his foreign policy. As part of that policy, Attorney General William French Smith ordered in 1981 that all undocumented immigrants applying for political asylum from Central America be held in INS detention centers. Within months, the country's immigration jails filled to overflowing, and the INS hastily erected makeshift detention camps to hold the excess. Still, the Salvadorans and Guatemalans kept coming. Those who managed to get past the Border Patrol opted for the uncertainty of hiding out illegally in this country over the risk of perishing at the hands of death squads or guerrillas back home.[18]

The Salvadoran community of Los Angeles, which numbered a mere 30,000 in 1979, mushroomed within four years to 300,000, mostly in the neighborhoods of Pico-Union, South-East, and South-Central. Others settled in Adams-Morgan in Washington, D.C., and the suburban towns of Long Island, New York, or Maryland. So many Salvadorans settled in a series of apartment complexes in Alexandria, Virginia—all of them from the same hometown of Chirilagua—that the immigrants eventually pooled together their resources, purchased the complex, and changed its name to Chirilandria.[19]

The Guatemalans carved out similar new communities in Los Angeles, northwest Chicago, and Houston, but they differed from the Salvadorans in several respects. For the most part, the Guatemalans were Indian peasants from that nation's underdeveloped highlands, whereas the Salvadorans were largely *mestizos* from the cities and towns of a country that was far more densely populated and much more cosmopolitan. Many of the Salvadorans even had previous experience as migrant workers in Honduras and thus were quicker to adapt to a new country than their fellow Guatemalans. The Salvadorans who settled in the Washington area went to work in the local hotel and restaurant industry, and, perhaps because of their country's extensive tradition of trade unionism, they soon became mainstays of the city's organized labor movement. A good number of Guatemalans, on the other hand, chose to settle outside the major cities, gravitating instead to the farm belts and small industrial towns of California, Florida, and North Carolina.

———

By the time the Central Americans arrived, the Latino immigrants of prior years had built stable ethnic enclaves, had perfected their English-speaking abilities, and even boasted an embryonic professional class with a basic grasp of its civil rights. The average Central American, on the other hand, spoke no English, was undocumented, unskilled, and desperate for any kind of work.

Take the Guatemalans of Houston, for example. They are largely highland Mayans from El Quiché and Totonicapán who were drawn to that city through kinship ties with earlier pioneers. They settled in the scores of low-rise and low-rent apartment complexes in Gulfton, a working-class neighborhood on Houston's southwest side that had been virtually emptied of whites during the oil bust period, and there they set about re-creating their old kinship-based society and Mayan customs. By 1990, two-thirds of Gulfton's forty thousand people were Latino, most of them Guatemalan.[20] Along with the Hondurans, the Guatemalans soon filled the ranks of the maintenance force in the city's downtown office buildings, and a considerable number found work with the Randall's supermarket chain.[21]

Around 1982, Mayans fleeing the scorched-earth policies of the Guatemalan military started to arrive in the Florida Everglades, where they gravitated to jobs in the tomato fields. Many settled in Indiantown and Immokalee near Lake Okeechobee, or in the area around Lake Worth on the east coast, so that by the mid 1990s, more than twenty-five thousand Guatemalan Indians were living in South Florida.[22]

Meanwhile, back in the Southwest, a modern version of the Underground Railroad was taking shape inside scores of U.S. churches whose members opposed our government's Central American policy. Church leaders called it the Sanctuary movement, and they date its official beginnings from March 1982, when the Reverend John Fife, minister of the Southside Presbyterian Church in Tucson, wrote a letter to the Justice Department. Fife's congregation, the letter said, had concluded that the federal government was violating the 1980 Refugee Act by jailing and deporting Central American refugees. Church members, Fife said, would begin using their building as a sanctuary for Central Americans. The protest movement spread quickly across the country. Within a few years, more than two hundred other churches had enlisted and were openly defying the government.

Although the Sanctuary movement appeared to be led by American priests and ministers, its inspiration and direction actually came from the refugees themselves, especially those who had been political opposition leaders back home. Carlos Vaquerano, for example, fled to the United States from El Salvador in November 1980, after one of his brothers was killed by a right-wing death squad. Vaquerano had been a university student leader from the town of Apastepeque in the department of San Vicente and sympathized with the left-wing guerrillas of the FMLN (The

Faribundo Martí National Liberation Front). Once he arrived in Los Angeles, he brought together fellow Salvadorans to educate North Americans about the war in hopes of bringing about a change in U.S. policies.[23] A network of Salvadoran groups, most of them organized in secret, arose in the refugee community. Members of those groups fanned out across the country, speaking to church, university, and labor organizations about the conditions in Salvador, and it was from those exchanges that the Sanctuary movement arose.

The sanctuaries, in turn, provided the basis for the first publicly known Central American organizations. Casa Maryland, for instance, was founded in 1983 as a sanctuary in the basement of a Presbyterian church in Takoma, Maryland. Today, it is the largest Salvadoran community agency in the region. That same year, Salvadoran Aquiles Magaña and other refugees in Los Angeles founded the Central American Refugee Center, popularly known as CARECEN. Staffed by Salvadorans who worked in tandem with progressive white American lawyers, the center offered valuable legal assistance, food pantries, and counseling to fellow immigrants. More CARECENs began to sprout up in Chicago, Washington, D.C., and Long Island.[24]

In 1983, a formal national congress of Sanctuary delegates in Chicago elected the movement's first coordinating body, which was composed of six North Americans, three Salvadorans, and three Guatemalans. The three Guatemalans, in turn, set about organizing their own subnetwork, which they christened La Red Atanasio Tzul (the Atanasio Tzul Network), after the leader of an early-nineteenth-century Mayan independence revolt against Spain.

Mario González, one of Atanasio Tzul's founders, is a Guatemalan psychologist who fled his homeland in the late 1970s. González was passing through Chicago on his way to study at the University of Berlin when a small circle of Guatemalan refugees living in the city convinced him to stay and organize the network. Those early refugees, like González, were mostly middle-class urban professionals or skilled workers who at first could only find jobs as laborers in Chicago factories. As more of their countrymen arrived in the 1980s, the Guatemalan *colonia* in that city began to take shape. At first, because they feared deportation home, most of the early migrants avoided any kind of civic involvement and sought to lose themselves among other Latinos.

"Those who lived in the Puerto Rican neighborhoods started acting and talking like Puerto Ricans, even claiming they were Puerto Rican," González recalls. "And those who lived in the Mexican neighborhoods swore they were Mexican."[25] The only exception to that anonymity was in sports, where the Guatemalans, who are avid soccer players, organized dozens of soccer leagues. Other than those soccer leagues, the new *colonia*'s first real organization in Chicago was the Guatemalan Civic Society, which was founded in the late 1970s, but which was confined mostly to the tiny professional sector and thus had only minimal impact on immigrant life.

Guatemalans in Florida likewise got their first impetus to organize from the Atanasio Tzul Network. Geronimo Campo Seco, a founding member of the network, is a Kanjobal Indian and former schoolteacher who fled northwestern Guatemala in 1980. He was one of the first from his country to be granted political asylum in the United States. Four years later, he moved to South Florida, where hundreds of Mayans and Kanjobal were already living as farmworkers. There, he met Nancy Couch, the director of the Catholic Committee for Justice and Peace in Palm Beach County.[26]

"I was in Indiantown working with the migrants, and Geronimo came up to me and asked if I could help him with his people," Couch recalled. She started by assisting Campo Seco with asylum applications and soon turned into a tireless advocate for the Guatemalans. Indiantown's three thousand residents included whites, Haitians, American blacks, and Mexican Americans, but each winter, when the harvest came, the population ballooned by as many as fifteen hundred Mayans.

In 1986, Congress succumbed to growing anti-immigrant sentiment by passing the Immigration Reform and Control Act (IRCA). The bill was intended to curb illegal immigration, but it produced unintended consequences. The bill's amnesty provision for longtime illegal residents, for instance, paved the way for Central American pioneers such as González to quickly legalize their status. Once those pioneers had a "green card," some were free to sneak a visit back home to relatives without fear of being unable to return. Most important, they were free to advocate openly for the rights of the new arrivals. After 1986, the Atanasio Tzul Network gradually separated itself from the underground Sanctuary movement and turned into a full-fledged Guatemalan organization.

Despite the efforts of the Reagan and Bush administrations, many Anglo Americans refused to endorse U.S. policy in Central America. Unflagging advocacy for the region's refugees by a combination of groups— from the Catholic Church and the Sanctuary movement, to civil rights lawyers, to left-wing political organizations like the Committee in Support of the People of El Salvador (CISPES)—finally culminated in two historic breakthroughs toward the end of 1990. That November, Congress relented to public pressure and granted Salvadorans a suspension

of deportation—temporary protected status (TPS)—and subsequently
extended it to Guatemalans and Nicaraguans as well.

Then, in December, a U.S. district court judge approved a consent decree in a pivotal class-action suit, *American Baptist Churches* v. *Thorn-
burgh,* which struck down as discriminatory the INS policy of deporting
Salvadorans and Guatemalans. The decree overturned 100,000 cases in
which the INS had denied asylum requests, the largest number of federal
judicial decisions ever negated by a single court case. Both the ABC decision and the TPS law proved to be stunning victories for human rights.
Along with IRCA's amnesty provision, they permitted Central Americans their first respite from the limbo of illegality they were confronting.

## FROM UNWANTED REFUGEES TO IMMIGRANT VOTING BLOC

With the threat of immediate deportation removed, immigrant leaders
turned their attention to putting down roots in their new society. González,
for instance, helped found Casa Guatemala, an uptown Chicago group
that sought to solve the day-to-day needs of the new arrivals. Today, his
full-time job is clinical director at Chicago's Kobler Center for the Treatment of Survivors of Torture, where he and his staff counsel hundreds of
Guatemalans who were subjected to rape, beatings, and electroshock
during the four-decade civil war.

"The terror in my country created a psychosocial disaster," González
told me. "So many were tortured to death that if the army took you into
custody and you survived, those in your circle would suspect you as a
traitor. Women who were raped were too ashamed to return to their
homes. Families and communities just disintegrated. Even though we
live in this country, most Guatemalans still dare not organize themselves
in public."

In South Florida, a similar transition from clandestine to legal existence took place among the Mayans. As their settlement took root,
Campo Seco formed two organizations in the early 1990s: CORN Maya,
an activist group in Indiantown, and the Guatemalan Center in Lake
Worth. The efforts of all the Guatemalan immigrant leaders received a
huge boost in 1992 when fellow Mayan Rigoberta Menchú was awarded
the Nobel Peace Prize.[27]

The post-ABC period also saw the stirrings of a civil and labor rights
movement among both Salvadorans and Guatemalans. At first, that movement took a chaotic and violent form. Three urban riots erupted in the
early 1990s in which Latinos played a significant role, and two of those

involved Central American neighborhoods. In May 1991, several hundred Latinos rampaged and looted a four-square-block area of the Mount Pleasant area of northwest Washington, D.C., after a police officer shot a Latino. In the days following the disturbances, Hispanic leaders complained of racism and insensitivity by the District's police and government officials. Reaction from the mostly black political leadership was sharply divided. "After listening to the Hispanic young people I went home and told my wife it was like listening to myself 20 years ago," said Councilman John Wilson, a former member of the Student Non-Violent Coordinating Committee. "If they [Hispanics] don't appreciate our country, get out," said another black councilman, H. R. Crawford. [28]

A year later, when the acquittal of four cops who beat black motorist Rodney King touched off the Los Angeles riot, thousands of Hispanics, most of them Central American, joined in the four days of arson and looting. Two of the hardest-hit areas, South-Central LA and Pico-Union, were largely immigrant communities. There were actually more Latinos among the twelve thousand arrested during the riot than there were blacks, and police identified the most deadly street gang involved in the rioting as the Mara Salvatrucha, a Salvadoran group. During the week that I spent covering that riot, I was amazed that the older Mexican American neighborhoods, like East LA and Echo Park, experienced no problems. A middle-aged Mexican American and Vietnam War veteran, whom I met while he was standing armed guard over the photo store he owned to protect it from looters, explained to me, "A community only riots once. When you realize it takes twenty years to recover, you never want to see that again." The other major civil disturbance involving Latinos was the riot mentioned previously that occurred in the Washington Heights section of New York City in July 1992, among another immigrant community—Dominicans.

Those early lawless eruptions by angry youths, however, soon gave way to more orderly demands for justice. In 1990, Ana Sol Gutiérrez became the first Salvadoran-born elected official in U.S. history when she won a seat on the school board of Montgomery County, Maryland. Ironically, Montgomery County is one of the richest counties in the United States, Gutiérrez was not a war refugee, and her victory did not depend on Latino voters. The daughter of a former Salvadoran ambassador to the United States, she came to this country in 1948 at the age of three. Her father, a founder of the World Bank, also worked for the Organization of American States during the Kennedy years. His diplomatic assignments kept the family traveling back and forth between San Salvador and Washington, so that Gutiérrez grew up largely in suburban

Chevy Chase and attended American schools, where she graduated with degrees in both chemistry and engineering.

Her election to the school board, she says, had "more to do with my credentials than being Salvadoran; the voter realized I was totally into math and science." Nonetheless, her victory signaled the beginning of Central American empowerment. As she went door-to-door in suburban Montgomery County soliciting votes, Gutiérrez was astounded to discover that many of those answering her knocks were Salvadorans who had settled in the county almost invisibly after moving there from cramped apartments in Washington, D.C.

The earliest Salvadorans in the nation's capital, Gutiérrez notes, arrived as domestic workers for Latin American diplomats and other Latinos in the federal government. "I've had three housekeepers from El Salvador over the years, all of whom are now citizens and residents in this area," she said. Once the civil war erupted, however, the legal residents brought as many of their relatives into the country as they could. The first types of immigrant organization in the Washington area, as in almost every U.S. city, were soccer leagues—there are more than fifty now. After the soccer teams came a local CARECEN center in the Adams-Morgan area.

Once she got elected, Gutiérrez became the most prominent advocate for Central Americans in the metropolitan area. She founded the Hispanic Alliance, the first Salvadoran group aimed at influencing domestic policy and education issues, a group that initially drew its membership from more middle-class Salvadorans. Gutiérrez soon realized, however, that the community's future would be determined by its far greater number of working-class immigrants.

"There is a real thirst to participate, an eagerness to become citizens among all the immigrants," Gutiérrez insists. Those who arrived in the early 1980s, who worked hard and managed to become legal residents after IRCA passed in 1986, were moving to the suburbs and buying their own homes ten years later. More than 46,000 Latinos have applied for citizenship in Montgomery County in recent years, turning the immigrants into a potent new electoral force.

Casa Maryland, for which Gutiérrez serves as board chairman, reflects the changing emphasis on domestic issues. The agency has developed a sophisticated array of services for the Latino community. Among the first of those services was a day laborer program that responded to local concerns that many Salvadorans were congregating on street corners in several county towns while they waited for contractors to hire them for a day's work. White residents saw the clusters of foreigners on their streets as a potential source of crime, and some of the immigrants became targets of racially motivated attacks. Those who did manage to land work were often cheated out of wages by unscrupulous employers but had no place to go to complain. Nowadays, Casa staff organize and supervise specific locations where the employers can hire their help and where the workers can obtain legal counseling. The program proved so successful that the agency launched training programs in carpentry, drywall, and asbestos removal to improve the immigrants' skills and earning power. Subsequently, the agency branched out into adult education, English and computer classes; and now it has even launched a program to challenge housing discrimination.

Perhaps nothing characterizes the Central Americans so much as their dedication to hard work. The labor force participation rate of Salvadorans and Guatemalans is among the highest of any ethnic group, whether immigrant or native-born.[29] And once on the job, even when confined to the lowest-paying work, they have shown a remarkable ability to organize for better conditions. In Los Angeles, for instance, Salvadoran and Guatemalan janitors became the mainstay of the Justice for Janitors Campaign, a union drive that recruited thousands of new members into the Service Employees International Union.

Guatemalan workers at a poultry plant in Morganton, North Carolina, electrified the labor movement in 1996 and 1997 with their militant campaign for union recognition. Officials at the chicken plant, Case Farms, had begun in 1990 to offer Guatemalan migrants from South Florida higher pay and free transportation to Morganton. Five years later, 85 percent of the plant's 450 workers were Guatemalan. Once they arrived, however, the new workers found lower pay rates than promised and working conditions so terrible that they launched an effort to bring in the Laborers International Union. Despite fierce company opposition, the workers mounted repeated strikes, picketed company plants in other states, and even demonstrated outside the Wall Street offices of the firm's biggest lender, the Bank of New York. Their persistent campaign caught the attention of the new AFL-CIO leaders in Washington, who pointed to the Case Farms battle as symbolic of the increasing influence Central American immigrants are poised to exert in the U.S. labor movement.[30]

Throughout the rest of the country, major manufacturers took to recruiting undocumented Central Americans in the 1990s. They did so by ignoring the employer sanction provisions of IRCA, secure in the knowledge that the federal government was unlikely to monitor their plants or to penalize them too harshly if they were caught. Many of those employers believed the Central Americans would be more docile than native African Americans or earlier groups of Latino immigrants. But those corporate policies, propelled by the constant search for lower wage costs, have brought unexpected consequences to the heartland of America, as white communities that had never known any Latinos are suddenly coping with a fast-growing Hispanic presence. In North Carolina, Hispanics now comprise 40 percent of the state's construction workers. Since 1990, the state's Hispanic population has increased by 70 percent and the number of Hispanic children in state schools has tripled. Even the smallest town in the state now has a burgeoning Latino population where only a few years ago everyone was either black or white. In 1998, Latinos were an estimated 33 percent of the residents of Dalton, Georgia; 45 percent of Lexington, Nebraska; and 40 percent of Dodge City, Kansas. The Latino population of Arkansas grew by 104 percent between 1990 and 1996, that of Tennessee by 58 percent, and Vermont's by 55 percent.[31]

The last of the Central American civil wars came to an end by 1996. But the full extent of U.S. involvement in the human carnage there was not publicly acknowledged until 1999. On February 25 of that year, a stunning report was issued by an international truth commission that had been set up as part of the United States–supervised peace accord in Guatemala.

The commission, which spent eighteen months reviewing Guatemalan and U.S. government declassified records, accused the Guatemalan military of "acts of genocide" and "massive extermination of defenseless Mayan communities" during that country's thirty-six-year war. Furthermore, the commission reported, the United States, "through its constituent structures, including the Central Intelligence Agency, lent direct and indirect support" to many of those "illegal state operations."

Some 200,000 Guatemalans died during the civil war, the commission estimated. In 90 percent of the 29,000 deaths it had directly investigated, the commission found the government and its allies were responsible. One month later, during a visit to several Central American countries, President Clinton publicly apologized to the Guatemalan people for past U.S. support of repressive governments in the region.[32]

But the changes wrought on both the sending and receiving nations by the massive Central American exodus of the 1980s have become irreversible. Today, the Salvadoran populations of Los Angeles and Washington, D.C., are bigger than any place except San Salvador itself. Guatemalans and Hondurans have forever altered the ethnic panorama of Houston, Chicago, and the Florida farm belt, and Nicaraguans of Miami. The Central Americans have had enormous influence on the older

Latino groups by breaking down the tribal battles and divisions that once existed between Mexicans, Cubans, and Puerto Ricans. Their arrival, in short, is forcing a gradual amalgamation of the various Hispanic immigrant groups into a broader Latino mosaic, where each ethnic group maintains its separate ethnic identity but all of them together comprise a new linguistic subset within the complex reality of twenty-first-century American society.

# 9

# Colombians and Panamanians: Overcoming Division and Disdain

Cartoons in the newspapers depicted the canal being dug by cheerful white Americans with picks and shovels . . . in truth, the colorline, of which almost nothing was said in print, cut through every facet of life in the Zone, as clearly drawn and as closely observed as anywhere in the Deep South or the most rigid colonial enclaves of Africa.

—*David McCullough*
The Path Between the Seas

Colombians and Panamanians seem unusual migrants to consider in the same breath—at least until you delve into their history.

Panamanians started arriving in the United States during the 1950s, most of them settling in Brooklyn, New York. By 1965, they numbered between fifteen thousand and thirty thousand, yet they went virtually unnoticed by the white society. Most were descendants of West Indian canal workers, and they assimilated rapidly into New York's African American neighborhoods.[1]

Colombian immigration came a little later but proved far more extensive and durable. More than 72,000 arrived during the 1960s, another 77,000 the following decade, and 122,000 in the 1980s.[2] Thousands more came here illegally. Typically, Colombians would fly into New York or Miami on tourist visas and simply overstay their allotted time. Today, more than 300,000 Colombians reside in our country, mostly in New York and South Florida.

Unlike Cubans and Dominicans, Colombians were not fleeing political persecution, nor were they contract laborers or migrant farmers as were so many Puerto Ricans and Mexicans, and, unlike the Panamanians, most were middle-class professionals, skilled workers, and white.

But what made the Panamanians and Colombians emigrate in the 1960s and 1970s? And why to the United States, not to some other country? What was distinct about their experience from that of other Latinos? Once they arrived here, where did they settle? How did they relate to African Americans, to other Latinos, and to Anglo Americans? As with other Latinos, we begin our search for answers by tracing how U.S. policy affected both Colombia and Panama. The modern history of both nations, after all, began in 1903, when Teddy Roosevelt paved the way for building his transoceanic canal by fomenting the creation of an "independent" Panama, one that was severed from Colombian territory.

The following accounts of some early Colombian and Panamanian migrants, the White and Méndez families, may supply some insights and some answers.

## THE WHITE FAMILY, WORKING ON THE CANAL

McKenzie White and his wife, Wilhemina, were both born in the Virgin Islands in the 1880s, but migrated to the Dominican Republic after the turn of the century when White signed on as a contract laborer to cut sugarcane for a U.S.-owned Dominican plantation.[3] While in the Dominican Republic, the young couple, unable to conceive a child, adopted a baby girl whom they named Monica. A decade or so later, they migrated again. This time, McKenzie took his wife and daughter to Panama, where he landed a job with the dredging division of the U.S. canal project that was then nearing completion.

The Panama Canal has long been acknowledged as one of the technical marvels of the twentieth century, a triumph of Yankee vision, audacity, and engineering that enabled a massive expansion of oceanic commerce and helped to unite North American society by sharply reducing the time needed for the transit of people, goods, and information between the Pacific and Atlantic coasts.

But the canal also led to profound fissures in the lives of the Panamanian people. West Indian migrants, as we have noted, provided the bulk of the canal workers and suffered the greatest casualties during its construction. Canal administrators preferred the West Indians because they spoke English and because it was believed they could better withstand the tropical heat. Yet those same West Indians, when it came to chronicling the almost mythical saga of the canal, were virtually forgotten. As one historian who tried to set the record straight noted, "To judge by the many published accounts, the whole enormous black underside of the caste system simply did not exist. Cartoons in the newspapers depicted the canal being dug by cheerful white Americans with picks and shovels and many came to Panama expecting to see just that" only to learn of "the awful gulf that separates the sacred white American from the rest of the Canal Zone world."[4]

Blacks were the canal's overwhelming labor force, more than three-fourths of the 45,000 to 50,000 employees in the last years of construction. They were so numerous that, according to historian David McCullough,

> [visitors] could not help but be amazed, even astounded, at the degree to which the entire system, not simply the construction, depended on black labor. There were not only thousands of West Indians down amid the turmoil of Culebra Cut or at the lock sites but black waiters in every hotel, black stevedores, teamsters, porters, hospital orderlies, cooks, laundresses, nursemaids, janitors, delivery boys, coachmen, icemen, garbage men, yardmen, mail clerks, police, plumbers, house painters, gravediggers. A black man walking along spraying oil on still water, a metal tank on his back, was one of the most familiar of all sights in the Canal Zone. Whenever a mosquito was seen in a white household, the Sanitary Department was notified and immediately a black man came with chloroform and a glass vial to catch the insect and take it back to a laboratory for analysis.[5]

From the first days of construction, the white American supervisors created a racial apartheid system that dominated canal life for half a century. The centerpieces of that system were separate racially based payrolls, a "gold" category for white American citizens and a "silver" one for the West Indians. All benefits were segregated according to those rolls—housing, commissaries, clubhouses, health care, schools for children of workers.[6]

Black workers were shunted into segregated company towns or into slums in the cities of Colón and Panama City, while whites lived surrounded by tropical opulence in planned communities like Pedro Miguel, Cristóbal, and Gamboa, with everything from housing to health care to vacations subsidized for them by the federal government.

"For black children, our schools stopped at the eighth grade," recalled Monica White, daughter of Wilhemina and McKenzie White. "We only had black teachers and we didn't get top priority for many things." The separate black schools kept the West Indians isolated from their new Panamanian homeland, since they were taught only in English, and pupils learned the same subject matter taught in U.S. public schools.[7]

By the time it opened in 1914, the canal had turned into a cauldron of

labor unrest. West Indians, unhappy over their pay, their working conditions, and by the racism of the U.S. soldiers and administrators, launched
several militant strikes, each walkout ending with massive evictions of
strikers from the Zone. Periodic layoffs forced thousands of others to
move into Panama's cities in search of work, and as they did so, their relations with native Panamanians rapidly deteriorated.[8]

"The Panamanians were prejudiced against the West Indians," Monica
White recalled. "They were determined to get us out of their country, back
where we came from. It was like there were two countries, one was Panama
and the other was the Canal Zone." Actually there were three, since
the Zone itself contained separate and unequal white and black worlds.

Panamanians, meanwhile, felt discriminated against in their own country. They resented how canal authorities employed only West Indians on
construction and maintenance, jobs that invariably paid higher wages
than most others in Panama. In response, a succession of Panamanian
governments attempted to ban further West Indian immigration, or at
least to prevent the immigrants' children from attaining Panamanian citizenship. After 1928, West Indian children born in Panama had to wait
until age twenty-one to be naturalized. Even then, the government required them to pass a test demonstrating their competency in Spanish
and Panamanian history.

The new naturalization law prompted Monica White to move out of
the Canal Zone soon after her son, Vicente, was born, so he could be educated in Panamanian schools and get his citizenship. By then, she was
separated from Vicente's father, and she opened a beauty salon in
Panama City in 1935. A few years later, she married another West Indian,
Ernest Manderson.

Not until the early 1940s did Washington lawmakers finally begin to
question the Canal Zone's Jim Crow segregation system. President
Franklin D. Roosevelt issued an executive order in 1941 ending discrimination in the defense industries and he specified in that order the Canal
Zone. But canal administrators, most of them white southerners, resisted
any change. Fearful that integration of their gold and silver rolls would
undermine labor control, they persisted with the "apartheid" system well
into the 1950s.[9]

"Even the toilets and water fountains were segregated," recalled Vicente White. "You walked in a building and you saw a sign: gold, silver.
Gold toilets were clean and their drinking fountains always had cold water. The silver ones were dirty and the water was always warm."[10]

By the mid-1950s, Monica Manderson and many other West Indians
found themselves caught in the middle between the demands of Latin

Panamanians for more control over the canal—the country's most vital resource—and recalcitrant Zone officials who were determined to prevent integration.

Ironically, it was a key victory by the U.S. civil rights movement that ended up forcing many black Panamanians to emigrate. In 1954, after the Supreme Court's ruling in *Brown* v. *Board of Education* outlawed separate but equal public schools throughout the nation, the federal government ordered Canal Zone authorities to integrate their schools as well. To avoid that, the canal's governor changed the language of instruction in the black schools to Spanish, and forcibly relocated many blacks out of the Zone, thus shifting the burden of housing and educating their children onto the Panamanian government.[11] A new canal treaty in 1955 made matters even worse for the West Indians—it required them for the first time to pay Panamanian taxes.

After four decades in Panama, Monica Manderson decided she was fed up with the racism from both white Anglo Americans and Spanish-speaking Panamanians. Like many West Indians, she was proud of her Anglo Caribbean culture. She wanted to retain her English tongue and her involvement in the Protestant church and benevolent societies that formed the core of her heritage. But she couldn't do it in Panama. So in 1957 she left for the United States.

## THE PANAMANIAN ENCLAVE IN BROOKLYN

Monica Manderson was not alone. From the mid-1950s to the mid-1960s, an estimated thirty thousand West Indians emigrated to the United States, about three-quarters of them settling in New York City. While not a huge migration compared to the Puerto Ricans and Cubans who came around the same time, it represented, according to prominent West Indian leader George Westerman, the most talented of Panama's black community.[12]

Until she got settled in the United States, Manderson left her son, Vicente, with his father in Panama. She moved into an apartment on Schenectady Avenue in the Bedford-Stuyvesant section of Brooklyn, which was the first *colonia* for the new immigrants. For the next twenty years, until her retirement in 1974, she worked at a variety of low-paying jobs—laundry worker, school aide, home care attendant—and she devoted herself to the many church and civic groups that sprang up to minister to the needs of the Panamanian enclave. Among those groups was Las Servidoras (the Servants), a women's group that provided college scholarships to needy Panamanian youths.

Initially, the immigrants had trouble fitting in to either the Latin American or African American communities, so they founded their own hometown social clubs. One of the first, the Pabsco Club, was located at Schenectady Avenue and Sterling Place. It became the main gathering place for expatriates to unwind on weekends, dance to their own *cumbia* and *guaracha* music, and organize group excursions to their homeland.

The Panamanians' mastery of English made their transition easier than that of other Latin Americans. It facilitated their finding better-paying jobs, especially in government civil service, and it eased their assimilation into the city's larger black community. "Gradually, the white people started moving out of Bedford-Stuyvesant," Manderson recalled, but new tension arose. "The American blacks were always jealous of us West Indians," she said. "We were trying to better our jobs and better ourselves and they hated that."

Vicente, who followed his mother to New York a few years later, has a different view. "Some Jamaicans and Barbadians believe that stuff and begin to feel superior to American blacks," he said. "And some blacks, only a few, fall for that, too. They say, 'Here you come, banana boy, taking our jobs.'"

Vicente's views reflect the third generation of West Indians. Because his mother enrolled him in Panama City schools, he grew up not only writing and speaking Spanish but also feeling more a part of Panamanian than of West Indian society. As a boy, he and the neighborhood children would play in a park near the National Assembly in Panama City. Behind the huge building ran a street that divided Panamanian territory from the Canal Zone.

"On the other side of the street stood a row of giant mango trees," White recalled. "We Panamanian kids would cross over to pick mangoes, and each time, the Zone police would chase and beat us." Decades later, he still recalled with bitterness the foreigners who forbade him as a boy to pick fruit in his own country.

Ironically, after he finished high school, White ended up a policeman in the Canal Zone.

"I worked in the jails in Gamboa," he said. "When they had no prisoners the white officers would tell the troops, 'Go and bring me some damn Panamanians so we can get some maintenance here.' We would have to go out in the Zone and arrest any Panamanian walking around and charge them with loitering. *Holgazaneando,* that's the term we used. By six in the morning, from an empty jail, you'd have twelve people. I became disgusted with it."

In 1959, the first signs of Panamanian resentment against U.S. control erupted. That year, students rioted after U.S. soldiers stopped them from hoisting the Panamanian flag beside the American flag in the Zone. White, a cop in the Balboa garrison at the time, followed the orders of his North American commanders to chase down and arrest the protesters. The shame that overcame him during the following weeks over what he'd done to his own countrymen sealed his decision to leave Panama.[13]

His father died a few months later. White, who was newly married, migrated to New York with his bride, and moved into his mother's apartment in Brooklyn. Shortly afterward, he enlisted in the air force. Because of his Canal Zone experience, he was assigned to the military police and stationed in Fairbanks, Alaska. That's where he was still stationed in January 1964, when he heard the news that protests had broken out again over Panamanians hoisting their national flag in the Canal Zone. This time, though, U.S. soldiers fired on the young demonstrators, killing twenty-four and wounding hundreds. The killings sparked an uproar in Panama and throughout Latin America.

"I thought right away that the riot was just," White recalled. "There was too much abuse by Americans in the Canal Zone. But being in the service, I kept to myself and said nothing."

President Johnson concluded that unless he granted Panamanians a voice in the running of the canal, he would risk another Cuba-style revolution, so he authorized negotiations that culminated in the Carter-Torrijos Treaty of 1977. As a result of that treaty, U.S. troops were gradually withdrawn, Panama regained sovereignty over the Zone, and nearly a century after Roosevelt's machinations, Panamanians regained complete control over the vital waterway.

White resigned from the air force after the 1964 riot and returned to New York. There he took a job as an undercover investigator with the state attorney general, eventually moving on to the Brooklyn district attorney's office, which is where I met him during one of New York's most infamous racial-bias trials. It was called the Yusuf Hawkins case. Hawkins, a black sixteen-year-old, had wandered into the all-white neighborhood of Bensonhurst, where he was attacked and killed by a gang of neighborhood whites. I was covering the trial for the *New York Daily News,* and White, who had fled Panama to get away from racism, was an investigator assigned to the prosecution team.

Most white Americans, White reminded me as we talked about his homeland one day in court, have no idea about the racially segregated system our leaders permitted there for so long. As for the antagonism his mother and the older generation of West Indians feel for the Latin Panamanians, White believes they became unwitting dupes of white Canal

Zone administrators and the *rabiblancos,* the Panamanian term for the tiny compliant white elite who traditionally ran politics there. "It was the U.S. who tried to paint the Panamanians as antiblack, anti–West Indians, and antiwhite," he said. "I never had a problem with Hispanics," White continued. "Once, I was down in Miami picking up a prisoner and went into a Cuban restaurant with a black partner. At first, they were stand-offish, like they didn't want to serve us. But then I started speaking Spanish and right away they changed. The language, it's a bonding thing between Hispanics."

## THE MÉNDEZ FAMILY AND COLOMBIA'S CYCLE OF VIOLENCE

Héctor and Pedro Méndez were born in the countryside of Colombia's western department of Tolima, into a typically large peasant family of eighteen children. Their father was Lázaro Méndez, a prosperous *mestizo* landowner descended from the Piajo tribe of that area. Pedro was born in 1940 and Héctor five years later. At the time, Colombia was relatively prosperous and peaceful, and the mountainous region around Tolima and neighboring Antioquia—of which Medellín is the capital—was a veritable "democracy of small farmers," according to one historian.[14]

That tranquillity was shattered on April 9, 1948, with the assassination of the charismatic Liberal Party leader Jorge Eliecer Gaitan. The murder so enraged his supporters that mobs attacked and burned the capital of Bogotá in the worst urban riot in Latin American history, leaving two thousand dead and millions in property damage. That touched off ten years of brutal civil war between Liberals and Conservatives, a bloodletting so horrific that all Colombians simply refer to it as La Violencia. No one knows how many died. Estimates range from 180,000 to more than 200,000, making it far more devastating, given Colombia's size, than the U.S. Civil War. Death squads, called *pájaros,* roamed the countryside on orders of the landed oligarchy, butchering any farmer suspected of being a Liberal, while guerrilla bands of Liberal Party supporters targeted the biggest landowners.[15] Every family was torn apart by the conflict, but those living in Tolima and Antioquia suffered the brunt of the killing. Lázaro Méndez's relatives were all Liberals, those of his wife Conservatives. Once the conflict erupted, the Méndez children were never again permitted to see their mother's family. "To this day, we've never known what happened to them," Héctor Méndez acknowledged in 1995.

The civil war destroyed agricultural production and emptied the countryside as millions fled to the cities. Ibagué, Bogotá, and Cali, which had been sleepy towns until La Violencia began, turned into sprawling metropolises overnight, brimming with dislocated farmers and landless peasants. The Méndez family fled to Cali in 1953. Lázaro and his wife purchased a plot of land in a mountainous area on the city's outskirts and he embarked on a new career as a moneylender. The family's house was so isolated the children had to walk more than a mile down the mountain to the nearest bus stop to get downtown. Their parents sent Héctor and Pedro to a school run by Salesian priests, and since the priests required all the students to learn a trade, Héctor became a linotypist and Pedro a pressman.

La Violencia ended in 1957 after Liberal and Conservative leaders reached an agreement to alternate power. But the years of bloodshed had uprooted and permanently disfigured much of Colombian society. The sons and daughters of the peasants who had fled the countryside when the fighting began were now urban dwellers and no longer tied to tradition. Many finished their studies during the 1960s only to find there were no jobs. Héctor Méndez was luckier than most. He found work as a linotypist at *El País,* one of Cali's big daily newspapers. The pay was good by Colombian standards—he was earning 4,500 pesos a month when the minimum wage was 350. But it was far inferior to printers' salaries in other parts of the world. Nearly all of Héctor's coworkers at *El País* started leaving for Australia when that country's publishers dangled offers of all-expense-paid travel, free housing, and top pay to any Colombian who would emigrate. Others accepted similar offers from Venezuela.

Violence, meanwhile, emerged as an accepted Colombian way of settling disputes, not just in the countryside where the civil war had raged but in the cities and shantytowns created by the war's refugees. Disaffected youths from those slums became easy recruits for new left-wing guerrilla groups, such as M-19, while in the countryside, the FARC (Armed Forces of the Colombian Revolution) and other revolutionary organizations wrested control of whole regions from the government. Several of the new revolutionary groups were started by former Liberal Party members who did not accept the power-sharing truce that ended La Violencia, while others were newly inspired by the Cuban revolution. In its effort to wipe out the guerrillas, the army killed or jailed every dissident it could find. In 1964, soldiers crushed the independent republic of Marquetalia, one of several peasant secessionist movements in Colombian history. But the repression against left-wing groups left behind thousands of leaderless slum youths whom the guerrillas had trained.

In the late 1970s, when drug lords from Cali and Medellín coalesced into competing cartels that battled each other for control of the world's cocaine market, they recruited thousands of those same youths as their foot soldiers, using them as *mulas* (drug couriers) and *sicarios* (assassins).[16] Medellín, long the nation's industrial center, was mired in crisis-level unemployment at the time so it was easy for the drug lords to recruit with promises of fast money.[17] Meanwhile in the countryside, the Colombian army, unable to stamp out the guerrillas, launched a "dirty war" against their supporters. Thousands were abducted, killed, or jailed by both soldiers and right-wing paramilitary groups on the slightest suspicion that they were sympathetic to the guerrillas.[18] The result was a second low-intensity civil war that has lasted for more than thirty-five years and produced a murder rate in Colombia unparalleled in the rest of the world. One Bogotá newspaper reported in 1987 that "43 people were killed on the streets of Bogotá, Cali and Medellín, the three largest cities, assassinated by armed hoodlums who indiscriminately gunned down women, children, beggars, and garbage collectors for fun and target practice."[19] In 1997 alone, 31,000 people were killed in Colombia, approximately equal to the U.S. murder toll that year, although our population is seven times larger.[20]

One by one, the Méndez brothers decided to emigrate. They chose the United States because it seemed more stable and peaceful than the rest of Latin America and because they knew there was already a large number of Hispanics living there. First to leave was their eldest brother, Gregorio, who arrived in 1964 with a legal resident's visa and went to work in the accounting department of a major bank. Pedro Méndez, his wife, Aurora, and his brother Héctor arrived in the early 1970s and quickly secured their legal residency permits.

## SETTING ROOTS AND FIGHTING WEEDS

Unlike Puerto Ricans and Dominicans, who found mainly low-paying jobs in restaurants and the garment industry, many of the early Colombians were skilled and middle-class, they commanded excellent salaries from the start, and they prospered rapidly. Before long, the printing industry and major newspaper linotype shops in many U.S. cities were filled with journeymen Colombian printers.

Carlos Malagón, a friend of the Méndez brothers, arrived in this country in 1967 at the age of thirty-five. He left behind a thriving hairstyling shop in downtown Bogotá and headed for New York City, he recalls, "on a whim, to seek out adventure."[21] A former Malagón employee who had visited the United States convinced him he could spend three or five years in El Norte, strike it rich, and return home. Malagón went to work for a German barber in Woodside, Queens. After only eight months, he had enough money to open his own shop. It was situated a block away from the giant Bulova watch company, where hundreds of newly arrived Colombians worked, and before long they all became Malagón's customers. Thirty years later, his Granada Hair Stylist was an immigrant landmark and Malagón a respected elder of the Colombian diaspora.

Those who came illegally faced greater obstacles. The Uribe sisters, for instance—Gloria, Norelia, and Beatrice—grew up in middle-class comfort in Medellín. Their mother, who owned a small garment factory, sent all seven of her daughters to private school but also trained them in seamstress work so they would have a salable skill.[22] Norelia emigrated first. In 1970, a Jewish textile owner for whom she worked helped find her a job in New York. The next year, her sister Gloria, pining from the breakup of a marriage, followed.[23] Then Beatrice, who owned a delicatessen in Medellín, visited New York on vacation and decided to stay. All three moved in with another Colombian woman, into a one-bedroom apartment on Queens Boulevard, and from there they landed factory jobs in the industrial parks of Long Island City. By the late 1970s, young Colombian women were being recruited avidly by factory managers in Queens because of their reputation for industriousness. Since most were in the country illegally and their bosses knew it, the women were often forced to endure low wages and constant sexual harassment by their supervisors.

Their greatest fear was being caught and deported by INS agents. "That was the panic in everyone," Beatrice recalled. "You never went to the movies because of rumors immigration was waiting there. We never took the subways since we heard agents might check your papers—only the buses."

By the late 1970s, smugglers were moving as many as five hundred Colombians a week illegally into the United States by way of Bimini and the Bahamas, charging their clients as much as $6,000 apiece. Typically, the *coyote* would take off from a South Florida airport in a small private plane on a purported domestic flight, then scamper over to one of the Caribbean islands by flying under U.S. radar, where he would pick up the Colombians. Once he was back in Florida, he would land on a deserted road in the Everglades where a van would be waiting to take the clients to Miami or straight to New York City. Many of the smugglers later realized that bringing in kilos of cocaine instead of people was far more lucrative, so they graduated to drug trafficking.[24]

Eventually, as a way to obtain legal residency, each of the Uribe sisters paid for so-called marriages of convenience to strangers who were U.S.

citizens. In 1984, for instance, Beatrice married a Puerto Rican she barely knew—the union had been arranged through a professional marriage broker—and she became a U.S. citizen nine years later.

The first attempt at civic organizing by the Colombian pioneers was in the late 1960s, when a small group of professionals who called themselves Colombianos en el Exterior (Colombians Abroad) began meeting at the Colombian consulate in Manhattan. Their fledgling effort collapsed in 1971 due to political differences between those allied with the Liberal and Conservative parties back home.

The next attempt was El Comité 20 de Julio (The 20th of July Committee, the date of Colombian independence), of which barber Carlos Malagón served as secretary-treasurer for several years. That group began the tradition of having hundreds of Colombian children march in New York's annual Día de La Raza Parade. The Comité grew to as many as four hundred members and held regular meetings at Club Millonario, a nightclub partly owned by the famous Colombian orchestra leader Arti Bastias, but internal squabbling eventually brought its demise.

The Méndez brothers, meanwhile, were prospering. They opened their printing shop, the first Colombian-owned business on the Roosevelt Avenue shopping strip in Jackson Heights, in 1980. That same year, the first permanent émigré organization in the United States, the Colombian Civic Center, was founded by expatriate members of the Conservative Party. The immigrants called it Centro Cívico. Despite its politically connected origins, the organization, located in a small building in Jackson Heights, flourished as a nonpartisan gathering place for the whole community. Both Malagón and the Méndez brothers were among its early leaders. In the decade after it was founded, Colombian businesses and restaurants mushroomed all along Roosevelt Avenue.

Meanwhile, back home, the cycle of violence in Colombian society was throwing the country into virtual anarchy. Shooting wars between the drug cartels, between the cartels and the government, between the guerrillas and the cartels, and between the guerrillas and the government led to constant outbreaks of bombings, kidnappings, hijackings, and assassinations, as well as complex and labyrinthine alliances between those responsible. As drug trafficking pumped more than $3 billion a year into Colombia during the 1980s, virtually any figure in the country became susceptible to corruption, including police, prosecutors, generals, and politicians. So large was the influx of drug money that Colombia was the only country in Latin America to maintain positive economic growth during that decade. The boom allowed the country to maintain a first-rate infrastructure of roads, public utilities, and all the accoutrements of a modern consumer society—glistening skyscrapers, sprawling suburban shopping malls, and a glittering nightlife. Hundreds of U.S. firms, especially chemical companies, fueled the boom by setting up operations there despite the escalating violence.

Those Colombians who refused the cartels' bribes were simply terrorized into submission or killed. No one was safe. During the 1980s alone, nearly fifty judges, numerous journalists, and several presidential candidates were assassinated. Violence escalated to the point that in the early 1990s more than two thousand members of the leftist Patriotic Union were killed by right-wing assassins. Most of the right-wing groups were financed by the country's richest landowners with tacit army approval.[25] In August 1989, after Liberal Party leader Luis Carlos Galán was gunned down on orders of drug lord Pablo Escobar, the Colombian government declared all-out war on Escobar's Medellín cartel, the most violent of the two drug mobs. Hundreds of midlevel Medellín traffickers and *sicarios* fled the country and hid in the Colombian communities of New York City and Miami. As they did so, turf wars escalated between the Cali and Medellín networks for control of the wholesale cocaine trade in America's cities. The war led to an explosion of both laundered drug money and bullet-ridden bodies in the Colombian immigrant neighborhoods.[26]

"Jackson Heights became a boomtown overnight," Héctor Méndez recalls. "That's when migrants of low quality began arriving. Many of the businesses that sprang up, you wondered if they weren't from drugs. People like us, who used to be so proud of having studied and worked hard to make it, found this new type of immigrant, [and we] knew they didn't have the money or education to come themselves. We called them *los nuevos ricos* [the nouveau riche]. They looked at the rest of us like we were garbage."

"You would go to the beauty parlor and all you'd hear about were drugs," recalled another early immigrant.

In the Centro Cívico, Héctor Méndez had launched classes to provide guidance to new immigrants who wanted to set up businesses. But everywhere the Méndez brothers went they began to notice how suspected drug traffickers were trying to legitimize themselves by infiltrating the few honest organizations, the Centro Cívico, the Liberal Party, the Conservative Party, the Colombian Merchants Association, even local community newspapers.

"Everyone started to lose trust in everyone else," Méndez said. "You never knew if the person you were talking to was involved in that business."

In the summer of 1991, Pedro Méndez accused one of the new immigrants who had joined the Centro Cívico, Juan Manuel Ortiz Alvear, of using a false identity in the United States to hide a criminal record back home. At the time, Ortiz was the publisher of *El Universal,* a local Queens Spanish-language newspaper, and he was trying to control the Centro's board of directors. Ortiz had been a controversial fixture in the community since his arrival from Cali in 1985. Many were accustomed to seeing him speeding around the neighborhood in his white Mercedes and spending huge sums of money night after night at a half-dozen Queens nightclubs. Usually he was accompanied by a group of armed bodyguards who sometimes abducted and raped women at gunpoint from those clubs yet they were never arrested. He and his band had the entire neigborhood living in fear.

After Méndez's public accusation, the leaders of the Centro Cívico expelled Ortiz. Enraged by their action, Ortiz, who insisted he was a legitimate businessman, launched a campaign in his newspaper against the group. Soon, Pedro Méndez began receiving telephoned death threats, and a few months later, on August 6, 1991, as he was returning home one night from his printing shop, Méndez was shot to death. The next day, none of the city's daily English-language newspapers mentioned the murder of one of the Colombian community's most respected businessmen. Queens homicide detectives, overwhelmed by the rash of unsolved killings in Jackson Heights, hardly paid much more attention. The murder remains unsolved.

Six months later came a second and even bigger murder. On March 11, 1992, Manuel de Dios Unanue, a Cuban-born journalist and former editor of *El Diario–La Prensa,* New York's oldest Spanish-language newspaper, was shot to death by a hooded assassin in a Jackson Heights restaurant. At the time of his death, De Dios had been publishing two muckraking magazines in whose pages he gave considerable space to exposing the inner workings and the hierarchy of the Medellín and Cali networks in this country. Organizational charts; names and photos of traffickers who were posing as legitimate Queens businessmen; narratives of drug conspiracies culled from federal indictments; even gossip about gangsters who were not yet indicted—De Dios published them all in detail, something no mainstream English-language publication had done until then. What police did not know at the time was that a few Colombian pioneers in Queens who were fed up with the growing influence of the drug traffickers in their community had been feeding De Dios information.

The murders of Méndez and De Dios, two such prominent Hispanics, were signals that Colombia's uncontrolled violence was reaching into the United States. A few courageous Colombians, aided by Latino political leaders and journalists from the around the city, kept pressure on the Police Department and federal agencies to solve the murders. Several immigrants took enormous risks by joining public marches in the community in memory of De Dios. One of those was the son of Beatrice Uribe, William Acosta, one of the first Colombian-born members of the New York Police Department. Acosta, who had worked in both U.S. military intelligence and with U.S. Customs before becoming a cop, had far better knowledge of what was going on among Colombian drug dealers in New York than most of the veteran Drug Enforcement Administration agents in the city. But like many Latino cops in law enforcement, his information and even his loyalty were often questioned, and his attempts to volunteer in solving the Manuel De Dios and Pedro Méndez murders were repeatedly rebuffed. After nearly ten frustrating years in the NYPD, Acosta resigned in the late 1990s and sued the department for discrimination.[27]

Public pressure and dogged work by several Latino detectives eventually solved the De Dios murder. Six people were convicted in federal court of arranging and carrying out the assassination on orders of José Santa Cruz Londoño, a leader of the Cali cartel who was subsequently killed by Colombian police. And while the Méndez murder was never solved, Ortiz Alvear, the man who had waged a campaign against him, was later convicted of drug trafficking and money laundering for the Cali cartel as well as of the attempted murder of another Colombian immigrant, and was sentenced to long prison terms for each conviction.

The jailing of Ortiz and the solving of the De Dios murder went a long way toward breaking the stranglehold of the cartels over the immigrant Colombian community. Drug trafficking did not end, but attempts by the drug bosses to terrorize and intimidate the hardworking majority were drastically reduced. From that point on, Colombians in this country could breathe a little easier, and the Colombian diaspora ceased being an aberration within the wider Latino immigrant saga.

# PART III

*Harvest*
(La Cosecha)

# 10

## *The Return of Juan Seguín: Latinos and the Remaking of American Politics*

At every hour of the day and night my countrymen ran to me for protection against the assaults or exaction of those adventurers. Sometimes, by persuasion, I prevailed on them to desist; sometimes, also, force had to be resorted to. How could I have done otherwise? Could I leave them defenseless, exposed to the assaults of foreigners who, on the pretext that they were Mexicans, treated them worse than brutes?

—*Juan Seguín*[1]

Every American recognizes the name Davy Crockett, the frontier legend who died defending the Alamo, but Juan Seguín, who fought with Crockett and survived, is virtually unknown.

Seguín's ancestors settled present-day San Antonio fifty years before the American Revolution. A rich landowner and federalist opposed to Mexican president Santa Anna, Seguín was part of the small group of Mexicans who joined the Texas rebels at the Alamo, but he was dispatched from the fort with a message to Sam Houston before the shooting began and thus escaped the massacre. Seguín went on to fight with Houston's army at the Battle of San Jacinto, was later elected a senator of the Texas Republic and served several terms as mayor of San Antonio. Then, in 1842, Anglo newcomers chased him from office at gunpoint, seized his land, and forced him to flee to Mexico, making him the last Hispanic mayor of San Antonio until Henry Cisneros took office 140 years later.[2]

Seguín is the forgotten father of Latino politics in the United States. The story of his life and career has left Mexican Americans with a somewhat different political legacy than that which Washington, Jefferson, and the Founding Fathers bequeathed to white Americans, or which Nat Turner, Sojourner Truth, and W. E. B. Du Bois symbolize for black Americans. How our nation comes to terms with that legacy will determine much of American politics during the twenty-first century.

The reason is simple. The political influence of Hispanic Americans is growing at breakneck speed. Between 1976 and 1996, Hispanic voter registration in the United States increased 164 percent compared to only 31 percent among non-Hispanics; voter turnout among Hispanics grew by 135 percent compared to only 21 percent among non-Hispanics. The number of votes cast by non-Hispanic whites decreased by 9,887,000 from 1992 to 1996, while it increased by 690,000 among Hispanics and only by 15,000 among blacks.[3]

In a mushrooming democratic revolution that is echoing what African Americans accomplished in the 1970s and 1980s, Latino candidates have been gaining majority control of school boards and rural governments throughout the Southwest, while Florida, the Northeast, and Midwest are experiencing similar upheavals. By the end of the decade, several Hispanics will be sitting in the U.S. Senate; four of the country's ten biggest cities—New York, Los Angeles, Dallas, and San Diego—will witness formidable campaigns for City Hall by Latino candidates; and the mayors of state capitals as scattered as Hartford, Sacramento, and Trenton could be Hispanic.

This political revolution will not be halted by the rise of anti-Hispanic sentiment among some white and black Americans nor by the spate of restrictive immigration laws Congress passed in the mid-1990s. It will not be turned back by Supreme Court decisions that negated as "racial gerrymandering" a handful of congressional districts redrawn after the 1990 census. If anything, the anti-Hispanic backlash at the end of the twentieth century—most symbolized by the English-only and anti-immigration movements—has only heightened the clamor of Latinos for full political equality.

Several new factors have fueled the spread of this peaceful revolution:

1. *A rush to citizenship.* Legal Hispanic immigrants, fearing the threat from initiatives like California's Proposition 187, moved in record numbers to acquire full citizenship during the 1990s rather than remain prey to laws that targeted noncitizens.

2. *Demographics.* With a median age far younger than the rest of the U.S. population, Hispanics are rapidly increasing their portion of the U.S. electorate, a trend that will continue throughout the first half of this century regardless of changes in future immigration levels.

3. *The consolidation of a cohesive national Latino lobby.* Historically disparate Hispanic ethnic groups have begun to master the art of build-

ing intra-Latino coalitions to affect the policies of Washington lawmakers.

4. *The emergence of a socially oriented Hispanic middle class.* During
the 1980s, a significant Latino professional and business class arose
that—perhaps with the unique exception of the Cuban American wing—
still identifies both its roots and its future with the masses of blue-collar
Latinos. Those Latino professionals, marginalized for years by white critics who kept labeling them the inferior products of affirmative action,
have now spent decades accumulating wealth and technical skills, and
they have matured into a burgeoning middle class that is insisting on ac-
countability to the Latino population by both government and other institutions within society.

5. *The rise of the Latino Third Force.* The growing ability of Latino
leaders and voters to function as an unpredictable "swing factor" in the
political landscape—refusing to be taken for granted by either the Democratic or Republican parties, or by those who see all politics in the country through the flawed prism of a white-black racial divide.

Fifty years ago, Latino registered voters in the United States could be
counted in the thousands; today, they number more than 6.5 million. In
1950, there were a few hundred Latino elected officials, almost none in
major cities. Today, there are more than six thousand; and Latinos comprise the biggest ethnic voting blocs in Los Angeles, New York, San Antonio, and Miami. Fifty years ago, no presidential candidate bothered to
worry about issues affecting Hispanics, while in the presidential campaign of 2000, both George W. Bush and Al Gore, the early favorites for
the Republican and Democratic nominations, boast of their bilingualism
and heavily court Latino voters.

This revolution did not happen overnight. It has been building since
the end of World War II and has passed through several stages during
that time. Unfortunately, the way those stages unfolded has until now escaped most political observers, for there have been few systematic studies of Latino politics in the U.S.

In this chapter, I identify and analyze each stage of the modern Latino
political movement: the people, organizations, ideas, and methods that
dominated each stage, and the important lessons each generation carried
forward from one stage to another. Hopefully, my effort will prod others
to produce more comprehensive studies. While the periods of development do not exactly coincide for each Latino group, the parallels among
them are far more striking than the differences. I have divided the past
fifty years into five major periods:

- The Integration Period: 1950–1964
- The Radical Nationalist Period: 1965–1974
- The Voting Rights Period: 1975–1984
- The Rainbow Period: 1985–1994
- The Third Force Period: 1995–present

## THE INTEGRATION PERIOD: 1950–1964

The most decisive influence on Latino politics this century was World War II. Thousands of Mexican Americans and Puerto Ricans who served their country in that war—and in the Korean War a few years later—returned from the battlefield with a new confidence regarding their rights as Americans. These veterans refused to accept the blatant anti-Hispanic segregation that had been the rule for generations, especially in the Southwest. In 1949, for instance, when a funeral home in Three Rivers, Texas, refused to bury war veteran Felix Longoria, civic leaders such as Dr. Hector García, attorney Gus García, and other veterans founded the American G.I. Forum, a civil rights and veterans advocacy group that won a wide following among Mexican Americans.[4] The Longoria incident, much like the controversy over Sergeant José Mendoza, the Congressional Medal of Honor winner from Brownsville, galvanized Mexican American anger throughout the nation.

The veterans not only threw themselves into organizations like the Forum and the older League of United Latin American Citizens, but they also turned to politics and began to challenge the historic exclusion of Mexicans from the voting booth. The infamous Texas poll tax and other measures to restrict ballot access (such as the all-white primary and annual voter registration months before an election) had been rammed through the Texas legislature at the beginning of the century by the Democratic Party's white elite to counter the growth of the Populist movement among blacks, Mexicans, and poor whites. At the height of the People's Party in 1896, for instance, its candidate for governor of Texas carried 44 percent of the vote, with an amazing 88 percent of voting-age adults going to the polls. But after the poll tax became law, turnout in Texas elections plummeted by as much as two-thirds and it failed to reach higher than 40 percent for the first half of the twentieth century. Poor whites, blacks, and Mexicans simply could not afford to pay a tax that in some cases equaled almost 30 percent of the average weekly factory wage in the South.[5] The tax remained in effect until 1966, when a federal judge ruled it unconstitutional. Its elimination made it possible for blacks and Mexican Americans to finally return to the voting rolls in large numbers.

Before World War II, only New Mexico could claim any tradition of Mexican Americans holding federal elected office. Dennis Chavez, for instance, served in the U.S. House of Representatives from 1935 to 1962. But few Hispanics held public office anywhere else in the country. Puerto Rican Oscar García Rivera, the only example in New York, was elected to the state assembly in 1937. After the war, the giant *barrios* of Los Angeles and San Antonio emerged as the centers of Hispanic ferment. In San Antonio, Henry B. González, a war veteran and former juvenile probation officer, began organizing the *tejanos* of the West Side through his Pan American Progressive Association, while in Los Angeles, social worker Edward Roybal, another war veteran, rallied *mexicanos* to register and vote. They were the first Latino councilmen in their respective cities since the mid-nineteenth century—Roybal in 1949 and González in 1953.

John F. Kennedy's nomination as the Democratic Party's presidential candidate in 1960 was the watershed moment of the Integration Period. Until then, Mexican Americans had backed liberal candidates in state elections but had made no visible impact on a national election. In Texas, for instance, Mexicans were loyal backers of populist Democratic senators Ralph Yarborough and Lyndon B. Johnson. But the campaign of Kennedy, a charismatic, liberal Catholic, gave Roybal, González, and the other World War II veterans the opportunity to show the growing clout of Latinos. They formed Viva Kennedy clubs throughout the Southwest to back the young Massachusetts senator against Vice President Richard Nixon.

In a close election, Kennedy swept 91 percent of the 200,000 Mexican votes in Texas, which helped him carry the state. And while he managed only a minority of the white vote in neighboring New Mexico, he garnered 70 percent of the Mexican vote, enough for a razor-thin margin there. Nationwide, he amassed 85 percent of the Mexican vote. Kennedy, in turn, threw his support to González in his victorious run for Congress in a special election the following year; and he provided similar support to Roybal in 1962, enabling him to win a congressional seat from a district that was only 9 percent *mexicano*. Then in the Democratic landslide that propelled Lyndon Johnson to victory over Barry Goldwater in 1964, Eligio "Kika" de la Garza won a second Texas congressional seat and Joseph Montoya, the congressman from New Mexico, captured a U.S. Senate seat.

That handful of victories during the early 1960s opened the gates for the modern Hispanic political movement. At the time De la Garza was elected, *tejanos* held only 31 of 3,300 elected positions in the state and only 5 of 11,800 appointed posts. By 1994, just three decades later, the number of Texas Hispanic officeholders had skyrocketed to 2,215.[6] To this day, you will find Mexican homes in the Southwest where a faded photo of John Kennedy hangs prominently near one of the Virgin of Guadalupe—a testament to Kennedy's role as the first U.S. president to address the concerns of Latinos within the American family.

Those early political gains, however, were largely confined to Mexican Americans. Although nearly a million Puerto Ricans lived in the United States by the late 1950s, they were concentrated in New York City and more concerned with political events on the island than with those in their new home. In August 1936, for instance, more than ten thousand people joined a march for Puerto Rican independence organized by radical East Harlem congressman Vito Marcantonio, and throughout the 1950s the debate over the status of Puerto Rico dominated the *barrios* of New York.[7] After Marcantonio's ouster, the few Puerto Ricans who won elective office in that city were all handpicked by the old-line Tammany Hall machine. None had the pioneering zeal exhibited by Mexican Americans González and Roybal at the other end of the country. Among those machine candidates were Felipe Torres, who captured a Bronx state assembly seat in 1954, and J. López Ramos, who went to the assembly from East Harlem in 1958.[8] The first citywide Puerto Rican civic associations, the Puerto Rican Forum, the Puerto Rican Family Institute, and the Puerto Rican Association for Community Affairs, were founded around that time. The machine's grip on Puerto Rican voters was not challenged until 1965, when Herman Badillo won the borough presidency of the Bronx as a candidate of the reform wing of the Democratic Party, thus becoming the first Puerto Rican to hold a major city post. Badillo's victory, however, depended largely on liberal Jewish and black voters instead of Puerto Ricans, who remained a tiny electoral force.

During the 1960s, the Johnson administration, under pressure from a rising civil rights movement and from the rioting of disaffected blacks, pushed a series of landmark bills through Congress. Those laws, the Civil Rights Act of 1964, the Voting Rights Act of 1965, and the Fair Housing Act of 1968, toppled the legal underpinnings of discrimination against both blacks and Hispanics. Some conservatives challenged the inclusion of Hispanics under those laws, especially under the Voting Rights Act, and they continue to do so to this day. Linda Chavez, for instance, in her book *Out of the Barrio*, claims that "Hispanics had never been subject to the same denial of their basic right to vote that blacks had suffered."[9] That assertion somehow ignores the genuine obstacles to political representation Mexicans faced from the caste system in place since the days of Juan Seguín.

Chavez even ignores major federal court decisions that finally struck down that caste system. In 1954, two weeks before its *Brown* v. *Board of Education* decision, the Supreme Court decided a seminal case affecting Mexican Americans. In *Peter Hernandez* v. *Texas,* the Court ruled that Mexicans were "a distinct class" who could claim protection from discrimination. The Court found that of six thousand jurors called in the previous twenty-five years in Jackson County, Texas, none had been a Mexican, even though Mexicans comprised 14 percent of the county's population. To attribute that to "mere chance," wrote Chief Justice Earl Warren for the Court's majority, "taxes our credulity." Instead, the Court found ample proof that the political system of the county discriminated against Mexicans as a distinct class from either whites or blacks.

A restaurant in town, Warren noted, had signs saying: NO MEXICANS SERVED, toilets in the local courthouse were segregated, with one men's toilet marked COLORED MEN and HOMBRES AQUI (MEN HERE) and "until very recent times, children of Mexican descent were required to attend a segregated school for the first four grades."

The Court thus reversed the murder conviction of plaintiff Peter Hernandez due to the systematic exclusion of Mexicans from juries in the county. In doing so, the Court's majority noted that "the Fourteenth Amendment is not directed solely against discrimination due to a 'two-class theory'—that is, based upon differences between 'white' and Negro."[10] Three years later, in *Hernandez et al.* v. *Driscol Consolidated Independent School System,* a federal district court outlawed segregated schools for Mexicans, which the court said had been a fact of life in Texas since the Anglo settlers first arrived.[11]

While new laws and federal court decisions during the Kennedy-Johnson era spurred Latino political involvement by eliminating legal discrimination, they did little to alter the economic and social inequities that had accumulated from both the Mexican caste system and Jim Crow segregation. Meanwhile, the pervasive new influence of television—whether in transmitting stories of dilapidated Harlem tenements, Bull Connor's dogs, or the riot in Watts—suddenly made social inequity more glaring. The 1965 Watts riot, in fact, signaled the end of the incremental Integration Period. Hispanics, along with everyone else in America, entered a new psychological and political era—one of rebellion and social polarization.

## THE RADICAL NATIONALIST PERIOD: 1965–1974

Watts sparked the greatest period of civil unrest in the United States during the twentieth century. For several years, riots became an annual reality for the inner cities, and, as they did, many white Americans began to regard protests by blacks and Hispanics as a threat to the nation's stability. At the same time, African American and Latino youth concluded that their parents' attempt at integration within the political system had failed. Only through massive protests, disruptive boycotts, and strikes or even riots, the new generation decided, could qualitative (some called it revolutionary) change be accomplished.

Within a few years, a whole gamut of new organizations arose to compete with the more established groups such as LULAC, the GI Forum, and the Puerto Rican Forum. The brash new groups—the Brown Berets, La Raza Unida, the Alianza, the United Farm Workers, the Young Lords, Los Siete de La Raza, Crusade for Justice, Movimiento Pro Independencia, MECHA, August Twenty-ninth Movement—were invariably more radical, their membership younger and usually from lower class origins, than the established civic organizations. They saw the older organizations as too tied to the status quo, too concerned with appearing to be respectable and reasonable to Anglo society.

The radical groups sprang up almost overnight in every urban *barrio* and Southwest farm community, rarely with much organizational connection. Inspired by the black power and anti–Vietnam War movement at home and by the anticolonial revolutions in the Third World, especially the Cuban revolution, most offered a utopian, vaguely socialist vision of changing America, and all of them called for a reinterpretation of the Latino's place in U.S. history. They insisted that both Puerto Ricans and Mexicans were descendants of conquered peoples who had been forcibly subjugated when America annexed their territories during its expansion. Because of those annexations, the rebels insisted, Puerto Ricans and Mexicans were more comparable to the Native Americans and the African Americans than to Scotch, German, Irish, or Italian immigrants.

This was also the period when the Latino community itself became more ethnically diverse. Dominican and Cuban refugees arrived in massive numbers to New York and Florida in the late 1960s, followed by Colombians, Salvadorans, Guatemalans, and Nicaraguans in succeeding decades. Meanwhile, Mexican immigrants—both legal and illegal—as well as Puerto Ricans, spread beyond their original enclaves in the Southwest and Northeast.

The Mexican Americans and Puerto Ricans tended to form nationalist groups with left-wing orientations, while the Cubans formed groups with almost exclusively right-wing outlooks. For Cubans, the failed Bay of Pigs invasion in 1961 was a seminal moment. Many blamed lack of support from the Kennedy administration for its failure. That resentment resulted in Cuban leaders allying themselves with the Republican Party.

For the next two decades the overriding goal of Cuban immigrants was returning to a homeland free from Castro and Communism. That obsession gave them more the character of an exile group than a traditional immigrant community.[12] The organizations they formed reflected that preoccupation. They had names like Omega 7, Alpha 66, Comando Zero, Acción Cubana, and at one time they even formed a grand coalition under the name Bloque Revolucionario. Their threats, bombings, and assassinations against those within the exile community whom they considered traitors, or against those in the broader society whom they perceived as agents of Communism, had enormous impact in forcing near unanimity in the public posture of the exile community.[13]

It did not take long for Cubans to make their presence felt in local politics, thanks to Public Law 89-732, which Congress passed in 1966. The law made it easier for Cubans to secure U.S. visas and it shortened the normal five-year waiting period for citizenship. An instant surge of Cuban naturalizations followed, and with it an explosion of Cuban voting power.[14] By the early 1970s—only a decade after their immigration started—Cuban Americans had captured their first seats on the Miami Board of Education, the city governments of Miami and Hialeah, and the Dade County judicial system. By contrast, Dominicans waited more than twenty-five years to elect their first city councilman, and by 1998, Colombians still did not have a single elected official.

The Hispanic population was growing rapidly, but only Mexican Americans in the Southwest, Puerto Ricans in New York, and the Cubans of South Florida boasted a sufficient number of voters by the mid-1970s to draw the attention of Anglo politicians. Leaders of the three groups thus took on the role, for better or worse, of socializing agents and political advocates for the newer Latino immigrants. Because the three groups were concentrated in separate regions of the country, a tense competition arose between their leaders when it came to influencing national policy, with each group's spokesmen fearing that their specific interests or power would be sacrificed under the broader banners of "Hispanic" or "Latino."

As the civil rights movement and anti–Vietnam War movement deepened, however, divisions took root among the Latino radicals. The Young

Lords, Los Siete de La Raza, August Twenty-ninth, and the Brown
Berets refused to participate in the traditional electoral process and
sought alliances instead with revolutionary groups outside the Latino
community, such as the Black Panther Party, the Students for a Democratic Society, and other New Left organizations.

Eventually, those coalitions splintered and evolved into scores of
fringe Marxist factions, and in the case of Puerto Ricans those splinters
included several clandestine urban groups that resorted to terrorist
bombings, such as the FALN (Fuerzas Armadas de Liberación Nacional)
and Los Macheteros. In the Cuban community, the most extreme coun-
terrevolutionaries began taking actions jointly with other non-Cuban
anti-Communist movements in the United States and Latin America, often with CIA sponsorship.[15] These radical factions, whether from the left
or from the right, became increasingly divorced not only from each other
but from the everyday reality that Latinos were facing. All failed to understand that despite the inequality and stubborn racism Latinos faced
in the United States, conditions here, even for the most destitute, were
substantially better than in the Latin American nations from which
they'd emigrated, a reality that to this day has doomed revolutionary
Marxist movements in our country to tiny followings.

A second trend was represented by Rodolfo "Corky" González's Crusade for Justice in Colorado, by Reies Tijerina's Alianza de los Pueblos,
and by La Raza Unida Party in Colorado and Texas. While their rhetoric
mirrored the militant nationalism of the Marxists, these groups opted for
working within the system of U.S. elections. But they rejected both the
Democratic and Republican parties as bankrupt and sought instead to
build independent Chicano organizations that would try to win elected
office in what the movement called Aztlán, the original Aztec homeland
that encompassed the old territory ceded by the Treaty of Guadalupe
Hidalgo. As we have seen, the party they formed, La Raza Unida, made
some impressive showings in small towns in South Texas, but it proved
unable to spark widespread *mexicano* desertions from the Democratic
Party.

A third trend was represented by Cesar Chavez's United Farm Workers Organizing Committee, by the National Council of La Raza, and by
Puerto Rican civic leaders like Gilberto Gerena Valentín. Members of
that trend concentrated on winning the basic rights that *mexicano*s and
Puerto Ricans had as American citizens—the right to unionize, the right
to vote, the right to basic government services like schools, public housing, sewers, and drinking water. Chavez, the foremost representative of

that trend, eventually became the most admired Hispanic leader in the country.

Out of NCLR's work emerged two pivotal organizations, the Mexican American Legal Defense and Education Fund (MALDEF), formed in 1967 by Pete Tijerina and Gregory Luna, and the Southwest Voter Registration and Education Project (SVREP), whose founder was San Antonio's Willie Velázquez. While NCLR became the main lobbying group for Hispanic issues in Washington, MALDEF and SVREP concentrated in the Southwest, where they provided Mexican Americans at the grassroots level the legal and organizational tools to enter the third period of Hispanic political development.

Meanwhile, Puerto Ricans in several Northeast cities were founding similar new civil rights groups. Gilberto Gerena Valentín, a longtime labor leader, united the various island hometown social clubs into a loose federation that pressured city government for better services; educator Antonia Pantoja founded Aspira, a youth organization to train a new generation of leaders; John Olivero, César Perales, and Luis Alvarez founded the Puerto Rican Legal Defense and Education Fund. Where *puertorriqueños* lagged behind *mexicanos* was in failing to involve themselves significantly in electoral politics, the major exception being Herman Badillo, who in 1969 became the first Puerto Rican elected to Congress.

## THE VOTING RIGHTS PERIOD: 1975–1984

After 1975, Latino involvement with revolutionary organizations and nationalistic independent politics declined. Most leaders returned to integrationist and reformist goals, a stage I have labeled the Voting Rights Period. Once again, the movement reverted to political equality as a primary goal, only now it was infused with the cultural and ethnic pride awakened by 1960s radicalism. Admittedly, the militancy was more muted, for America had changed. The reforms the federal government conceded to the civil rights, feminist, and peace movements during the Vietnam War era had in turn spawned a New Right backlash. That backlash began in 1964 with Barry Goldwater, gathered force with George Wallace's presidential campaign in 1968, and spread with the aid of Protestant fundamentalist sects into a nationwide conservative populist movement.

Meanwhile, on the economic front, U.S. companies in search of cheap labor began relocating industrial jobs to the Third World. Faced with rising unemployment and a declining standard of living, white workers searched for someone to blame, so African Americans and Hispanics became the convenient scapegoats. The issues minority community leaders were raising—equal housing opportunity, school busing for desegregation, affirmative action, equal political representation, bilingual education—were all blamed for subverting established "old values" and principles of fairness in American society. The nation entered a conservative period wherein millions of whites called for restoring that traditional America, yet few stopped to consider how a good portion of that tradition had been based on the subjugation of others.

In this new climate, the second generation of postwar Latino leaders discarded its illusion of overthrowing political power and sought instead a proportional share of it. But theirs was not simply a replay of the earlier Integration Period, for each generation absorbs lessons from its predecessors. Several new factors distinguished the Voting Rights Period: first, Latino leaders filed an unprecedented number of federal civil rights lawsuits; second, they formed the first lasting national coalitions across ethnic and racial lines; third, they expanded their movement beyond just middle-class professionals into poor Latino communities by combining 1960s-style mass protests with voter registration and election campaigns.

On the legal front, the Southwest Voter Registration and Education Project, the Mexican American Legal Defense and Education Fund, and, some years later, the Mid-West Voter Registration and Education Project filed and won numerous voting rights suits against at-large election systems that prevailed in many municipalities. Those systems had effectively shut out Mexican Americans from office for decades. Since Latinos were historically segregated into *barrios,* they could best increase representation by electing candidates from compact geographic districts, not at-large ones.

Those court victories, together with massive voter registration drives launched by SVREP in Mexican American towns and counties of South Texas, produced a virtual revolution in that state's politics, one best symbolized by the 1982 election of Henry Cisneros in San Antonio.[16]

At the other end of the country, Puerto Ricans renewed their own efforts at building civil rights or advocacy groups. By then, their *colonias* had spread to many Rust Belt cities and farming counties. The new groups devoted considerably more attention to voter registration and lobbying than had previously occurred in the Puerto Rican communities. Among that new generation of organizations were the National Puerto Rican Coalition (formed by Luis Alvarez, Luis Nuñez, and Amalia Betanzos in 1973 with seed money from the Ford Foundation), the Coalition in Defense of Puerto Rican and Hispanic Rights (founded in New York City in the late 1970s by lawyer Ramón Jiménez, Manuel Ortiz, and others); the National Congress for Puerto Rican Rights (founded in 1981 by scores of former Young Lords and other 1960s radicals, including myself), and the Institute for Puerto Rican Policy (a research and public policy think tank founded by political scientist Angelo Falcon).

The new groups worked closely with the Puerto Rican Legal Defense and Education Fund on several voting rights suits. As a result, in both New York and Chicago, federal judges ruled in the early 1980s that apportionment of municipal districts had discriminated against Hispanics and African Americans. In Chicago, that led to the creation of seven new aldermanic districts—three with majority black populations and four majority Hispanic. A special election in 1984 resulted in the number of Hispanic aldermen increasing from one to four: Miguel Santiago (the only incumbent), Jesús García, Juan Soliz, and Luis Gutiérrez. The Gutiérrez victory rocked the city because it gave a one-vote majority in the city council to the new black mayor, Harold Washington, and thus symbolized the potential of a developing alliance between black and Hispanic politicians.[17]

In New York, the Puerto Rican Legal Defense and Education Fund was able to halt the 1981 municipal elections and get the federal courts to eliminate at-large council seats.[18] The redrawn council districts opened the way for increases in Puerto Rican representation on the council. Since New York has always been the trendsetter for Puerto Ricans, the battle sparked a new awareness of voting rights throughout the East Coast. As a result of both the activism of the new organizations and other voting rights court victories, by the mid-1980s New York had a new, more independent group of Puerto Rican officials, such as city councilman José Rivera and state assemblymen José Serrano and Israel Ruiz. Similar victories occurred in other eastern and midwest cities.[19] Usually, the victories resulted from alliances the Hispanic candidates struck with a strong African American electoral campaign. Such was the case with Gutiérrez in Chicago, with Angel Ortiz, who won an at-large city council seat as part of Wilson Goode's victorious 1983 mayoral campaign, and with Nelson Merced, the first Hispanic to capture a seat in the Massachusetts House of Representatives, from a predominantly black Boston district.

The climax of the Voting Rights Period came in 1983, with the stunning mayoral victories of Harold Washington in Chicago and Wilson Goode in Philadelphia. Suddenly, the nation awoke to a new reality. Power in the Democratic Party's urban areas had slipped from organizations of white politicians and their ethnic constituencies to coalitions of African Americans and Hispanics. In both Chicago and Philadelphia, Hispanic voters, who until then had been ignored by political candidates, demonstrated a newfound ability to tip an election by registering and voting in startling numbers. Washington, who had received only 25 percent of the Hispanic vote in winning a hard-fought Democratic primary, went on to capture 74 percent of that vote—the margin of his victory— in the general election against conservative Republican Bernard Epton.[20]

Likewise, in Philadelphia, Goode eked out a victory in a close Democratic primary against former mayor Frank Rizzo, thanks to a black-Hispanic-liberal alliance, then he romped against a weak Republican opponent. In both cases, Hispanic voters, mostly Puerto Rican, opted for Goode by more than two to one.

In South Florida, meanwhile, Cuban exile leaders, who at first had limited their political goals almost exclusively to ousting Castro and returning to Cuba, began a drastic change in the mid-1970s. That change was sharply influenced by the new generation of Cubans who had been born or raised in this country. Between 1973 and 1979, according to one study, those who said they planned to return to Cuba if Castro should be overthrown plummeted from 60 to 22 percent.[21] This changing perception by Cuban émigrés was reflected in politics. By 1974, some 200,000 Cubans in South Florida had become citizens and many were voting regularly. After several unsuccessful attempts, the first two Cubans were elected to office in 1973—Manolo Reboso to the Miami City Commission and Alfredo Durán to the Dade County School Board. Not surprisingly, both were Bay of Pigs veterans. Then, in late 1975, Cuban professionals, aided by Hispanic media personalities, launched a citizenship campaign. The following year more than 26,000 exiles were naturalized. By 1980, more than 55 percent of the exiles had become citizens, double the percentage in 1970.[22]

Those new citizens quickly made their presence felt. At first, it was largely in symbolic ways. On April 15, 1973, the Metro Dade County Commission, which had no Hispanics among its nine members, bowed to Cuban pressure and declared the county "officially bilingual." But the symbols quickly turned real. In 1978, Jorge Valdés became the country's first Cuban American mayor when he captured the Sweetwater City Hall, and he was followed by Raul Martínez in Hialeah.[23]

This growth of Cuban voting power, together with the new wave of immigrants brought by the Mariel exodus, soon touched off a backlash among whites in Dade County, who struck back with a 1980 referendum

to nullify their commission's earlier bilingual declaration. The new referendum, which proposed to prohibit "the expenditure of county funds for
the purpose of utilizing any language other than English, or promoting
any culture other than that of the United States," instantly catapulted the
issue of language onto the national stage. It passed handily, with the vote
polarized almost exclusively along ethnic lines—71 percent of non-
Hispanic whites voted for it and 85 percent of Latinos voted against.[24]

While they found increased resistance from whites on their domestic agenda, Cuban politicians had great success in pushing their anti-
Communist initiatives. The Miami City Commission passed twenty-eight
resolutions or ordinances against Communism in Latin America during
one sixteen-month period before May 1983.[25]

The anti-Cuban backlash, however, prompted some soul-searching by
first- and second-generation immigrant leaders, who decided to counter
the negative image of their community in the English-speaking press. In
1980, civic leaders founded both the Spanish American League Against
Discrimination (SALAD) and the Cuban American National Foundation (CANF), and two years later they launched Facts About Cuban Exiles (FACE).[26]

Ronald Reagan's election as president in 1980 signaled a new era for
the solidly anti-Communist Cuban Americans. With a friend like Reagan
in the White House, powerful Miami groups like CANF and the Latin
American Builders Association perfected a well-bankrolled behind-the-
scenes lobby in Washington for their special projects—Radio Martí, TV
Martí, and aid to the Nicaraguan Contras. At the same time, they adopted
a new pragmatism in public, focusing less on controversial issues like
bilingual education.[27]

Cuban voters diverged from Puerto Ricans and Mexican Americans in
another crucial way—their posture toward the black community. While
*mexicanos,* and even more so Puerto Ricans, managed to build tenuous
alliances with blacks in several major cities, Cuban Americans and African
Americans in Dade County turned into bitter enemies, especially as the
much older black community of Miami watched the newer Cuban immigrants catapult over them economically. During the early 1970s, a Puerto
Rican, Mauricio Ferré, the blond, blue-eyed scion of one of the island's
richest families, won the Miami mayor's seat by building an alliance of
the black and liberal Jewish community to stave off the burgeoning conservative Cuban political movement.

When riots erupted in Miami's black communities several times in the
1970s and 1980s, allegations by blacks of mistreatment by Cubans were
usually raised as underlying factors. By the mid-1980s, Cuban immi-

grants had turned South Florida into the center of Hispanic conservative power throughout the country. Nothing reflected that more than the election of the first Cuban American to Congress in 1989. Ileana Ros-Lehtinen, a conservative Republican, narrowly won the race despite her Democratic opponent's getting 88 percent of the Anglo vote and 94 percent of the black vote. Ros-Lehtinen's margin of victory was made possible by a Latino turnout of nearly 60 percent.[28]

## THE RAINBOW PERIOD: 1985–1994

When Jesse Jackson began his first campaign for the Democratic nomination for president in 1984 by calling for a new "Rainbow Coalition," Washington experts dubbed his attempt a meaningless protest. He promptly shocked all the experts by winning the majority of African American votes and a substantial minority of Latino and white votes. Jackson, who had witnessed the power of a black–Latino–liberal white coalition in both Chicago and Philadelphia, was determined to replicate it at the national level. Four years later, this time with widespread support from black and Latino politicians who had not supported him in 1984, Jackson garnered 7 million votes against the eventual Democratic presidential candidate, Michael Dukakis. In places like New York and Connecticut, Jackson won the majority of votes among Latinos, while in California, Texas, and elsewhere in the Southwest, he improved his showing but remained below 50 percent.[29]

The 1984 and 1988 Jackson campaigns, in addition, brought millions of first-time voters to the polls in the South and the northern ghettos, and those same voters sent blacks and Hispanics to Congress in record numbers. In some states, blacks showed higher election turnouts than white voters for the first time, and candidates who identified themselves as part of Jackson's Rainbow Coalition started to win isolated local elections. In Hartford, Connecticut, for instance, a Rainbow alliance captured control of the city council in the late 1980s and elected that city's first black mayor.

Then in 1989 came the most electrifying of local victories for the Rainbow movement. David Dinkins won the mayoralty of New York City—the first black to hold the post—and he did so by capturing 88 percent of the black vote, 64 percent of the Hispanic vote, and less than 35 percent of the white vote.[30] As blacks and Hispanics gained greater influence within the Democratic Party, however, white middle-class and suburban voters kept deserting the party.

The Rainbow's revolutionary potential came from its appeal to those sectors of the nation's voting-age population that had remained alienated and disenfranchised throughout most of the twentieth century—blacks, Hispanics, the young, and the poor. Our country has had for decades one of the lowest voter turnout rates of any industrial democracy, assuring that those elected to office, from either the Democratic or Republican party, represent only a minority of the voting-age adults. In 1972, for instance, 77 percent of middle-class property owners voted compared to 52 percent of working-class Americans. And well-educated Americans usually vote at twice the rate of less educated citizens.[31] Jackson's Rainbow movement, by contrast, placed prime importance not only on registering new voters but on removing legal obstacles in many states to simple and universal voter registration. But in both the 1988 and 1992 elections, Democratic presidential candidates chose to continue competing with the Republicans for the same small number of already registered voters who had fled the Democrats—the so-called Reagan Democrats—in the hope of getting them to "swing" back. Little attention was paid to Jackson's strategy of getting millions of new voters from the lower classes—where blacks and Hispanics are disproportionately concentrated—onto the rolls, so they could become the basis of a new political majority.

After that initial breakthrough of the late 1980s, however, the Rainbow Coalition stalled. In a country so long fixated on the contradictions between white and black society, the Rainbow fell victim to similar divisions. Jackson and many of the veteran black officeholders around him started treating the white, Hispanic, and Asian members of the Rainbow as permanent junior partners who could be mobilized as allies but who would not be permitted autonomy or opportunity to shape organizational strategy and policy. At the same time, a few black and Hispanic leaders started promoting ethnic competition for jobs and elected posts in a variety of cities. "The blacks want everything for themselves," was a common phrase of some Hispanic leaders, and "Latinos just want to ride to power on our coattails" was a refrain of too many of their black counterparts.

While the leaders argued, their followers clashed over government contracts and patronage jobs. The steady rise in the number of Hispanics elected to office, for instance, was not mirrored by a rise in the number who were appointed to jobs in local governments, as had happened with the Irish, Italian, and African American urban political machines of the past. After the riots of the 1960s, federal and municipal government employment had turned into a prime vehicle for many blacks to rise into the middle class. But Hispanics, perhaps in part because of the language barrier some had to overcome, did not witness a parallel progress. The few who did land government jobs invariably perceived blacks who were in supervisory positions over them as reluctant to aid their progress.

Differences in attitude toward race also tore at the Coalition. Jackson portrayed the Rainbow as a "common ground" for all Americans seeking economic justice; he urged an inclusive approach toward all minorities. Many African Americans, however, believe Latinos aspire to be considered white, while many Hispanics regard blacks as obsessed with race; and a good number, especially among Mexican Americans, even harbor deep prejudice toward blacks. In fact, Latinos simply view race relations from a historically different perspective. This country's stark white-black dichotomy is alien to Latinos. Rather, to varying degrees, based on the country of origin and even the region within the home country, ethnic identification, or nationality, remains much more at the core of Latino identity. This view is even mirrored by the physical locations of many Latino communities in U.S. cities; often, they have emerged almost as buffer areas between black and white neighborhoods. Rather than air these different views and resolve them through debate and education, the Rainbow swept them under the rug, thus undermining its own unity.

The sudden death of Chicago mayor Harold Washington in 1987 was the first signal that keeping the Rainbow Coalition together would be even harder than constructing it. Within a few years, some of the very Latino leaders who backed Washington deserted his splintered movement and joined a new alliance with the old Democratic Party machine, now headed by Richard Daley, son of the legendary mayor. Among those was Luis Gutiérrez, an activist in the Puerto Rican independence movement.[32] As a result of his switch, Gutiérrez would later win Daley's support for a new congressional seat created by reapportionment. At the same time, in New York City, another Puerto Rican leader, Nydia Velázquez, fought to keep the Rainbow Coalition together, winning key support from both Jackson and the Reverend Al Sharpton in a race for a new congressional seat. In 1992, Gutiérrez and Velázquez became the second and third Puerto Rican voting members of Congress, yet they used different electoral alliances to come to power.

In Philadelphia, the black-Latino alliance started to rupture in 1991. Of those Puerto Ricans who had supported Wilson Goode throughout his two terms, some backed a liberal black Democratic leader who attempted to succeed him, John White, Jr., while others backed the more moderate white Democrat, and eventual winner, Ed Rendell.

Finally, in 1993, the coalition of African Americans and Latinos in New

York City foundered during the reelection campaign of David Dinkins. While Dinkins retained a majority of Latino votes, his percentage was reduced, as was the voter turnout in the Latino community, enabling Republican Rudy Giuliani to squeak to victory with a very slim margin. Thus by 1995, the mayoralty in four of the country's largest cities—New York, Los Angeles, Chicago, and Philadelphia—had passed from a liberal or moderate black incumbent to a more conservative white leader. In each case, Hispanic voters shifted in significant percentages from the previous black mayor to the new white candidate, and each time the argument of those who switched sounded the same: "We weren't treated as equal by the black leaders." Meanwhile, the failure of Jesse Jackson to expand his Rainbow Coalition through a third presidential campaign in 1992 left the movement organizationally adrift at the national level. Even as the number of black and Hispanic leaders in Congress reached a record number, the cohesiveness of the alliance fractured, especially as black voters along with whites grew increasingly uneasy about the country's population of Hispanics and Asians. In November of 1994, for instance, a majority of black Californians voted for Proposition 187 to cut off all public benefits to illegal immigrants.

Thus, the Rainbow Coalition was dead as a vehicle for a new progressive alliance by early 1995, even though Jackson never officially declared its demise but simply folded it into his old Operation PUSH organization.

## THE THIRD FORCE PERIOD, 1995–PRESENT

Following the disintegration of the Rainbow, Latinos entered a new stage that I have dubbed the Third Force Period. The hallmarks of this new stage have been a massive rush to citizenship by Latino immigrants, a huge increase in voter participation levels, and a newfound independence by Latino leaders.

From 1994 to 1997, citizenship applications to the INS nearly tripled, from 543,353 to 1,411,981, the overwhelming majority from Hispanics.[33] This stampede to citizenship was caused by several factors. First and most important was the spate of restrictive immigration laws that began with Proposition 187 in California and then spread across the country. Until then, Mexicans had the lowest naturalization rates of any immigrant group. One study showed that only 3 percent of Mexicans admitted into the country in 1970 had become citizens by 1979.[34] Many Mexicans had lived and worked in this country for years, but since they invariably expected to return home someday, they rarely sought citizenship. Likewise, the Central Americans who fled civil wars in the 1980s expected to return once those wars ended.

But the new immigration laws sparked a Latino backlash. Of the 3 million illegal immigrants who became legal U.S. residents under the amnesty provisions of the Immigration Reform and Control Act of 1986 (IRCA), for instance, 2.6 million were from Latin America, and as soon as they were eligible for citizenship in 1992, most opted for it.[35] In addition, the Republican-sponsored ban in 1996 on federal benefits for legal permanent residents (it was later partially repealed) prompted hundreds of thousands who were here legally to seek citizenship. As soon as they were sworn in, those new citizens registered to vote.

The second factor in the rush to citizenship was the peace accords in Nicaragua, Salvador, and Guatemala, which ended the fighting but not the economic chaos in those countries. Once the wars ended, the Central American refugees suddenly turned into the main source of economic aid to their beleaguered countries through the billions of dollars in remittances they sent home each year. Because of that, both the immigrants and their home governments resisted their repatriation.

A third factor was the transformation of citizenship laws in Latin America, with governments there increasingly adopting dual citizenship provisions that allowed their nationals to retain home country rights even if they became U.S. citizens. Colombia, Mexico, and the Dominican Republic have already taken major steps in that direction.[36]

The combination of all those factors turned the dormant potential of Latino politics into reality starting in 1996, when the Hispanic vote astounded political experts with both its explosive growth and its unpredictability.[37] More than 5 million Latinos went to the polls that year, an astounding 20 percent increase over 1992.[38]

And turnout was higher in the new immigrant neighborhoods than in more established Latino areas. In New York City, for instance, overall Latino turnout was 48 percent of registered voters, but it reached 63 percent in the Dominican area of Washington Heights, and 60 percent in the Colombian section of Jackson Heights.[39]

Those who came to the polls voted overwhelmingly for Bill Clinton and the Democratic Party. Clinton garnered 72 percent of the Latino vote compared to 61 percent in 1992.[40] Even in Florida, where Cubans had always voted solidly Republican, he grabbed 44 percent to Bob Dole's 46 percent.[41] The seismic shift was best exemplified in California, where a relative unknown, Loretta Sánchez, narrowly defeated right-wing congressman Robert Dornan in Orange County, a historically conservative Republican stronghold.

The following year, local elections in many cities repeated the same pattern of high Hispanic turnout but also showed the Latino vote was becoming less predictable than in the past. In the New York and Los Angeles mayoral races, for instance, not only did the number of Latino votes exceed that of blacks for the first time, but Latinos gave substantial backing to victorious Republican incumbents—45 percent to New York's Rudy Giuliani and 48 percent to LA's Richard Riordan—while blacks voted heavily against both.[42]

Overall, the Latino nationwide vote has more than doubled since 1980 (from 2.1 million to 5 million), and it seems sure to continue that phenomenal rate of increase even if current immigration restrictions remain in force. The demographics leave no alternative. Those 5 million voters, after all, amount to less than a third of the 17.5 million voting-age Latinos in the country today, since many Hispanic adults are still not citizens, and a good portion of those who are have yet to register. Furthermore, with nearly half of all Latinos in the United States under twenty-five compared to just a third of non-Latinos, and with Hispanic fertility rates higher than non-Hispanics, the pool of potential voters will mushroom irreversibly for decades.[43]

Most experts argue that the new Latino electorate will never function in nearly the unified fashion that blacks have done historically. The terms "Hispanic" or "Latino," they note, are useless umbrella categories masking huge ethnic differences, and Latinos will gradually adopt voting patterns closer to the old European immigrants. While the first conclusion is certainly true, the second fails to grasp the emergence during the last several decades of a rich new Latino identity on U.S. soil. From what was at first largely a Mexican American population in the Southwest and a Puerto Rican enclave in New York City, the different Hispanic groups have undergone, and continue to undergo, cultural amalgamation among themselves—through intermarriage, through shared knowledge of one another's music, food, and traditions, through common language, through a common experience of combating anti-Hispanic prejudice and being shunted into the same de facto segregated neighborhoods. No longer do a handful of Mexican American or Puerto Rican or Cuban groups dominate the national political debate on Hispanics; rather, the leaders of once disparate groups are now speaking with a more unified voice through organizations like the National Association of Latino Elected and Appointed Officials, the National Hispanic Agenda, the National Hispanic Chamber of Commerce, the Labor Council for Latin American Advancement, and the National Hispanic Political Action Committee.

In 1994, nearly fifty years after Ed Roybal and Henry B. González pioneered modern Latino politics, there were 5,459 Latino elected officials in the nation. But that still represented little more than 1 percent of all elected officials in the country at a time when Latinos were 10 percent of the population.[44]

Some studies claim the Latino electorate is conservative at heart, but I would urge caution before accepting such conclusions. True, wherever Hispanic communities achieve relative prosperity—in places like Miami and Orlando, northern New Mexico, Contra Costa County, California—they inevitably become more conservative in their voting patterns. But Hispanics remain overwhelmingly concentrated among the country's working-class and lower-middle-class sectors. The economic quest of the majority for a better standard of living necessarily brings it into conflict with corporate America's drive to achieve maximum profit from fewer and fewer workers. Latinos are constantly influenced by news of how people in their homelands are struggling to survive within the new global economy. Those economic realities, together with the anti-Hispanic bias they confront each day in the United States, continually force Hispanics of all nationalities to bind together to defend their interests.

Furthermore, Latin American immigrants are more politically sophisticated than most of us realize. They come from countries where civil wars and political strife have forced them to pay attention to politics. In Puerto Rico, among the most peaceful of Latin American homelands, more than 80 percent of the voting-age population regularly goes to the polls. Everyone follows politics there with fervor more typical of football fans here. There, election day is a holiday; all establishments are shuttered, even movie theaters and restaurants, until the polls close; and the social and family pressures on everyone to vote are immense. The same kind of fanatical approach to voting exists in the Dominican Republic and many other Latin American countries.

Because the continuing economic crisis in Latin America means more immigrants will keep coming, and because of the maturing of this interethnic Hispanic identity here, I have no doubt that the twenty-first century will lead to a full awakening of the voting power of Latinos. During the next few years, Hispanic Americans will continue to register and vote in record numbers, energized by the historic sense that "our time has come." According to one recent study, by 2025, Latinos and African Americans will constitute 52 percent of the population of Texas, 50 percent in California and New Mexico, 43 percent in New York, 41 percent in Florida, 36 percent in Arizona, 34 percent in Nevada, and 31 percent in Illinois; and in each of those states, Latinos will be the dominant group.

Hispanic political leaders who understand this, and who refuse to fall into the ever-recurring black-white divide on racial issues or to be taken for granted as a permanent reserve of the Democratic Party, will succeed in turning the Hispanic voter, along with the growing number of Asian American voters, into the basis of a new interracial coalition, or "Third Force," in American political life. Such a Third Force movement would seek to build a genuinely multiracial, multiethnic civic majority. Its aim would be not just getting more people to vote, but getting them to participate actively in social and civic institutions, creating space and voice for citizens of all races and ethnic groups. Because such a coalition would reach out to those who so far have been alienated and disenfranchised, it would necessarily change the terms of national debate, providing an alternative to the corporate-conservative minority that has financed and run both major political parties for the past thirty years.

By building such a coalition to renew American politics, the descendants of Juan Seguín will not merely reclaim their role in American history, they will rewrite it.

# 11

## *Immigrants Old and New: Closing Borders of the Mind*

> For fifteen centuries they were the backbone of a continent, un-
> changing while all about them radical changes again and again
> recast the civilization in which they lived.
>
> *—Oscar Handlin,*
> The Uprooted

Immigration sparked red-hot public debate in the United States during the 1990s. Despite a roaring stock market during most of the decade, too many Americans suffered from prolonged stagnation in their incomes, corporate downsizing, and the loss of good-paying factory jobs as more and more U.S. production shifted overseas. Increasingly, the victims of the new global market directed their resentment at the record number of foreigners arriving on our shores, particularly from Latin America and Asia.

The new immigrants, many became convinced, were *different* from the past waves of Europeans. They were clinging to their native languages, refusing to assimilate, draining public services, and producing a disturbing share of criminals. Television news and radio talk shows stoked those fears, depicting immigration agents at our borders and airports as overwhelmed by the massive influx of illegal foreigners. As the panic spread, a gamut of conservative politicians, moderate academics, and even liberal environmentalists demanded a crackdown. The nation's way of life, its very identity, was under siege, they said.

California struck the first blow. In 1994, its voters overwhelmingly approved Proposition 187, banning all public services for illegal immigrants. Two years later, Congress enacted and President Clinton signed a series of draconian new laws meant to sharply reduce legal and illegal immigration and speed up deportation of those the government deemed undesirable.

Anti-immigrant backlashes are not new in U.S. history. Each major wave of newcomers to our shores has provoked consternation among previous settlers, who then justified periodic clampdowns with allegations against the immigrants that were very similar to the current ones. The current nativist backlash began around 1980 and is the third major eruption since the country's founding, though there have been several smaller ones.

Some of what the current nativists say is undoubtedly true. The latest immigration to the United States has been markedly different from previous waves. Twenty-one million foreigners settled here legally between 1960 and 1996 in the second-largest wave in our history. Half of those immigrants were from Latin America and the Caribbean, and another quarter from Asia and Africa.[1] They came in such numbers that they permanently transformed the long-held image of the United States as a nation of transplanted Europeans.

And some of those new immigrants do differ from the Europeans who came before them—even from today's Asian immigrants—but not because of some innate propensity to fall into crime and poverty or some conscious and stubborn refusal to learn English and enter the American mainstream. Rather, the Latin American and Caribbean immigrants confronted specific external factors in the nature and the timing of their migration that greatly influenced their integration—or lack of integration—into our national life. Unlike the Europeans and Asians, Latin Americans moved from the backyard of the U.S. empire to its heartland, from one part of the New World to another. Because their countries of origin were so much closer to the United States, in both geographical and political terms, Latin American migration has historically been more fluid and uncontainable than that of Europeans and Asians, involving more travel back and forth, more communication and physical connection between the migrants and their homelands, and that in turn has led to far stronger ties between them and their old cultures than previous migrants experienced.

In addition, since they came from countries that have been long dominated by the United States, the attitude of Latin American migrants toward North American society was invariably more ambivalent, certainly more critical, than those of newcomers from other parts of the world. Finally, the timing of their arrival, as the United States was entering a postindustrial information-based economy, had enormous impact on the ability of Latin Americans to integrate themselves into our national life in the same manner Europeans did during prior eras. No matter what restrictions are placed on it, Latin American immigration seems sure to continue at historically high levels deep into this new century, for it is fueled by political, economic, and demographic forces beyond the control of any set of immigration "reforms." Among those forces are:

1. A catastrophic economic crisis in Latin America that *pushes* migrants here;
2. Corporate globalization, which inexorably *pulls* Latin Americans here;
3. A declining birth rate and aging of the white population of the United States, which assures a continued *demand* for low-paid Latin American labor.

## FROM BACKLASH TO BACKLASH

In 1729, Pennsylvania's Quakers, who viewed the newly arrived Scotch-Irish immigrants as an unworthy and crime-prone lot, passed a law to penalize those who brought them in.[2] Shortly after the War of Independence, the descendants of the original colonists assumed the label "native" Americans to distinguish themselves from those who arrived later. It didn't take long for an influx of newcomers to alarm them. During the 1840s, Irish escaping the Great Famine and German workers and intellectuals fleeing the repression that followed the failed revolutions of 1848 began arriving in large numbers. These immigrants were Catholics, which worried the older settlers, and they quickly established their voice and strength at the voting booth. In fact, they built formidable urban political machines that openly challenged Protestant power by opposing public schools and temperance laws. Their rising influence led to anti-Catholic bigotry and provoked the founding of a new anti-immigrant party, the "Know-Nothings," or American Party. The Know-Nothings accused the pope and his followers of subverting this country's Protestant origins. The party grew rapidly in influence and its leaders soon advocated banning the immigration of paupers or criminals, a twenty-one-year wait for citizenship, the mandatory use of the Protestant Bible in all public schools, and a ban on immigrants holding office or receiving federal land grants.[3]

"Their Catholicism and their atheism produce a pest wherever they go," said one Boston Know-Nothing newspaper of the Irish and Germans.[4] One modern sociologist's review of crime convictions in New York City for the year 1859 by ethnic group clearly indicates which group was considered the greatest "threat" to society:

TABLE 5

| | |
|---|---|
| Canadians | 80 |
| Scotch | 118 |
| English | 666 |
| Germans | 1,403 |
| Irish | 11,305[5] |

The nativists found intellectual support for their prejudices from the growing body of eugenicists in the country, such as Edward Jarvis, who published studies showing high rates of lunacy among the new immigrants. In 1855, deadly riots erupted between Know-Nothings and German immigrants in Cincinnati, Columbus, and Louisville. By then, the Know-Nothings were so entrenched that they controlled the governorships or legislatures of seven states. Publisher Horace Greeley, their fiercest opponent, estimated that seventy-five congressmen were associated with the party.[6] Only the bitter debate between North and South over slavery finally eclipsed the burgeoning nativist movement; the Know-Nothings became so divided over that issue that they ruptured in 1857 and disappeared from sight.

The next nativist surge began around 1890 and lasted more than thirty years. The immigrant scapegoats this time were from southern and eastern Europe: Italians, Slovaks, and Jews from Poland and Russia. Racist theories found renewed support among older settlers, as yet another generation of eugenicists, purporting to base themselves on Social Darwinism, once again proclaimed immigrants and blacks as inferior. Among them was Dr. Harry Laughlin, who was appointed a consultant to the House Committee on Immigration and Naturalization in 1922. To buttress his anti-immigrant views, Laughlin reported to Congress that the foreign-born in federal and state hospitals had three times the insanity rate of American natives.[7]

"The European governments took the opportunity to unload upon careless, wealthy and hospitable America the sweepings of their jails and asylums," charged a typical writer of the period.

> The result was the new immigration . . . [which] contained a large and increasing number of the weak, the broken and the mentally crippled of all races drawn from the lowest stratum of the Mediterranean basin and the Balkans, together with hordes of the wretched, submerged populations of the Polish ghettos. Our jails, insane asy-

lums and almshouses are filled with this human flotsam and the whole tone of American life, social, moral and political, has been lowered and vulgarized by them.[8]

Bowing to this public outcry, Congress passed the most restrictive immigration law in U.S. history, with a racially based national quota system. Not surprisingly, this was also a period of intense oppression of blacks in the South, for it seems that anti-immigrant upsurges always seem to go hand in hand with high tides of antiblack prejudice. The Ku Klux Klan swelled to 6 million members. Jim Crow laws were enacted throughout the South. In 1919 alone, seventy-four blacks were lynched.[9]

Three-quarters of a century later, our nation is in the midst of another nativist tide, one that has been gathering steam since the Mariel boat lift of 1980. That year, *Time* magazine startled middle America with its proclamation that the eighties would be the "Decade of the Hispanic," while *Foreign Affairs* warned its influential readers that "50 percent or more of legal and illegal immigrants to the United States have come from a single foreign-language group [Spanish-speaking]" from 1968 to 1977.[10]

Five years later, former Colorado governor Richard Lamm launched a movement against Hispanic immigration in a much-publicized book, *The Immigration Time Bomb.* "Most of us would not want the United States to be unrecognizably different from the way it is today," Lamm wrote. "But if you don't believe that unassimilated immigrants have the power to change America, go to Miami, in Dade County, Florida." There, he said, white English-speaking Americans were fleeing and black Americans had become victims of the "culture clash, the feeling of being a foreigner within one's own country."[11] Lamm was among the first prominent U.S. leaders to charge that the new immigrants, unlike prior waves, were responsible for a rise in crime and were resisting assimilation.

Soon after Lamm's book appeared, the first federal attempt to clamp down on contemporary immigration was passed, the 1986 Immigration Reform and Control Act (IRCA), sponsored by Wyoming senator Alan Simpson. IRCA coupled an amnesty program for long-term undocumented immigrants with stiff fines against employers who hired illegal migrants. While it led to the legalization of 2.6 million people who were already in the country, IRCA failed to stem the tide of illegal entries.

Much of that failure was the government's fault. While federal officials beefed up border interdiction programs, they were slow to crack down on employers who knowingly broke the law by recruiting and hiring undocumented workers. Between 1989 and 1994, as part of federal policy to reduce the size of government, INS cut in half the number of agents assigned to enforce employer sanctions. Predictably, the number of fines issued dropped by the same amount. By 1994, INS was completing less than 2,000 investigations annually and had a backlog of 36,000 cases.[12]

In reaction to IRCA's inadequacy, whites near the Mexican border began to dramatize their frustration with uncontrolled immigration. Vigilante movements like "Light Up the Border" formed, in which groups of citizens living in Southern California gathered at night to shine their car headlights across the border and stop Mexicans from crossing illegally. In some cases, groups of white supremacists took to attacking immigrants.[13]

As alien menace stories proliferated, politicians responded.[14] Pat Buchanan became the first major presidential candidate to run on an anti-immigrant platform in the 1992 Republican primary. Two years later, Republicans incorporated his views into their Contract with America. By 1995, another much-ballyhooed book, Peter Brimelow's *Alien Nation,* staked out an even more radical stand. Our "white nation," Brimelow warned, was being subverted by uncontrolled Third World immigration. "There is no precedent for a sovereign country undergoing such a rapid and radical transformation of its ethnic character in the entire history of the world," he alleged.[15] Along with other populist conservatives, Brimelow blamed the liberal Democrats in Congress for opening the floodgates to Third World migrants through the Immigration and Control Act of 1965. He called for a 1920s-like retrenchment, a near-total moratorium on immigration to save white America from social and racial degeneration.

Views like Brimelow's and Buchanan's, fueled by right-wing talk radio hosts, resonated across the heartland. The result was a rash of 1996 immigration laws that have led to a virtual militarization of our border with Mexico, sharp reductions in legal immigration quotas, skyrocketing fees and other economic obstacles for those applying for legal residency or citizenship, and accelerated deportation procedures for noncitizens convicted of even the most minimal crimes.

In 1997, for instance, I reported the story of Jesus Collado, a businessman who had been a legal resident in New York City for decades. That April, after visiting family in his native Dominican Republic and returning home, Collado was arrested at Kennedy Airport by INS agents, who immediately sought to deport him. Collado, it turns out, had been found guilty by a New York City judge in 1974 of sexual abuse of a minor. He had been seventeen at the time, and the minor was his fifteen-year-old girlfriend. The girl's mother, a neighbor and friend of Collado's family, admitted in court that she filed charges against him solely to break up their relationship. The judge, recognizing that this was a case more of teenage love than of sexual abuse, sentenced Collado to probation. In the twenty-three years since then, Collado had never run afoul of the law. In the meantime, he had married someone else, raised four children, put two of them through college, and established a successful restaurant. But now, INS wanted to deport him as undesirable for a twenty-three-year-old misdemeanor.[16]

He spent seven months in an immigration jail before the intervention of several New York congressmembers convinced the Justice Department to at least release him on bond. But thousands of other legal residents guilty of past minor brushes with the law, people with children and wives who are legal U.S. citizens, have not been so lucky. They have been caught up in the escalating INS dragnet aimed at deporting anyone with a criminal record.

That dragnet appears to be increasingly directed at Latino immigrants. In 1997, the INS deported or excluded more than 110,000 aliens, most of them for past criminal convictions, and almost double the number removed in 1996. Latinos from eight countries comprised 90 percent of those 110,000. The disparity in treatment of Latinos can be seen when we compare how the agency handles Canadians. The INS estimates there are 120,000 illegal Canadians residing here, the fourth largest group of illegals, and 2.7 million Mexicans. Yet, in 1996, only 2,047 illegal Canadians were apprehended and repatriated at the U.S. border, compared to 1.5 million Mexicans.[17]

## SOME MYTHS AND REALITIES

This latest targeting of Latin Americans for mass deportation should come as no surprise given the way a new generation of nativists and eugenicists have whipped up anti-Latino fervor with recycled myths and stereotypes.

*Myth Number 1:* Latin Americans come to this country to get on welfare.

*Reality:* The labor force participation rate—the percentage of those working or actively seeking a job—is far higher for Latin American immigrants than for native-born Americans, and often higher than for other immigrants (see table 6).

TABLE 6
## LABOR FORCE PARTICIPATION RATES FOR
## SELECTED IMMIGRANT GROUPS, 1990[18]

| Country of Birth | % in U.S. Labor Force |
| --- | --- |
| United States average | 65.3 |
| Former Soviet Union | 39.7 |
| Canada | 52.1 |
| Japan | 54.2 |
| United Kingdom | 57.3 |
| Dominican Republic | 63.8 |
| Mexico | 69.7 |
| Colombia | 73.7 |
| India | 74.6 |
| Nicaragua | 74.7 |
| Guatemala | 75.7 |
| El Salvador | 76.3 |
| Philippines | 76.3 |

Not only are Latino immigrants more prone to work than native-born Americans, but a recent California study found that half of all immigrants from western Mexico, whether they are in the United States legally or illegally, return home within two years, and fewer than one-third stay for ten years.[19] Mexicans, remember, constitute nearly 60 percent of all Hispanic immigrants.

*Myth # 2:* Latino immigrants drain public resources such as education and government services.

*Reality:* Numerous studies demonstrate that immigrants in this country make enormous contributions to U.S. society in taxes and Social Security. The major problem is that those contributions are *unevenly distributed* between federal and local governments.

In New York State, for instance, immigrants, the bulk of them Latinos, made up 17.7 percent of the population in 1995, earned 17.3 percent of total state personal income, and paid 16.4 percent of total federal (including social security), state, and local taxes. The problem was that 69 percent of those taxes went to the federal government, while only 31 percent remained in local coffers. A similar study in 1990–1991 of illegal immigrants in Los Angeles County overwhelmingly showed that they contributed $3 billion in taxes, but 56 percent of the money went to Washington, while the local costs of dispensing health care, education, law enforcement, and social services to the county's illegal immigrant population far surpassed the immigrants' contributions.

In essence, young immigrant workers today are paying for the federal budget and Social Security benefits of native workers while local governments are being saddled with paying the social costs of services to those immigrants, and, in the case of illegal immigrants, the states rarely receive the proportionate share of federal funds to pay those expenses, because many of the immigrants do not qualify or are not even officially counted.

Furthermore, the New York study revealed that the state's 1 million immigrants who were naturalized citizens in 1995 had a higher average per capita income ($23,900) and paid more in taxes ($8,600) than native Americans ($18,100 and $6,500, respectively). Altogether, the 2.8 million foreign-born who resided in the state legally—whether as naturalized citizens, legal permanent residents, or political refugees—averaged $6,300 in taxes paid, only slightly less than natives. The big problem was an estimated 540,000 illegal immigrants—16 percent of the state's foreign-born—who averaged significantly lower income and taxes, $12,100 and $2,400. Those illegal immigrants, confined as they are to a low-wage underground economy, can rarely pay taxes without revealing themselves to the government, but neither are they eligible for, and rarely do they utilize, the usual gamut of social services. Many of them would gladly pay their share of taxes in exchange for being legalized.[20]

Two areas where both illegal and legal immigrants do utilize government services extensively are public schools and the health care system, and these areas have become the focus of the allegations that immigrants drain the nation's resources. Proponents of this theory rarely mention that most of the 20 million foreign-born residents of the United States in 1990 came here during the prime working years of their lives. The cost of their education was thus borne by the governments of their homelands, yet the sending countries lost the benefits of that investment in human capital when many of their brightest, most ambitious and resourceful citizens emigrated to the United States. Meanwhile, the United States gained young workers in whose education it did not have to invest any money. As for the children of those immigrants, *all children,* whether from immigrant families or native ones, are a drain on the resources of a country. Only when those children grow up and become productive citizens is the investment made by that society then repaid. So, logically, any calculation of the cost of educating immigrant children should include calculations of their future productivity to the general society.

*Myth #3:* Latino immigrants take jobs away from U.S. citizens.

*Reality:* While some studies do indicate that skilled Asian or West Indian immigrants have had a negative impact on white and black employment in some industries, Latino immigrants, especially those in the country illegally, have actually improved local economies for whites, according to several studies, because their willingness to work for lower wages has rejuvenated the profitability of ailing industries and thus prevented further job losses.[21] (How many big-city restaurants and service establishments, how many construction and landscaping businesses, for instance, could afford to stay in operation if they had to pay their immigrant workers wages comparable to those of native-born Americans?)

## WHY LATINO IMMIGRATION WILL CONTINUE INTO THE TWENTY-FIRST CENTURY

Exploding immigrant stereotypes is one thing. It is far more difficult to grasp what is distinct about Latino immigration and what forces are driving it. Consider these factors:

1. *The catastrophic economic crisis in Latin America.*

Latin America's population is exploding today more rapidly than Europe's did during the great nineteenth-century exodus to the United States, and the conditions its people face are even more dire.[22] As recently as 1950, the populations of the United States and Latin America were roughly equal. Since then, Latin America's has increased at nearly three times our rate (see table 7).

### TABLE 7
### ESTIMATED POPULATION OF THE UNITED STATES, LATIN AMERICA, AND CARIBBEAN

|  | 1950 | 1995 | Increase |
|---|---|---|---|
| United States | 151,000,000 | 263,000,000 | 74% |
| Latin America and Caribbean | 166,000,000 | 481,000,000 | 190% |

The living conditions of that population, especially during the past two decades, have steadily deteriorated. More than 40 percent lived in poverty in 1990, according to the United Nations Economic Commission for Latin America.[23] The region's per capita gross domestic product has actually declined since 1980.[24] Millions of peasants, forced off the land by competition from American agribusiness, have fled to the major cities, where enormous shantytowns have sprouted.

While the majority of Latin Americans suffer deprivation, a tiny elite benefits from an economic boom brought about in large measure by the selling of public assets and the opening of the region's labor market to multinational corporate investment. More of Latin America's wealth is being siphoned to El Norte each day. U.S. corporations and their subsidiaries in the region earned (excluding Puerto Rico) $16.2 billion in profit in 1995, while the total foreign debt of the countries in the region that year was $575 billion, a 25 percent increase from 1992.[25] U.S., West European, and Japanese banks are now owed $1,100 for every man, woman, and child in Latin America.

Among many Latin American families, emigration is no longer simply a question of better opportunity, it is a matter of survival. In some villages and urban neighborhoods of the Caribbean, Mexico, and Central America almost every family has someone working up North and sending money back home to feed those left behind. Between 1980 and 1994, immigrant remittances to just five countries—Colombia, the Dominican Republic, El Salvador, Guatemala, and Mexico—jumped from $700 million to $5.5 billion a year. Add to that as much as $800 million annually that Cuban Americans are believed to send family members in their homeland despite the U.S. trade embargo, plus those amounts that reach Honduras, Nicaragua, and Panama, and the total to the Spanish-speaking Caribbean rim nations approaches perhaps $7 billion. And that's not counting the value of consumer goods, appliances, and clothing that immigrants regularly ship home or take back as gifts when they visit. The cash remittances alone are so large that between 1978 and 1980, they totaled more than all U.S. foreign aid in the world. In El Salvador, remittances are already the number-one source of foreign income, exceeding the value of export revenues.[26]

Latin American immigrants, in short, are preventing the total collapse of their homelands. The only way to keep more of them from leaving for the United States is through economic policies that assure that a greater portion of the wealth their countries produce stays home.

2. *Latino immigration is a movement of urban workers within the New*

*World, not a rural movement of peasants, as was the old European and much of the modern Asian influx.*

The Europeans who came here at the beginning of the century were mostly poor farmers. They left their homelands prepared to sever their ties with the Old World and remake their lives in the New. As Oscar Handlin, the consummate chronicler of their exodus, wrote, "From the westernmost reaches of Europe, in Ireland, to Russia in the east, the peasant masses had maintained an imperturbable sameness; for fifteen centuries they were the backbone of a continent, unchanging while all about them radical changes again and again recast the civilization in which they lived."[27]

Latin American immigration, on the other hand, is a movement of people from the New World's impoverished southern, Spanish-speaking periphery to its more prosperous northern, English-speaking hub. The cultural traditions and national identities of both regions—no matter how immutable some may claim them to be—are still relatively young and in a constant process of change.

Precisely because of their geographic proximity to the United States and their long historical relationship to it, Latin Americans do not come here planning to stay, or planning to integrate into a new and higher civilization. Rather, they come looking to survive, to find a better-paying job. Within every migrant heart beats the hope of returning home someday. Some do, as often as once a year, laden with holiday gifts for relatives. Those who cannot afford the trip keep in regular touch with loved ones by telephone.

This has meant a new fluidity in the migration process unknown among Europeans, one that finds numerous expressions. A son falls into drugs or gangs in South-Central Los Angeles, so the immigrant mother sends him back home to live with a relative in Guatemala or Honduras for a few years. A young woman gets pregnant out of wedlock or is abandoned by her husband in the Dominican Republic, so she leaves for the United States to escape the shame or to find a job to support herself and her child. A Mexican travels back and forth each year from a small farm in Sonora to work in the grape fields of California at harvesttime. A Dominican livery cabdriver in New York City spends the summers driving fares around Manhattan, then spends the winters relaxing in the new house he's built back home in El Cibao.

To a far greater extent than most people realize, this constant movement back and forth—itself a reflection of the removal of restraints to both capital and labor in our new global economy—serves to both rein-

force and undermine aspects of the cultures of the sending and receiving
countries alike. Just as corporations pride themselves on their abilities to
move about the world with ever-increasing rapidity, migrant labor has
become increasingly mobile, and Latin American labor the most mobile
of all.

Latin Americans, moreover, can hardly be considered peasants from
an unchanging countryside, as were the early Europeans. They are, with
the exception of Indians from Mexico, Guatemala, and Peru, largely city
dwellers, a reflection of the fact that since World War II, Latin America
has been transformed into the planet's largest urban ghetto. While in 1930
more than two-thirds of its people lived in the countryside, now more
than three-quarters inhabit cities. Four of the world's ten largest metropolises are located in the region—Rio de Janeiro, Brasília, Buenos Aires,
and Mexico City—each with more than 10 million inhabitants. A staggering thirty-nine other cities contain more than a million residents.[28] By
comparison, the United States had only eight cities in 1990 with more
than 1 million people. The Latin American city is usually a gleaming
downtown core whose infrastructure is bursting at the seams and is en-
veloped by sprawling megaslums of cardboard and corrugated tin.

Before they ever head North, Latin Americans have been exposed to
years of social conditioning about the dream life that awaits them. Hollywood films, U.S. programs on local television, Anglo music on local radio, outdoor billboards plastered with Madison Avenue fashion models,
Spanish translations of U.S. magazines, all combine to create a thirst for
a lifestyle beyond anything that could be satisfied at home.

Moreover, Latin American immigrants, while generally less educated
than migrants from other regions, are usually better educated than their
compatriots who stay behind. Studies of Mexican illegal immigrants, for
instance, show that from 3 to 10 percent are illiterate, whereas illiteracy
in Mexico is at 22 percent.[29] Many Latin American migrants have
worked for years for an American firm in one of the free trade zones,
have studied English, and have thus been socialized into American
methods before arriving. In short, they are far more urbanized, educated,
and socially prepared to adapt to postindustrial U.S. society than were
the Europeans who came here at the beginning of the century. What they
lack, and what their European predecessors found plentiful in the automobile, steel, rubber, and coal factories of the early twentieth century,
are a sufficient number of semiskilled jobs that pay a decent wage and
provide some measure of job security.

3. *Mexicans, the largest of Latino immigrant groups, have historically
been "pulled" here only to be treated as easily deportable labor.*

As we have seen, Mexicans were recruited from south of the border between the 1880s and the 1930s to work on the railroads and in the fields of the southwestern and midwestern United States. More than a million crossed the border between 1920 and 1930 alone.[30] Then the Depression hit, domestic unemployment skyrocketed, and the migrant laborers found they were no longer welcomed. During the 1930s, an estimated 1 million Mexicans were forcibly deported back home.[31] When World War II closed off European and Asian immigration, however, our corporations convinced the federal government to renew the massive importation of Mexican and Latin American labor. Thus began the wartime *bracero* program in 1942. That first year, it brought in 52,000 Mexicans to work in railroad maintenance and agriculture, and after the war, the program became a regular feature of American life, for the Southwest was growing rapidly and agribusiness needed more low-wage workers. In 1950 alone, 450,000 people passed through Mexico's three main *bracero* recruitment centers, and hundreds of thousands more entered the United States illegally to look for work.

Almost as soon as it was reopened, however, the door was slammed shut once again after the Korean War, when a new recession led to anti-Mexican protests by unemployed Anglos. In July 1954, the federal government unleashed one of the darkest periods in immigrant history— "Operation Wetback." Brutal dragnets were conducted in hundreds of Mexican neighborhoods as migrants were summarily thrown into jails, herded into trucks or trains, then shipped back to Mexico. Many of those abducted were American citizens of Mexican descent. The government, ignoring all due process, deported between 1 and 2 million people in a few short months. As soon as the recession ended, however, the demand for Mexican labor picked up again and the *bracero* program was resuscitated. And so it was that the United States perfected two contradictory—some would say hypocritical—policies toward Mexican immigration: while southwestern businesses welcomed cheap Mexican labor and lobbied Congress to allow more migrants in, the federal government, reacting to periodic outbursts of public frustration over the boom-and-bust cycles of our capitalist economy, conducted periodic dragnets to throw them out.

By 1960, thanks in large measure to the "pull" aspect of the *bracero* program, one-quarter of the workforce in the Southwest was immigrant labor from Mexico.[32] President Johnson finally ended the program in 1964, but agribusiness merely supplanted it with a scaled-down version called the H-2 guest worker program. Finally, American manufacturers and the Mexican government came up with a new strategy: instead of bringing Mexicans to work here, they would shift production to Mexico. And so the border industrialization program began in 1966 (see chapter 13).

But the pull factor is not just a reality with Mexicans. Immigration to the United States has always served first and foremost the labor needs of capitalist expansion and contraction. The ever-changing religious, ethnic, and racial composition of the various immigrant waves has historically made it easier for farmers and manufacturers to thwart the inevitable demands of their workers for better wages and working conditions simply by pitting one group of native-born employees against another of newly hired immigrants.

Our contemporary era has been marked by two major upheavals that have intensified the worldwide mobility of labor and capital: the fall of the Communist bloc and the computer/digital revolution. Today, multinational corporations pit whole nations against each other in the competition to get the lowest wages and least restrictive labor and environmental regulations for their new factories. The same governments that face external pressure to reduce all barriers to capital flow also face internal pressures from their own populations for similar freedom of movement.

Here at home, corporations try to drive down costs by hiring more and more low-wage Latino immigrants. Corporate battles against trade unions in the meatpacking and other industries during the 1980s, for instance, led to two-tier wage systems in many areas of the country. Over time, industry managers gradually push the better-paid white workers into early retirement, then replace them with Latino immigrants at the lower-tier wage. Today, employers still pay labor recruiters at the Mexican border to sign up new hands for factories and farms in the South and Midwest, and they rarely care whether those workers are legal or not. INS raids of meatpacking plants in Iowa and Nebraska, for instance, led to the arrest of more than one thousand illegal immigrants between 1992 and 1996, but INS officials estimated that at least twelve thousand undocumented immigrants, most of them Mexicans, were still working at meat plants in those two states alone.[33]

Another example is the former Waste Management, Inc. (now called U.S.A. Waste Management, Inc.), the world's largest disposer of waste. I reported in late 1997 that more than five hundred workers at a WMX plant in Brooklyn, New York—almost all of them South American immigrants and many of them undocumented—were being paid the minimum wage, while a small group of white truck drivers from the company's old workforce earned nearly three times the salary of the Latinos. That year, three of the Latino workers were killed in separate accidents at the plant. The federal government repeatedly fined WMX for safety violations, yet the city administration granted the company a $26 million contract to haul all household trash from the Bronx.[34]

4. *The United States, faced with an aging white population, will need an increasing number of Latin American workers to fill unskilled jobs.*

Along with all the other major powers that fought World War II, the United States confronts a looming demographic crisis in the first half of the twenty-first century—a shortage of young workers. The country's white population is growing inexorably older; median age among whites in 1992 was thirty-four, while among Hispanics it was twenty-six. At the same time, births to Hispanic women are at record levels and increasing. In 1995, Hispanics made up 10.3 percent of the population in the fifty states, but 18 percent of all new births.[35]

By the time most baby boomers retire, 20 percent of the population will be over sixty-five. This demographic reality not only threatens the viability of the Social Security system, but it will also create a huge demand for workers in the health and social service fields, especially for unskilled workers who can take care of an aging population. "Retiring baby boomers need people who can contribute more in taxes than they consume in services," noted one conservative writer.[36] This explains why our classical conservatives have split with neoconservatives over the issue of immigration, with the neoconservatives, who represent the more far-sighted internationalist views of the major corporations, favoring immigration, while classical conservatives such as Pat Buchanan oppose it. Because Latin America contains the closest pool of such ready labor, workers who are easiest to repatriate when they are no longer needed, it will continue to function as a labor reserve for the United States, no matter how loudly the classical conservatives may roar.

In summary, the more that U.S. corporations, U.S. culture, and the U.S. dollar penetrate into Latin America, the more that laborers from that region will be pulled here, and the more that deteriorating conditions in their own homelands will push the migrants here. The effect of this push-and-pull phenomenom creates an irresistible force, and that force produces a constant stream of migrants heading North. Whether we regard this human stream as curse or fortune does not matter, for it is the harvest of empire and it will not be stopped until the empire's expansion is redirected and its prosperity shared more equitably.

# 12

## *Speak Spanish, You're in America!*: El Huracán *over Language and Culture*

It matters not that they be cultivated men
Or rude, wild, barbarous, and gross,
For 'tis enough, and more, to know that they are men
And know that, except for the Fiend himself,
They all are the worst beast, when they do wish,
Of all the ones that God created . . .
　　　　　*—Gaspar Pérez de Villagrá,*
　　　　　　Historia de la Nueva México, *1610*

On August 28, 1995, during a child-custody hearing in a divorce case in Amarillo, Texas, state district judge Samuel Kiser ordered Martha Laureano, a U.S. citizen of Mexican descent, to speak English at home to her five-year-old daughter. "[You are] abusing that child and relegating her to the position of a housemaid," the judge told Laureano after she acknowledged that she spoke only Spanish to the girl. "It's not in her best interest to be ignorant," Kiser said, threatening to end Laureano's custody unless she changed her method of communicating. Newspaper reports of the courtroom exchange rocked Latino households around the country and sparked an outcry from community leaders. While the judge toned down his order and issued a partial apology a few days later, he was only echoing what many white Americans have believed for years.[1]

No issue so clearly puts Hispanic Americans at odds with English-speaking white and black Americans as this question of language. Backers of a constitutional amendment that would make English our official language say that the rising number of immigrants, especially the flood of Latin Americans during the past few decades, is threatening to balkanize the nation into warring linguistic groups, to make English speakers strangers in their own land.

This debate over language, of course, is not unique to the United States. Virtually every modern nation-state confronts linguistic minorities within its borders. In fact, we are in the unique position of being not only the largest English-speaking country in the world, but also the fifth-largest Spanish-speaking one, surpassed only by Mexico, Spain, Argentina, and Colombia.[2]

In this country, however, the squabble over language has been intertwined for years with the even deeper discord over how we interpret and teach the American experience—some call it the dispute over multicultural education. Language, after all, is at the heart of an individual's social identity. It is the vehicle through which the songs, folklore, and customs of any group are preserved and transmitted to its descendants. Given the historic diversity of this country's immigrant populations, our leaders have long perceived English as a critical thread in the national fabric, one that not only provides common means of communication but that also helps to bind the different immigrant groups into one American tapestry.

In his 1991 polemic, *The Disuniting of America,* historian Arthur Schlesinger, Jr., rails against the rising "cult of ethnicity" or "compensatory history" by contemporary advocates of multiculturalism and bilingualism. In the process, Schlesinger serves up his version of the creation story of America: "Having cleared most of North America of their French, Spanish, and Dutch rivals, the British were free to set the mold. The language of the new nation, its laws, its institutions, its political ideas, its literature, its customs, its precepts, its prayers, primarily derived from Britain."[3]

Unfortunately, whether the mythmaking comes from Bible Belt conservatives like Judge Kiser or eastern liberals like Schlesinger, it suffers from the same flaw—a failure to accept that the quest for empire, fueled by the racialist theory of Manifest Destiny, divided and deformed the course of ethnic relations from our nation's inception, fragmenting and subverting any quest for one "national language" and "national culture."

Few of us would disagree that English is the *common* language of the country. Yet the very process of territorial expansion—not just immigration—created repeated battles throughout U.S. history over whether English should be the only recognized tongue. A number of ethnic groups have attempted to preserve their native languages at the same time they adopted English, while our government, especially at the federal level, sought just as strenuously to suppress efforts at bilingualism.

Those language battles from prior eras do not all fall under one neat category—rather, a close examination of them reveals three main trends, and the qualitative differences between those trends gets lost in the rhetoric of the current debate. The first category includes the millions of immigrants who came here from Europe and Asia voluntarily seeking American citizenship, and who, by doing so, were cutting ties with their homelands, adopting the language of their new country and accepting a subsidiary status, if any, for their native tongues.

The second category was made up of the slaves from dozens of African nations who were brought here in chains, forced from the start to give up their various mother tongues, and not permitted even to acquire a reading or writing knowledge of English so that the slaveowners could more easily control and dominate them.

The third category, and the one least understood, encompasses those people who were already living in the New World when their lands were either conquered or acquired by the United States: the Native Americans, the French Creoles of Louisiana, the Mexicans, and the Puerto Ricans. These latter groups became American citizens by force. Congress declared them so without any vote or petition on their part; it did not care what language they spoke nor did it seek their public oath of allegiance.

Since a new sovereignty was imposed on them while they were they still residing on their old lands, these "annexed" Americans could hardly consider themselves foreigners. This turned them into persistent defenders of the right to use their own language, and the new Anglo authorities who took over administration of the states or territories in which they resided occasionally understood that viewpoint and accommodated them. The federal government, on the other hand, reacted with hostility to any linguistic diversity.

Throughout the past two centuries, Anglo historians consistently relegated the languages of these conquered nationalities to the margins of the American experience, dismissing their cultures as either primitive or nonexistent. Despite that marginalization, Latinos in particular managed to preserve their language and traditions by fashioning a parallel subterranean storehouse of music, dance, theater, journalism, literature, and folklore—in English, as well as Spanish. Over time, the culture of Mexicans, Puerto Ricans, Cubans, and other Latinos who resided here gradually fused with one anothers', while continuing to borrow elements from their Latin American homelands. At the same time, this emerging U.S.-Latino culture combined with and reshaped aspects of African American and Euro-American music, dance, and theater, creating in the process a dazzling array of hybrid forms that are today uniquely American, and which are most evident in musical genres such as Tex-Mex,

Cubop, Latin jazz, Latin rock, bugaloo, salsa, rap, and even country rock, but which have spread to other areas of the arts as well. Only in recent years, with the phenomenal growth of Latino immigration, has this underground cultural stream finally surfaced and begun to sweep away the melting-pot myth of the United States. Despite that resurgence, Latinos remain invisible to mainstream chronicles of American culture, and they are virtually absent from the culture's most influential contemporary media, Hollywood movies and television.

## THE EARLY BATTLES OVER LANGUAGE

From the very beginning, the thirteen colonies confronted a quandary over language. Before independence, German was virtually the only tongue spoken throughout fifteen thousand square miles of eastern Pennsylvania, while Dutch was widely used in the Hudson River Valley. Between 1732 and 1800, at least thirty-eight German-language newspapers were published in the Pennsylvania colony, and the University of Pennsylvania established a program in German bilingual education as early as 1780. So widespread was the use of German that the first U.S. Census reported 8.7 percent of Americans spoke it as their first language, almost identical to the proportion of Hispanics in our country in 1990.[4]

The prevalence of a German linguistic minority continued into the twentieth century. By 1900, as many as 600,000 children in American public and parochial schools were being taught in German, nearly 4 percent of the country's school population.[5] Only with the Americanization policy that accompanied World War I was German finally eliminated as a language of instruction.

The experience of European immigrants, however, is not as relevant to the modern-day language debate as that of the annexed nationalities. When Louisiana became a state in 1812, for instance, the majority of its residents spoke French. As a result, until the 1920s, all laws and public documents in the state were published in French and English. The courts, the public schools, even the state legislature operated in two languages. Louisiana's second governor, Jacques Villere, spoke no English and always addressed the legislature in French. As more settlers moved in, and English speakers became the majority during the 1840s, the use of French declined, but it did so through the evolution of the population, not through government fiat, and the rights of French-speaking children continued to be recognized in the public schools.[6]

After the Treaty of Guadalupe Hidalgo imposed American citizenship

on the Mexicans living in the annexed territories, Congress did not require its new subjects to swear allegiance to their new nation or adopt a
new language. Those who did not want to become citizens had to publicly
register their refusal but the lives of the *mexicanos* continued pretty
much as before. As late as the 1870s, more than a quarter century after
annexation, New Mexico's legislature operated mostly in Spanish. By
then, only two of fourteen counties had switched to jury trials in English
and most of the public schools conducted instruction either all in Spanish or bilingually.[7] This did not mean that New Mexicans resisted learning English, only that their opportunities to learn the language were
minimal in isolated rural communities where they composed the overwhelming majority. Because of that, New Mexico was one of the last territories to become a state, in 1913, but it boasted a *mexicano* majority
until 1940. A similar process evolved in the Rio Grande Valley of Texas,
only there *mexicanos* have remained the overwhelming majority for 250
years, with most residents still retaining the use of Spanish while also being fluent in English.

Then there is the language experience of some Native Americans. Oklahoma's Cherokees built a public school system in the 1850s in which 90
percent of the children were taught in their native language while also
learning English. So successful was the effort that Cherokee children of
that era registered higher levels of English literacy than white children in
the neighboring states of Texas and Arkansas. But in the late 1800s, the
federal government initiated a policy of Americanization. It forcibly removed thousands of Indian children from their families and shipped
them to boarding schools to learn English. The disastrous result, as documented by repeated studies during the second half of the twentieth
century, was that 40 percent of Cherokee children became *illiterate in
any language* and 75 percent dropped out of school.[8]

Finally, there is Puerto Rico's forgotten language saga. Shortly after
the U.S. occupation of the island in 1898, Congress declared the territory
officially bilingual, even though its population had spoken Spanish for
four hundred years and almost no one spoke English. Military governor
Guy Henry promptly ordered all public school teachers to become fluent
in the language of their new country, and he instituted an English-
proficiency test for high school graduation. Despite widespread resistance from island politicians, educators, and students, the territory's
Anglo administrators proceeded to make English the language of instruction in all island schools. The result was a near-total breakdown of
the education system as thousands of students stopped attending classes,

and those who stayed struggled to learn academic subjects in a language they did not understand.

Efforts to force Puerto Ricans to learn English continued unsuccessfully for nearly half a century, with only a brief reversion to Spanish instruction in the 1930s when José Padin, the island's education commissioner, tried to reintroduce Spanish. But President Roosevelt promptly fired Padin on the advice of Secretary of the Interior Harold Ickes and brought back the English-only policy. Things remained that way until 1949, when the island's first native-born elected governor, Luis Muñoz Marín, finally ended the hated policy of language suppression. Even though Muñoz and the local legislature reinstituted Spanish as the language of instruction, they still required pupils to learn English as a second language. The Popular Democrats took their reforms one step further in 1965; they brought back Spanish as the official language of the island's local courts. Congress, however, insisted that English remain as the language of the federal courts on the island.[9]

The mere existence of Puerto Rico—an entire U.S. territory whose residents speak Spanish—has created enormous problems for theorists of a monolingual U.S. nation. In 1917, the same year Congress established a literacy test for all foreigners applying for citizenship, it declared Puerto Ricans citizens without requiring them to demonstrate any English proficiency! Once Puerto Ricans began moving to the United States in big numbers after World War II, this contradiction of U.S. citizens who spoke no English was exacerbated. The situation produced such a dilemma that Congress had to include a special "Puerto Rican" provision in the Voting Rights Act of 1965. That law, which suspended literacy tests in southern states where they had been used to prevent blacks from voting, also had a part, Section 4(e), introduced by New York senator Robert Kennedy, that prohibited New York State, which had a sixth-grade education requirement for voters at the time, from denying the vote to any citizen whose education had been in an American-flag school where "predominant classroom instruction was other than English." Through that provision, Congress acknowledged that, at least in the case of Puerto Ricans, U.S. territorial expansion had created Spanish-speaking citizens with a claim to certain linguistic rights.

The Mexican, Puerto Rican, French Creole, and Native American language experiences, then, are markedly different from that of European immigrants, who, as Schlesinger notes, "stayed for a season with their old language" before the next generation adopted English.[10] Spanish, Cajun, and the surviving Native American languages are not "foreign." They are the tongues of long-settled linguistic minorities who were absorbed by an expanding multinational state.

International law has long recognized that linguistic minorities within a multiethnic state like ours have a right to protection against discrimination. Article 53 of the United Nations Charter, for example, urges member states to promote "universal respect for and observance of human rights and fundamental freedom for all without distinction as to race, sex, *language* or religion" (my emphasis). Similar descriptions can be found in the UN Universal Declaration of Human Rights and in proclamations of the European and Inter-American states.[11]

Those principles, however, are routinely violated in this country, where federal courts prohibit discrimination because of a person's race, religion, or national origin, but continue to permit language discrimination. A classic example occurred in Texas in 1975 in the case of *García* v. *Gloor*. Héctor García, the plaintiff in the case, was a twenty-four-year-old native-born Texan who attended public schools in Brownsville and who spoke both English and Spanish. His parents, however, were Mexican immigrants and the family always spoke Spanish at home, so he felt more comfortable in Spanish.

García was hired as a salesman by Gloor Lumber and Supply, Inc., specifically because he could speak Spanish to its customers, but the company had a policy that employees could not speak Spanish *to one another* on the job, though they were free to speak whatever language they wanted off the job. In June 1975, García was dismissed after violating the company rule several times, whereupon he filed a federal discrimination complaint. At the trial, the U.S. district court found that seven of the eight salesmen Gloor employed, and thirty-one of its thirty-nine employees, were Hispanic, that 75 percent of the customers in the Brownsville business area also were Hispanic, and that many of Gloor's customers wished to be waited on by salesmen who spoke Spanish. Alton Gloor, an officer and stockholder, testified that there were business reasons for the Spanish ban, among them: English-speaking customers objected to communications between employees that they could not understand; pamphlets and trade literature were only in English, so employees needed to improve their English skills; and supervisors who did not speak Spanish could better oversee their subordinates. The court ruled in Gloor's favor, finding no discrimination.

The case eventually went to the U.S. Court of Appeals for the Fifth Circuit, which agreed in a May 1980 decision that "Mr. Garcia's use of Spanish was a significant factor" in his firing. The court concluded, however, that García had not suffered national discrimination, even though he presented an expert witness who testified that the "Spanish language is the most important aspect of ethnic identification for Mexican Americans," and even though he was backed in his contention by the Equal Employment Opportunity Commission. The court's decision went on to say

> Mr. Garcia was fully bilingual. He chose deliberately to speak Spanish instead of English while actually at work. . . . Let us assume, as contended by Mr. Garcia, there was no geniune business need for the rule and that its adoption by Gloor was arbitrary. The EEO Act does not prohibit all arbitrary employment practices. . . . It is directed only at specific impermissible bases of discrimination, race, color, religion, sex, or national origin. National origin must not be confused with ethnic or sociocultural traits or an unrelated status, such as citizenship or alienage . . . a hiring policy that distinguishes on some other ground, such as grooming codes or how to run his business, is related more closely to the employer's choice of how to run his business than to equality of employment.

In other words, because García was bilingual, he had lost any right to speak his language—the language for which he was hired and the majority language in the community—at work. Spanish was a "preference" of his, the court said, and an employer could legally ban it just as he could ban "persons born under a certain sign of the zodiac or persons having long hair or short hair or no hair at all."[12] The court thus performed a Solomon-like miracle—severing García's nationality from his language.

## CHICO AND THE MAN—THE WAR OVER IMAGE AND REALITY

The language debate is a nagging reminder that conquering a territory by force does not guarantee the assimilation of that territory's original inhabitants, nor does the passing of a few generations assure the gradual disappearance of their culture. For if conquered people feel themselves systematically mistreated by their conquerors, they inevitably turn their language and culture into weapons of resistance, into tools with which they demand full equality within the conquering society. This is precisely what happened with Latinos in America toward the end of the twentieth century.

Unfortunately, even some of the best Anglo historians have misread that movement as one that is seeking separation rather than inclusion.

Take Pulitzer prize–winner Arthur Schlesinger's response to the multicultural movement. "It may be too bad that dead white European males have played so large a role in shaping our culture," Schlesinger writes in *The Disuniting of America*. "But that's the way it is. One cannot erase history."

The alarmism of Schlesinger and others notwithstanding, no one in the multicultural movement except a few bizarre ethnocentrists ever sought to erase the historical role of "dead white European males" in American history. Rather, most exponents of that movement have endeavored to undo the damage created by several centuries of what Edward Said, one of America's most perceptive social critics, has properly called "cultural imperialism."

A culture's music, song, fiction, theater, and popular lore, Said notes, together with specialized disciplines, sociology, literary history, ethnography, and the like, comprise the narratives by which a people understand the best of themselves, their place in the world, their identity. But over the course of civilization, culture became attached to specific nations and states, and at least since the time of the Greeks, those attachments have led to classifications, often antagonistic notions of "us" and "them," of superior and inferior societies, thus turning culture into another weapon by which the strong dominate the weak. As Said notes,

> The main battle in imperialism is over land, of course; but when it came to who owned the land, who had the right to settle and work on it, who kept it going, who won it back, and who now plans its future—these issues were reflected, contested, and even for a time decided in narrative [culture] . . . the power to narrate, or to block other narratives from forming and emerging, is very important to culture and imperialism and constitutes one of the main connections between them.[13]

In the United States, the link between culture and empire has been harder to grasp, partly because our heterogeneous immigrant society has made even the definition of a "dominant" culture more difficult to distill, but that link is just as strong as it was between the former European powers and their colonies, insists Said:

> Before we can agree what the American identity is made of, we
> have to concede that as an immigrant settler society superimposed
> on the ruins of considerable native presence, American identity is
> too varied to be a unitary and homogeneous thing; indeed the bat-

tle within it is between advocates of a unitary identity and those who see the whole as a complex but not reductively unified one. . . .

Partly because of empire, all cultures are involved in one another; none is single and pure, all are hybrid, heterogeneous, extraordinarily differentiated, and unmonolithic. This, I believe, is as true of the contemporary United States as it is of the modern Arab world.[14]

In his pioneering literary analysis, *Culture and Imperialism,* Said goes on to demonstrate how many of the West's greatest fiction writers, Defoe, Conrad, Kipling, Austen, Malraux, T. E. Lawrence, Melville, and Camus, all unconsciously promoted in their works the imperial ambitions of their separate nations, while they ignored or overlooked the intrinsic value of the colonial cultures in which their novels were set.

Much the same has happened in this country with both classical and popular traditions and culture. During the nineteenth century, Anglo settlers in the Southwest readily adapted the Spanish hacienda styles of architecture, Spanish names for cities, rivers, and even states, Mexican food, the *vaquero* life of the Mexican *rancho,* or the hunting, camping, and solitary worship of nature so prevalent among Native Americans, while they refused to regard the Mexicans or Indians among them as equals. The job of justifying that outlook fell to the dime-store novelists of frontier life, to the travel writers, and to the journalists.

During the twentieth century, Hollywood films and television replaced newspapers and novels as the primary tools for banishing Hispanics to the shadows of American culture. A half-dozen major surveys since the 1970s have documented the virtual absence of Hispanics on television. In *Watching America,* a study of thirty years of television programming from 1955 to 1986, the Center for Media and Public Affairs found that Hispanics averaged barely 2 percent of all characters. Worse, the center discovered that the percentage had steadily decreased, from 3 percent in the 1950s to 1 percent in the 1980s, even as the Hispanic population was skyrocketing. A survey by the Annenberg School for Communication found that Hispanics averaged 1.1 percent of prime-time characters on television from 1982 to 1992, compared to 10.8 percent for African Americans. Since Hispanics comprised at least 9 percent of the population in 1990, that means they were nine times less likely to appear on your living room tube than in real life.

Those few Latino characters who do make it to the screen are disproportionately unsavory. The Center for Media and Public Affairs reviewed 620 fictional television shows from 1955 to 1986 and found that 41 percent of Hispanic characters were portrayed negatively, compared to 31 percent of whites and 24 percent of blacks. A review of 21,000 television characters over a twenty-year period by the Annenberg School of Communications revealed seventy-five Hispanic villains for every one hundred "good" Hispanic characters, compared to thirty-nine white villains for every one hundred "good" white characters.[15]

In Hollywood films, Latinos actually received more prominent leading roles and a wider variety of parts during the 1940s and 1950s than later in the century. Part of that was due to the fact that during and after World War II, Latin Americans were regarded as "Good Neighbors," as important allies against Fascism, so there was pressure to portray them more sympathetically than in the past. In addition, the war cut off the European market for the United States, so studios scrambled to make up for lost revenues by boosting film sales in Latin America. Among the great Latino parts in those years were Anthony Quinn as the daring *vaquero* in *The Ox-Bow Incident* (1943); Ricardo Montalban as the heroic Mexican government official in *Border Incident* (1949); José Ferrer in the Oscar-winning *Cyrano de Bergerac* (1950); Katy Jurado as the savvy businesswoman in *High Noon* (1952); a whole Mexican community in the labor classic *Salt of the Earth* (1953); Cesar Romero, Duncan Renaldo, and Gilbert Roland, all of whom starred in the *Cisco Kid* television series; and perhaps the most famous of all, Desi Arnaz as the charming, hot-tempered Latin husband in *I Love Lucy*.

Once those golden years ended, few identifiably Hispanic actors were able to find work beyond stereotypical and unflattering roles. One major exception was Rita Moreno, who played a Hungarian in *She Loves Me*, a midwestern WASP in *Gentry*, and an Irishwoman in *The Miracle Worker*. There were, of course, those actors whom film viewers rarely considered Hispanic and who thus encountered greater opportunities and a richer variety of roles, among them Quinn, Rita Hayworth, Raquel Welch, and Linda Carter.

By the 1970s, the rash of films portraying Latinos as criminals, drug addicts, or welfare dependent became endless: *Dirty Harry* and *The French Connection* (1971), *The New Centurions* (1972), *The Seven-Ups, Badge 373*, and *Magnum Force* (1973), *Death Wish* (1974), *Boardwalk* (1979), *The Exterminator* (1980), *Fort Apache: The Bronx* (1981), *Colors* (1988), and *Falling Down* (1993).[16]

Whether Hollywood producers realized what they were doing or not is irrelevant. The fact remains that the stunted images and unsympathic portrayals of Latinos the industry produced during the 1970s and 1980s had a devastating impact. To a generation of young Hispanics, they glorified a violent, outlaw, marginal identity. To white Americans, they reinforced prejudices that have accumulated in white folklore since the days of Manifest Destiny. For both groups, they created the "us" and "them" cultural construct Said has revealed as a critical part of imperialist cultural domination. Nowhere to be found in any of these films by Anglo producers and directors was any inkling that Latinos have been a positive force in U.S. society, that we possessed a culture of any value before we were conquered, or that we contributed to or expanded the culture of this nation.

## LATINO CULTURE RIGHT HERE—NOTES ON AN UNTOLD STORY

Latino literary heritage in this country dates back to 1610, when Gaspar Pérez de Villagrá penned the first epic poem in U.S. history, *Historia de la Nueva México*. A Mexican-born *criollo,* Pérez de Villagrá accompanied the expedition of *conquistador* Juan de Oñate, which colonized New Mexico and conquered the Pueblo Indians in 1599. The poem, written fourteen years before Captain John Smith's *General History of Virginia,* is an account of that expedition and of the capture of the Pueblo city of Acoma.[17] Although a Spanish court subsequently convicted Oñate for atrocities against the natives and banished him from New Mexico,[18] Pérez de Villagrá's epic remains a frightening yet stirring tale of its times. It is written in the classical *canto* style of Spain's Golden Age, using hendecasyllabic verse (metrical lines of eleven syllables each). While much of it gets bogged down in mundane events that lose any poetic quality, some of the best passages rival those found in the *Iliad* or *Paradise Lost.* Yet few American-literature students have heard of the poem.

Some of that is understandable, given that Pérez de Villagrá wrote in Spanish and this epic dates back nearly four hundred years, but the same cannot be said of Felix Varela's work. Perhaps no single Latino left a greater imprint on nineteenth-century American culture than Varela, the father of the Catholic press in the United States. A Cuban-born priest, philosophy professor, and revolutionary, Varela fled his native country in 1823 to avoid arrest by the Spanish Crown and settled in Philadelphia. There he published Cuba's first proindependence newspaper, *La Habanera,* and dedicated himself to translating important English works into Spanish, including Thomas Jefferson's *A Manual of Parliamentary Practice* and Sir Humphry Davy's *Elements of Agricultural Chemistry.*

Eventually, he was appointed pastor of his own church in New York City, where he developed a legendary reputation for his work among New York's Irish immigrants, creating dozens of schools and social services for the city's poor and even founding the New York Catholic Temperance Association in 1840. He rose to become vicar-general of the New York Archdiocese, but it was in the realms of theology and literature that Varela left his most important legacy. Among the pioneering publications he founded and edited were *The Protestant's Abridger and Annotator* (1830), the country's first ecclesiastical review; the weekly *Catholic Observer* (1836–1939); and the first two literary and theological Catholic journals, *The Catholic Expositor and Literary Magazine* (1841–1843) and the *Catholic Expositor* (1843–1844). Even as he juggled his amazing workload, Varela found time to encourage and mentor a generation of patriots back in his homeland, where he is still revered as the greatest Cuban thinker of his time. He died in 1853 in Saint Augustine, Florida, without ever getting to seeing his Cuba free of Spanish rule.[19]

Meanwhile in the Southwest, the *mexicanos* living in the annexed territories saw their cultural ties with Mexico become stronger, not weaker, after 1848, for they often traveled back and forth across the border and drew consistent nourishment from Mexico's well-established theater, music, art, and folklore traditions. At the same time, they came under increasing influence from black, Anglo-Saxon, and immigrant European culture.

The first Latino-owned theater in this country was in Los Angeles, where *mexicano* theatrical companies had been mounting professional performances since the early 1820s. Antonio Coronel, a wealthy *californio* who served for a time as the city's mayor, opened his three-hundred-seat Coronel Theater in 1848. Perhaps because of the influence of his Anglo wife, Mariana Williamson, Coronel staged his plays in both Spanish and English. By the late 1850s, his theater had competition from several others, including Vicente Guerrero's Union Theater, Abel Stearn's Arcadia Hall, and Juan Temple's Temple Theater, all of which staged performances in Spanish. The state's Spanish-theater movement became so well known that by the 1860s a few top Mexican and Latin American companies relocated there.[20]

The heyday of Mexican American theater, however, was the 1920s, when the Mexican revolution sparked an artistic renaissance that spilled over into the *mexicano* communities of the Southwest. Those communities had expanded in size with migrants who came North to work in American factories during World War I. After the war, thousands of Mexican Americans returned home from the European battlefields. The returning veterans had a more cosmopolitan view of the world and enough money in their pockets to support a fledgling entertainment industry.

Something else had happened in Latin America at the turn of the century. A new generation of writers and artists began to define a literary and social view of the world that was distinct from both Europeans and Anglo Americans. This new philosophy, the *modernista* movement, a form of Pan Latin–Americanism, drew on the unique mixture of African, Indian, *mestizo,* and *mulato* traditions of the region. In 1900, Uruguayan positivist José Enrique Rodó published *Ariel,* one of the most famous works of Latin American literature, in which he claimed the United States had lost its original idealism to materialist values, and that it was up to Latin America to preserve the idealism the New World represented. Rodó and Nicaraguan poet Rubén Darío were the most celebrated of the modernists. Six years before Rodó's *Ariel,* José Martí published his seminal essay "Our America," in which he argued that Latin American artists, intellectuals, and political leaders needed to draw inspiration from the real history of their own countries, not by importing theories and views of Europe and the Old World.

"The European university must bow to the American university," Martí declared. "The history of America, from the Incas to the present, must be taught in clear detail and to the letter, even if the archons of Greece are overlooked. Our Greece must take priority over the Greece which is not ours. . . . Let the world be grafted onto our republics, but the trunk must be our own."[21]

In response to that new awareness here and below the border, playwrights like Esteban Escalante, Gabriel Navarro, Adalberto Elias González, and Brigido Caro created the first theatrical works depicting Mexican life in this country rather than using themes from Spain. Stylistically, the new playwrights experimented with a variety of forms, from old Spanish *zarzuelas,* to *bufos cubanos,* to *revistas,* to *comedias*. Caro's classic *Joaquin Murieta,* for instance, told the tragic story of the heroic California rebel most white Americans knew only as a bandit. Similar theater movements arose in San Antonio and Tucson as well. And the renaissance was not confined just to Mexicans; whites often attended theater performances.[22]

At the other end of the country, Cuban, Spanish, and Puerto Rican actors and playwrights also created a thriving theater movement in New York City and Tampa. Cuban Alberto O'Farrill was the master of *bufos cubanos,* perfecting the classic role of a poor, comic Afro Cuban in 1920s New York. During the same decade, Puerto Rican actor Erasmo Vando and playwrights Juan Nadal and Gonzalo O'Neill garnered a wide following from the city's small but growing Hispanic community. O'Neill's

1928 play, *Bajo una sola ḫandera,* electrified theatergoers with its daring advocacy of Puerto Rican independence from the United States.

But the greatest advances in Latino culture, the area in which Latinos most often intermingled with, borrowed from, and greatly transformed American culture, has been in music. It is hard to overstate the immense influence Latin American music has had—from the mid-nineteenth century to the present—on the various forms of popular music in the United States, whether among whites or among blacks.

Critic John Storm Roberts, in his brilliant study, *The Latin Tinge: The Impact of Latin American Music on the United States,* traces the earliest influences to two places, South Texas and New Orleans. Along the Rio Grande Valley, Mexicans developed *corrido* music, folk ballads that were sung to the polka, waltz, or march music, and whose lyrics chronicled real events of the day, from gun battles and wars, to crimes and love affairs, to cattle drives and the coming of the railroads. The average *corrido* was usually so filled with dates, names, and factual details that it functioned not only as entertainment but also as a news report, historical narrative, and commentary for the mass of Mexicans who were still illiterate. One of the earliest *corridos* told the story of General José Antonio Canales and his guerrilla attacks against the U.S. Army in the Mexican-American War. Another related the life and times of Juan Cortina, while others recounted the atrocities of the Texas Rangers and the exploits of Mexican outlaws. Perhaps the most popular *corridos* were of Gregorio Cortez, the early-twentieth-century outlaw falsely accused of being a horse thief.

On the southwestern frontier, it was not unusual for wagon trains of Mexicans and Anglo cowhands to cross paths, camp together for the night, and start a friendly campfire competition between *corrido* singers and Anglo ballad singers, thus initiating musical exchanges between the two cultures.[23]

In New Orleans, one of the first piano virtuosos in the United States, Louis Moreau Gottschalk (1829–1869), started introducing Cuban elements into his classical American compositions in the 1850s, creating such works as "Ojos Criollos" and "Escenas Campestres Cubanas," an orchestra suite, as well as "Marche des Gibaros," which was based on a Puerto Rican folk song. New Orleans emerged as a center for more than just the fusion of classical music themes. By the end of the nineteenth century, Mexican and Cuban musicians, together with descendants of the original Spanish residents of Louisiana, were playing major roles in the flourishing ragtime scene of the city's Latin Quarter. "Latin rhythms have been absorbed into black American styles far more consistently than into white popular music, despite Latin music's popularity among whites," Roberts notes.[24] Perlops Nuñez, for instance, ran one of the city's first black bands in the 1880s, and Jimmy "Spriggs" Palau played with famous jazzman Buddy Bolden. As New Orleans ragtime and then jazz evolved, they drew considerable inspiration from Mexican, Cuban, and later Brazilian music.

By the early twentieth century, a succession of Latin music forms captivated the American public. In 1913, Vernon and Irene Castle, a husband-and-wife dance team, performed their first tango at New York's Knickerbocker Theater, touching off a nationwide tango craze. Then, in the late 1920s, the Hurtado brothers of Guatemala started recording and performing the *marimba* music of Guatemala; soon a half-dozen *marimba* bands were touring the country to huge receptions. The Cuban composer Ernesto Lecuona became popular with Broadway composers, who soon took to imitating Lecuona's *habanera* songs. George Gershwin's "Argentina" and Richard Rodger's "Havana" are only two examples from that decade.[25]

By the late 1920s, Caribbeans were fusing their arrangements with the ragtime and jazz greats of New York City. Writer Ruth Glasser has reconstructed the little-known saga of how a group of great Puerto Rican musicians, all products of a rich tradition of classical training on the island, migrated to New York and initiated collaborations with African American musicians that reshaped the musical history of the city.

That collaboration was started by Lieutenant James Reese Europe, the composer and bandleader who conducted the most famous musical group of World War I, the 369th Infantry "Hellfighters" Band. While he was putting together the band, Europe convinced his commander, Colonel William Hayward, to let him travel to Puerto Rico in 1917 to recruit some wind instrument players. Europe had heard that Puerto Rico was brimming with talented musicians, thanks to a long tradition of army and municipal marching bands under the Spaniards. Better yet, all the Puerto Ricans could read sheet music—and they usually played more than one instrument. During a quick trip to the island, Europe recruited eighteen young men, among them Rafael Hernández, who would become Puerto Rico's greatest composer, singer, and bandleader; Hernández's brother, Jesús; and clarinetist Rafael Duchesne, the scion of an illustrious family of composers and conductors.

After the war, Hernández and the other Puerto Ricans moved to New York. Several of them ended up playing for Broadway pit bands or in jazz orchestras of the day. Their success prompted more Puerto Rican and Cuban musicians to leave home for New York's bright lights. Puerto Rican trombonist Francisco Tizol, for instance, played for the 1922 show

*Shuffle Along,* and both he and fellow trombonist Fernando Arbelo were regulars in Fletcher Henderson's band; tuba player Ralph Escudero worked in the orchestra of *Chocolate Dandies* in 1928; and clarinetist Ramón "Moncho" Usera in *Blackbirds.*[26]

In 1929, Cuban Mario Bauza, already a veteran of Havana's symphony orchestra, arrived in New York. He spent the next ten years playing for the greatest bandleaders of the era, among them Noble Sissle, Don Redman, Cab Calloway, and Chick Webb. While in Calloway's band, Bauza played alongside another young trumpet player, Dizzy Gillespie. Likewise, Augusto Coen, the Ponce-born son of an American Jew and Afro–Puerto Rican mother, arrived in New York in the 1920s. A virtuoso with the guitar, trumpet, and several other instruments, Coen went on to perform with Sissle, Duke Ellington, Henderson, and others.

The tango rage of the 1920s was followed by the rumba craze of the 1930s, a sound pioneered by Cuban big-band leaders like Don Azpiazu, Xavier Cugat, and later, Desi Arnaz. In its first Broadway performance in 1930, Azpiazu's orchestra introduced what would become the most famous Cuban tune in U.S. history, "El Manicero" ("The Peanut Vendor"). Those early bands exposed American audiences for the first time to the powerful and exotic combination of Cuban instruments—*maracas, claves, güiros, bongós, congas,* and *timbales*—many of which would later be adopted by countless white and black musical groups. By adopting English lyrics to their tunes, and often by featuring American women as vocalists, Azpiazu, Cugat, and Arnaz pioneered the first successful commercial crossover bands among Anglos. Throughout the 1940s, Hollywood produced dozens of movies with Latin tunes and themes, making bandleaders like Cugat *(Holiday in Mexico, The Three Caballeros)* and Arnaz *(Cuban Pete)* stars in the process. Bing Crosby and Bob Hope starred in *Road to Rio* (1947), and Groucho Marx and Carmen Miranda were paired in *Copacabana.*

But for serious lovers of music, the most exciting experiments were happening uptown in Harlem and in the jazz clubs of Manhattan, where the great Afro-Cuban and Afro–Puerto Rican musicians, still ignored by a race-conscious country, were exploring new forms with the great black bands. By the 1940s, some of those Cubans and Puerto Ricans, Bauza, Coen, Frank "Machito" Grillo, and Alberto Socarrías, began to form their own orchestras. Their groups fused the big-band sound of American music—with its clarinet, saxophone, and trumpet sections—to island instruments such as *panderetas, maracas, güiros and bongós;* they adapted the Cuban *guarachas* and *son* and the Puerto Rican *danzas* and *plenas t*o lyrics of their new American reality, and out of all that came new hybrid musical genres.

No major musician in the country, whether on Broadway, in Hollywood, at the major recording studios, or in the concert halls, escaped the influence of the new Latino music they created. Glenn Miller, Cab Calloway, Charlie Parker, Woody Herman, all of them experimented with fusing jazz and Cuban music—and later the Brazilian samba. Nat "King" Cole recorded his first Latin-inspired album, *Rumba a la King,* in Cuba in 1946 with "Chocolate" Armenteros, one of the greatest of Cuban trumpet players. Out of those experiments, two separate but interrelated musical styles emerged by the 1950s, the mambo, which was popularized by musicians like Perez Prado, Tito Puente, and Tito Rodriguez, and Cubop or Afro-Cuban jazz, whose creative founders were Machito, Stan Kenton, Dizzy Gillespie, Chano Pozo, Puente, and others.

Meanwhile, British pianist George Shearing, who had been experimenting with Latin music for a decade, organized a new quintet in 1953 to play Latin-oriented jazz in California. The musicians Shearing recruited would became a virtual musical hall of fame decades later. They included Cubans Mongo Santamaria on *conga* and Armando Peraza on *bongó,* Puerto Rican Willie Bobo on *timbales*, and Swedish-American Cal Tjader on vibraphones.[27]

A simultaneous but distinct fusion of Latin and Euro-American music occurred in South Texas, where the *norteño* music of Mexico gave rise to *conjunto,* or Tex-Mex. The development of *conjunto* is explored in Manuel Peña's incisive study, *The Texas-Mexican Conjunto: History of a Working Class Music.* Peña traces how the accordion, a European instrument, was adopted into Mexican music as early as the 1850s. But it was not until South Texan Narciso Martinez, a master of the Chicano accordion style, combined in 1928 with Santiago Almedia, who played the Mexican *bajo sexto,* that the main instrumental components of *conjunto* were created. The other major *conjunto* musician of the 1930s was Santiago "Flaco" Jimenez.[28] The *ranchera, corrido,* and *conjunto* forms gradually spread beyond the Mexican border towns and seeped into American country music. In the Southwest, Roberts notes, country music "took both guitar techniques and songs from Mexican sources. The 'Spanish Two-Step' has been suggested as the origin of 'San Antonio Rose,' and 'El Rancho Grande' was played by almost all western swing bands and has become a 'standard' in country music."[29]

The Chicano influence on American music, especially on rock and country, continued from the 1950s on, from the Latin rock of Carlos Santana, to the country rock of Linda Ronstadt, to the wild Tex-Mex rock and roll of Freddy Fender, to the fusion style of "Little Joe" Hernandez and La Familia, finally, to the pop Tex-Mex of Selena Quintanilla.

———

If the period between World Wars I and II marked the rise of Latino theater and music, the 1960s saw the rise of Latino literature, marked by classics such as José Antonio Villareal's *Pocho* (1959), Piri Thomas's *Down These Mean Streets,* and Rudolfo Anaya's coming-of-age classic, *Bless Me Ultima.* The long delay in the rise of English-language Latino literature should come as no surprise. It is one thing to learn a new language, quite another to develop a literary tradition in that language.

Since then, we have witnessed a surge of Latino creativity—from the novels and stories of Nicolasa Mohr, Sandra Cisneros, Danny Santiago, Oscar Hijuelos, Cristina García, Julia Alvarez, and Ana Castillo, to the poetry of Pedro Pietri, Tato Laviera, and Martín Espada, to the theater and films of Luis Valdéz, Dolores Prida, and Edward James Olmos.

The Mariel exodus, in addition, brought some of Cuba's finest writers and artists to the United States. Refugees Reinaldo Arenas, author of the classic *Hallucinating World,* Juan Abreu, Carlos Alfonzo, Victor Gómez, and Andrés Valerio sparked a revival of the arts in the émigré community soon after their arrival, and with it, a renewal of pride in Cuban culture.[30]

In summary, Latino artists accomplished several simultaneous fusion movements, whether in theater, music, literature, or film. They borrowed and absorbed lessons from one another's separate national experiences. They found reinforcement and new approaches from the artistic traditions of Latin America. And they explored and adapted the styles and content of African American and Anglo American artists. Out of all these fusion efforts, they created a new, many-faceted, and vibrant Latino branch of American culture. Yet none of these accomplishments show up in high school texts, Hollywood films, or network television shows.

## BILINGUALISM AND THE HUNGER TO FORGET LANGUAGE

Unfortunately, most of the debate around language has centered on the "threat" of bilingualism, even though, according to virtually all studies, most Latinos believe that mastery of English is critical for their progress in this country. They believe it so fervently that 75 percent of Hispanic immigrants are speaking English on a daily basis by the time they have lived in the United States for fifteen years, and 70 percent of the children of those immigrants become dominant in or only speak English.[31]

Even in the nineteenth century, Mexican newspapers rejected a separatist philosophy and embraced the need to learn English. Francisco Ramirez's newspaper, *Clamor Público*, added a page in the 1850s to help its readers learn the language. But those early *mexicanos* rejected the view that Spanish was a "foreign" tongue, so they defended its continuing use. *El Independiente*, of Las Vegas, Nevada, for instance, urged its readers to learn English while not allowing Spanish "to be trampled underfoot." A major goal of LULAC, the nation's oldest Hispanic civil rights group, since its founding early in the century, has been to teach English to all immigrants.

In his 1982 best-selling autobiography, *Hunger of Memory*, writer Richard Rodriguez recounts how he immersed himself in the English language from his earliest years in school as a way of willing himself to become "a middle-class American man. Assimilated."[32]

Those 1950s English immersion programs did succeed in one sense. They turned Richard Rodriguez, myself, and thousands of others from our generation into skillful users of the English language. But what of the many who faltered and were left back in school again and again, only to end up illiterate in two languages? Or who were tracked into special education or vocational programs only because they could not master English and ended up dropping out of school?

Those childhood memories of sink-or-swim immersion programs turned me into a consistent advocate of bilingual education. By that, I do not mean the most extreme form, the "maintenance model," which seeks to maintain Spanish literacy often to the detriment of rapid English acquisition and thus leads to government-subsidized cultural enclaves, but of the "transitional" model instead.

Bilingual education, in fact, was born not among poor Hispanics but among upper-class Cuban refugees who arrived in Miami in the 1960s. Initially financed by the federal government, the program sought to make what was then considered a temporary stay by the refugees as easy as possible. Over the years, the policy turned into a vast jobs program, first for Cuban professionals and then for other middle-class Latin Americans who were recruited from abroad to teach in the bilingual programs that proliferated across the country.

Had most schools adopted the "transitional" bilingual model, which instructs in the native language for a limited amount of time—two to four years—while the child masters English, the acrimony of the current debate might have been mitigated. But extreme positions on both sides drew the most media attention. In the new climate of "Americanization," proponents of total immersion have gained momentum. Under this system, children are placed in intensive English-language courses until they gain a basic knowledge of the language, which means they fall behind in their other subjects. It also means their knowledge of Spanish is treated as a handicap, not as an asset.

Critics of bilingual education correctly point to the excesses of a bilingual bureaucracy that feeds on itself.[33] They point to New York City, for instance, where studies show that 25,000 students were kept in bilingual programs for four or more years. But changing a child's language is not as simple as learning to dress differently. It involves a complex switching of cultural markers that, if not handled properly, can lead to years of psychological repercussions. The older a child is when he or she begins the transition, the more difficult it becomes to achieve mastery in the new language. In the case of Puerto Ricans and Mexican Americans who have been born and raised as American citizens in households where Spanish has been a part of family life for generations, language becomes integral to a sense of who one is.

Native language retention is no doubt higher among Hispanics than other immigrants, but that is caused by very real factors—proximity to the cultural influence of Latin America and fifty years of continued massive immigration. Throughout the Mexican border region, for example, broadcasts from television and radio stations in Mexico can be picked up on the American side (just as broadcasts from the U.S. side can be heard in Mexico). In a small city like El Paso, Texas, which sits across the Rio Grande from the far larger Mexican metropolis of Juárez, it should surprise no one that the Spanish language and Mexican culture exercise a dominant influence.

The fear of some Americans that English will soon be replaced as the country's language is more than wrong, it borders on paranoia. If anything, the global reach of American commerce and communications is accomplishing the opposite. Throughout Latin America, English is virtually the second language of all public schools, the main language of many private academies, and the principal language on the Internet. It is everywhere in the mass media and in advertising. It is already the lingua franca of empire. At night, in cities throughout the southern half of the hemisphere, hundreds of thousands of young Latin Americans eagerly pack private schools to learn it. Young Latinos who are raised in this country are proud of their English and often recoil with greater disgust than white students at the idea of having to study Spanish in high school. In a strange way, those Latino students have internalized the broader society's scorn of Spanish, as if admitting that you speak a language different from that of the majority relegates you to a status of less than American.

What is needed in our country is not some constitutional amendment declaring English the official language and giving the green light to employers and xenophobic politicians to persecute the use of Spanish. Rather, we need a renewed emphasis on Spanish instruction among English-speaking Americans as part of a newfound appreciation for our own country's multicultural roots. The public schools should be providing a broader education to our youth by inculcating them with an appreciation of the significant Hispanic cultural contributions to our nation. They should be dissecting and analyzing the new hybrid cultural trends that emerged in the twentieth century from the amalgamations and fusions of Latino, Anglo, and black arts. From Tex-Mex, bugaloo and mambo, to Latin jazz, reggae, rap, and hip-hop, these new musical genres are our best examples of cultural bridges. History is filled with examples of other great nations that sought to stamp out "differences" of race, religion, language, only to end up destroying themselves. We fool ourselves to think our fate will be any different from that of those who preceded us.

As Pérez de Villagrá, the first poet on American soil, wrote more than 350 years ago as he described the battle at Acoma between the Spanish and the Pueblos:

> *It matters not that they be cultivated men*
> *Or rude, wild, barbarous, and gross,*
> *For 'tis enough, and more, to know that they are men*
> *And know that, except for the Fiend himself,*
> *They all are the worst beast, when they do wish,*
> *Of all the ones that God created . . .*[34]

# 13

## Free Trade: The Final Conquest of Latin America

After two centuries, England has found it convenient to adopt free trade *because* it thinks that protection can no longer offer it anything . . . my knowledge of our country leads me to believe that within two hundred years, when America has gotten out of protection all that it can offer, it too will adopt free trade.

—*Ulysses S. Grant*

During the second half of the twentieth century a momentous shift occurred in American economic life. U.S. transnational firms searching for cheap labor and maximum profit shifted much of their manufacturing to Third World countries, especially to Latin America. As part of that shift, the U.S. government led a worldwide campaign to convince developing nations to lower the high tariffs protecting their domestic industries and to adopt "free trade" policies. That campaign, as we will see in this chapter, has further distorted Latin America's economic development, increased the income gap between rich and poor, and accelerated labor migration to our shores.

North Americans at first ventured into Mexico, the Caribbean, and Central America during the nineteenth century to buy up land and build massive transportation projects: Vanderbilt's Nicaraguan Transit Company, Minor Keith's Central American Railroad, Aspinwall's Panama Railroad, for example. By the early twentieth century, the main methods of exploitation had shifted to extracting raw materials—bananas, sugar, coffee, oil—and to financing the operations of Latin American governments. The region grew to be so important that by 1914, U.S. companies had $416 million in direct investments in Mexico alone, the highest of any country in the world, and Latin America overall accounted for nearly half of all U.S. foreign investment in the world.[1]

The period after World War II brought a third shift, as U.S. apparel, then electronics, plastics, and chemical companies, started closing down factories at home and reopening them abroad. That offshore production is at the heart of the free trade model the United States has promoted and perfected in Latin America. It is a model that has developed in four stages:

1. Panama and Puerto Rico (1947).
2. Mexico's border industrialization program (1965).
3. The Caribbean Basin initiative (1985).
4. NAFTA (1994).

As quickly as industrial plants were shuttered in the Northeast and Midwest, scores of shiny new industrial parks and factory towns, usually called free trade zones (FTZs) or export processing zones (EPZs), sprang up south of the border. By 1992, there were more than 200 of these zones in Mexico and the Caribbean Basin. They housed more than 3,000 assembly plants, employed 735,000 workers, and produced $14 billion in annual exports to the United States.[2]

These free trade zones were allowed to operate as virtual sovereign enclaves within the host countries, routinely ignoring the few local labor and environmental laws that existed. Inside the zones, child labor was reborn and the most basic rights of workers trampled. As agricultural production in many Latin American countries fell under the sway of foreign agribusiness, millions of Latin America's young people abandoned the countryside to find work in or near the zones. But the cities to which the migrants moved lacked infrastructures of roads, sewage systems, housing, and schools to sustain the surge in population. Worker shantytowns sprang up overnight, and with the shantytowns and the factories came industrial pollution, untreated human waste, disease, crime—in short, a public health nightmare.

Thus free trade, which was supposed to stabilize the economies of the countries involved, has actually made conditions worse, and the free trade zones, instead of providing Latin Americans with living wage jobs, have probably fueled massive Latin American emigration to the United States.

Typically, the young Latin American worker from the countryside arrives in the local city and finds work in a free trade zone in factories now commonly known as *maquiladoras* or *maquilas*. There, the worker is trained in rudimentary industrial skills—the rigors of assembly production, the discipline of time, the necessity for obedience to instructions. At night, the worker begins studying English in the scores of private language schools that abound in the new urban environment. He or she becomes immersed in American shows on the newly bought television—

*maquila* workers in Honduras are more likely to own a television (67 percent) than non-*maquila* workers (60 percent); in fact, they are more likely to own a television than a stove (49 percent) or a refrigerator (24 percent).[3] Each day, the worker devours the Spanish-language magazines and newspapers that are easily available in the cities and which glorify life in the United States. The worker quickly learns she can earn ten times the salary she gets in the *maquila* doing the same job in a factory across the border. Eventually, filled with her new consciousness and disgusted with her dead-end shantytown existence, the worker saves up the money to pay a *coyote* and risks the trip to El Norte.

## DO AS I SAY, NOT AS I DO

The term "free trade" seems innocuous at first glance. Who could be against the idea that nations should seek the maximum freedom to trade with each other? Or that increased trade will bring with it increased prosperity? Unfortunately, the history of most major industrialized nations is just the opposite. None of them practiced free trade during their early period of economic growth. Instead, they used high tariffs to protect their domestic industries from foreign competition, often engaging in tariff wars against rivals.

"In the early days, when British industry was still at a disadvantage, an Englishman caught exporting raw wool was sentenced to lose his right hand, and if he repeated the sin he was hanged," Uruguayan journalist Eduardo Galeano reminds us.[4]

Only when England gained a decided advantage over all other countries in world commerce did its government begin advocating free trade in the nineteenth century. During the early days of Latin American independence, England used the slogan to justify bullying the new *criollo* governments. In the 1850s, for instance, British and French warships sailed up the Río Paraná to force the protectionist government of Argentine leader Juan Manuel de Rosas to open his country's prospering market to British bankers and traders.[5] Eventually, the British concentrated on controlling the South American market, ceding control over most of the Caribbean region to the United States.

In our own country, Congress pursued protectionist policies throughout the post–Civil War period, an era of extraordinary industrial growth for the nation. "In every year from 1862 to 1911, the average [U.S.] duty on all imports exceeded 20 percent ... [and] in forty-six of those fifty years ... [it] exceeded 40 percent," notes economist Alfred Eckes, who served on the International Trade Commission under President Reagan.[6] Germany pursued a similar protectionist policy during its nineteenth-century industrial expansion. Not surprisingly, both the German and the U.S. economies experienced higher growth rates during that century than did England, the era's main proponent of free trade.

Despite the historical record, most neoliberal economists in the advanced industrial nations continue to praise the fall of tariffs and the growth of free trade during the past few decades. They contrast the new open global marketplace to the "bad old days" of 1970s, when Third World governments resorted to high tariffs to protect their own fledgling industries, a strategy called import substitution.

But does expanded world commerce automatically spur an increase in wealth, as the free traders say? And just who are the main beneficiaries of today's surge in international trading?

Free trade proponents would have us believe this unfettered commerce is occurring between millions of businessmen in scores of countries and that the money changing hands is creating more and better-paid workers, who then have more money to consume, which in turn means that markets expand. But the reality is quite different. Two-thirds of all the trade in the world today is between multinational corporations, and one-third of it represents multinational corporations trading with their own foreign subsidiaries! A General Motors plant in Matamoros, for example, moves parts and finished cars between itself and the parent company in the United States; or Zenith ships machinery to expand one of its twelve assembly plants operating in Reynosa. Between 1982 and 1995, exports of U.S. multinational corporations more than doubled, but the portion of those exports that represented intracompany trading more than tripled. As a result of this enormous expansion of multinationals, the largest private traders and employers in Mexico today are not Mexican firms but U.S. corporations.[7]

Furthermore, if free trade leads to greater prosperity, why has economic inequality soared and poverty deepened in virtually every Third World country that adopted neoliberal free trade policies? According to the United Nations, the 225 richest people in the world had a net worth in 1997 equal to the income of 2.5 billion people, 47 percent of the world's population.[8]

---

Latin America now suffers from the most uneven distribution of wealth in its history. Before the 1980s, Latin Americans generally protected their domestic industries through heavy government ownership, high tariffs, and import substitution. Mexico pursued that policy from 1940 to 1980, and during that time it averaged annual growth rates of more than 6 percent, with both manufacturing output and real wages for industrial workers growing consistently. But then came the debt crisis of the 1980s. Along with other Latin American countries, Mexico was gradually pressured by U.S.-controlled international financial institutions to adopt neo-liberal, free trade policies. Those policies included selling public assets and increasing exports to pay down its debt. Between 1982 and 1992, the Mexican government sold off eleven hundred of fifteen hundred state-owned companies and privatized more than eighteen banks. This fire sale, instead of bringing prosperity, only deepened the chasm between rich and poor, as a new crop of Mexican billionaires emerged, real wages plummeted, and 200,000 Mexicans lost their jobs.[9]

Mexico, however, was not the birthplace of Latin America's free trade model. Rather, it started in two territories the United States directly controlled.

## THE FIRST EXPERIMENTS—PUERTO RICO AND PANAMA

The first attempts by American corporations to operate offshore factories on any grand scale started in the late 1940s in the Panama Canal Zone and Puerto Rico, where pliant local governments cooperated in setting up corporate oases that included: no tariffs or local taxes; super-low wages; minimal enforcement of environmental and labor laws; financial incentives from Washington for companies to relocate there; and federal tax exemption for the repatriated income of the company. By the 1980s, six hundred firms had factories operating in the Colón Free Zone on the Atlantic Coast, where they could take advantage of Panama's 75-cent-an-hour wages.[10]

But Puerto Rico's experiment was far more extensive. The whole island was turned into a virtual free trade zone, thanks to a little-known loophole in the Internal Revenue Service Code—called Section 936 in its last incarnation—which exempted from federal taxes the income of U.S. subsidiaries.

First to arrive was Textron, which relocated to the island in 1947 after shutting six of its U.S. mills and laying off 3,500 workers. By the early 1950s, more than one new factory a week was being inaugurated. But the job boom proved ephemeral. As more U.S. companies opened up, Puerto Rican–owned factories, unable to compete, were driven out of business.

During the first ten years of the program, new U.S. factories created 37,300 island jobs, but the job losses among Puerto Rican manufacturers totaled 16,600.[11]

And something else happened. The new jobs the factories created were not sufficient to dent the soaring unemployment caused by the rapid mechanization of agriculture and the flight of people to the cities. As a result, both the U.S. and Puerto Rican governments actively encouraged migration to the mainland as a safety valve to prevent social unrest. They offered cheap air fares and facilitated large-scale labor contracting by American companies through offices of the Commonwealth of Puerto Rico, which were established in several U.S. cities.[12] The result was that at the height of the new U.S. investment, the greatest number of Puerto Ricans in history migrated to the United States.

Puerto Rico thus set the mold for a trend that has now repeated itself throughout the Caribbean region for two generations: American corporations move in and set up low-wage factories, the factories draw laborers to the cities from the impoverished countryside, the migrants come in greater numbers than the jobs available, and the surplus workers begin leaving for the United States, either as contract laborers or as illegal immigrants.

Puerto Rico had one wrinkle that set it apart, however—it was still a U.S. territory. That meant federal labor and environmental laws protected factory workers' health and safety and their right to unionize. By the 1960s, as the island's labor movement became increasingly militant, workers demanded wages and working conditions closer to U.S. levels, which caused many U.S. firms to sour on the "Puerto Rican miracle." The firms started moving to other Caribbean countries willing to offer lower labor costs and more lax environmental and safety laws. The shift away from Puerto Rico production, however, failed initially to address one important cost area—tariffs. Once they left U.S. territory, manufacturers could not count on duty-free entry to the American market. To replicate their Puerto Rican oasis, therefore, American industrialists needed steep tariff reductions wherever they were going next.

## THE RISE OF THE *MAQUILAS*

Beginning in 1965, the manufacturing scene shifted to Mexico. That country's new border industrialization program spawned the "miracle" of the *maquiladoras,* a swath of industrial parks just across the U.S. border.

In colonial Mexico, *maquiladora* denoted the share of grain a miller would charge a farmer for processing his harvest. Over time, the word came to represent a step in a larger operation that occurred elsewhere.[13] As envisioned in the original BIP legislation, the first *maquilas* were supposed to be "twin plants," each with a partner factory on the U.S. side. The Mexican plant would assemble a product from components imported from its twin plant in the United States, then ship the finished product back across the border for sale in the American market, and when the product crossed the border only the value added by the Mexican labor would be subject to a tariff.

Since this was a very specific and limited form of tariff reduction, the Mexican government initially permitted it only in areas near the border. That way, supporters argued, jobs would be created on both sides of the border, and the *maquilas* would reduce immigration because Mexicans would choose to stay and work in their own country with the new North American subsidiaries.

But the BIP turned instead into a way for the corporations to evade U.S. labor and environmental laws while manufacturing hundreds of yards from our own country. From Tijuana on the Pacific Coast to Matamoros near the Texas Gulf, the *maquiladora* zone emerged as a giant industrial strip all along that border.

Too often, the twin plant on this side of the border became nothing more than a warehouse, providing jobs to only a few people.[14] General Electric Corporation, which opened its first *maquiladora* in 1971, had eight Mexican plants within a decade, where 8,500 workers made circuit breakers, motors, coils, and pumps.[15] In one year alone, the General Motors Corporation opened twelve new *maquilas* while closing eleven factories in the United States and laying off 29,000 people. By the early 1990s, GM was the biggest private employer in Mexico, with fifty *maquila* plants and 50,000 workers.[16] On the eve of Congress's approving the North American Free Trade Agreement in late 1993, more than 2,000 factories were employing 550,000 Mexicans.[17] Thus, in little more than two decades, the industrial heartland of North America was unceremoniously uprooted from America's Midwest to Mexico's northern border.

Unlike the old U.S. factories that largely employed men, the *maquilas* took to recruiting young Mexican women who traditionally had not been part of Mexico's labor force. Their U.S. managers considered Mexican men more difficult to control and hired as few as possible.[18] Thus, Mexico's unemployment problem, which had always been more severe for its men, was barely dented by the *maquila* program. Drawing so many young women from the countryside to the border factories disrupted social organization in rural villages, where women historically provided critical unpaid labor. Even though the young men had no job prospects, they ended up following the women to the cities, and once they arrived at the border towns, many of them decided to cross into the United States. As economist Saskia Sassen notes: "People first uprooted from traditional ways of life, then left unemployed and unemployable as export firms hire younger workers or move production to other countries, may see few options but emigration—especially if export-led strategies have weakened the country's domestic economy."[19]

Those who managed to find jobs in the *maquilas* soon found that their meager wages bought less and less each day. Real wages in the industry plummeted during the past fifteen years when measured against the U.S. dollar. They dropped 68 percent between 1980 and 1992 even though *maquila* productivity increased 41 percent. Most of the drop resulted from two separate devaluations of the Mexican peso in the 1980s—and all that was before the huge December 1994 devaluation, where the peso lost an additional 50 percent value.

Contrary to the glowing predictions of our government and business leaders in 1965, the explosion of *maquiladoras* has done nothing to slow Mexican emigration. Instead, emigration has escalated side by side with *maquila* growth—exactly as happened with Puerto Rico (see table 8).

### TABLE 8
### LEGAL MEXICAN IMMIGRATION TO THE UNITED STATES
#### (BY FISCAL YEARS)[20]

| | |
|---|---|
| 1961–1970 | 453,000 |
| 1971–1980 | 640,000 |
| 1981–1990 | 1,655,000 |
| 1991–1996 | 1,653,000 |

The miracle prosperity that lower trade barriers were supposed to bring never reached the majority of Mexicans outside the *maquilas* either. Per capita domestic product for the whole country dropped from $2,421 annually in 1980 to $2,284 in 1994.[21] While in the Far East factory wages rose throughout the 1980s, Mexican wages plummeted, making the country and the whole Caribbean region the most desirable place in the world for U.S. direct investment.[22]

Meanwhile, Mexico's government, thanks to its tight control over national unions, assured foreign investors that no one would challenge the super-low-wage structures of the *maquilas*. In most free trade zones along the border, only government unions are allowed to operate. In those rare cases where independent unions gain a foothold, such as the northeastern state of Tamaulipas, the workers see immediate benefit. *Maquila* workers there earn 30 percent more than their counterparts in other Mexican states for a forty-hour week, while workers in other states are required to work forty-eight hours.

But even in Tamaulipas, union leaders know their limits. In 1993, Agapito González, the seventy-six-year-old leader of the Union of Day Laborers and Industrial Workers of Matamoros, found out what happens when you exceed them. That January, he pulled out his 35,000 members in an unprecedented strike against the *maquila* owners' attempt to rein-stitute the forty-eight-hour week.[23] The strike was so successful the owners relented within a few days. Soon afterward, the federal government arrested the popular labor leader, flew him to Mexico City, and imprisoned him without bail for six months on tax evasion charges. President Carlos Salinas released González only after he agreed to turn over day-to-day operations of the union to his son. When I interviewed Agapito González, Jr., in June 1993, at the union headquarters in Matamoros, the son spoke with obvious caution about the need for "cooperation" with the *maquila* owners and the government.

## NIGHTMARE ON THE BORDER

The other side of Mexico's industrial transformation is the social and environmental disaster created by unrestrained growth.

Sleepy border towns have been catapulted helter-skelter into the industrial age. Just across the Rio Grande from El Paso, for instance, is Juárez, whose population, just 250,000 in 1960, jumped fivefold in thirty years.[24] Reynosa, across the river from McAllen, Texas, zoomed from 4,800 inhabitants in 1930 to 280,000 in 1990. And that's according to the official government count. Estimates by the McAllen Economic Development Corporation put the population closer to 600,000! So frenetic has been the pace of growth that 60 percent of Reynosa's *maquila* workers have lived in the city less than five years, and 20 percent less than a year.[25]

The same population explosion has been replicated in the border cities of Tijuana, Mexicali, Nogales, Nuevo Laredo, and Matamoros. As thousands have flocked to the farrago of *maquiladoras* in search of work, the border towns have simply been overwhelmed by the lack of roads, housing, electrical power, schools, even clean drinking water for the new migrants. The result has been urban anarchy on a scale almost unimaginable to Americans. In Reynosa, one researcher counted two hundred separate shantytowns in 1992, most without cement roads. More than a third of the city's population had no indoor plumbing and 15 percent no electricity.[26] As late as 1998, no major city along the border had a sewage treatment plant fully operational, including Juárez, with its 1.5 million residents.

Added to the human waste and garbage created by the population surge has been the pollution released from the unprecedented concentration of factories. The most cursory summary of the worst contamination would fill scores of pages. Among them are: the repeated escapes of deadly toxic gas clouds from Dupont's Quimica Flor plant in a densely populated neighborhood of Matamoros; the 80,000 tons of lead sulfate found illegally dumped in 1992 outside Tijuana by Los Angeles–based Alco Pacific, which ran a lead-processing plant there for more than a decade; the discharges of xylene—a highly toxic industrial solvent—by the General Motors' Rimir plant into the sewers of Matamoros, where a Boston-based environmental group found xylene at 6,300 times the level permitted by U.S. drinking water standards.[27]

The human impact of so much toxic pollution is inescapable:

- In the mid-1980s, Mexican health professionals in Matamoros discovered that deformities in many of the city's children might be traced to one of the first *maquiladoras,* Mallory Mexicana S.A, an Indiana-based plant that had produced capacitors for televisions during its early years and in the process exposed employees to various toxic chemicals, including PCBs.

  At least 70 severely disabled Mallory children had been identified in 1992 when I visited Matamoros. Since then, the number has climbed to 120. All the children were born between 1970 and 1977 to mothers who had worked while pregnant on the assembly line. Those children are all adults now, but many still wear diapers; others move and talk normally but possess the minds of seven-year-olds. Their facial features are flat and listless and some communicate in bone-chilling shrieks, their spindly arms and legs constantly convulsing.

  By the time the mothers realized the source of their problem, the plant had closed and the company had been sold in a string of deals to several U.S. firms.[28] On August 27, 1995, more than a half-dozen *maquiladora* firms agreed to pay $17 million to settle a lawsuit by twenty-seven of the families, though the companies insisted no proof had been established of an environmental link.[29]

- In 1993, American Rivers, a national conservation group, concluded that the Rio Grande "poses a greater threat to human health than any other river system in North America." The report blamed industrial waste from *maquiladoras* for much of the problem.[30]

- From 1991 to 1993, childhood cancers in the Brownsville public schools increased 230 percent.[31]

- Gallbladder problems, liver cancer, and hepatitis rates are higher along the thirty-three Texas counties near the Rio Grande than in the rest of the state and the nation.[32]

- Abnormal clusters of anencephalic births have been identified in Cameron County on the U.S. side of the border and in the adjacent state of Taumalipas on the Mexican side. Though a few studies by U.S. medical experts have so far found no link to pollution, many residents and environmental activists remain convinced the birth defects are related to the toxins produced by the *maquilas*.[33]

- Mexico's industrial accident and illness rate is among the highest in the world, 23 cases per 100,000 workers annually between 1987 and 1991, according to the International Labor Organization, and the rate has been rising.[34] Moreover, under Mexican law, foreign companies are absolved from court suits for work-related injuries. With workers only allowed to collect legally capped disability payments from the government, American companies thus face little threat from huge liability suits.[35]

## THE CARIBBEAN BACKYARD

By the mid-1980s, American industrialists convinced our federal government to replicate the Puerto Rico and Mexico experiments throughout the rest of the Caribbean and Central America. The Reagan administration called this next stage the Caribbean Basin Initiative (CBI). Under the program, Congress provided direct federal aid to countries in the Caribbean that established free trade zones and eliminated tariffs for manufactured goods entering the United States from those zones. Passage of the bill fueled an immediate expansion of offshore production. Many of the new manufacturers were direct subsidiaries of U.S. firms or Korean and Taiwanese middlemen supplying the U.S. market.

But CBI went much further than the Mexico program. U.S. officials actually enticed U.S. companies to close down their U.S. factories and eliminate American jobs. The policy became public late in 1992, when a coalition of labor unions pulled off the first labor sting in American history. The sting, organized by the National Labor Committee, involved the creation of a fictitious firm, New Age Textiles. The "executives" of the fake firm attended textile industry trade shows, where they caught on secret cameras officials of the U.S. Agency for International Development and the U.S. Commerce Department urging their firm to locate production in the Caribbean region. The federal officials offered to arrange financing, feasibility studies, and even site selection trips to the Caribbean free trade zones, and they even boasted how union activists were blacklisted and unions kept out of the zones.

When the sting was finally revealed on a network television news program, it turned out that the federal government had spent nearly $700 million since 1980 on projects aimed at promoting Caribbean *maquiladoras*.[36] The revelations, coming in the midst of a recession and just before the 1992 presidential elections, threw Washington into an uproar and sparked Congress to enact new restrictions on economic aid under CBI. A decade after the program had been established, more than five hundred companies had utilized CBI incentives to set up their first production facilities in the region's FTZs, and another three hundred had expanded operations.[37]

By the time of my first trip to the Dominican Republic in 1992, that country already boasted twenty-three free trade zones, which employed 170,000 people. Few of those jobs had existed a decade earlier. The largest FTZ was in the southeastern city of San Pedro de Macorís. It contained ninety plants and was brimming with 40,000 workers, most of them teenagers and young women who worked ten- and twelve-hour shifts for as little as $4 a day.

Once again, however, the staggering growth in jobs did nothing to stem emigration. The same decade that saw the most *maquila* jobs created in the Dominican Republic also saw the greatest Dominican exodus to the United States; from 1981 to 1990, 252,000 immigrated legally to this country and an unknown number illegally—more than in the previous two decades combined.

With *maquila* profits booming, you might expect some meager prosperity to find its way to the average Dominican. Just the opposite occurred. Dominican gross national product declined almost every year between 1982 and 1992, and per capita consumption dropped 22 percent during that time.[38]

Central Americans have not fared much better. At first, the civil wars in the region dampened foreign investment interest, but since the end of the fighting, Central America has joined the *maquila* bandwagon, with free trade zones sprouting in several countries.

Today, the Caribbean Basin is the world's largest supplier of clothing to the U.S. market.[39] Name an American retailer whose soaring profits have made it a darling of Wall Street and in all likelihood its garments are produced by teenagers in Central America. Average hourly wages in those zones have been caught in a spiraling race to the bottom. In 1992, they were 45 cents for El Salvador; 39 cents for Honduras; 26 cents for Costa Rica; and 62 cents for Guatemala.[40]

Among the U.S. firms that closed domestic plants and flocked to the region were Farah, Haggar, GTE, Kellwood, Levi Strauss, Leslie Fay, Sara Lee, Oxford, and Arrow. In 1981, for instance, Kellwood Industries, a St. Louis–based manufacturer of apparel and home furnishings, employed 16,000 people in sixty-two U.S. plants and it had no overseas production. Eleven years later, Kellwood had closed fifty of those plants and eliminated 9,500 domestic jobs and replaced them with 8,900 new workers in the Dominican Republic, Honduras, Haiti, and Costa Rica. Today, 58 percent of Kellwood's workforce is offshore, where its workers earn only a few dollars a day.[41]

The frenetic pace of factory expansion in the region is astounding. A 1993 U.S. AID study of the free trade zones in Honduras reported that the number of Honduran *maquila* workers had skyrocketed by 43 percent in just one year, to more than 22,000, and was expected to triple by 1996. Those Honduran workers were overwhelmingly women (71 percent) and under twenty-five years of age (83 percent), with nearly half of them teenagers.[42]

Claudia Leticia Molina was one of those teenagers. She was a rail-thin sixteen-year-old who weighed ninety-three pounds when she began working at a Honduran factory called Orion Apparel in one of the zones outside San Pedro Sula. Her supervisors sometimes forced Claudia to clock into work at 7:00 A.M. on a Friday, and she would not leave the factory until 4:00 A.M. the next morning. Her only rest was catching a few hours' sleep on the floor by her machine. A week of such work earned her $43. In neighboring El Salvador, Judith Yanira Viera, eighteen, would work as many as seventy hours at Mandarin International, a Taiwanese-owned plant that produced shirts for such well-known American retailers as Eddie Bauer, the Gap, and JCPenney. Her average pay was 56 cents an hour.[43]

Physical and sexual abuse against women in the zones is commonplace. In some factories, women are fired when they become pregnant, and there have been documented instances of factory owners requiring employees to take birth control pills each morning as they report to work.

In San Salvador, the Human Rights Office of the Catholic Archdiocese denounced an incident in which numerous female employees at Mandarin International were beaten with pistol butts on June 29, 1995, by a factory manager and a Salvadoran army colonel who was a partner in the firm. At the time, the women were protesting the firing of 350 of their coworkers for trying to organize a union.[44] The outcry by Church and labor groups both in El Salvador and the United States led to a boycott against the Gap, one of Mandarin's principal customers. As the boycott appeared to gather steam, image-conscious Gap officials offered to settle the dispute and get the workers rehired. The Gap also agreed to a pioneering set of employee rights, which the firm pledged all its future contractors would honor.

The growth of factories in the free trade zones has been so great that one federal study warned of a looming shortage of female workers. The report, compiled for the U.S. Agency for International Development by Price Waterhouse, predicted that in Honduras, where 50 percent of young females in the Sula Valley are already working in the factories, "it is likely that the female participation rate will level off between 65 percent and 70 percent, so future labor force growth will depend on vegetative population increase plus immigration."[45]

Yes, unbridled growth of free trade zones has led a U.S. government agency to worry about the need for "vegetative" population increases!

Unfortunately, the phenomenal profits being made by the multinational corporations and their middlemen producers have not trickled down to the average Central American worker. While foreign investment in the free trade zones has boomed, overall annual exports from the region to the United States dropped by more than $1 billion from 1984 to 1991, and per capita income in the Caribbean Basin fell at a rate two and a half times faster than the rest of Latin America. The United Nations estimates that 60 percent of the people of Central America and the Caribbean live below the poverty line.[46]

Meanwhile, just as in Puerto Rico, Mexico, and the Dominican Republic, *maquiladora* growth in Central America has not slowed immigration. During the decade of the 1980s—at the height of the region's civil wars—468,000 Central Americans came to the United States legally and many more illegally. After the fighting stopped, however, the flood of migrants did not slow down. Between 1991 and 1996, another 344,000 arrived legally. The conclusion is inescapable. The neoliberal industrialization strategy has done nothing to improve basic conditions in the region. If anything, it has only accelerated migration and rootlessness among the region's workers, who, once they have fled their villages for the *maquilas*, find it even easier to flee the *maquilas* for El Norte.

## NAFTA: WHERE DID ALL THE PROMISES GO?

None of the prior phases of this free trade juggernaut compares in scope to what has happened since the U.S. Congress approved the North American Free Trade Agreement (NAFTA). The treaty, which took effect on January 1, 1994, created a new common market whose aim was to remove all tariff barriers between Mexico, Canada, and the United States by 2010.[47]

During the bitter fight in Congress over the treaty, NAFTA's advocates promised a new era of prosperity for what they billed as the world's biggest economic bloc. President Clinton predicted 170,000 new jobs would be created for Americans from increased exports to Mexico just in NAFTA's first year.[48] During the initial ten years, some experts claimed, Mexico would gain more than 1 million new industrial jobs. Clinton and Vice President Al Gore lobbied fiercely for the treaty and they were joined by several former Republican and Democratic presidents. They all assured the public, just as previous leaders had with the border industrialization program, that the economic boom from NAFTA would benefit Americans and that it would slow the tide of illegal immigration, because Mexicans who earned more at home would not come here looking for jobs.

The same day NAFTA took effect, Mayan peasants in Chiapas launched their Zapatista revolt. One of the demands of the rebels was for protection against NAFTA's expected impact on agriculture. The treaty's provisions, the Zapatistas and some American critics insisted, had the potential to devastate close to 2 million Mexican peasants who produced corn, the country's food staple, on small individual plots. By reducing agricultural tariffs, NAFTA would drive the farmers out of business, since they would not be able to compete with the expected surge of American corn and wheat, crops whose harvests here are highly mechanized.[49]

The guerrilla uprising jolted world financial experts who had long trumpeted Mexico as an economic miracle and a model for Latin America.[50] What those experts refused to acknowledge was that Mexico remains a nation divided by immense disparities of wealth. In 1992, for instance, the top 10 percent of Mexicans took in 38 percent of total income, while the bottom half received only 18 percent.[51]

The Mexican leader most in tune with corporate America's desire for NAFTA, and the man who shepherded the treaty through the Mexican legislature, was former president Carlos Salinas. Throughout his presidency, Salinas fueled the Mexican miracle with risky gambits, high-interest, short-term bonds sold to foreign investors and denominated in U.S. dollars. By 1995, Mexico owed $29 billion in those bonds. It needed another $9 billion a year just to service the interest on its regular long-term debt, already one of the biggest in the world. The combined debt, together with a ballooning trade deficit, drove the country to the brink of insolvency by late 1993 and early 1994.

Both the Clinton and Salinas administrations, however, ignored the crisis, for they were determined first to win passage for NAFTA in the American Congress, then to salvage another victory for Salinas's chosen successor for president, Ernesto Zedillo, in the August 1994 election—so they dared not risk any belt-tightening financial reforms that would anger the Mexican electorate. Salinas's failure to act left Mexico's economy in such shambles that his successor, Zedillo, was forced to order an open-ended devaluation of the peso, only months after assuming the presidency. His action stunned world markets and propelled the country into economic free fall.

President Clinton hastily engineered a $50 billion international bailout, $20 billion of which he offered from the U.S. Treasury, so that Mexico could pay off its foreign creditors. The bailout was conditioned on the Zedillo government's ramming a severe austerity program onto its people. By midyear 1995, the Mexican peso had plummeted 50 percent against the dollar, a million Mexicans had lost their jobs, and interest rates had skyrocketed to the point that Mexican consumers were paying as much as 100 percent interest for credit card loans. All predictions of immediate post-NAFTA prosperity vanished in the meltdown. Four years later, the average Mexican had still not regained his precrisis standard of living.

Many economists in this country have tried to separate the NAFTA accords from the Mexican financial meltdown. By doing so, they overlook the fundamental weakness of the common market that the treaty created when it married Mexico, an underdeveloped country still torn by severe poverty and class conflict, to the richest economy in the world. Such an unequal union can only lead to economic instability for both countries.

Five years after the new union started, workers in all three countries have seen the various pre-NAFTA promises turn to smoke. Canada has watched helplessly as thousands of jobs relocate to Mexico, and the U.S.

Department of Labor has had to admit that 214,000 layoffs in U.S. factories have been due to jobs transferred south of the border between 1994 and 1998. Labor unions, however, insist the government's measuring standards are too narrow, and they claim twice as many jobs were lost. Worse, they say, industrial wages at home have been kept artificially low because those employers who remain often threaten workers that they'll move to Mexico if their unions demand unreasonable pay increases.[52] The number of new jobs in the United States directly attributable to NAFTA trade is so embarrassingly small the Commerce Department stopped keeping track of it.

Meanwhile, Mexico has been gaining new *maquila* jobs at a breathtaking pace. By January 1998, four years into NAFTA, the number of *maquiladora* workers had doubled from 546,000 to nearly 1 million.[53] In other words, nearly as many *maquila* jobs were created during the last four years as in the previous three decades. Since the peso devaluation of 1994, Mexican workers are poorer than ever. In 1997, the purchasing power of their wages was still one-third below 1993 levels. The depression that followed devaluation threw 1.8 million people out of work and bankrupted a third of all businesses. Today, nearly half of Mexico's 92 million people live on less than $5 a day, and 65 percent of the labor force is unemployed or underemployed.

Only the strong growth of the U.S. economy in other parts of the world has obscured the seriousness of NAFTA's failure. Instead of all the new jobs promised, we have a tidal wave of imports from Mexico. The U.S.-Mexico trade surplus, which stood at $1.7 billion in 1993, evaporated into a $14.7 billion trade deficit by 1998.

More *maquilas* below the border have produced an even more dangerous environment. The volume of hazardous waste produced has surged to a third higher than pretreaty levels. In 1995, forty-four tons a day of hazardous waste, one-quarter of the total produced in the *maquiladora* zone, was unaccounted for—neither returned to the United States for disposal nor properly processed in Mexico by the factories that produced it.[54]

As the polluting industries multiply, the social and health consequences are predictable. In Cameron County, which includes the city of Brownsville, hepatitis A rates jumped 400 percent between 1993 and 1997. In Maverick County, across the Rio Grande from the Piedras Negras *maquiladora* zone, they rose 122 percent.[55] All along the border, new sewage treatment plants promised by Mexico as part of NAFTA's environmental improvements were postponed or cancelled because of the peso devaluation and the country's financial collapse.

Unfortunately, the farm crisis that NAFTA's opponents warned about has come true. In 1995, Mexico imported nearly 30 percent more basic grains than it did the previous year. According to one report, there was "a wave of immigration of indigenous peasants . . . no longer able to survive producing corn and beans."[56] At the same time, food exports by agribusiness to the United States have exploded. Nearly 96 percent of all U.S. strawberries and 52 percent of all other fruits and vegetables now come from Mexico. Yet food inspections on both sides of the border have declined precipitously, leading to several major outbreaks of food poisoning in the United States. In one outbreak in 1997, 270 people in five states were sickened by a potentially fatal hepatitis A from frozen Mexican strawberries.[57]

The grand promises NAFTA advocates made about slowing down immigration have also come to naught. Since the *maquiladoras* are the only part of the Mexican economy that is consistently expanding, the border industries continue to function as a magnet drawing Mexicans north in search of jobs. While Mexican women form the bulk of the *maquila* workers, Mexican men head for the United States for jobs. Border interdictions by the INS are at record levels. Much of this is due to beefed-up enforcement, more Border Patrol agents and more sophisticated surveillance technology, but there is little doubt that Mexico's worst depression during this century has forced even more of its army of unemployed to leave for the United States.

Compared to the barrage of media attention that accompanied the original debate over NAFTA, most news outlets have ignored the horrendous aftermath. White Americans, it seems, were much more captivated in 1999 by the continuing bull market on Wall Street. But in the *barrios* and shantytowns of Latin America, fifty years of empty promises about free trade prosperity have brought only increased misery and made more people than ever desperate to escape to El Norte.

# 14

## Puerto Rico, U.S.A.:
## Possessed and Unwanted

> Colonialism is not satisfied merely with holding a people in its
> grip and emptying the native's brain of all form and content. By
> a kind of perverted logic, it turns to the past of the oppressed
> people, and distorts, disfigures, and destroys it. . . .
> —*Frantz Fanon,* The Wretched of the Earth

North Americans have known two contrasting images of Puerto
Rico for most of the past century. One is the vacation paradise of
shady beaches, turquoise waters, and glittering casinos, a U.S. island that boasts Latin America's second highest standard of living. The
other is the welfare basket case, the U.S. territory whose residents drain
$5.3 billion a year in government assistance while paying no federal
taxes. In this other Puerto Rico, 60 percent of the people live in poverty,
the murder, drug addiction, and AIDS rates rival the worst in our own
country, and so many residents have emigrated that nearly half of all
Puerto Ricans now live in the fifty states.[1]

Little else is known about the island, since news outlets in this country
rarely report events there, except for the periodic hurricanes that bedevil
the tourist trade or the occasional bizarre story that strikes some State-
side curiosity. During 1995, for instance, the Puerto Rico story generating
most attention was the infamous *"Chupacabras,"* the vampire that supposedly sucked the blood of animals it killed. Island affairs are so obscure here that the Associated Press normally carries stories about
Puerto Rico on its "international" wire, even though its residents are U.S.
citizens. Hollywood hasn't helped either. More often than not, its films
depict Puerto Ricans as welfare-dependent and violence-prone, certainly not the stuff of sympathetic copy.[2]

From the days of sociologist Oscar Lewis's best-selling *La Vida: A
Puerto Rican Family in the Culture of Poverty, San Juan and New York,*[3]
a host of academics has cultivated an equally grim portrait. Former Reagan White House staff member Linda Chavez, for instance, wrote of the

"Puerto Rican Exception" in her 1992 book, *Out of the Barrio:* "Puerto Ricans are not simply the poorest of all Hispanic groups; they experience the highest degree of social dysfunction of any Hispanic group and exceed that of blacks on some indicators."[4] Chavez attributed much of this "dysfunction" to the "self-inflicted" wounds of welfare dependency and out-of-wedlock childbirth.

Are Puerto Ricans as socially problematic, and dependent, as Chavez asserts? Is it true that island residents have milked this country's federal entitlement programs while giving little back, as some conservatives have claimed in recent years?[5]

Both "vacation paradise" and "welfare sinkhole" are easy labels and catchy sound bites for pundits and network news broadcasts. The only problem is they're grossly inaccurate. They are labels that mask a profound and disquieting reality: that Puerto Rico remains the biggest, the most lucrative, and the oldest colony of the United States in an age when colonies were supposed to have disappeared.

As we will see in this chapter, Puerto Rico has provided perhaps more wealth to the United States than any country in history. That wealth, together with the numerous U.S. military bases to which the island has been home for fifty years, and the enormous sacrifices made by Puerto Rican veterans who fought in U.S. wars throughout the twentieth century, dwarfs the value of any federal aid its residents have received.

While the U.S. presence in Puerto Rico has brought some undeniable benefits, it has also deformed the island's economy and the psychology of its people, fostering the very dependent relationship for which Puerto Ricans are blamed. Only now, a century after occupying the island, are U.S. policy makers seeking to rid themselves of their last major overseas possession. Yet, a decade of sporadic debate in Congress over bills to determine Puerto Rico's final status has accomplished very little. Leaders in both Washington and San Juan remain sharply divided over the choices: statehood, independence, or a more autonomous form of the current commonwealth. They are divided because no matter the option—and all sides acknowledge the current relationship is unsatisfactory—any change will produce far-reaching repercussions for both Puerto Rico and the United States. Acquiring a colony, it turns out, is considerably easier than relinquishing it.

## THE RICHEST COLONY IN AMERICAN HISTORY

As an American possession—belonging to the United States but not being a part of it—Puerto Rico has historically had a unique position in U.S.

politics. Island residents are U.S. citizens at birth, but they do not have the same rights and protections, nor the same responsibilities, as other Americans. They do not, for example, vote in federal elections, and because of that they are exempt from paying federal taxes. Trade between the island and the continental United States has always been exempt from import duties, so Puerto Rico's economy is wholly integrated into that of this country.

Federal tax exemption, as we saw in the previous chapter, created an irresistible draw for investment, with the arrival of hundreds of U.S. firms after World War II spurring an economic miracle that made Puerto Rico the envy of the developing world. As a result of industrialization, the *Populares* under Governor Muñoz Marín built a first-class port, highway and communications systems, public schools for all, an advanced health care network, a huge tourist industry, and an imposing array of government-owned corporations, all of which helped create a model living standard for Latin America.

But the miracle evaporated quickly. Annual growth rates dropped from an average of 6 percent in the 1950s, to 4 percent in the 1970s, and they were stagnant throughout the 1980s.[6] Despite that stagnation, manufacturing continued to grow as a portion of the island's economic activity. By the 1970s, as the federal minimum wage gradually covered the island's workers, and as labor unions became better organized, many of the U.S. firms fled to Mexico or the Dominican Republic in search of even cheaper labor.[7]

The firms that remained tended to be larger multinational corporations involved in the manufacture of chemicals, pharmaceuticals, electronics, and scientific equipment. Companies in those sectors quickly realized that they could turn the loophole of the Section 936 federal tax exemption into a secret gold mine.[8]

The secret was simple. Firms with high research, development, and marketing expenses but low production costs farmed out factory production to wholly owned subsidiaries in Puerto Rico, then transferred the patents and trademarks from their U.S. headquarters to the subsidiaries as well, thus shielding all revenue from the product from federal taxes.[9] The tablets in that bottle of prescription pills from your local pharmacy, for example, may have cost only pennies apiece to manufacture in Puerto Rico, but the lion's share of the bottle's $20 price tag, which represents the sum of the research and marketing costs the firm spent in the United States, plus the production costs on the island, were all tax-exempt under Section 936. The loophole proved to be such a gravy train that by 1974 more than 110 of the *Fortune* 500 companies had Puerto Rico subsidiaries.[10]

Hundreds of pharmaceutical and medical plants opened on the out- skirts of virtually every small town on the island, employing more than 100,000 workers by the early 1990s. Between 1960 and 1976, tiny Puerto Rico catapulted from sixth to first in Latin America for total direct U.S. investment. With island workers registering some of the highest produc- tivity levels in the world, the results were profit levels unheard-of at home. By 1976, Puerto Rico accounted for 40 percent of all U.S. profit in Latin America—more than the combined earnings of all U.S. sub- sidiaries in Brazil, Mexico, and Venezuela.[11] So great were the windfall returns that several major multinationals reported in 1977 that more than a quarter of their worldwide profits were coming from the island.[12]

Chemicals and pharmaceuticals benefited most. For every $30,300 drug companies paid in salary and benefits to a Puerto Rican worker in 1985, they got back $85,600 in federal tax benefits.[13] From its 4,000 work- ers in Puerto Rico alone, pharmaceutical giant Johnson & Johnson saved $1 billion in federal taxes between 1980 and 1990. Smith-Kline Beecham saved $987 million; Merck & Company, $749 million; Bristol-Myers Squibb, $627 million.[14]

The cost in lost taxes to the federal treasury mushroomed to nearly $3 billion annually in 1992, as Puerto Rico rapidly turned into the number- one source of profit in the world for U.S. companies. By 1986, the island's profitability had surpassed even industrial giants such as Germany, Canada, Japan, and the United Kingdom. That year, U.S. companies earned $5.8 billion from their Puerto Rico investments.[15]

A decade later, the island was still at the top. Net profits from direct in- vestments of nonresidents in Puerto Rico (largely American corpora- tions) ballooned to $14.3 billion in 1995, just ahead of the United Kingdom and nearly double that of any other country (see table 9). That amount is breathtaking when you compare Puerto Rico's minuscule population of 3.8 million to the United Kingdom's 58 million, Germany's 81 million, or Brazil's 150 million. The reason is simple: Puerto Rico is among the most industrialized and most captive economies in the Third World—99.3 percent of its exports are manufactured goods, and 90 per- cent of all those exports go to the United States.

But island employment never kept pace with that amazing industrial- ization. As sugar production declined after 1950, Puerto Ricans fled the countryside for the cities, where the number of job seekers always ex- ceeded the number of new factory jobs. The disparity led to massive emigration to the United States. Despite that emigration, island unemployment has rarely dipped below 11 percent in a quarter century, and during times of recession in the United States, it has surpassed 20 percent.

---

TABLE 9

### NET INCOME FROM U.S. DIRECT INVESTMENT*
### IN SELECTED COUNTRIES, 1995
#### (IN MILLIONS OF DOLLARS)[16]

| | |
|---|---|
| Puerto Rico | 14,339† |
| United Kingdom | 13,773 |
| Ireland | 7,440 |
| Germany | 5,271 |
| Brazil | 4,579 |
| Japan | 4,237 |
| France | 4,077 |
| Hong Kong | 3,005 |
| Mexico | 916 |

*For majority-owned nonbank foreign affiliates.
†Since Puerto Rico is not considered a foreign country, figures are for direct investments of nonresidents (overwhelmingly U.S. corporations).

---

What did grow was income inequality. A distressing share of the income Puerto Ricans produce never touches Puerto Rican hands. In 1995, nearly four out of every ten dollars made on the island ended up in the bank account of a U.S. firm.[17] So much wealth has been siphoned off that today the salaries of Puerto Rican factory workers represent a mere 21 percent of the income of their firms, far less than the 63 percent they received in 1970.[18] By comparison, U.S. workers, even after all the corporate downsizing and union busting of the past twenty years, still retain an average of 70 percent of their employers' income as salaries.

Despite record-breaking growth in productivity and corporate profits for U.S. companies on the island, 60 percent of Puerto Ricans still live below the poverty level. That impoverished majority, unable to find enough living-wage jobs to meet its basic needs, was forced into depending on a gamut of federal entitlements to survive. Those federal payments started escalating around 1975, just as the gap between the Puerto Rican worker's income and corporate income began to widen.[19]

In summary, the colonial status of Puerto Rico turned the island, with its combination of duty-free trade, low wages, and tax loopholes, into a corporate bonanza unlike any other in the world. At the same time, the federal government was forced to spend nearly $6 billion annually in federal welfare and transfer payments to alleviate the island-wide poverty the greed of these very corporations perpetuated.[20]

But there are other examples of how Puerto Rico's colonial status has created unnecessary hardship for its people.

Among the most obvious are:

1. *Shipping.* Since its early days as a U.S. possession, Puerto Rico has been deemed by Congress to be under the coastal shipping laws of the United States, even though the island is more than a thousand miles from the North American coast and surrounded by dozens of other island countries. Those laws require that all trade between the island and the fifty states must be on U.S.-made ships manned by U.S. crews. While the rest of the world transports much of its cargo on low-cost Panamanian- and Liberian-flag freighters, island residents end up paying as much as 25 percent higher prices for imported goods because of their higher freight costs. This loophole in maritime law has turned tiny Puerto Rico into the main subsidizer of the U.S. merchant fleet. In 1991, island shipping represented 21.7 percent of all U.S.-flag shipments even though the island's population was barely 1 percent of the total U.S. population (see table 10).

### TABLE 10
### U.S.–PUERTO RICO SHIPPING TRADE, 1991
#### (IN BILLIONS OF DOLLARS)[21]

| Trade flow | Value of U.S. Merchant Fleet Shipments (Total) | (with Puerto Rico) | Puerto Rico as a % of U.S. Merchant Fleet Shipments |
|---|---|---|---|
| U.S. exports | $29.1 | $8.0 | 27.4% |
| U.S. imports | $60.1 | $11.4 | 18.9% |
| Total | $89.2 | $19.3 | 21.7% |

2. *Trade.* As a Caribbean nation, Puerto Rico's trade needs are vastly different from those of the United States, yet the island has always been subject to the same commercial treaties and import tariffs as the fifty

states. Congress has repeatedly rejected requests by the Puerto Rican
government to be able to negotiate separate trade agreements beneficial
to the island, a right Puerto Rico already enjoyed as a possession of
Spain back in 1897.

Because their island is a captive economy, Puerto Ricans are the
largest per capita importers of U.S. goods in the world. According to one
study, trade between the two countries creates 487,000 jobs in the United
States and 322,000 jobs on the island. The United States not only gains
one-third more jobs from the relationship, but American workers earn
two to three times more income than the Puerto Ricans.[22]

3. *Courts.* Spanish is the language of the island's local courts, but English is the language of the U.S. District Court in San Juan. This effectively excludes the majority of island residents who do not speak English
from serving on federal juries. It also requires all litigants who file appeals of lower court decisions to the federal courts to switch language in
midstream. Furthermore, all appeals from the U.S. District Court in
Puerto Rico are handled thousands of miles away in Boston, instead of
at a closer jurisdiction, such as Atlanta or Washington, which would be
less of a hardship for litigants.

4. *Federal programs.* In recent years, Congress has attempted to reduce federal spending by capping scores of entitlement programs, such
as Medicaid, welfare, and federal aid to education, at lower levels for
Puerto Rico than for the fifty states, while it has completely excluded the
island from federal highways construction funds, supplemental security
income, or revenue sharing.[23] Those congressional restrictions have sent
a clear message to island residents that while they may be U.S. citizens,
they are citizens of a lesser category. Only by moving to the United
States can they receive equal treatment from the federal government.

5. *Military.* Puerto Rico has proportionally more military installations
than any other part of the United States—14 percent of its land. As late
as 1999, the navy was still using much of Vieques, a small island inhabited
by nearly 9,400 Puerto Ricans, for frequent air and ship-to-shore bombing target practice, despite decades of opposition by a succession of island governments. Nearly sixty years of constant bombardment on
Vieques has destroyed marine life, ruined its pristine beaches, caused numerous civilian injuries from abandoned munitions, and decimated the
local fishing and tourist economies.[24] Beyond the issue of bases is the
U.S. military itself. Puerto Ricans were drafted or volunteered to fight in
every U.S. war of the twentieth century (see table 11). In the Korean and
Vietnam wars especially, Puerto Rican soldiers distinguished themselves
often in combat. In Korea, Puerto Ricans suffered the second-highest ca-

sualty rate (Hawaii had the highest), 1 for every 600 soldiers, while in the rest of the United States, the rate was 1 for every 1,125. Yet the island's people have never had a vote in the Congress that declared any of those wars.[25]

---

### TABLE 11
## MILITARY SERVICE OF PUERTO RICANS IN U.S. WARS

|  | Number Served | Number Killed |
|---|---|---|
| World War I | 17,855 | 1 |
| World War II | 65,034 | 23 |
| Korea | 61,000 | 731 |
| Vietnam | 47,000 | 342 |

---

## HAVE WE EVER AMOUNTED TO ANYTHING?

A century of economic and political control has left a deep psychological imprint on all Puerto Ricans and has affected the way North Americans regard the island and its people. Those views have turned markedly negative since Puerto Ricans began migrating here in large numbers after World War II.

Take, for instance, this article from *New York* magazine in 1972:

> These people were "Spanish." They came in swarms like ants turning the sidewalks brown, and they settled in, multiplied, whole sections of the city fallen to their shiny black raincoats and chewing-gum speech. We called them "mee-dahs," because they were always shouting "mee-dah, mee-dah" . . .
>
> I only knew they grew in numbers rather than stature, that they were neither white nor black but some indelicate tan, and that they were here, irrevocably; the best you could do to avoid contamination was to keep them out of mind.[26]

Or take Oxford University professor Raymond Carr, an expert on Latin American studies, who wrote in 1984:

> Few Americans take seriously the claims of Puerto Rican culture. They arrive in an island where they are offered rum and Coca-Cola

by English-speaking waiters and where they see book shops crammed with American paperbacks. Puerto Rican culture appears to them merely quaint folklore kept alive for the tourist trade.

Puerto Ricans' culture may be a poor thing, but it is their own; less as an intellectual construct than as a bundle of attitudes, of feelings, that make the life of the tribe comprehensible to its members.[27]

Or Chavez in *Out of the Barrio:* "So long as significant numbers of young Puerto Rican men remain alienated from the work force, living by means of crime or charity, fathering children toward whom they feel no responsibility, the prospects of Puerto Ricans in the United States will dim."[28]

This theory that Puerto Ricans have allowed a culture of poverty to take root, that whole sectors are eagerly dependent on government handouts, has made amazing inroads among many white Americans. How else, asks Chavez, do you explain Puerto Ricans' lack of progress even when compared to other Latinos? Dependency, however, has little to do with the specific culture of any people and much to do with the outside forces those people confront. It is something that is taught, nurtured, and reinforced. Frantz Fanon, the psychiatrist and theorist of Algerian independence, best analyzed how colonial systems have historically created a psychology of dependence in their subjects:

Colonialism is not satisfied merely with holding a people in its grip and emptying the native's brain of all form and content. By a kind of perverted logic, it turns to the past of the oppressed people, and distorts, disfigures, and destroys it. . . . The effect consciously sought by colonialism [is] to drive into the natives' heads the idea that if the settlers were to leave, they would at once fall back into barbarism, degradation, and bestiality.[29]

To be independent, to stand on one's own, a person, a group, a nation must first conceive of themselves as whole, as separate and unique from others. Unlike other immigrants, even other Latin Americans, Puerto Ricans have always suffered from deep ambivalence and insecurity when it comes to something as basic as who we are. Several studies have shown that Puerto Ricans suffer from extremely high rates of mental and personality disorders—three times the U.S. average—and that schizophrenia is by far the most treated psychosis. In a speech to the American Academy of Psychoanalysis in 1980, Dr. Hector R. Bird said:

The present state of Puerto Rican society is one of identity diffusion and identity confusion.

Numerous social indicators reflect the depth and breadth of the Puerto Rican crisis and suggest a collectivity in a state of psychosocial disintegration. Criminality is rampant, divorce rates are among the highest in the world, as are the rates of alcoholism and drug abuse and the high incidence of psychopathology and emotional malfunction. . . . We do not mean to imply that identity conflicts are the sole explanation for all of Puerto Rico's social ills. Such a highly complex situation is evidently multidetermined and a host of other factors contribute (such as overpopulation, the stresses of repeated uprootings in the pattern of back-and-forth migration, rapid social change, and so forth). But many of these factors are directly or indirectly related to the colonial status and to the absence of the aforementioned "mutually supportive psychosocial equilibrium" to which identity conflicts contribute.[30]

How could this identity confusion be otherwise? Before they came to this country, for instance, Mexican, Dominican, and Colombian immigrants all learned in their public schools, libraries, and mass media about their own national history and culture. The poorest Mexican laborer swells with pride at the mention of Moctezuma, Our Lady of Guadalupe, of Benito Juárez and Zapata, and of those giants of twentieth-century art, Orozco and Rivera. But generations of Puerto Ricans have learned only about Washington, Lincoln, and the Roosevelts, about Whitman and Hemingway and Poe. For the first fifty years of the U.S. occupation, public schools on the island sought to bury any memory of a culture and history that existed before the U.S. flag was planted. They even tried unsuccessfully to bury the most critical vehicle for preserving that history and culture, the island's language. In this country, meanwhile, few children in the public schools, including Puerto Rican children, are taught anything about Puerto Rico except for its geographical location and the fact that it "belongs" to the United States.

Given that century of cultural oppression, it is amazing that Puerto Ricans on the island have preserved *any* knowledge of their cultural heritage, from Alonso Ramírez's 1849 masterpiece, *El Jíbaro,* to the works of poets José Gautier Benítez (1851–1880) and Lola Rodríguez de Tió (1843–1924); to painters Francisco Oller (1833–1917) and Ramón Frade (1875–1956); to essayists and historians like Eugenio María de Hostos (1839–1903) and Salvador Brau (1842–1912).[31] Much of the credit for preserving that cultural legacy is owed to government organizations that developed under the Popular Party toward the second half of the twentieth century, such as the Institute for Puerto Rican Culture, and to the research and writings of scores of scholars, many of them proindependence, at the University of Puerto Rico.

At the popular level, island culture has shown special resilience in the fields of music and dance; the classical *danzas* of Julio Arteaga (1867–1923) and Juan Morel Campos (1857–1896); the *plena,* with its hypnotic staccato beat; the early-twentieth-century songs of Joselino "Bumbun" Oppenheimer (1884–1929), to César Concepción and Rafael Hernández in the 1940s; to Rafael Cortijo and Ismael Rivera in the 1950s and 1960s; to the legions of first-class salsa and jazz musicians of today.

While Puerto Ricans on the island had to battle to preserve their culture from annihilation, Puerto Ricans here were denied even the most rudimentary access to it, and thus grew up with virtually no understanding of our unique relationship to the United States.

"Citizenship, which should have enhanced Puerto Rican achievement," posits Chavez, "may actually have hindered it by conferring entitlements, such as welfare, with no concomitant obligations."[32] As proof, Chavez points to the disproportionate level of welfare dependency among New York Hispanics (42 percent of all recipients of Aid to Families with Dependent Children in 1977, when Hispanics were only 12 percent of the population). No doubt, a dependent mentality toward government, pessimism about one's ability to change the future, self-hatred, and self-deprecation have become ingrained in too many Puerto Ricans. But these did not originate from the breakup of the family and out-of-wedlock births, as Chavez, Moynihan, and others claim. They are symptoms of a more deep-rooted malady—the structure of colonialism itself. How else could the U.S. government justify to its people the continued possession of a colony except by cultivating an image of Puerto Ricans as helpless and unable to care for themselves?

As for the "breakup" of the family, we would do well to ask what the ideal Puerto Rican family was like before mass migration to the United States, or how economic and class forces affected it. We have already noted how consensual unions were always more prevalent in Latin American society, especially among the poorer classes, than in Anglo-Saxon society. But rapid industrialization itself had a debilitating impact on the Puerto Rican family structure. U.S. firms chose to hire mainly Puerto Rican women for their island factories while ignoring the men. In 1980, women represented 36.5 percent of Puerto Rico's labor force but 48.3 percent of its factory workers. From the end of World War II to 1980, the labor force participation rate of the island's adult males dropped from 70.6 percent to 54.4 percent.[33] Those men who had trouble landing jobs at home found the U.S. migrant farm labor program eager and ready to transport them to the fields of New Jersey, New York, Connecticut, Massachusetts, and Ohio, a process that separated them from their families for months out of every year and often led to permanent breakups of marriages.

Added to the strains of a migrant labor existence was the decline of industrial employment in this country. Deindustrialization took hold in the Northeast and Midwest shortly after Puerto Ricans migrated to those regions. In New York, for example, 60 percent of Puerto Rican workers in 1960 had factory jobs, so they were particularly vulnerable over the succeeding decades as those jobs disappeared.[34] As the nature of work changed in urban America, Puerto Ricans found themselves shut out of the growing areas of white-collar financial, professional, and government jobs. This was due not so much to their own volition as it was to language barriers, lack of education, and racial discrimination.

In both Puerto Rico and urban America, the welfare system emerged during the 1970s as a key vehicle for the federal government to prevent starvation and social unrest by granting subsistence income to the long-term unemployed. Unfortunately, many Puerto Ricans, already psychologically deformed by colonialism, found it far too easy to rely on those government handouts.

In addition, the ease by which Puerto Ricans move back and forth on the "air bridge" connecting the island and the mainland—an option other Latino immigrants lack—brought unique problems of instability. Those migrant pioneers who were successful in business found it easier just to pack up and return to Puerto Rico. Once there, with their modest savings and their newfound fluency in English, they joined the island middle class as employees in the fast-growing tourist industry, as managers of American companies, or just as comfortable retirees. Their return home, however, depleted the Puerto Rican *barrios* in the mainland of a developing middle class. As new waves of unskilled laborers moved up from the island, those *barrios* remained disproportionately filled with the unemployed and poor, and thus appeared to outsiders as almost stuck in time, unable to progress.

By the late 1970s, Puerto Rican professionals, unable to find work at home, started migrating here as well. But these new professionals often settled far from the old Puerto Rican *barrios,* or in cities where Mexicans or Cubans predominated. A considerable number of island-trained engineers, for instance, went to work for NASA in Houston or the burgeoning computer industry in California (Orlando, Florida, now boasts the fastest-growing Puerto Rican community). The result of this back-and-forth migration has been a Puerto Rican middle class here that is less stable and less connected to institution building among the masses of poor people than in, say, the Mexican and Cuban immigrant communities. Cuban businessmen, as previously noted, routinely hire fellow Cubans, develop their businesses, and spend their money within the Cuban community, as do Mexicans, Salvadorans, and other Latinos.

The above factors should indicate why Puerto Ricans, more than any other Latino group, feel such an intimate bond to their homeland, and why they should be regarded by the rest of American society as one people. The experiences of the 2.8 million Puerto Ricans in this country cannot be separated from those of the 3.8 million on the island. All 6.6 million of us, after all, are U.S. citizens, and all continue to live with the effects—whether the rest of American society realizes it or not—of one hundred years of colonialism.

## FREEDOM OF CHOICE AND THE DEBATE OVER STATUS

For nearly half a century, Congress has insisted that Puerto Ricans wanted that relationship, that island residents voluntarily chose to be a dressed-up colony, or commonwealth, and voted accordingly in previous status referendums. That claim was finally unmasked in 1989 when the island's three major political parties jointly declared that Puerto Ricans had never really exercised their right of self-determination. That year, the three parties, the Popular Democratic, the New Progressive, and the Puerto Rican Independence Party, jointly petitioned Congress for a new referendum to decide the island's final status.

As any serious student of Puerto Rican history knows, two prior referendums in 1952 and 1967 were so unfairly stacked for one option that they mocked the idea of free choice. The 1952 vote offered Puerto Ricans only the choice of remaining a direct colony or accepting the limited self-rule that now exists under the commonwealth. Neither statehood nor independence were put on the ballot by Congress. In fact, government repression of the independence movement was at its height at the time. Even peaceful advocates of separation were systematically blacklisted from government jobs. The infamous 1948 "gag law," passed by the precommonwealth legislature, made it a crime to publicly advocate violent opposition to the U.S. occupation. After the failed Jayuya independence revolt of 1950, the law was invoked to declare virtual martial law and imprison thousands of nationalists and their sympathizers. Despite that repression, candidates of the proindependence party garnered an amazing 20 percent of the vote in island elections in the 1950s, and they managed to keep the issue of Puerto Rico's colonial status alive at the United Nations.[35]

By the 1960s, as more African and Asian colonies secured their independence and joined the UN, the new member states began to ask pointed questions of the U.S. delegation about Puerto Rico's status. The pressure prompted President Johnson in 1964 to appoint a blue-ribbon U.S.–Puerto Rico Status Commission, which recommended a new plebiscite in which, for the first time, independence, statehood, and commonwealth would all be offered as options of "equal dignity and equal status." That referendum was held on July 23, 1967. Governor Muñoz Marín campaigned strenuously for what he called "enhanced commonwealth," which he described as having greater autonomy than the federal government had approved in 1948.

While the choices were a vast improvement over those offered in 1952, they still suffered from fundamental flaws. First, Congress refused to commit itself before the vote to accept whatever decision the Puerto Rican people made, insisting instead on its sovereign right to decide the island's status. Second, Congress refused to clarify how the federal government would treat the island economically under a transition period to each of the three choices. Because of those flaws, the Puerto Rican Independence Party and a section of the statehood party boycotted the referendum, thus assuring a 60 percent margin for "enhanced commonwealth."

Only years later was a third and even more serious flaw revealed—a conspiracy by federal officials to subvert the vote. FBI agents conducted a campaign of dirty tricks and harassment against the Puerto Rican Independence Party aimed at weakening its support.[36] Even for Muñoz Marín and the Popular Democrats, however, the referendum proved to be a hollow victory, as Congress repeatedly rebuffed Muñoz's efforts to achieve the greater autonomy that the voters had approved.

Shortly after Jimmy Carter became president in 1977, his Latin America experts privately counseled a reexamination of Puerto Rico. Not only was the island's status creating repeated embarrassment before the United Nations Decolonization Committee but its intractable poverty was becoming a drain on the federal treasury. Some advisers urged steering the island toward a form of sovereignty, but one that would preserve U.S. influence and control.[37] Before a Carter commission could complete its work, however, Carter lost the 1980 presidential election, and his two immediate successors, Ronald Reagan and George Bush, both endorsed statehood for the island. But the Reagan-Bush vision of statehood differed markedly from annexationist leaders on the island. Those leaders, such as former governor Carlos Romero Barceló, advocated *un estado criollo,* a "Creole state." For them, Spanish would remain the island's language even after it joined the union, and this was something conservatives in Congress refused to accept.[38] As a result, the 1980s passed without federal action because the White House and Congress couldn't agree.

It was their frustration over the zigzags in U.S. policy that thus prompted the three island parties to unite in 1989 and petition Washington for a new plebiscite. In response to that petition, U.S. lawmakers began crafting a "Puerto Rico Self Determination Act" under the leadership of Louisiana senator J. Bennett Johnston. This time, Puerto Rican leaders demanded the specific definitions of each status, something that prior plebiscites had avoided. Those specifics, they argued, were the meat and potatoes of any real choices. How Congress spelled out the economic and cultural ramifications of each alternative would shape the voters' decision.

Under statehood, for instance, what kind of transition period would Congress grant before residents began paying federal taxes? What incentives would it offer to prevent American companies from abandoning the island once their federal tax exemptions evaporated? Would public schools and local government continue using Spanish as the primary language of instruction? Even such things as sports came under the spotlight: Would Puerto Rico retain its own Olympic team if it became the fifty-first state?

In case voters chose independence, what would happen to the American citizenship of those who already have it? Was a form of dual citizenship, or at least unrestricted entry in and out of the United States, possible? What would be the fate of the Social Security, pension, and veterans' benefits, or federal mortgage insurance programs, to which Puerto Ricans were already entitled? Would the U.S. government negotiate new treaties and agree to pay for the military bases it wished to keep in Puerto Rico? Would an independent Puerto Rico get special preferences for trade and foreign aid, such as Mexico, Jordan, and Israel now enjoy?

Under enhanced commonwealth, would island governments finally achieve a greater say over their local affairs, the kind of broad autonomy Puerto Rico enjoyed under Spain before the U.S. occupation?[39] Could Puerto Rico, for instance, negotiate its own trade and tariff agreements with other countries? Would it participate in international organizations such as the UN? Would it have a say over federal appointments on the island or in how federal laws were applied? More importantly, Puerto Rican leaders wanted the bill to be "self-executing." That is, Congress had to agree beforehand to implement the voters' choice, not reserve for itself ultimate power to veto or alter it. The Puerto Rican leaders were sure Washington could not ignore their concerns as it had in 1952 and 1967. After all, a whole civil rights revolution had occurred since then. Dozens of Latinos and African Americans were sitting in Congress as a result. There was even a Puerto Rican representative, José Serrano of New York City, who was managing to forge an influential minority alliance around the issue of Puerto Rican self-determination.

They were wrong. The Senate committee drafting the bill rejected most of the key requests of all sides. It dismissed statehooders' insistence that Spanish remain the language of instruction in the public schools, any phase-in period for the paying of federal taxes, or any special tariffs to protect Puerto Rican coffee farmers from imports. Likewise, it rejected virtually all the "enhanced commonwealth" proposals as unconstitutional and a usurpation of U.S. sovereignty.

More importantly, the Senate insisted that whatever choice Puerto Ricans eventually made must cost the federal government no additional funds. When a Congressional Budget Office study revealed that statehood would require an additional $18 billion over nine years to equalize Medicaid and other benefits to the island, the Senate's reluctance to approve any bill increased. The most cost-effective alternative, the CBO concluded, was independence, since it would save the Treasury $1 billion annually.[40] Two years of dogged negotiations and contentious public hearings followed, with the Senate's Natural Resources Committee finally failing to approve the plebiscite bill by a 10–10 vote.

A second effort to pass a referendum bill failed in 1991. By then, conservative Republicans started voicing concerns that Puerto Rican statehood would lead to another Quebec.[41] Not lost on leaders of both parties was the reality that most of the pro-statehood and all the pro-commonwealth politicians on the island were affiliated to the Democratic Party. A Puerto Rican state was thus likely to elect two Democratic senators and six Democratic members of Congress. It might even fuel long-standing demands by African Americans for statehood for the District of Columbia. The whole issue, in short, threatened a major expansion of the voting franchise to millions of Hispanics and African Americans and an almost certain realignment of federal political power.

Soon after the plebiscite bill's defeat, island elections swept the pro-statehood New Progressive Party into power. The new governor, Pedro

Rosselló, decided to ignore Congress and immediately organize his own own status referendum in November 1993. Even though the vote had no congressional sanction, Rosselló hoped it would keep the pressure on Washington for a final resolution, and he was confident that statehood would finally achieve a majority. But the final tally showed 48.4 percent for commonwealth, 46.25 percent for statehood, and 4.4 percent for independence. An astounding 80 percent of the electorate had turned out. For the third time in fifty years, commonwealth supporters had won a referendum, and once again, Washington simply ignored the island's vote.

The Republicans captured control of Congress the following year, and bitter battles over the federal budget temporarily relegated Puerto Rico's status to the political shadows. The new Republican majority subsequently rammed through a series of bills that were viewed as anti-Hispanic, which caused Latinos to turn out in record numbers in the 1996 election, thus helping reelect President Clinton. All the polls after that election confirmed that Republicans were losing support among Hispanics, the country's fastest-growing group of voters. Party consultants warned House Speaker Newt Gingrich that the slim Republican majority in Congress might slip away in the 1998 election unless the party got more Hispanic votes. So, against the wishes of the party's most conservative wing, Gingrich agreed to bring a new Puerto Rican plebiscite bill to a vote in the full House. The Clinton administration, in an unusual display of bipartisanship, backed Gingrich's plan and marshaled all the Democrats it could to vote for the bill.

In the months leading up to that vote, Puerto Rican leaders lobbied feverishly over the bill's content, while conservative groups seeking to head off statehood lobbied just as hard to kill any legislation. The final version, sponsored by Alaska Republican Don Young, passed on March 4, 1998, by a razor-thin 209 to 208 margin. The Senate, however, shelved any action on the bill.

## THE YOUNG BILL—THE FIRST ADMISSION THAT COLONIALISM MUST END

Even though the Young Bill eventually died in the Senate, it was a major milestone in the century-long status debate. For example, the bill's preamble conceded that the United States has never allowed Puerto Ricans genuine self-determination. For the first time, Congress was offering island voters a choice between commonwealth, statehood, and "separate sovereignty." And for the first time, Congress stated that commonwealth was not a permanent solution in the eyes of the United States, nor was the greater self-rule implied by "enhanced commonwealth" constitutional. According to the bill, should Puerto Ricans choose commonwealth, a new referendum would be held every ten years until a majority chose either statehood or "separate sovereignty."

Under the Young Bill, before Puerto Rico could be admitted as a state, it would have to adhere to whatever U.S. law exists at the time on official language. And while English is not yet the official language of the country, the message between the lines was clear: it *will* be by the time Puerto Rico becomes a state.

The "separate sovereignty" provision of the bill recognized two alternatives as equally viable: complete independence or free association. Under the second, the island would be recognized as a separate nation in a voluntary union with the United States. Both independence and free association, however, would put an end to automatic American citizenship for those born on the island after the new status took effect. At first glance, that provision appears to doom the "separate sovereignty" option, since the overwhelming majority of Puerto Ricans want to retain their U.S. citizenship. But the federal courts long ago ruled that children of American citizens born anywhere in the world can claim U.S. citizenship, so any Puerto Rican who wished to do so could grandfather citizenship into his or her immediate family from generation to generation.

The marathon twelve-hour debate that preceded the House vote was televised over C-Span in both Puerto Rico and the United States, which meant that the American people witnessed the first public debate by our leaders over what to do with the nation's most important colony. And this time the debate was led by four members of the House of Representative who had been born in Puerto Rico. The four mirrored the same deep divisions and passion over status that exist among all Puerto Ricans. Chicago's Luis Gutiérrez, an advocate of independence, and New York's Nydia Velázquez, a defender of commonwealth, vehemently opposed the Young Bill. They labeled it a sham because it undermined commonwealth as a legitimate permanent option. New York's José Serrano, who has never stated his preference for a final status, and Carlos Romero Barceló, the island's nonvoting resident commissioner and most passionate advocate of statehood, eagerly backed the bill, but they differed strongly over whether Puerto Ricans living in the United States should be allowed to vote. Serrano insisted that a plebiscite to decide the future of a nation is not a normal election; it should be open to all people born on the island—no matter where they now live. Romero Barceló argued that only residents of the island, no matter their nationality, should vote, because only they would have to live with the plebiscite's results. Serrano's amendment was overwhelmingly defeated.

The rest of Congress was just as sharply divided as the Puerto Ricans. The close final vote reflected deep uncertainty over this country's continued relationship to the island. Some congressmen even questioned why the matter of Puerto Rico was coming up for debate at all—as if the issue could be tabled for another hundred years.

Pro-statehood governor Pedro Rosselló, however, refused to be deterred by inaction in Congress. He scheduled yet another referendum on status for the end of 1998, the hundredth anniversary of the U.S. occupation, in hopes of pressuring Washington for action. He even rejected requests to postpone the referendum after Hurricane Georges plowed through the Caribbean that September and devastated Puerto Rico and a dozen other islands. Rosselló alienated voters further by excluding the "commonwealth" option favored by the Popular Democrats from the ballot. The result was a massive voter protest against the entire process, with more than 50 percent choosing "none of the above" and statehood getting just 46 percent. The bizarre tally only confounded Congress, permitting its members to postpone any new debate on the island.

But that decision cannot be avoided for much longer. The current colonial status, marked by economic stagnation and cultural confusion, is no longer acceptable to anyone. All leaders on the island are demanding a change. Unfortunately, getting a majority in either Puerto Rico or the United States for one option has so far proved elusive. Public-opinion polls show Puerto Ricans are against any choice that gives up either their American citizenship or their right to speak Spanish in island schools and courts. To most English-speaking Americans, those two "rights" are mutually exclusive, an insoluble contradiction. But to Puerto Ricans, they are no less a contradiction than the current position of Congress and the Supreme Court that Puerto Rico "belongs to but is not a part of the United States." No ethnic or territorial group, Puerto Ricans are now saying, can remain the "property" of another nation forever, and if the cost of ending that colonial relationship ends up inconveniencing the colonizing nation, perhaps forcing it to change its Constitution, then so be it.

But another factor is propelling Congress to act: the U.S. no longer needs Puerto Rico as a colony. Just as slavery is ultimately more costly than wage labor, since the master must pay for the food and lodging of his slaves, so does possessing a colony involve huge costs of upkeep that sooner or later become a burden on the colonial administrator. As we have noted, it is easier today for U.S. corporations to exploit laborers in the Dominican Republic or Mexico than in Puerto Rico, whose workers now enjoy the labor rights of other Americans, so the continued cost of possessing Puerto Rico can no longer be justified.

Finally, Puerto Rico's strategic value as a military outpost against Communism has diminished considerably with the end of the Cold War.

So why not end colonialism by welcoming Puerto Rico as the fifty-first state, as the annexationists want? Haven't Puerto Ricans proved our loyalty by fighting in every major U.S. war this century? José Trías Monge, a former chief justice of the Supreme Court of Puerto Rico, insists that statehood was never intended by Congress for the island. In a recent book reviewing congressional law and Supreme Court decisions on Puerto Rico, Trías Monge notes that unlike Hawaii and Alaska, which Congress deemed incorporated territories and slated for annexation from the start, Puerto Rico was kept "unincorporated" specifically to avoid offering it statehood.

President Taft made that policy clear during his annual message to Congress in 1912, when he said:

> I believe that the demand for citizenship is just, and that it is amply earned by the sustained loyalty on the part of the inhabitants of the island. But it should be remembered that the demand must be, in the minds of most Porto Ricans is, entirely dissociated from any thought of statehood. I believe that no substantial public opinion in the United States or in Puerto Rico contemplates statehood for the island as the ultimate form of relations between us.[42]

How much truer Taft's words seem today. With our government clamping down on the flood of Latin American immigrants, it is almost unthinkable that a congressional majority would be prepared to admit an entire state whose people are racially mixed and who speak Spanish as their main language. Hawaii petitioned Congress for statehood for the first time in 1919. Its residents voted overwhelmingly for it in a plebiscite as early as 1940. Yet Congress denied that plea for nineteen more years because the territory had a substantial native and Asian population.[43] How much more difficult will statehood be for Puerto Rico, when the population of Anglo Americans there is still tiny and not even a bare majority of islanders is petitioning for statehood after a hundred years?

Well, then, what about independence? Any concept of a Puerto Rican republic that fails to preserve U.S. citizenship for most islanders is doomed to fail in the foreseeable future. The reason is simple. The United States is the richest and most powerful nation in the world. At a time when millions of people in other countries will travel any distance, make any sacrifice, overcome any obstacle to achieve U.S. citizenship, or at least permanent residence here, Puerto Ricans are unlikely to give theirs up voluntarily.

How, then, can a solution be found that meets the contradictory needs of both the American and Puerto Rican people? A small but highly influential group of island leaders has urged for years that the only solution out of this quagmire is a new status, one that incorporates aspects of the three historic choices. They call it the associated republic, *república asociada,* an arrangement chosen in 1986 by the Pacific Trust Territories of the United States. It is the equivalent in the United Nations decolonization process to a "free associated state."

The associated republic begins with the premise that Puerto Rico is a separate nation with the right to "sovereignty and self-government." It posits that the people of the United States and of Puerto Rico have chosen to maintain a "close and mutually beneficial relationship in a voluntary association."

The main elements of that new union would be:

- Puerto Rico conducts its own international affairs, including its own treaties, customs duties, and participation in the United Nations and other international organizations;
- Dual American and Puerto Rican citizenship for those born on the island;
- A common market, common currency, and common postal system between the two nations;
- No immigration barriers to citizens of either country;
- It grants U.S. "authority and responsibility for international security and defense" of the island, but requires consent of the Puerto Rican legislature to involve the island in a war;
- Negotiated use and adequate rent for U.S. military bases;
- Foreign investment incentives to replace the Section 936 tax exemption;
- Elimination of the U.S. maritime monopoly on Puerto Rican shipping;
- Block grants of foreign aid to replace current federal transfer payments;
- A twenty-five-year lifetime for the compact, after which it would be renegotiated.[44]

The associated republic offers a new common ground. In many ways, it is the logical extension of Muñoz Marín's thirty-year-old dream of "enhanced commonwealth," but it does require U.S. leaders to recognize the obvious, that Puerto Rico is a separate nation from the United States. At the same time, the new status would not sever all citizenship ties with this country, and would not challenge the military's desire for long-term bases. It would provide some of the reforms sought by commonwealth supporters in customs and treaties, and it would eliminate the maritime monopoly. It would put an end to the second-class status abhorred by statehooders while maintaining the island's Spanish language and culture. By giving up the quest for statehood, Puerto Ricans could ease the fears of millions of Americans on the mainland that complete annexation of the island will fragment further the nation's cultural unity, and they would dispel concerns that Puerto Rico will remain an enclave of poverty laying annual claim to ever-larger doses of federal aid.

Puerto Ricans cannot be the only ones to make concessions, however. The American people should enthusiastically endorse long-term federal assistance to the island. Given the enormous sacrifices Puerto Ricans have made in this country's wars and the immense wealth U.S. corporations secured from island labor, a free associated Puerto Rico deserves at least as much federal assistance as Israel or Egypt, nations with more distant and less enduring relationships to this country. Free association could pave the way for moving the world's oldest colony toward equality in the world of nations. To generations of Puerto Ricans, the psychological benefit that will accompany the end of this netherworld of colonial dependency will be incalculable. For Americans, it would wash away an old and ugly stain on this nation's most cherished ideals.

A hundred years, after all, is time enough to decide.

# Epilogue

The Chinese spent almost two thousand years perfecting their Great Wall, the Spanish endured eight centuries of foreign occupation before finally expelling the Moors, and the dazzling civilization of Teotihuacán flourished for seven centuries before suddenly disappearing, so the mere two centuries that have elapsed since the Americas broke away from European colonialism barely amount to a crawling stage on the road to nationhood.

The new American states were all unprecedented social experiments into which were amalgamated the cultures, races, and political traditions of both settlers and indigenous peoples. The societies that arose from those experiments are still in search of solid identities today, still extracting and refining the ore that will become their legacy to civilization. The United States is no exception. No matter what the leaders of this nation may claim about its immutable Anglo-Saxon character, fresh waves of immigrants arrive each year, flinging themselves and their customs into the mix, recombining and redefining, ever so slightly, the locus of shared memories that make up the definition of America. This process of growth and change, of cross-fertilization and amalgamation, is more likely to speed up in the twenty-first century than to slow down.

During those first two hundred years, the United States emerged as the world's only superpower and its richest nation. No empire, whether in ancient or modern times, ever saw its influence spread so far or determined the thoughts and actions of so many people around the world as our nation does today. That spectacular success was due in large measure to the unique brand of representative democracy, the spirit of bold enterprise, the respect for individual liberty, and the rugged devotion to hard work that characterized so many of the early American settlers. But there was another aspect to that success, as I have tried to show, the details of which most Americans knew nothing about, but which was always carried out in their name. It was a vicious and relentless drive for territorial expansion, conquest, and subjugation of others—Native Americans, African slaves, and Latin Americans—one that our leaders justified as Manifest Destiny for us.

That expansion transformed the entire hemisphere into an economic satellite and sphere of influence of the United States. The empire that expansion created produced an unexpected harvest here at home toward the end of the twentieth century—massive Latin American immigration. As U.S. capital penetrated the region, it dislocated Latin Americans from their land, impoverished them, then recruited them into a ragtag army of low-priced labor wandering along carefully charted migratory circuits. The best wages in the hemisphere, and the lion's share of its wealth, remained in the United States, so the hardiest of those uprooted workers inevitably headed here, some drawn by corporate recruiters, others pushed by political repression.

By seeking a piece of our prosperity, however, Latin Americans were merely reliving our immigrant creation story. They came by the millions, desperate, unarmed, heads bowed, not dictating terms at gunpoint or declaring their independence in filibuster revolts as did the Anglo pioneers who ventured into Latin America before them, yet the peaceful transformation they have achieved has been just as inexorable. It is nothing less than Latinization of the United States from the bottom up. If current trends continue, Latinos, who now compose one of every ten Americans, will increase to one of every four by the year 2050, and could even approach one-half of the population by 2100.[1]

All attempts to stem this immigration explosion will fail, so long as nothing is done to control the unfettered spread of U.S. corporate power below the Rio Grande. Those who keep trying to block immigration with exclusionary laws risk inciting the very ethnic balkanization and domestic civil strife they fear. In seeking to defend the "old America," they risk permanently damaging the current one.

It does not have to be this way. Profound change in our country's ethnic makeup need not undermine its deepest-held beliefs. Just as the abolition of slavery signaled a new beginning, a chance to make democracy more universal, so too can a policy of embracing the Latin American masses with whom U.S. history has always been so intertwined. White Anglo leaders must begin by rejecting cultural intolerance and margin-

alization of Latinos. They must move quickly to reduce a growing alien-
ation between Hispanic Americans and the rest of the nation. They must
stop regarding Latinos as a linguistic caste within the empire, as conquered peoples, and they must press for specific economic and social reforms that have gone ignored for too long.

Only radical change will bring about qualitative progress in Latino
economic life. That change has little to do with the behavior-based solutions of conservatives, with catchy slogans like "family values," "work
ethic," or "personal responsibility," or with the Band-Aid solutions of liberals: bigger and better government social programs, school integration,
affirmative action. The reforms I am suggesting may seem at first to be-
long more in the realm of foreign than domestic policy. Yet they are essential reforms precisely because the Latino presence here is so directly
connected to our nation's foreign conquest. Only by changing the nature
of the American empire can Latino equality and assimilation become
real. The following changes in national policy are the ones I consider essential for this new century.

1. *End the predatory dual labor market in cheap Mexican labor*. The
only way to prevent the continued exploitation of millions of Mexicans,
both in this country and across the Rio Grande, is with the complete mobility of labor between the two nations and the gradual equalizing of
their respective environmental and labor laws. In 1994, NAFTA created
a common market for goods but not a common market for people. The
former essentially benefits small elites in both countries, while the latter
would be a boon to the majority of workers in both. A common labor
market—perhaps even with cross-border labor unions or alliances such
as the American-Canadian AFL-CIO unions already in existence—will
reduce the gap between wages and labor standards in the United States
and Mexico. As wages rise south of the border, Mexicans will consume
more U.S. goods and fewer of them will seek to emigrate North. Abol-
ishing the concept of "illegality" among Mexicans, who are overwhelmingly the largest source of undocumented labor, will drive up wages at
the bottom of our society. How? Because U.S. employers will find it
harder to exploit those who can freely organize unions and petition the
courts and government for their legal rights. It is just that kind of a common labor market that the European Union is moving toward.

2. *End the colonial status of Puerto Rico.* Congress should immediately
schedule a plebiscite on Puerto Rico's permanent status. It should agree
beforehand to implement whatever status Puerto Ricans decide, whether
that be a sovereign associated state, a fully autonomous commonwealth,

an independent nation, or the fifty-first state. Should Puerto Ricans choose either free association or independence, Congress, in recognition of the immense wealth islanders provided this country for one hundred years, and out of gratitude for the thousands of Puerto Ricans who fought in U.S. wars, should commit itself to provide transitional federal assistance, the right of all islanders to retain dual U.S. citizenship, and a free trade market with the United States. Should Puerto Ricans choose statehood, Congress should not delay in granting it, one in which English and Spanish become co-official languages. Only through genuine decolonization can the second-class limbo Puerto Ricans experience finally end.

3. *Recognize the rights of language minorities and promote the widespread study of Spanish.* Unlike many nations in the world, the United States has yet to recognize the right of language minorities to protection against discrimination. Puerto Ricans, Cubans, and Mexicans in this country are each ethnic minorities, but all Hispanics together comprise a linguistic minority, one whose origins predate the founding of the country. Spanish is not a foreign tongue in the United States. It is the principal language of the Western Hemisphere and the second language of the United States, and should finally be recognized as such. Instead of passing anachronistic English-only laws, our leaders should, at the minimum, be embracing bilingualism. American public schools, for instance, should foster the teaching of Spanish as a main secondary language, maybe even requiring its study in those regions or states where Hispanics are a substantial minority. Doing so will not in any way reduce the pivotal role English performs as the country's main language. On the contrary, it will foster greater understanding among Americans of all races. As more whites and blacks in this country learn Spanish, as they taste the greater cultural sophistication and intellectual power that comes from breaking out of an English monolingual ghetto, they will turn into bridge builders and healers within our own population.

4. *Reinvest in U.S. cities and public schools.* The bulk of Latinos live, work, and learn in urban America. Our future is tied to that of the cities. A federal program aimed at rebuilding urban America's infrastructure and at investing in its public schools would provide jobs and upward mobility into the middle class for many Latinos now caught at the economic margins, just as the building of the suburbs in the 1950s helped create the white middle class.

5. *End U.S. militarism in Latin America.* From the days of gunboat diplomacy to the era of the *jefes,* from the secret wars of the CIA to the current War on Drugs, the U.S. military has always sought to dictate the affairs of Latin America, installing or propping up unpopular leaders, de-

fending rogue Yankee businessmen, or simply spurring sales of U.S. weapons to local governments and private paramilitary groups. Our government must renounce this militarism once and for all. Only such an about-face would begin to ameliorate the estrangement felt by Salvadoran, Guatemalan, Colombian, and Dominican immigrants, many of whom continue to harbor bitter feelings about this country's role in recent civil wars in their countries of origin.

6. *End the economic blockade of Cuba.* Given the flourishing economic and political relations our government has cultivated with socialist countries such as China and Vietnam in recent years, Washington's stubborn forty-year blockade of Cuba remains a glaring example of how Uncle Sam still regards Latin America as its own backyard and refuses to tolerate dissent in the region. The blockade is almost universally condemned by the rest of the world. While the extraordinary government assistance provided to Cuban immigrants in the past has helped turn them into the most successful Latino group economically, it has also led to a dual standard in immigration policy and resentment from all other Latinos. Ending the blockade and normalizing relations would improve economic conditions in Cuba and pave the way for an end to that dual standard.

These solutions are not likely to find receptive ears in the current conservative era. Nowadays, our leaders prefer to search for the causes of crime and poverty in the actions or inaction of those at the very bottom of society. The obscene transfers of wealth over the past thirty years from that bottom to a privileged few at the top—and from much of the Third World to financial elites in the West—are all excused as the natural evolution of the Market, when, in fact, they are products of unparalleled greed by those who shape and direct that Market.

That is why my solutions aim directly at that all-powerful and invisible Market and the empire we have created in its name. Immigrant labor has always been critical to the Market's prosperity. The Market recruits it, exploits it, abuses it, divides it, then ships it back home when no longer needed. Only by reining in that Market, by challenging its relentless grasp, by humbling its colossal power, can Latinos in this country move from incremental to qualitative progress, only then can they shatter the caste system to which they have been relegated. Only by taming the Market can the people of the Americas, north and south, move beyond our ethnic, racial, and linguistic divisions. Only then can we grasp our common humanity, realize our common dreams.

America, after all, never did end at the Rio Grande.

# Acknowledgments

Many thanks to my various editors at Penguin Putnam: Don Fehr, who guided me during the first few years in making the transition from newspapers to books, and whose meticulous analysis and uncanny sense of organization and structure turned my primitive and chaotic initial drafts into a coherent whole; Jane von Mehren, whose constant support and careful reviews of the manuscript helped shape my sense of audience; and Sarah Baker, whose probing questions repeatedly exposed the weaknesses in my thinking and copy.

For improving the content, I am grateful to several friends who read various drafts of chapters over the years and offered their suggestions: Tom Acosta, Stephen Handelman, and Dennis Rivera in New York; Gil Cedillo and David Sandoval in California; *New York Daily News* editors James "Hap" Hairston and Albor Ruiz; Greg Tarpinian of Labor Research Associates; Clara Rodríguez of Fordham University; Héctor Cordero Guzmán of the New School for Social Research; and two of Puerto Rico's most brilliant journalists, Juan Manuel García Passalacqua and Jesús Dávila.

I am especially indebted to my friend and agent, Frances Goldin, whose relentless defense of her writers is matched only by her untiring devotion to social justice.

Many thanks to Amilcar Tirado at the Center for Puerto Rican Studies Library at Hunter College in New York, to Yolanda González at the Arnulfo Oliveiras Memorial Library at the University of Texas at Brownsville, to Margo Gutiérrez at the Benson Latin American Collection of the University of Texas at Austin, and to Faigi Rosenthal, chief librarian at the *New York Daily News,* for their invaluable help in locating source material, and to Esther (Nequi) González, my research assistant for several years. Without Nequi's commitment and dedication to detail, this book might never have reached print.

My wife and *compañera,* Niurka Alvarez, did a marvelous job cataloging and completing all the final source notes, correcting my frequent lapses in Spanish usage, and prodding me to keep writing whenever I became discouraged. She even found time to give birth to our wonderful daughter, Gabriela, in the midst of it all.

Countless Latinos in this country, as well as in Mexico, Central America, and the Caribbean, welcomed me into their homes and opened their hearts to me over the past few decades. Whether I was reporting for a newspaper or doing research for this book, they willingly recounted little-known family tales in hopes that the rest of America would more fully understand their story. Many of the best-known leaders of the Latino community—too many to mention here—have generously shared their thoughts with me over the years and thus helped to shape the views in this book.

But special thanks go to the lesser-known Latinos who facilitated my getting to know the families whose migration stories form the emotional core of the book. People like Domingo Gonzáles in Brownsville, Texas; Sandra Garza in El Paso; Estela Vázquez, Alfredo White, Héctor Méndez, and William Acosta in New York City; Luis Del Rosario in Miami; Mario González in Chicago; Ignacio Soto and Heraclio Rivera in the Dominican Republic, Víctor Alfaro Clark in Mexico.

Finally, thanks to my own family—especially my mother, Florinda Guillén, and my deceased father, Juan González, for never letting me forget how far we've come.

# *Notes*

## INTRODUCTION

1. Sam Howe Verhovek, "Tiny Stretch of Border, Big Test for a Wall," *New York Times,* December 8, 1997; also Verne G. Kopytoff, "A Silicon Wall Rises on the Border," *New York Times,* January 14, 1999; also Gregory Gross, "Shifting to the East: U.S. Fights to Close Gaps from Otay to Jacumba," *San Diego Union-Tribune,* May 26, 1996.
2. Author's interview with Jorge Giovanni López, March 1990.
3. Author's interview with Silvestre Reyes, June 1995. Reyes is now a U.S. representative from El Paso.
4. U.S. Department of Justice, *1996 Statistical Yearbook of the Immigration and Naturalization Service* (Washington, D.C.: U.S. Government Printing Office, 1997), 27–28.
5. U.S. Census Bureau, *Current Population Survey,* March 1994.
6. Ellen L. Lutz, *Human Rights in Mexico: A Policy of Impunity* (New York: America's Watch, June 1990), 87.
7. John Darnton, "Western Europe Is Ending Its Welcome to Immigrants," *New York Times,* August 10, 1993; also Alan Riding, "France, Reversing Course, Fights Immigrants' Refusal to Be French," *New York Times,* December 5, 1993; also John Tagliabue, "Sunny Italy Turns a Scowling Face to Immigrants," *New York Times,* January 5, 1995.

## CHAPTER 1: CONQUERORS AND VICTIMS

1. Tzvetan Todorov, *The Conquest of America* (New York: HarperCollins, 1984), 4–5; Adam Smith, *The Wealth of Nations* (1776), ed. Edwin Cannan, vol. 2 (London: University Paperbacks, 1961), 141. (The other for Smith was the discovery of a passage to India.)
2. William M. Denevan, *The Native Population of the Americas in 1492* (Madison: University of Wisconsin Press, 1992), xvii–xxix. Also Jack Weatherford, *Indian Givers: How the Indians of the Americas Transformed the World* (New York:

Fawcett Columbine, 1988), 158; Alvin Josephy, Jr., *The Indian Heritage of America* (Boston: Houghton Mifflin, 1991), 71; and Francis Jennings, *The Invasion of America: Indians, Colonialism and the Cant of Conquest* (New York: W. W. Norton, 1976), 30.

3. Estimates range from 7 to 18 million. See David Weber, *The Spanish Frontier in North America* (New Haven: Yale University Press, 1992), 28. Also Jennings, *The Invasion,* 30.

4. Bernal Díaz del Castillo, *The Conquest of New Spain* (London: Penguin Books, 1963), 235.

5. Josephy, *The Indian Heritage,* 164.

6. Robert S. Gottfried, *The Black Death* (New York: The Free Press, 1993), 133–56, provides a provocative analysis of how the plague transformed medieval Europe.

7. Geoffrey Elton, *The English* (Cambridge: Blackwell Publishers, 1995), 111.

8. Ibid., 138–39; also Nicholas Canny, *The Ideology of English Colonization: From Ireland to America,* quoted in Jennings, *The Invasion,* 46.

9. Alvar Núñez Cabeza de Vaca, *Adventures in the Unknown Interior of America,* ed. and trans. Cyclone Convey (Albuquerque: University of New Mexico Press, 1990), 67.

10. Ibid., 123.

11. Todorov, *The Conquest,* 5.

12. Samuel M. Wilson, *Hispaniola: Caribbean Chiefdoms in the Age of Columbus* (Alabama: University of Alabama Press, 1990), 91–93, summarizes the dispute over Hispaniola's population, whose estimates run from 200,000 to 5 million; also Eric Williams, *From Columbus to Castro: The History of the Caribbean 1492–1969* (New York: Vintage Books, 1984), 33.

13. Jennings, *The Conquest,* 24–27.

14. Miguel León-Portilla, *The Broken Spears: The Aztec Account of the Conquest of Mexico* (Boston: Beacon Press, 1992), 124.

15. Ibid., 117–20.

16. Bartolomé de las Casas, *A Short Account of the Destruction of the Indies* (London: Penguin Classics, 1992), 19.

17. John A. Crow, *The Epic of Latin America* (Berkeley: University of California Press, 1992), 157–60.

18. Josephy, *The Indian Heritage,* 302–3; Alice B. Kehoe, *North American Indians: A Comprehensive Account* (Englewood Cliffs, N.J.: Prentice-Hall, 1992), 251–52.

19. Ibid., 252–53.

20. Bernard Bailyn, *The Peopling of British North America* (New York: Vintage Books, 1988), 116.

21. Weatherford, *Indian Givers,* 158; and Josephy, *The Indian Heritage,* 322.

22. Díaz, *The Conquest,* 82.

23. Kathleen Deagan, "St. Augustine and the Mission Frontier," *The Spanish Missions of Florida,* ed. Bonnie G. McEwan (Gainesville: University of Florida, 1993), 99.

24. Simon Collier, Thomas E. Skidmore, and Harold Blakemore, *The Cambridge Encyclopedia of Latin America* (New York: Cambridge University Press, 1992), 193.

25. Jennings, *The Invasion,* 111.

26. Ibid., 53–56.

27. Ibid., 247.

28. Ibid., 251.

29. William Bradford, *Of Plymouth Plantation, 1620–1647,* ed. Samuel E. Morrison (New York: Alfred A. Knopf, 1952), 24.

30. Crow, *The Epic,* 192–208, gives an excellent summary of the Spanish missionary experience.

31. Josephy, *The Indian Heritage,* 319–20.

32. Weber, *The Spanish Frontier,* 106, 307, 309.

33. Bailyn, *The Peopling of British North America,* 96.

34. Nancy Rubin, *Isabella of Castile: The First Renaissance Queen* (New York: St. Martin's Press, 1991), 11–12; also Crow, *The Epic,* 149.

35. Hugh Thomas, *Conquest: Montezuma, Cortés and the Fall of Old Mexico* (New York: Simon & Schuster, 1993), 652, n. 17.

36. Leslie Bethell, ed., *Colonial Spanish America* (New York: Cambridge University Press, 1987), 20; also Clara E. Rodríguez and Héctor Cordero-Guzmán, "Placing Race in Context," *Ethnic and Racial Studies* 15, no. 4 (London: Routledge, October 1992), 527.

37. Verena Martínez-Alier, *Marriage, Class and Colour in Nineteenth-Century Cuba: A Study of Racial Attitudes and Sexual Values in a Slave Society* (Ann Arbor: University of Michigan Press, 1989), 42–79.

38. Herbert S. Klein, "Anglicanism, Catholicism, and the Negro Slave," in *Slavery in the New World,* ed. Laura Foner and Eugene D. Genovese (Englewood Cliffs, N.J.: Prentice-Hall, 1969), 146.

39. Herbert S. Klein, *African Slavery in Latin America and the Caribbean* (Oxford: Oxford University Press, 1986), 169–70.

40. Klein, *African Slavery,* 224, says there were 1.3 million whites, 658,000 slaves, and 32,000 free colored, while the British West Indies had nearly half a million slaves by the 1780s, only 53,000 free whites, and a mere 13,000 free blacks.

41. Some 60 percent of freed slaves, and virtually all of those freed unconditionally by masters, were young women—suggesting that personal unions between white masters and female slaves played a critical role in forging the freed population of the Iberian colonies. See Klein, *African Slavery,* 227.

42. Santo Domingo counted 80,000 free colored and 15,000 slaves in 1788; Puerto Rico, 22,000 slaves and 104,000 free colored in 1820; and Mexico, 10,000 slaves and 60,000 free colored in 1810. Klein, ibid., 221.

43. Louis A. Pérez, Jr., *Cuba: Between Reform and Revolution* (New York: Oxford University Press, 1995), 86.

44. Klein, *African Slavery,* 225–26.

45. Crow, *The Epic,* 216.

46. J. H. Elliot, *The Old World and the New, 1492–1650* (New York: Cambridge University Press, 1970), 75–77.

47. Larry Neal, *The Rise of Financial Capitalism: International Capital Markets in the Age of Reason* (Cambridge: Cambridge University Press, 1990), 10.

48. Herbert Aptheker, *The Colonial Era* (New York: International Publishers, 1959), 10–12.

49. Philip Foner, *Labor and the American Revolution* (Westport, Conn.: Greenwood Press, 1976), 7; also Bailyn, *The Peopling,* 120–22.

50. Bailyn, *The Peopling,* 37–42.

51. Ibid., 147, n. 40.

52. Crow, *The Epic,* 217.

53. Aptheker, *The Colonial Era,* 36, 40; also Bailyn, *The Peopling,* 60–61.

54. Patricia Nelson Limerick, *The Legacy of Conquest: The Unbroken Past of the American West* (New York: W. W. Norton, 1987), 68–69.

55. Bailyn, *The Peopling,* 66–67.

56. Aptheker, *The Colonial Era,* 56.

57. For discussion of *mayorazgos,* see Bethell, *Colonial Spanish America,* 283–85; Crow, *The Epic,* 162, 257.

58. Thomas, *Conquest,* 8.

59. Quoted in Bruce E. Johansen, *Forgotten Founders: How the American Indians Helped Shape Democracy* (Boston: Harvard Common Press, 1982), 9.

60. Clark Wissler, *Indians of the United States: Four Centuries of Their History and Culture* (New York: Doubleday, Doran, 1940); Henry Steele Commager, *The Empire of Reason: How Europe Imagined and America Realized the Enlightenment* (New York, Anchor Press/Doubleday, 1977); Felix Cohen, "Americanizing the White Man," *American Scholar* 21, no. 2 (1952); Weatherford, *Indian Givers,* 132–50.

61. Johansen, *Forgotten,* 13.

62. Ibid., 128.

63. Ibid., 54.

64. Thomas Jefferson, *Notes on the State of Virginia,* 9th American ed. (Boston: H. Sprague, 1802), 287.

## CHAPTER 2: THE SPANISH BORDERLANDS AND THE MAKING OF AN EMPIRE

1. George W. Crichfield, *American Supremacy: The Rise and Progress of the Latin Republics and Their Relations to the United States under the Monroe Doctrine* (New York: Brentano's, 1908), vol. 1, 268–99.

2. Jack Ericson Eblen, *The First and Second United States Empires: Governors and Territorial Government, 1784–1912* (Pittsburgh: University of Pittsburgh Press, 1968), 17–51, summarizes the pressures on the Founders to expand the country's territory; Malcolm Rohrbough, *The Land Office Business: The Settlement and Administration of American Public Lands, 1789–1837* (New York: Oxford University Press, 1968), says, "Land was the most sought after commodity in the first half-century of the republic, and the effort of men to acquire it was one of the dominant forces of the period"; Charles Grant, *Democracy in the Connecticut Frontier Town of Kent* (New York: Columbia University Press, 1961), 13–27, documents how land speculation was rampant among settlers from earliest colonial times; and Arthur Preston Whitaker, *The Spanish-American Frontier: 1783–1795* (Lincoln: University of Nebraska, 1927), 47, says, "The importance of the land speculator in the history of westward expansion in the United States . . . can hardly be exaggerated."

3. Lester D. Langley, *The Americas in the Age of Revolution, 1750–1850* (New Haven: Yale University Press, 1966), 107, 111, 163.
4. Jacques Barbier and Allan J. Kuethe, eds., *The North American Role in the Spanish Imperial Economy, 1760–1819* (Manchester: Manchester University Press, 1986), 16.
5. Peggy Liss, "Atlantic Network," in *Latin American Revolutions, 1808–1826,* ed. John Lynch (Norman: University of Oklahoma Press, 1994), 268–69. Also Crow, *The Epic,* 418–20.
6. In the Viceroyalty of Peru, where natives made up 90 percent of the population, Inca chief José Gabriel Condorcanqui killed the local governor in 1780 and proclaimed the reestablishment of the Inca Empire. He crowned himself Tupac Amaru II, after the last Inca emperor (who had been beheaded by the Spaniards), abolished slavery, and raised an army of thousands with which he attacked the colonial capital of Cuzco. Spanish troops finally captured and beheaded him in 1781, but it took three years of fighting and eighty thousand deaths to restore order. The same year Tupac Amaru was executed, twenty thousand Indians and *mestizos* from the area around Socorro in the Viceroyalty of New Granada (Colombia) marched on the city of Bogotá to protest escalating sales taxes. For a fine summary of the Tupac Amaru rebellion, see Crow, *The Epic,* 404–8; and for an unsympathetic view, see "What Is an Indian?" in Lynch, *Latin American,* 191–205.
7. The only place Spain seemed to welcome Creoles was its colonial army, where they made up 60 percent of its officers. See Lynch, *Latin American,* 17; also Tulio Halperin-Donghi, *The Contemporary History of Latin America* (Durham: Duke University Press, 1993), 6–7.
8. Successive wars between Spain and England in the 1790s and early 1800s repeatedly cut the colonies off from trade with the mother country. Those interruptions gradually forced the Crown to allow contraband merchants from England and North America to trade openly with the colonies. As early as 1776, the United States was already Cuba's main trading partner. See Barbier, *The North American Role, 1760–1819,* 15; also Lynch, *Latin American,* 10–11; also John Fisher, *Commercial Relations Between Spain and Spanish America in the Era of Free Trade, 1778–1796* (Liverpool: Centre for Latin American Studies, University of Liverpool, 1985), 16; also Halperin-Donghi, *The Contemporary,* 80–83.
9. David J. Weber, *The Mexican Frontier, 1821–1846: The American Southwest Under Mexico* (Albuquerque: University of New Mexico Press, 1982), 159; Alexander von Humboldt, *Political Essay on the Kingdom of New Spain* (Norman: University of Oklahoma Press, 1988), 37; and Desmond Gregory, *Brute New World: The Rediscovery of Latin America in the Early Nineteenth Century* (London: British Academic Press, 1992), 133.
10. Crow, *The Epic,* 609.
11. Ibid., 675.
12. R. W. Van Alstyne, *The Rising American Empire* (Chicago: Quadrangle Books, 1965), 87.
13. Quoted in Langley, *The Americas,* 240.
14. Henry Marie Brackenridge, *South America: A Letter on the Present State of*

*That Country to James Monroe* (Washington, D.C.: Office of the National Register, October 15, 1817), 24.

15. Apolinar Díaz-Callejas, *Colombia–Estados Unidos: Entre La Autonomía y La Subordinación. De La Independencia a Panamá* (Bogotá: Planeta Colombiana Editorial S.A., 1997), 93–98.

16. For a summary of how Henry Clay and Brackenridge urged immediate recognition of the United Provinces of Río Plata, but President Monroe refused their entreaties, see William F. Keller, *The Nation's Advocate: Henry Marie Brackenridge and Young America* (Pittsburgh: University of Pittsburgh Press, 1956), 221–22.

17. Harold A. Bierck, Jr., *Selected Writings of Bolívar.* Vol. 1: *1810–1822* (New York: Colonial Press, 1951), 213.

18. Langley, *The Americas,* 194–95, 244–45 ; Halperin-Donghi, *The Contemporary History,* 76; for Venezuela policy, see Barbier, *The North American Role,* 174–75.

19. Bierck, *Selected Writings of Bolívar,* Vol. 2: *1823–1830,* 603.

20. Chile abolished slavery in 1823, Central America in 1824, and Mexico in 1829; Venezuela, Ecuador, Peru, and Colombia took until the 1840s and 1850s because of resistance from slaveholder groups. See Simon Collier, *The Cambridge Encyclopedia of Latin America,* 142.

21. Gregory, *Brute New World,* 90–93; also Brackenridge, *South America,* 42.

22. At their apogee in the mid-seventeenth century, the Spanish missions numbered forty and ministered to 26,000 Christianized Indians. See Bonnie G. McEwan's *The Spanish Missions of La Florida* (Gainesville: University of Florida Press, 1993), xv. For an account of the escaped-slave problem, see Theodore G. Corbett's "Migration to a Spanish Imperial Frontier in the Seventeenth and Eighteenth Centuries: St. Augustine," *Hispanic American Historical Review* 54, no. 3 (August 1974).

23. Weber, *The Spanish Frontier,* 289; also Whitaker *The Spanish-American Frontier,* 33–46, for a discussion of the interplay between Indian, Spanish, and North American.

24. Weber, *The Spanish Frontier,* 280–81, notes that between 1782 and 1792 the population of Louisiana more than doubled, from 20,000 to 45,000, largely as a result of Anglo American immigration, and Spain appointed an English-educated officer, Manuel Gayoso de Lemos, as commander of the Natchez District specifically so he could communicate with its many foreign subjects there.

25. Ramiro Guerra y Sánchez, *La expansión territorial de los Estados Unidos a expensas de España y de los paises hispanoamericanos* (Habana: Editorial del Consejo Nacional de Universidades, 1964), 102; also Weber, *The Spanish Frontier,* 297.

26. For a summary of Jackson's early land speculation, see Michael Paul Rogin, *Fathers and Children: Andrew Jackson and the Subjugation of the American Indian* (New York: Alfred A. Knopf, 1975), 81–100.

27. Among the early Texas filibuster attempts were: Philip Nolan, who was captured and shot with his band of invaders by Spanish soldiers in 1801; Aaron Burr, who tried without success to organize an invasion in 1806 and was ordered arrested by President Jefferson. For those, see Charles H. Brown, *Agents*

*of Manifest Destiny: The Lives and Times of the Filibusters* (Chapel Hill: University of North Carolina Press, 1980), 6–7; Mexican Bernardo Gutiérrez and former U.S. Army Lieutenant Augustus Magee, who with more than eight hundred North Americans, Frenchmen, and Mexican revolutionaries invaded the territory from Tennessee and seized San Antonio in 1812 before being routed, and Connecticut adventurer Henry Perry, who in 1817 invaded Texas and marched on La Bahia. See Odie B. Faulk, *The Last Years of Spanish Texas, 1778–1821* (London: Mouton & Co., 1964), 134–37; and Mississippi merchant James Long, who invaded with three hundred men in 1819 in a failed attempt to establish the Republic of Texas. See Rodolfo Acuña, *Occupied America: A History of Chicanos* (New York: HarperCollins, 1988), 6.

28. Jorge Roa, *Los Estados Unidos y Europa en Hispano América: Interpretación Política y Económica de la Doctrina Monroe, 1823–1933* (Havana: Carasa, 1933), 167–78.

29. Henry Steele Commager, *Documents of American History.* Vol. 1: *To 1898* (Englewood Cliffs, N.J.: Prentice-Hall, 1988), 236–37.

30. Examples of where the United States either failed to act or supported outside intervention were: Britain's seizure of Argentina's Malvinas (or Falkland) Islands in 1833; its seizure of Central American territory to expand British Honduras in 1835 and 1838; the French blockade and occupation of Veracruz in 1838; and Spain's reannexation of the Dominican Republic in 1861. In one especially outrageous case, the Clayton-Bulwer Treaty of 1853, the United States and England agreed to jointly control any Central American canal construction without consulting a single Central American leader. Only after the French occupation of Mexico in 1862, and Louis-Napoleon's installation of Austria's archduke as emperor, did the United States openly condemn a major European aggression, but even then Washington did little more than register official objections, embroiled as the nation was in its own Civil War. It was left to Benito Juárez and the Mexican people to defeat the French invasion. For a detailed examination of the violations, see Gaston Nerval, *Autopsy of the Monroe Doctrine* (New York: Macmillan, 1934), 155–81; also Luis Quintanilla, *A Latin American Speaks* (New York: Macmillan, 1943) 117–22.

31. Bierck, *Selected Writings of Bolívar,* vol. 2, 732.

32. John Francis Bannon, *The Spanish Borderlands Frontier 1513–1821* (Albuquerque: University of New Mexico Press, 1974), 213–14.

33. The Stillman family partner, Daniel Smith, the U.S. consul in Matamoros, had already begun to oversee more than thirty New Orleans companies that were buying wool and hides from the Mexican ranchers and shipping lumber to the United States. See Chauncey Devereaux Stillman, *Charles Stillman, 1810–1875* (New York: C. D. Stillman, 1956), 4–20.

34. Milo Kearney, *More Studies in Brownsville History* (Brownsville: Pan American University, 1989), 47–48, mentions some of those early Anglo settlers: In 1829, Henry Austin, a cousin of Stephen Austin, began running a ship from New Orleans up the Rio Grande to Mier; John Southwell initiated a newspaper in Matamoros in 1834; and Robert Love a hat factory shortly afterward. Englishman William Neale arrived in 1834 and set up a stagecoach line from Matamoros to Boca del Río.

35. Acuña, *Occupied America,* 89, notes that of 784 marriages in Sonora (Arizona)

between 1872 and 1899, 148 were of Anglo men to Mexican women, and only six of Mexican men to Anglo women. By the twentieth century, however, most intermarriage had stopped.

36. Carlos Castañeda, *Our Catholic Heritage in Texas, 1519–1933,* vol. 6 (New York: Arno Press, 1976), 217–18.

37. Ciro R. de la Garza Treviño, *Historia de Tamaulipas: Anales y Efemérides* (Mexico City: Princeton University Press, 1956), 96.

38. Quoted in Weber, *The Mexican Frontier,* 170.

39. Ibid., 10.

40. John Hoyt Williams, *Sam Houston: A Biography of the Father of Texas* (New York: Simon & Schuster, 1993), 81–100; also Guerra y Sánchez, *La expansión,* 199.

41. Frederick Merk, *Slavery and the Annexation of Texas* (New York: Alfred A. Knopf, 1972), 206. See also José María Tornel y Mendivil, "Relations Between Texas of the United States of America and the Mexican Republic," 1837, in Carlos Castañeda, *The Mexican Side of the Texas Revolution* (Washington, D.C.: Documentary Publications, 1971), 328.

42. Reginald Horsman, *Race and Manifest Destiny: The Origins of American Racial Anglo-Saxonism* (Cambridge: Harvard University Press, 1981), 117–228, gives an excellent overview of the racial supremacist theories prevalent in the United States at midcentury and how they were used to rationalize territorial expansion.

43. Anson Jones, *Memoranda and Official Correspondence Relating to the Republic of Texas, Its History and Annexation* (New York: Arno Press, 1973), 97–98.

44. John S. D. Eisenhower, *So Far from God: The U.S. War with Mexico 1846–1848* (New York: Doubleday, 1989), xviii.

45. Ulysses S. Grant, *Personal Memoirs of U.S. Grant,* vol. I (New York: Charles A. Webster & Co., 1885), 53.

46. Railroad interests in the East who were trying to build a southern railroad line to gold-rich California began pressing President Franklin Pierce for more Mexican land not included in the original Treaty of Guadalupe Hidalgo. Pierce authorized his ambassador to Mexico, James Gadsden, to negotiate the purchase of flatlands south of the Gila River in Sonora and Coahuila provinces, which would provide the best transit route. Gadsden, himself a railroad executive, succeeded in getting a strip of thirty thousand square miles—a territory equal in size to Scotland—for $10 million, and it was through that area that the Southern Pacific Railroad built its line. Weber, *The Mexican Frontier,* 274–75.

47. Juan Gómez-Quiñones, "The Origins and Development of the Mexican Working Class in the United States: Laborers and Artisans North of the Río Bravo, 1600–1900, in Elsa Cecilia Frost et al., *Labor and Laborers Through Mexican History* (Tucson: University of Arizona Press, 1979), 482–83.

48. Carey McWilliams, *North from Mexico: The Spanish-Speaking People of the United States,* edition updated by Matt S. Meier (New York: Praeger, 1990), 144–45. Also David Montejano, *Anglos and Mexicans in the Making of Texas 1836–1986* (Austin: University of Texas Press, 1987), 80–84.

49. McWilliams, *North from Mexico,* 136–39; also Gómez-Quiñones, "The Origins," 486–87.

50. Acuña, *Occupied America,* 148.

51. McWilliams, *North from Mexico,* 135–36; also Gómez-Quiñones, "The Origins," 492–93.

52. In 1826, New York businessman Aaron H. Palmer founded the Central American and United States Atlantic and Pacific Canal Company, with Governor DeWitt Clinton as a board member. The firm won a concession to build a canal across the isthmus, then failed to get financing. See Karl Bermann, *Under the Big Stick: Nicaragua and the United States since 1848* (Boston: South End Press, 1986), 15–16.

53. Lester D. Langley, *The United States and the Caribbean in the Twentieth Century* (Athens: University of Georgia Press, 1989), 32–33.

54. Gustavus Myers, *History of the Great American Fortunes,* vol. 2 (Chicago: C. H. Kerr, 1910), 117–23; and Wheaton J. Lane, *Commodore Vanderbilt: An Epic of the Steam Age* (New York: Alfred A. Knopf, 1942), 85–86, summarize the steamship company shenanigans in Central America by Law, Vanderbilt, and others; for the Panama Railroad, see "History of the Panama Railroad," by Fessenden N. Otis, in *The Panama Canal: Readings on Its History,* ed. Paul Scheips (Wilmington, Delaware: Michael Glazier, Inc., 1979), 25–52.

55. Albert Z. Carr, *The World and William Walker* (New York: Harper & Row, 1963), 33, 70; David Folkman, Jr., *The Nicaragua Route* (Salt Lake City: University of Utah Press, 1972), 43.

56. Quoted in Bermann, *Under the Big Stick,* 43–46.

57. Ibid., 46–50.

58. *New York Times,* December 15, 1854, 3.

59. Bermann, *Under the Big Stick,* 63.

60. Brown, *Agents of Manifest Destiny,* 352–55.

61. Ibid., 348.

62. Bermann, *Under the Big Stick,* 71; Brown, *Agents of Manifest Destiny,* 346–58.

63. Michael L. Conniff, *Black Labor on a White Canal: Panama, 1904–1981* (Pittsburgh: University of Pittsburgh Press, 1985), 17.

64. Díaz-Callejas, *Colombia–Estados Unidos,* 215–30.

65. Thomas Karns, *Tropical Enterprise: The Standard Fruit and Steamship Company in Latin America* (Baton Rouge: Louisiana State University Press, 1978), 3–4.

66. Aviva Chomsky, *West Indian Workers and the United Fruit Company in Costa Rica, 1870–1940* (Baton Rouge: Louisiana State University Press, 1996), 17–19.

67. Acuña, *Occupied America,* 146–49; also John Kenneth Turner, *Barbarous Mexico* (Chicago: C. H. Kerr, 1910), 251–69.

68. Arturo Morales Carrión, *Puerto Rico: A Political and Cultural History* (New York: W. W. Norton, 1983), 114.

69. John Quincy Adams, *The Writings of John Quincy Adams,* vol. 7, ed. Worthington C. Ford (New York: Macmillan, 1913–17), 372–79.

70. Philip S. Foner, *The Spanish-Cuban-American War and the Birth of American Imperialism,* vol. 1: 1895–1898 (New York: Monthly Review Press, 1972), xvi.

71. Ibid., 42.

72. Louis A. Pérez, Jr., *Cuba and the United States: Ties of Singular Intimacy* (Athens: University of Georgia Press, 1990), 18, 19, 24. Pérez reports that William Stewart of Philadelphia acquired La Carolina estate near Cienfuegos, a plantation of about two thousand acres, worked by five hundred slaves. Au-

gustus Hemenway of Boston purchased San Jorge estate near Sagua la Grande in 1840, a property of more than 2,500 acres with 160 slaves. J. W. Baker from Philadelphia owned the 1,200-acre San Jose estate near Cienfuegos, which was worked by seven hundred slaves.

73. According to Pérez, the number of North American residents in Cárdenas increased from 1,256 in 1846 to almost 2,500 in 1862. So many arrived that "in 1855, a new hospital was established in Havana exclusively to serve the needs of the North American community in Cuba." Ibid., 19–21.

74. Ibid., 47.

75. Eighteen hundred came in 1858 and 3,106 in 1859, according to Pérez. Ibid., 22.

76. Boston banker Edwin Atkins, for instance, began foreclosing on more than a dozen sugar estates in Cienfuegos in the 1880s. Eaton Stafford, a New York banking firm, gobbled up properties in the Cienfuegos-Trinidad area. The E&L Ponvert Brothers of Boston bought or foreclosed on several in Palmira, including the four-thousand-acre Homiguero plantation. And, in 1893, New Yorkers Benjamin Perkins and Osgood Walsh gained control of one of the largest sugar plantations in the world, the sixty-thousand-acre Constancia estate. Ibid., 57–63.

77. Stephen Schlesinger and Stephen Kinzer, *Bitter Fruit: The Untold Story of the American Coup in Guatemala* (New York: Doubleday, 1983), 66.

78. Lester D. Langley, *The United States and the Caribbean in the Twentieth Century,* 12.

79. Alfonso Lockward, *Documentos para la Historia de las Relaciones Dominico Americanas,* vol. 1: *1837–1860* (Santo Domingo: Editora Corripio, 1987), ix.

80. Bruce J. Calder, *The Impact of Intervention: The Dominican Republic During the U.S. Occupation of 1916–1924* (Austin: University of Texas Press, 1984), 2.

81. Emilio Rodríguez Demorizi, *Luperón y Hostos* (Santo Domingo: Editora Taller, 1975), 14, 31.

82. Carlos M. Rama, *La Idea de la Federación Antillana en los Independentistas Puertorriqueños del Siglo XIX* (Río Piedras: Librería Internacional, 1971), 15–16; also Harold J. Lidin, *History of the Puerto Rican Independence Movement,* vol. 1: *19th Century* (Hato Rey: Master Typesetting of Puerto Rico, 1981), 108–9.

83. Charles C. Tansil, *The United States and Santo Domingo, 1798–1873: A Chapter on Caribbean Diplomacy* (Baltimore: John Hopkins Press, 1938).

84. For a colorful account of the fight between Grant and Sumner, see William S. McFeely, *Grant: A Biography* (New York: W. W. Norton, 1981), 332–55.

85. Roberto Marte, *Cuba y la República Dominicana: Transición Económica en el Caribe del Siglo XIX* (Santo Domingo: Editorial CENAPEC, 1988), 350.

86. Roger Plant, *Sugar and Modern Slavery: A Tale of Two Countries* (London: Zed Books, 1987), 13–14; also Marte, *Cuba y la República Dominicana,* 436–37.

87. See Frank Moya Pons, *The Dominican Republic: A National History* (New York: Hispaniola Books, 1995), 265–78.

88. Foner, *The Spanish-Cuban-American War,* vol. I, 261.

89. Ibid., 258–59.

90. Ibid., 270.

91. Perez, *Cuba and the United States,* 100.

92. Foner, *The Spanish-Cuban-American War,* vol. 2, 368–70.

93. Foner, *The Spanish-Cuban-American War,* vol. 1, 281–310.

94. Schlesinger, *Bitter Fruit,* 67.

## CHAPTER 3: BANANA REPUBLICS AND BONDS

1. Scott Nearing and Joseph Freeman, *Dollar Diplomacy: A Study of U.S. Imperialism* (New York: B. W. Huebsch, 1925), 16.

2. Angel Rivero, *Crónica de la Guerra Hispano Americana en Puerto Rico* (New York: Plus Ultra Educational Publishers, 1973), 502.

3. Mini Seijo Bruno, *La Insurrección Nacionalista en Puerto Rico, 1950* (Río Piedras: Editorial Edil, 1989), 8–9.

4. James L. Dietz, *Economic History of Puerto Rico: Institutional Change and Capitalist Development* (Princeton: Princeton University Press, 1986), 87–88; also José Trías Monge, *Puerto Rico: The Trials of the Oldest Colony in the World* (New Haven: Yale University Press, 1998), 12–13.

5. Some estimates are that coffee farms in Puerto Rico lost 40 percent of their real worth through that devaluation. Delma S. Arrigoitia, *José De Diego, El Legislador: Su Visión de Puerto Rico en la Historia, 1903–1918* (San Juan: Instituto de Cultura Puertorriqueña, 1991), 322–26.

6. Juan R. Torruella, *The Supreme Court and Puerto Rico: The Doctrine of Separate and Equal* (Río Piedras: Editorial de la Universidad de Puerto Rico, 1988), 53.

7. Dietz, *Economic History,* 88.

8. Torruella, *The Supreme Court,* 59.

9. Dietz, *Economic History,* 94–95.

10. Norma Valle Ferrer, *Luisa Capetillo: Historia de una Mujer Proscrita* (San Juan: Editorial Cultural, 1990), 66.

11. Charles H. Allen, "First Annual Report, Charles H. Allen, Governor of Puerto Rico," in *Documents of the Puerto Rican Migration,* ed. Centros de Estudios Puertorriqueños (Research Foundation of the City of New York, 1977), 11.

12. The agents for the planters were New York labor brokers Williams, Dimond and Company and Macfie and Noble, a plantation equipment importing company that had offices in several Puerto Rican port cities. See Norma Carr, *The Puerto Ricans in Hawaii: 1900–1958* (University of Michigan doctoral dissertation, 1989), 87; also *Documents of the Puerto Rican Migration,* 13–42; also Blase Camacho Souza, "Boricuas Hawaiianos," in *Extended Roots: From Hawaii to New York, Migraciones Puertorriqueñas,* ed. Centro de Estudios Puertorriqueños (New York: CUNY, 1988), 8–10.

13. The bulk of those contracted cane workers came from the coffee-growing sections of the island, which had been devastated by the worst hurricane in the island's history, San Ciriaco. The storm struck Puerto Rico on August 8, 1899, and killed three thousand. See Dietz, *Economic History,* 99.

14. Congressional Record, 64th Congress, 1st session, May 5, 1916. Cited in Ronald Fernandez, *Cruising the Caribbean: U.S. Influence and Intervention in the Twentieth Century* (Monroe: Common Courage Press, 1994), 113.

15. Pérez, *Cuba and the United States,* 118.

16. Langley, *The United States and the Caribbean,* 38.

17. Foner, *The Spanish-Cuban-American War,* vol. 2, 481; Langley, *The United States and the Caribbean,* 38.

18. Nearing and Freeman, *Dollar Diplomacy,* 178–81.
19. Langley, *The United States and the Caribbean,* 64–65.
20. Louis A. Pérez, Jr., *Cuba Under the Platt Amendment, 1902–1934* (Pittsburgh: University of Pittsburgh Press, 1986), 140.
21. Ibid., 229.
22. Gary R. Mormino and George E. Pozzetta, *The Immigrant World of Ybor City: Italians and Their Latin Neighbors in Tampa, 1885–1985* (Urbana: University of Illinois Press, 1987), 64–69.
23. "There were, of course, innumerable demands for American armed intervention, especially from certain people representing commercial interests," he recalled. "Every request was flatly rejected." What Welles never divulges in those memoirs were his repeated requests to Roosevelt—later revealed in his secret State Department correspondence—for an American invasion, all of which the president rebuffed. For Welles's account, see Sumner Welles, *The Time for Decision* (New York: Harper, 1944), 193–99. For a detailed version of Welles's insidious role, see Pérez, *Cuba and the United States,* 186–201.
24. Louis A. Pérez, *Cuba Between Reform and Revolution* (New York: Oxford University Press, 1995), 276–312, provides an excellent summary of the Batista years.
25. Luis A. Diez Castillo, *El Canal de Panamá y Su Gente* (Panama: 1990), 26.
26. Langley, *The United States and the Caribbean,* 35–37. Also, Walter LaFeber, *The Panama Canal: The Crisis in Historical Perspective* (New York: Oxford University Press, 1970), 29–46.
27. Some twenty thousand came from Barbados, amounting to 40 percent of all the adult males on that island at the time! See Conniff, *Black Labor on a White Canal,* 29; also David McCullough, *The Path Between the Seas: The Creation of the Panama Canal, 1870–1914* (New York: Simon & Schuster, 1977), 476.
28. During those ten months, 656 West Indians died, compared to 34 Americans. While blacks were three times the number of white workers, they had nearly twenty times the number of deaths. See McCullough, *The Path Between the Seas,* 501.
29. Ibid., 31–35.
30. Calder, *The Impact of Intervention,* 3; also Frank Moya Pons, *The Dominican Republic: A National History,* 279–82.
31. In 1921, when some marines shot a British citizen—a black plantation worker from Saint Kitts—in cold blood, C. M. Ledger, the British chargé d'affaires in San Pedro, demanded an investigation of the "reign of terror" by the marines. See Calder, *The Impact of Intervention,* 133–83, for an in-depth view of the occupation and guerrilla war.
32. Already a subsidiary of the U.S-owned South Porto Rico Sugar Company, Central Romana would nearly quadruple in size to more than half a million acres by the 1960s and would later become one of the Caribbean pearls in the worldwide empire of the giant Gulf and Western Corporation, Plant, *Sugar and Modern Slavery,* 14.
33. Calder, *The Impact of Intervention,* 91–114, gives an excellent overview of land and sugar policy during the occupation; also Edward S. Herman and Frank Brodhead, *Demonstration Elections: U.S.-Staged Elections in the Dominican Republic, Vietnam, and El Salvador* (Boston: South End Press, 1984), 19.

34. Plant, *Sugar and Modern Slavery,* 14–15.

35. For the 1902–1903 sugar harvest, for instance, the planters imported three thousand laborers from the English-speaking Caribbean to the Dominican Republic. See Plant, *Sugar and Modern Slavery,* 17.

36. Calder, *The Impact of Intervention,* 99.

37. Following his arrival in the country in 1922, Welles got the military government to secure $6.7 million in public works bonds through the U.S. firm of Lee, Higginson & Company; in 1924, after the new civilian president Horacio Vázquez took office, Welles pressured him to borrow another $3.5 million through Lee, Higginson and use part of the money to pay an inflated price for the assets of the failed American-owned Water, Light and Power Company of Puerto Plata and Santiago; subsequently, Welles convinced Vázquez, despite the president's dissatisfaction with Lee, Higginson, to arrange a new $10 million loan in 1926; he even got Vázquez to pay $150,000 to the firm of a lady friend to erect a luxurious Dominican Embassy in Washington. See Jose Ortega Frier, *Memorandum Relativo a la Intervención de Sumner Welles en la República Dominicana* (Santo Domingo: Ediciones de Taller, 1975), 89–94. According to Dominican historian Frank Moya Pons, by the time the occupation ended, the country's $10 million foreign debt had climbed to $15 million. See Moya Pons, *The Dominican Republic,* 339.

38. Ramón Alberto Ferreras, *Trujillo y sus mujeres* (Santo Domingo: Editorial del Nordeste, 1982), gives an account of Trujillo's many attacks on women.

39. By 1899, five U.S. companies had investments of nearly $3 million in Bluefields. See Langley, *The United States and the Caribbean,* 46–49; Bermann, *Under the Big Stick,* 123–50; Gregorio Selser, *Sandino: General of the Free* (New York: Monthly Review Press, 1981), 28–40.

40. Bermann, *Under the Big Stick,* 137–40.

41. Ibid., 142–45.

42. Ibid., 143.

43. Ibid., 144; Langley, *The United States and the Caribbean,* 50–52. Bermann and Langley cite more active involvement by the U.S. government in the revolt, while Dana Munro in *Intervention and Dollar Diplomacy in the Caribbean* (1964), 167–86, ascribes less imperialist motives to U.S. actions.

44. They awarded themselves and their cronies in Nicaragua exorbitant payments for damages incurred during the war against Zelaya. Chamorro alone got $500,000.

45. Bermann, *Under the Big Stick,* 157–61.

46. Langley, *The United States and the Caribbean,* 102–3.

47. H. H. Knowles, a former ambassador to both Nicaragua and the Dominican Republic, condemned the U.S. presence during a speech at Williamstown, saying: "We have used the Monroe Doctrine to prevent European countries sympathetic to those republics from coming to their aid. Instead of sending them teachers, instructors, and elements of civilization, we send them hunters of usurious banking concessions, avaricious capitalists, corrupters, soldiers to shoot them down, and degenerates to infest them with every disease." See Selser, *Sandino: General of the Free,* 80–81.

48. Langley, *The United States and the Caribbean,* 109; Selser, 174–77; also Tom

Barry and Deb Preusch, *The Central America Fact Book* (New York: Grove Press, 1986), 272.

49. By 1920, there were ninety-nine branches of American banks in the region. See Barbara Stallings, *Banker to the Third World: U.S. Portfolio Investment in Latin America, 1900–1986* (Berkeley: University of California Press, 1987), 65–67.

50. Ibid., 71.

51. Eduardo Galeano, *Open Veins of Latin America: Five Centuries of the Pillage of a Continent*, trans. Cedric Belfrage (New York: Monthly Review Press, 1973), 124–29.

52. Stallings, *Banker to the Third World*, 84, 187. In the early 1950s, Latin America represented only 4 percent of annual "portfolio investments" of U.S. companies in the world; that figure skyrocketed to nearly 41 percent of world investments by 1979.

53. Galeano, *The Open Veins*, 246–47.

54. Schlesinger and Kinzer, *Bitter Fruit*, xii.

55. McWilliams, *North from Mexico*, 152.

56. Ibid., 169; also Acuña, *Occupied America*, 177; Zaragosa Vargas, *Proletarians of the North: A History of Mexican Industrial Workers in Detroit and the Midwest, 1917–1933* (Berkeley: University of California Press, 1993), 6.

57. McWilliams, *North from Mexico*, 169.

58. Acuña, *Occupied America*, 153.

## CHAPTER 4: PUERTO RICANS

1. The Census Bureau counted 7,364 in Manhattan's Spanish Harlem and around the Brooklyn Navy Yard. Joseph Fitzpatrick, *Puerto Rican Americans: The Meaning of the Migration to the Mainland* (Englewood Cliffs, N.J.: Prentice-Hall, 1987), 38.

2. This and much of the early González family history is pieced together from extensive interviews by the author during 1992–1993 with Graciela Ramos, Pura Morrone, Sergio González, and Ana Meléndez, the surviving children of Teofilo and María González, with my mother, Florinda Guillén, with her brother, Heraclio "Pancho" Rivera, with my uncle Charley Meléndez, and with several members of the González clan of the second generation, my many cousins.

3. Dietz, *Economic History of Puerto Rico*, 55.

4. For an account of the role of the Puerto Rican scouts in the U.S. invasion, see Rivero's *Crónica de la Guerra Hispano Americana en Puerto Rico*, 473–87.

5. Earl Parker Hanson, *Puerto Rico: Land of Wonders* (New York: Alfred A. Knopf, 1960), 77.

6. Ibid.

7. While Puerto Ricans earned 63 cents daily in 1917, Hawaiian cane cutters earned 97 cents and Cubans $1.26. Between 1923 and 1930, the return on capital of the four largest U.S. corporations averaged 22.5 percent; and from 1920 to 1925, three U.S. sugar growers (Central Aguirre, South Porto Rico, and Fajardo) distributed more than $60 milllion in dividends to shareholders while accumulating only $20 million for reinvestment. In other words, 75 percent of the companies' earnings were leaving the country to shareholders' pockets. See James Dietz, *Economic History of Puerto Rico*, 110–11, 139.

8. Ronald Fernández, *The Disenchanted Island: Puerto Rico and the United States in the Twentieth Century* (New York: Praeger, 1992), 116; also Dietz, *Economic History of Puerto Rico,* 175.

9. Kal Wagenheim and Olga Jiménez de Wagenheim, *The Puerto Ricans: A Documentary History* (Maplewood, N.J.: Water Front Press, 1998), 179–82.

10. Seijo, *La Insurrección,* 35.

11. Gerald Meyer, *Vito Marcantonio: Radical Politician, 1902–1954* (Albany: State University of New York, 1989), 27–29. Gives an in-depth look at Marcantonio.

12. Author's interview with Eugenio Morales.

13. See interview with Teodoro Moscoso, former head of industrial development for Puerto Rico in documentary *Manos a La Obra: The Story of Operation Bootstrap,* Center for Puerto Rican Studies of the City University of New York.

14. Juan Gonzalez, "The Turbulent Progress of Puerto Ricans in Philadelphia," *Bulletin of the Center for Puerto Rican Studies (CPRS)* 2, no. 2 (Winter 1987–1988): 34–41; and Eugene Rivera, "The Puerto Rican Colony of Lorain, Ohio," *Bulletin of CPRS 2,* no. 1 (Spring 1987): 12–14 .

15. Frank Santana was a teenage Puerto Rican gang member who made front-page headlines in 1955 when he murdered a white boy. Facing the electric chair if convicted, he pleaded guilty to second-degree murder and was sentenced to twenty-five years to life. See "Gangster, 17, Admits Slaying Model Boy, 15," *New York Daily News,* May 2, 1955. Likewise, Salvador "Capeman" Agron was captured after a sensational manhunt, and subsequently convicted for the fatal 1959 stabbing of two white boys in a gang fight in the Hells Kitchen area of New York. Agron, who was eventually pardoned by Governor Nelson Rockefeller after spending nearly two decades in jail, was the subject of a controversial and short-lived Broadway musical by Paul Simon. See "Slew Two 'Because I Felt Like It,' Says Capeman," *New York Daily News,* September 3, 1959.

16. Richie Perez, "From Assimilation to Annihilation: Puerto Rican Images in U.S. Films," *Centro Bulletin* 2, no. 8 (Spring 1990): 8–27.

17. Fortunato Vizcarrondo, *Dinga y Mandinga* (San Juan: Baldrich, 1942); Toni Morrison, "On the Backs of Blacks," *Time* 142, no. 21 (Fall 1993): 57.

18. While the definitive account of Puerto Rican involvement in the 1960s upheaval and how it affected the overall society has yet to be written, those interested in that period, and especially the Young Lords, should see Alfredo López, *Puerto Rican Papers: Notes on the Re-Emergence of a Nation* (New York: Bobbs-Merrill Company, 1973), 321–39; and Michael Abramson, *Palante: Young Lords Party* (New York: McGraw-Hill, 1971).

19. Author's interview with Eddie Palmieri.

20. The film *The Battle of Algiers* was regularly shown by the Young Lords in education classes within the organization and in street showings to the community.

## CHAPTER 5: MEXICANS

1. *1996 Statistical Yearbook of the Immigration and Naturalization Service* (October 1997), 28.

2. Conan T. Wood, "Cerralvo as the Mother City of the Lower Rio Bravo Valley," in *Selections from the Collected Papers of the Lower Rio Bravo Historical Soci-*

*ety: 1949–1979* vol. 1 (Harlingen, Tex.: Lower Rio Bravo Valley Historical Society, 1982). Wood presented this talk to the society on October 28, 1964, 1–3.

3. J. B. Wilkinson, *Laredo and the Rio Bravo Frontier* (Austin: Jenkins Publishing Company, 1975), 11–12.

4. Florence Johnson Scott, *Historical Heritage of the Lower Rio Grande* (San Antonio: Naylor, 1937), 8–21; *Royal Land Grants North of the Rio Grande, 1777–1821* (Rio Grande City: La Retama Press, 1969), 1–17.

5. Ana Josefa de la Garza, a relative of the captain, married a son of Blas Canales, Jr., José Antonio Canales, in 1755.

6. A Canales family member, José López, founded Lopeño, which still exists just outside Mier, according to family members and a Texas State Historical Society marker at Lopeño.

7. Wilkinson, *Laredo and the Rio Bravo Frontier,* 17–27; also Johnson Scott, *Historical Heritage of the Lower Rio Bravo,* 8–21; also Robert J. Rosenbaum, *Mexicano Resistance in the Southwest* (Austin: University of Texas, 1981), 33–39.

8. Johnson Scott, *Royal Land Grants North of the Rio Bravo,* 1777–1821, 7.

9. Jóse Joaquín Canales, great-grandson of the original pioneer, served as a town councilman in Monterrey for more than thirty years and as mayor three times. His cousin, Rev. Manuel María Canales, founded the area's first public school in 1812, led the citizens of Monterrey in publicly swearing allegiance to the new Mexican government after independence, and later represented the city in the national legislature. See Israel Cavazos Garza, *Diccionario Biográfico de Nuevo León,* vol. 1, *A–L* (Monterrey: Universidad Autónoma de Nuevo León, 1984), 70–71.

10. John S. D. Eisenhower, *So Far from God: The U.S. War with Mexico, 1846–1848* (New York: Doubleday, 1989), 103. Originally a Federalist who had twice rebelled against the tyranny of President Santa Anna and even welcomed Texas adventurers in his army, Canales made peace with the Mexican government by the mid-1840s and received a colonel's commission in the army. Soon after, along with the notorious General Ampudia, he turned back one invasion by a group of Texas filibusters at the Battle of El Rosillo in Mier. During that battle, Ampudia and Canales captured 250 Anglo prisoners and executed seventeen of them on orders of President Santa Anna. The victory earned Canales a promotion to general.

11. John C. Rayburn and Virginia Kemp Rayburn, *Century of Conflict, 1821–1913: Incidents in the Lives of William Neale and William A. Neale, Early Settlers in South Texas* (Waco: Texian Press, 1966), 57–61.

12. Pat Kelley, *River of Lost Dreams* (Lincoln: University of Nebraska Press, 1986), 46–71.

13. Montejano, *Anglos and Mexicans,* 43.

14. Author's interview with Canales family member Santos Molina.

15. *The Tejano Yearbook: 1519–1978: A Selective Chronicle of the Hispanic Presence in Texas.* Compiled and edited by Philip Ortego y Gasca and Arnoldo De León (San Antonio: Caravel Press, 1978), 41.

16. Imelda Garza, who was born in 1923 and is the great-granddaughter of Gervacio Canales, Sr., recalls one lynching her older brothers, Flavio and Fernando, told her they witnessed in 1917. "They were walking in the fields between two ranches," Imelda said, "and they came across a Texas Ranger who they'd never

seen before. They watched from hiding as the Ranger stopped a *mojaito* [wetback or illegal immigrant] and just hung him from a tree." Author's interview with Imelda Garza.

17. Montejano, *Anglos and Mexicans*, 28.
18. Johnson Scott, *Royal Land Grants North of the Rio Bravo, 1777–1821*, 62–67.
19. Judge J. T. Canales, "Juan N. Cortina Presents His Motion for a New Trial," in *Selections from the Collected Papers of the Lower Rio Bravo Valley Historical Society, 1949–1979*, vol. 1, 78–79.
20. Montejano, *Anglos and Mexicans*, 41.
21. Ibid., 79.
22. George Durham, *Taming the Nueces Strip: The Story of McNelly's Rangers* (Austin: University of Texas Press, 1962), 29.
23. Charles W. Goldfinch, *Juan N. Cortina, 1824–1892: A Re-Appraisal* (Chicago: University of Chicago, 1949), 33.
24. The U.S. government accused him of being a cattle thief and smuggler, but a Mexican Commission appointed by President Benito Juárez, which also investigated the conflict, concluded that while some men he recruited did engage in cattle rustling, Cortina had not promoted the stealing and was in fact the victim of a smear campaign by powerful Texans. The Mexican commission went on to accuse major Texas landowners King, Billy Mann, and Patrick Quinn of directing extensive theft of cattle on the Mexican side of the river. See Gabriel Saldivar, *Historia Compendiada de Tamaulipas* (Mexico: Academia Nacional de Historia y Geografía, 1945), 197–98.
25. Arnoldo De León, *Tejanos and the Numbers Game: A Socio-Historical Interpretation from the Federal Censuses, 1850–1900* (Albuquerque: University of New Mexico Press, 1989), 42–43.
26. Author's interview with Fiacro Salazar.
27. McWilliams, *North from Mexico*, 152.
28. Author's interview with Imelda Garza.
29. John Chavez, *The Lost Land: The Chicano Image of the Southwest* (Albuquerque: University of New Mexico Press, 1984) 113–15.
30. Author's interview with Santos Molina.
31. McWilliams, *North from Mexico*, 309–17.
32. Ibid., 232.
33. Chavez, *The Lost Land*, 121–24.
34. Author's interview with Sandra Garza.
35. Author's interview with Mary Velásquez.
36. Ignacio García, *United We Win: The Rise and Fall of La Raza Unida Party* (Tucson: Masrc, 1989), 161–64.
37. Author's interview with Diane Garza.
38. Robert R. Alvarez, Jr., *Familia: Migration and Adaptation in Baja and Alta California, 1800–1975* (Berkeley: University of California Press, 1991).

## CHAPTER 6: CUBANS

1. Alejandro Portes and Alex Stepick, *City on the Edge: The Transformation of Miami* (Berkeley: University of California Press, 1993), 129.
2. Mormino, *The Immigrant World of Ybor City*, 63–77.

3. Richard R. Fagen, Richard A. Brody, and Thomas J. O'Leary, *Cubans in Exile: Disaffection and the Revolution* (Stanford: Stanford University Press, 1968), 17.

4. The disparity in wealth between those who left and those who stayed was enormous. According to one study, at a time when 60 percent of Cuba's employed males earned less than $900 a year, only 7 percent of the heads of households among the refugees earned less than $1,000, while half earned more than $4,000. And this study probably understates the disparities, since the richest Cubans did not even pass through refugee centers on arrival and thus were never surveyed. See Fagen, *Cubans in Exile,* 21–22.

5. Thomas D. Boswell and James R. Curtis, *The Cuban-American Experience: Culture, Images and Perspectives* (Totowa, N.J.: Roman & Allanheld, 1984), 81.

6. Pérez, *Cuba and the United States,* 254; also, "The Cuban Immigration 1959–1966 and Its Impact on Miami–Dade County, Florida," The Research Insitutite for Cuba and the Caribbean Center for Advanced International Studies, University of Miami, July 10, 1967, xiv–xv.

7. Portes and Stepick, *City on the Edge,* 126.

8. And while more than half of Cubans on the island had less than a fourth-grade education, only 4 percent of the refugees had failed to reach the fourth grade. See Fagen, *Cubans in Exile,* 19.

9. Portes and Stepick, *City on the Edge,* 129–32.

10. In 1979, 63 percent of a group of Cuban immigrants in a survey bought everyday goods in Cuban stores, but in a similar group of Mexicans in the country just as long as the Cubans, only 32 percent bought at Mexican stores. Also, in 1979, 49 percent of a sample of Cubans in the same survey were employed in Cuban firms, whereas only 15 percent of the Mexicans worked for a Mexican firm. Ibid., 145–46.

11. Ibid., 127–28.

12. Ibid., 146.

13. Author's interviews with Luis Del Rosario, from August 1994 to May 1996.

14. A 1960 study of one thousand Cubans in urban and semiurban centers concluded 86 percent supported the revolutionary government, while a 1962 study of Cuban workers showed 70 percent backed the government. See Lloyd A. Free, "Attitudes of the Cuban People Toward the Castro Regime in the late Spring of 1960," Institute for International Social Research, Princeton, N.J., 1960; and Maurice Zeitlin, "Economic Insecurity and the Political Attitudes of Cuban Workers," *American Sociological Review* 31 (February 1966).

15. Author's interview with Manuel de Dios Unanue, May 1990, and Albor Ruiz, January 1998, both members of the Committee of Seventy-five.

## CHAPTER 7: DOMINICANS

1. Jorge Duany, *Los Dominicanos en Puerto Rico: Migración en la Semi-Periferia* (Río Piedras: Ediciones Huracán, 1990), 30–31.

2. Hamlet Hermann, *Francis Caamaño* (Santo Domingo: Editora Alfa y Omega, 1983), 253; Edward S. Herman, *Demonstration Elections,* 30; also John Stockwell, *In Search of Enemies: A CIA Story* (New York: W. W. Norton, 1978), 160, 236; and Víctor Grimaldi, *El Diario Secreto de la Intervención Norteamericana de 1965* (Santo Domingo: Amigo del Hogar, 1989), 39–40; also Ramón Gros-

foguel, "Migration and Geopolitics in the Greater Antilles," paper presented at Conference on Transnational Realities and Nation-States: Trends in International Migration and Immigration Policy in the Americas," the North-South Center, University of Miami, May 18–20, 1995.

3. Frank Moya Pons, *The Dominican Republic: A National History* (New Rochelle, N.Y.: Hispaniola Books, 1995), 392.

4. Stockwell, *In Search of Enemies,* 236; also Edward S. Herman, *Demonstration Elections,* 22; also Grimaldi, *El Diario Secreto,* 37–40.

5. Much of the following account of the Luciano family history is from a series of interviews by the author with Estela Vázquez, Ana María Luciano, Amparo Sención and Tony Sención, members of the Luciano family in New York and Santo Domingo.

6. John Bartlow Martin, *Overtaken by Events: The Dominican Crisis from the Fall of Trujillo to the Civil War* (New York: Doubleday, 1966), 35. See also Bernardo Vega, *Control y Represión en la Dictadura Trujillista* (Santo Domingo: Fundación Cultural Dominicana, 1986).

7. Author's interview with Arnulfo Reyes.

8. Hermann, *Francis Caamaño,* 145–47.

9. Ibid., 155–204. Also interviews with Estela Vázquez and Heraclio Rivera, an uncle of the author and survivor of the April revolution.

10. Grimaldi, *El Diario Secreto.*

11. Sherri Grasmuck and Patricia R. Pessar, *Between Two Islands: Dominican International Migration* (Berkeley: University of California Press, 1991), 24.

12. Ibid., 77.

13. Palmira N. Rios, "Acercamiento al Conflicto Dominico-Boricua," Center for Puerto Rican Studies Bulletin 4, no. 2 (Spring 1992), 46.

14. Amelia Estades Santaliz, "Sólido red para el tráfico de ilegales," *El Nuevo Día,* February 19, 1999.

15. Juan Gonzalez, *New York Daily News,* "Caribbean Labor Pains," August 2, 1991.

16. According to a study in one Dominican city, Santiago, 20 percent of the households in 1981 were receiving regular aid from family members abroad. See Grasmuck, *Between Two Islands,* 71.

## CHAPTER 8: CENTRAL AMERICANS

1. That number is nearly 400,000 fewer than the total estimated above to have arrived, but we must take into account that thousands inevitably returned home after a few years of working illegally in the United States. Others were discovered by the INS and deported, and some of the 1.1 million counted as entering most certainly crossed the border several time and may have been double- or triple-counted.

2. Inter-American Development Bank, *1996 Annual Report* (Washington, D.C.), 130–31; also Barry, *The Central America Fact Book,* 225.

3. Ibid., 251.

4. Robert S. Kahn, *Other People's Blood: U.S. Immigration Prisons in the Reagan Decade* (Boulder: Westview Press, 1996), 11.

5. Inter-American Development Bank, *1996 Annual,* 133.

6. Sarah J. Mahler, *American Dreaming: Immigrant Life on the Margins* (Prince-

ton: Princeton University Press, 1995), 174, shows INS approval rates for asylum requests from socialist countries that were not even at war were far more disparate—68.2 percent from Romania, 76.7 percent from the USSR, and 64.9 percent from China.

7. Maurice Belanger, "A Chronology of the Treatment of Central American War Refugees in the U.S.," National Immigration Forum, 1997.

8. Adam Clymer, "Poll Finds Americans Don't Know Positions in Central America," *New York Times,* July 1, 1983.

9. Between 1949 and 1964, 2,969 Nicaraguan officers were trained at the school. Costa Rica, with 1,639, was second. See Willard F. Barber and C. Neale Ronning, *Internal Security and Military Power: Counterinsurgency and Civic Action in Latin America* (Columbus: Ohio State University Press, 1966), 145.

10. John A. Booth and Thomas Walker, *Understanding Central America* (Boulder: Westview Press, 1993), 135–39, summarizes the pivotal role of grassroots Church activism.

11. Mario Lungo Ucles, *El Salvador in the Eighties: Counterinsurgency and Revolution* (Philadelphia: Temple University Press, 1996), 97.

12. Piero Gleijeses, *Shattered Hope: The Guatemalan Revolution and the United States, 1944–1954* (Princeton: Princeton University Press, 1991), 88–90.

13. Carol Smith, ed., *Guatemalan Indians and the State: 1540 to 1988* (Austin: University of Texas Press, 1992) 141–42.

14. For more on the Arévalo period, Walter La Feber, *Inevitable Revolutions: The United States in Central America* (New York: W. W. Norton, 1993), 113–19; also Schlesinger and Kinzer, *Bitter Fruit,* 37–43; and Booth, *Understanding Central America,* 42–43.

15. Gleijeses, *Shattered Hope,* 32–38.

16. Barry, *Central American Fact Book,* 225. For details of the 1954 CIA coup, see Schlesinger and Kinzer, *Bitter Fruit;* also Richard H. Immerman, *The CIA in Guatemala: The Foreign Policy of Intervention* (Austin: University of Texas Press, 1982), 161–86.

17. U.S. General Accounting Office, "Cental American Refugees: Regional Conditions and Prospects and Potential Impact on the United States," July 29, 1984, 3.

18. Kahn, *Other People's Blood,* 11–24, provides a summary that is highly critical of U.S. refugee policy. Aristide R. Zolberg, "From Invitation to Interdiction: U.S. Foreign Policy and Immigration Since 1945," in *Threatened Peoples, Threatened Borders: World Migration and U.S. Policy,* ed. Michael S. Teitelbaum and Myron Weiner, 137–52, shows how refugee policy for Central America, much as in the rest of the world, has always been dictated by U.S. foreign policy interests.

19. Author's interview with Ana Sol Gutiérrez, August 18, 1998.

20. Jacqueline María Hagan, *Deciding to Be Legal: A Mayan Community in Houston* (Philadelphia: Temple University Press, 1994), 48–68; also Roberto Suro, *Strangers Among Us: How Latino Immigration Is Transforming America* (New York: Alfred A. Knopf, 1998), 38.

21. Suro, *Strangers Among Us,* 44–48.

22. Anne-Marie O'Connor, "Refugees in Florida Cheer Prize, Guatemalans Want Asylum," *Atlanta Constitution,* December 6, 1992.

23. Author's interview with Carlos Vaquerano, August 1998.

24. Author's interviews with Angela Sanbrano, CARECEN of Los Angeles, August 1998, and Benito Juárez, Guatemalan Support Network of Houston, May 1998.

25. Author's interview with Mario González, August, 1998.

26. Author's interview with Geronimo Campo Seco, August 1998.

27. "Researcher Says Mayans Adapt Well," United Press International, November 24, 1987; "Mayan Refugees Seek New Lives in the United States," Associated Press, July 10, 1984.

28. Juan Williams, "Black Power's New Dilemma: The D.C. Establishment That Fought for Civil Rights Faces a Latino Demand for Justice," *Washington Post*, May 12, 1991..

29. For Guatemalans, it was 75.7 percent, and for Salvadorans, it was 76.3 percent in 1990, while the U.S. average was 65.3 percent. See Portes, *Immigrant America,* 68.

30. Farhan Haq, "U.S. Labor: Guatemalan, U.S. Workers Unite Against Case Farms," Inter Press Service, August 16, 1996; also Craig Whitlock, "Immigrant Poultry Workers' Struggle for Respect Draws National Attention," *News & Observer,* Raleigh, North Carolina, November 30, 1996.

31. Edwin Garcia and Ben Stocking "Diaspora: The Latino Migration to Middle America," *San Jose Mercury News,* August 16–17, 1998.

32. Mireya Navarro, "Guatemalan Army Waged 'Genocide,' New Report Finds," *New York Times,* February 26, 1999; also John M. Broder, "Clinton Offers His Apologies to Guatemala," *New York Times,* March 11, 1996.

## CHAPTER 9: COLOMBIANS AND PANAMANIANS

1. Conniff, *Black Labor on a White Canal,* 137.

2. U.S. Department of Justice, *1996 Statistical Yearbook of the Immigration and Naturalization Service* (Washington, D.C.: U.S. Government Printing Office, 1997), 27–28.

3. Author's interview with Monica Manderson, January 21, 1995.

4. David McCullough, *The Path Between the Seas: The Creation of the Panama Canal 1870–1914* (New York: Simon & Schuster, 1977), 575.

5. Ibid.

6. Conniff, *Black Labor,* 31–35; also McCullough, *The Path Between,* 576–81.

7. Conniff, *Black Labor,* 6.

8. Ibid., 49–61.

9. Ibid., 91.

10. Author's interview with Vicente White, February 10, 1993.

11. Conniff, *Black Labor,* 121–23.

12. Ibid., 136–37.

13. Ibid., 140–41.

14. Galeano, *The Open Veins of Latin America,* 116.

15. Alonso Salazaar, *Born to Die in Medellín* (New York: Monthly Review Press, 1990), 6–8; also Galeano, *Open Veins,* 116–19; and Crow, *The Epic,* 800.

16. Salazaar, *Born to Die,* 7.

17. Alan Gilbert, *The Latin American City* (London: Latin American Bureau, 1994), 63.

18. Human Rights Watch, *War Without Quarter: Colombia and International Humanitarian Law* (New York: 1998).

19. Quoted in Crow, *The Epic,* 803.

20. *New York Times,* "Bogotá Halts Unit Faulted Over Rights," May 25, 1998; also, "Colombia—A Killing Every 20 Minutes," Reuters, January 14, 1997.

21. Author's interview with Carlos Malagón, January 27, 1995.

22. Author's interview with Beatrice Uribe, February 4 and 6, 1995.

23. Author's interview with Gloria Uribe, May 1992.

24. Germán Castro Caycedo, *El Hueco: La entrada ilegal de colombianos a Estados Unidos por México, Bahamas y Haití* (Bogotá: Planeta Colombiana Editorial S.A., 1989), 13–34, gives a Colombian journalist's extraordinary eyewitness account of how the immigrant smuggling operation worked.

25. James Petras and Morris Morley, *Latin America in the Time of the Cholera: Electoral Politics, Market Economics, and Permanent Crisis* (New York: Routledge, 1992), 21; also Crow, *The Epic,* 803–4.

26. Author's interviews with several New York City detectives and Colombian community leaders during 1991 and 1992.

27. Author's interview with William Acosta, March, May, December 1992, November 1995, February 1998.

## CHAPTER 10: THE RETURN OF JUAN SEGUIN

1. *A Revolution Remembered: The Memoirs and Selected Correspondence of Juan N. Seguín,* ed. Jesús F. de la Teja (Austin: State House Press, 1991), 90.

2. Ibid., 1–70. De la Teja provides an excellent summary of Seguín's life. For Cisneros's election, see Thomas Weyr, *Hispanic U.S.A.: Breaking the Melting Pot* (New York: Harper & Row, 1988), 116.

3. United States Hispanic Leadership Institute, *Latino Electoral Potential 2000–2025,* Report No. 312 (Chicago: 1998).

4. Juan Gómez Quiñones, *Chicano Politics: Reality & Promise, 1940–1990* (Albuquerque: University of New Mexico Press, 1990), 60.

5. The average factory wage in the South in the early 1900s was $10 a week, while the city and state poll taxes sometimes totaled $2.75. See Chandler Davidson, *Race and Class in Texas Politics* (Princeton: Princeton University Press, 1990), 18–23.

6. Gómez Quiñones, *Chicano Politics,* 53–60, 73; and National Association of Latino Elected Officials, *1996 Election Handbook,* 20.

7. James Jennings and Monte Rivera, *Puerto Rican Politics in Urban America* (Westport, Conn.: Greenwood Press, 1984), 31–32.

8. Sherrie Baver, "Puerto Rican Politics in New York City: The Post–World War II Period," in Jennings and Rivera, *Puerto Rican Politics in Urban America,* 44.

9. Linda Chavez, *Out of the Barrio: Toward a New Politics of Hispanic Assimilation* (New York: Basic Books, 1991), 40.

10. *Rodriguez v. Texas,* May 3, 1954, 347 U.S. 475.

11. Gómez Quiñones, 87. Also Manuel Del Valle, "Developing a Language-Based National Origin Discrimination Modality," in *Journal of Hispanic Policy,* John F. Kennedy School of Government, Harvard University, vol. 4, p. 75, n. 22.

12. John F. Stack and Christopher L. Warren, "Ethnicity and the Politics of Sym-

bolism in Miami's Cuban Community," *Cuban Studies* 20 (Pittsburgh: University of Pittsburgh Press, 1990), 13.

13. Examples were the Miami assassinations of Luciano Nieves and Rolando Masferrer in 1975 and of Ramon Donesteves in 1976; and the murders of Carlos Muñiz Varela and Eulalio Negrín in Union City, New Jersey, in 1979; for furthering dialogue with Cuba, see Max Azicri, "The Politics of Exile: Trends and Dynamics of Political Change Among Cuban-Americans," *Cuban Studies* 11 (Pittsburgh: University of Pittsburgh Press, 1981 and 1982), 62–66.

14. From 1961 to 1965, an average of 2,400 Cubans became citizens each year, but after the new law, those numbers grew steadily each year. In 1970 alone, 20,888 Cubans became citizens. See Silvia Pedraza Bailey, "Cubans and Mexicans in the United States: The Functions of Political and Economic Migration," *Cuban Studies* 11 (Pittsburgh: University of Pittsburgh Press, 1981), 89.

15. Among the most well known of many actions taken by members of the Cuban underground in non-Cuban issues were: the 1973 Watergate break-in, which included three former CIA Cubans in Howard Hunt's "plumbers'" group; the fatal bombing that same year of the Chilean ambassador to Washington, Orlando Letelier, where two members of the Cuban Nationalist Movement were initially convicted, then acquitted in a retrial. See Azicri, "The Politics of Exile" 62–66; also Peter Dale Scott and Jonathan Marshall, *Cocaine Politics: Drugs, Armies, and the CIA in Central America* (Berkeley: University of California Press, 1991), 23–50.

16. Dan Balz, "Hispanics Use New Voting Rights Act to Reshape Texas Politics," *Washington Post,* April 25, 1983.

17. Gary Rivlin, *Fire on the Prairie: Chicago's Harold Washington and the Politics of Race* (New York: Henry Holt, 1992), 348–57.

18. Jennings and Rivera, *Puerto Rican Politics,* 54.

19. Among the victories were those of Ralph Acosta and City Councilman Angel Ortiz in Philadelphia, State Representative Americo Santiago in Bridgeport, City Councilman Eugenio Caro in Hartford, State Representative Nelson Merced in Boston, Board of Education member Nancy Padilla in Rochester, Gutierrez and Santiago in Chicago.

20. But even among Hispanic voters, Puerto Ricans (79 percent) were the most pro-Washington, followed by Mexicans (68 percent) and Cubans (52 percent). Rod Bush, *The New Black Vote: Politics and Power in Four American Cities* (San Francisco: Synthesis, 1984), 150–51.

21. Alejandro Portes, Juan M. Clark, and Manuel M. López, "Six Years Later, the Process of Incorporation of Cuban Exiles in the United States: 1973–1979," in *Cuban Studies,* July 1981–January 1982, 11.

22. María Cristina García, *Havana USA: Cuban Exiles and Cuban Americans in South Florida, 1959–1994* (Berkeley: University of California Press, 1996), 113–15.

23. Thomas D. Bowell and James R. Curtis, *The Cuban American Experience: Culture, Images and Perspectives* (Roman & Allandheld Publishers), 69.

24. Stack and Warren, "Ethnicity and the Politics," 16–17.

25. Ibid., 19.

26. Alejandro Portes, "The Rise of Ethnicity: Determinants of Ethnic Perceptions

Among Cuban Exiles in Miami," *American Sociological Review* 49, no. 3 (June 1984): 395.

27. Ibid., 20–24.
28. Stack and Warren, "Ethnicity and the Politics."
29. Institute for Puerto Rican Policy, *The Puerto Rican and Latino Vote in the 1984 NYS Democratic Presidential Primary* (New York: April 5, 1984); also Institute for Puerto Rican Policy, "Puerto Ricans and the 1988 Presidential Elections," (New York: November 7, 1988); also Univision Network Poll, June 1, 1988.
30. Institute for Puerto Rican Policy, *The 1989 Mayoral Election and the Charter Revision Vote in New York City* (New York: November 1989).
31. Frances Fox Cloward and Richard A. Piven, *Why Americans Don't Vote* (New York: Pantheon, 1988), 115–16.
32. Institute for Puerto Rican Policy, *The Dinkins Administration and the Puerto Rican Community: Lessons from the Puerto Rican Experience with African-American Mayors in Chicago and Philadelphia* (New York: February 1990).
33. Author's interview with INS spokesman, March 1998; also "A Record Backlog to Get Citizenship Stymies 2 Million," *New York Times,* April 20, 1998.
34. Alejandro Portes and Rubén G. Rumbaut, *Immigrant America: A Portrait* (Berkeley: University of California Press, 1996), 117–18.
35. *Hispanic Americans Today,* U.S. Census Bureau Current Population Reports, P23–183 (Washington, D.C.: U.S. Government Printing Office, 1993), 15.
36. Louis Aguilar, "Mexican Congress Approves Dual Nationality," *Hispanic Link Weekly Report,* December 23, 1996; also Deborah Sontag and Larry Rohter, "Dominicans May Allow Voting Abroad," *New York Times,* November 15, 1997.
37. *New York Times,* November 10, 1996: "The Expanding Hispanic Vote Shakes Republican Strongholds."
38. National Association of Latino Elected Officials, *1996 Latino Election Handbook,* 4.
39. Angelo Falcón, "Beyond *La Macarena:* The New York City Latino Vote," *Hispanic Link Weekly Report,* November 25, 1996, 4.
40. *New York Times,* "Expanding Hispanic Vote Shakes Republican Strongholds"; also *Wall Street Journal,* September 30, 1996, "Despite Rapid Growth, Hispanic Vote May Play Only a Limited Role in Fall Presidential Contest."
41. Falcón, "Beyond *La Macarena.*"
42. Los Angeles voter exit poll conducted by the Tomas Rivera Policy Institute, *La Opinión,* and KVEA-TV, April 8, 1997.
43. *Hispanic Americans Today,* U.S. Census Bureau, 7.
44. *1994 National Roster of Hispanic Elected Officials* (NALEO Education Fund, 1995), viii.

## CHAPTER 11: IMMIGRANTS OLD AND NEW
1. U.S. Department of Justice, *1996 Statistical Yearbook of the Immigration and Naturalization Service* (Washington, D.C.: U.S. Government Printing Office, 1997), 25–28.
2. Pastora San Juan Cafferty, "The Language Question: The Dilemma of Bilingual Education for Hispanics in America," in *Ethnic Relations in America: Im-*

*migration, The Cities, Lingualism, Ethnic Politics, Group Rights,* ed. Lance Liebman (Englewood Cliffs, N.J.: Prentice-Hall, 1982), 106.

3. Carl Wittke, *Refugees of Revolution: The German Forty-eighters in America* (Philadelphia: University of Pennsylvania Press, 1952), 185.

4. Ibid., 182, citing *Westbote,* July 28, 1854; also *New Yorker Staatszeitung,* April 1, 1854.

5. Joseph Fitzpatrick, *The Stranger Is Our Own: Reflections on the Journey of Puerto Rican Migrants* (Kansas City: Sheed & Ward, 1996), 99–100.

6. Wittke, *Refugees of Revolution,* 178.

7. Alejandro Portes, *Immigrant America,* 159–64.

8. Michael Novak, *The Rise of the Unmeltable Ethnics: Politics and Culture in the Seventies* (New York: Macmillan, 1972), 86.

9. Ibid., 86; also Harold Cruse, *Plural But Equal: Blacks and Minorities in America's Plural Society* (New York: William Morrow, 1987), 104–5.

10. Michael Teitelbaum, "Right Versus Right: Immigration and Refugee Policy in the United States," *Foreign Affairs* 59, no. 1 (Fall 1980): 26–27.

11. Richard D. Lamm and Gary Imhoff, *The Immigration Time Bomb: The Fragmenting of America* (New York: Truman Talley Books, 1985), 85, 93.

12. *Washington Post,* February 2, 1995, "INS 'Enforcement Deficit' Tied to Law; Voluntary Compliance Provision Fails to Deter Hiring of Illegals."

13. "Sealing Our Borders, the Human Toll," American Friends Service Committee, 6–7.

14. "The Browning of America," *New York Times,* April 9, 1990; "A Land of Immigrants Gets Uneasy About Immigration," *New York Times,* October 14, 1990; "Calculating the Impact of California's Immigrants," *Los Angeles Times,* January 8, 1992; "A Flood of Illegal Aliens Enters U.S. Via Kennedy," *New York Times,* March 18, 1992; "Fixing Immigration," *New York Times,* June 8, 1993; "Politicians Discovering an Issue: Immigration," *New York Times,* March 8, 1994.

15. Brimelow obviously has no idea that at least one Latin American country, Panama, watched its entire ethnic and racial character transformed by the United States in the early 1900s when our country imported massive numbers of West Indians to build the Panama Canal. See Peter Brimelow, *Alien Nation: Common Sense About America's Immigration Disaster* (New York: Random House, 1995), 57.

16. Juan Gonzalez, "INS Fouls with a '74 Strike," *New York Daily News,* September 7, 1997. Collado was eventually released as a result of public pressure; see Juan Gonzalez, "Learning from Immigrant's Saga," *New York Daily News,* October 26, 1997.

17. *1996 Statistical Yearbook of the Immigration and Naturalization Service,* 174, 198.

18. Alejandro Portes, *Immigrant America,* 68.

19. Belinda I. Reyes, "Dynamics of Immigration: Return Migration to Western Mexico," Public Policy Institute of California, January 28, 1997.

20. Jeffrey S. Passel and Rebecca L. Clark, *Immigrants in New York: Their Legal Status, Incomes and Taxes, Executive Summary* (Washington, D.C.: The Urban Institute, 1998), 4–8; also "Calculating the Impact of California's Immigrants," *Los Angeles Times,* January 8, 1992.

21. Alejandro Portes, *Immigrant America,* 285–90.
22. Europe's population jumped from 140 million to 260 million in the hundred years between 1750 and 1850. By 1900, it had increased to 400 million. (See *World Almanac and Book of Facts,* 1993 (New York: Pharos Books, 1992). We can only imagine what social conditions would have been like in a twentieth-century Europe if emigration had not been available as a safety valve. In contrast, Latin America, which counted 100 million inhabitants in 1930, skyrocketed to nearly 450 million in 1990. (See Alan Gilbert, *The Latin American City,* 26–27.) Thus, the region took a mere sixty years to achieve a population increase that took Europe 150 years. That population explosion has been worsened by economic stagnation of the past few decades.
23. James Petras, *Latin America in the Time of the Cholera,* 14.
24. In 1980, per capita gross domestic product was $2,315, but fourteen years later, it had dropped to $2,218. See Inter-American Development Bank, *Annual Report, 1994,* 103.
25. Raymond J. Mataloni, "U.S. Multinational Companies: Operations in 1995," in *Survey of Current Business,* October 1997, 62–63; also Inter-American Development Bank, *Annual Report, 1996,* 126.
26. Rodolfo de la Garza, Manuel Orozco, and Miguel Baraona, "The BiNational Impact of Latino Remittances," Report of the Tomas Rivera Policy Institute (Claremont, Calif.: March 1997); for Cuba, see Anita Snow, "U.S. Dollar Takes on Central Role in Cuban Economy," Associated Press, July 20, 1998.
27. Handlin, *The Uprooted,* 7.
28. Alan Gilbert, *The Latin American City,* 26–36.
29. Alejandro Portes, *Immigrant America,* 11. Similar patterns have been found in studies of Dominican immigrants.
30. James D. Cockcroft, *Outlaws in the Promised Land: Mexican Immigrant Workers and America's Future* (New York: Grove Press, 1986), 49.
31. Francisco E. Balderrama and Raymond Rodriguez, *Decade of Betrayal: Mexican Repatriation in the 1930s* (Albuquerque: University of New Mexico Press, 1995), 120–22.
32. Cockcroft, *Outlaws in the Promised Land,* 67–75; also McWilliams, *North from Mexico,* 238–40.
33. "The New Jungle," *U.S. News and World Report,* September 23, 1996, 38; also Steven A. Holmes, "In Iowa Town, Strain of Diversity: Local Jobs Attract Immigrants from Mexico and Southeast Asia," *New York Times,* February 17, 1996.
34. Juan Gonzalez, "Some Dying to Work There," *New York Daily News,* October 16, 1997.
35. "Hispanic Births in U.S. Reach Record High," *New York Times,* February 12, 1998.
36. Lawrence Auster, "The Forbidden Topic," *National Review,* April 27, 1992. "Immigration will have to become an increasing part of the solution, not just in the U.S. but throughout the industrial world," Auster warns.

## CHAPTER 12: SPEAK SPANISH, YOU'RE IN AMERICA!

1. Sam Howe Verhovek, "Mother Scolded by Judge for Speaking Spanish," *New York Times,* August 30, 1995.

2. India's population is larger, but the majority of its people speak neither English nor Hindi, the two official languages.

3. Schlesinger, *The Disuniting of America*, 27–28, 122.

4. James Crawford, *Hold Your Tongue: Bilingualism and the Politics of "English Only"* (Reading: Addison-Wesley, 1992), 30–39; also Pastora San Juan Cafferty, "The Language Question," in Liebman, *Ethnic Relations in America*, 108.

5. Crawford, *Hold Your Tongue*, 46.

6. Ibid., 42–44.

7. Ibid., 51–52.

8. Ibid., 44.

9. Loida Figueroa, *Tres Puntos Claves: Lares, Idioma y Soberanía* (San Juan: Editorial Edil, 1972), 37–51; Crawford, 241–45.

10. Schlesinger, *The Disuniting of America*, 107.

11. Manuel del Valle, "Developing a Language-Based National Origin Discrimination Modality," 54–56.

12. *Garcia v. Gloor*, 618 F. 2nd 264.

13. Edward W. Said, *Culture and Imperialism* (New York: Alfred A. Knopf, 1993), xii–xiii.

14. Ibid., xxv.

15. Clara Rodríguez, *Latin Looks: Images of Latinas and Latinos in the U.S. Media* (Boulder: Westview Press, 1997), 21–33, summarizes many of these studies.

16. Ibid, 73–179.

17. Ward Alan Minge, *Acoma: Pueblo in the Sky* (Albuquerque: University of New Mexico Press, 1991), 11–15.

18. Gaspar Pérez de Villagrá, *Historia de la Nueva México, 1610,* trans. and ed. Miguel Encinias, Alfred Rodríguez and Joseph P. Sánchez (Albuquerque: University of New Mexico Press, 1992).

19. Roberto Esquenazi-Mayo, ed., *El Padre Varela: Pensador, Sacerdote, Patriota* (Washington, D.C.: Georgetown University Press, 1990).

20. Nicolas Kanellos, *A History of Hispanic Theater in the U.S.: Origins to 1940* (Austin: University of Texas, 1990), 2–4.

21. José Martí, *Our America: Writings on Latin America and the Struggle for Cuban Independence,* ed. Philip S. Foner (New York: Monthly Review Press, 1977), 88.

22. Kanellos, ibid., 44–70.

23. John Storm Roberts, *The Latin Tinge: The Impact of Latin American Music on the United States* (New York: Oxford University Press, 1999), 24–27.

24. Ibid., 27–30, 36–41.

25. Ibid., 44–45, 50–55.

26. Ruth Glasser, *My Music Is My Flag: Puerto Rican Musicians and Their New York Communities, 1917–1940* (Berkeley: University of California Press, 1995), 54–82.

27. Roberts, *The Latin Tinge*, 76–126.

28. Manuel Peña, *The Texas-Mexican Conjunto: History of a Working-Class Music* (Austin: University of Texas Press, 1985), 51–59.

29. Roberts, *The Latin Tinge*, 97.

30. García, *Havana U.S.A.*, 117.

31. Crawford, *Hold Your Tongue*, 21.

32. Richard Rodriguez, *Hunger of Memory: The Education of Richard Rodriguez* (Toronto: Bantam Books, 1982), 3.
33. "New York's Bilingual Bureaucracy Assailed as School Program Grows," *New York Times,* January 4, 1993.
34. Pérez de Villagrá, *Historia de la Nueva México,* 120.

## CHAPTER 13: FREE TRADE

1. Mira Wilkins, *The Emergence of Multinational Enterprise: American Business Abroad from the Colonial Era to 1914* (Cambridge, Mass.: Harvard University Press, 1970), 110.
2. The National Labor Committee Education Fund, *Paying to Lose Our Jobs* (New York: September 1992), 7.
3. Price Waterhouse, *Update of Baseline Study of Honduran Export Processing Zones,* Report to United States Agency for International Development, (Washington, D.C.: 1993), 63.
4. Galeano, *Open Veins of Latin America,* 198.
5. Ibid., 203–6.
6. Alfred E. Eckes, Jr., *Opening America's Market: U.S. Foreign Trade Policy Since 1776* (Chapel Hill: University of North Carolina Press, 1995), 47, 52.
7. United Nations Conference on Trade and Development, *TNCs and World Development* (London: 1996), 4; also Kim Moody, *Workers in a Lean World: Unions in the International Economy* (New York: Verso, 1997), 48–49. Also Raymond J. Mataloni, Jr., "U.S. Multinational Companies: Operations in 1995," in *Survey of Current Business,* October 1997, 50; also Doug Henwood, "Clinton's Trade Policy," in *Free Trade and Economic Restructuring in Latin America,* ed. Fred Rosen and Deidre McFadyen (New York: Monthly Review, 1995), 32.
8. United Nations Development Programme, *Human Development Report 1998* (New York: Oxford University Press, 1998), 30.
9. Moody, *Workers in a Lean World,* 130–32.
10. Barry and Preusch, *The Central American Fact Book,* 309.
11. Dietz, *Economic History of Puerto Rico,* 210–12.
12. Ibid., 226–28.
13. Augusta Dwyer, *On the Line: Life on the U.S.-Mexican Border* (London: Latin American Bureau, 1994), 6.
14. Author's interview with Othal Brand, mayor of McAllen, Texas, and president of Griffin and Brand, June 1993.
15. Dwyer, *On the Line,* 8.
16. Ibid., 42.
17. *NAFTA's Broken Promises: The Border Betrayed* (Washington, D.C.: Public Citizen Publications, 1996), 5–6; also *La Industria Maquiladora en Reynosa y Matamoros,* Centro de Estudios Fronterizos y de Promoción de los Derechos Humanos (Tamaulipas, Mexico: 1992), 5.
18. Centro de Estudios Fronterizos, *La Industria Maquiladora . . . ,* 10; also *Mexico, No Guarantees: Sex Discrimination in Mexico's Maquiladora Sector* (New York: Human Rights Watch, August 1996).
19. Saskia Sassen, "Why Migration?" in *Free Trade and Economic Restructuring in Latin America,* 277–78.

20. U.S. Justice Department, *1996 Statistical Yearbook of the Immigration and Naturalization Service,* 27–28.

21. Inter-American Development Bank, *Annual Report* (Washington, D.C.: 1994), 103.

22. In 1981, the average hourly factory wage in Mexico and Hong Kong was the same, $1.80. But, by 1987, the Hong Kong wage had risen to $2.11, while Mexico's had dropped to $.71. See *La Industria Maquiladora en Reynosa y Matamoros,* 3.

23. Juan González, *New York Daily News,* June 11, 1993.

24. Dwyer, *On the Line,* 17.

25. *La Industria Maquiladora,* 34.

26. Ibid., 36.

27. Sanford J. Lewis, *Border Trouble: Rivers in Peril, A Report on Water Pollution Due to Industrial Development in Northern Mexico* (Boston: National Toxic Campaign Fund, 1991), 4–8.

28. Michael Beebe, "Mallory Plant Is Long Gone: Some Say It Left Grim Legacy," *Buffalo News,* March 11, 1987; also Juan González, "The High Costs of 'Free' Trade," *New York Daily News,* January 22, 1992; also Dwyer, *On the Line,* 66–68.

29. *NAFTA's Broken Promises,* 25.

30. *Endangered Rivers of America: The Nation's Ten Most Endangered Rivers and Fifteen Most Threatened Rivers for 1993,* American Rivers (Washington: April 20, 1993,) 1.

31. Author's interview with Domingo Gonzáles, Coalition for Justice for the Maquiladora Workers, Brownsville, Texas, June 1993; also Sanford J. Lewis, *Border Trouble,* 8.

32. *NAFTA's Broken Promises,* 29–34.

33. Ibid., 20–25; also The Texas Department of Health, *An Investigation of a Cluster of Neural Tube Defects in Cameron County, Texas,* July 1, 1992; also Linda Diebel, "Mexico's Futuristic Nightmare," *Toronto Star,* March 13, 1993.

34. Dwyer, *On the Line,* 67.

35. Ibid., 5.

36. National Labor Committee, "Paying to Lose Our Jobs," 17–22.

37. Ibid., 23.

38. Ramona Hernández, Francisco Rivera-Batiz, and Roberto Agodini, "Dominican New Yorkers: A Socioeconomic Profile," Dominican Research Monographs (New York: CUNY Dominican Studies Institute, 1995), 14.

39. Apparel exports to the United States from the region increased 688 percent between 1980 and 1991. See *Paying to Lose Our Jobs,* 23–24.

40. National Labor Committee, *Paying to Lose Our Jobs,* 39–41.

41. National Labor Committee Education Fund, *Free Trade's Hidden Secrets: Why We Are Losing Our Shirts* (New York: November 1993) 9.

42. Price Waterhouse, *Update of Baseline Study,* 11–12.

43. Juan Gonzalez, "Exploitation's Always in Fashion," *New York Daily News,* July 25, 1995.

44. "Casos Especiales Durante el Período del 23/06/95 al 29/06/95" Oficina de Tutela Legal del Arzobispado, Comisión Arquidiocesana de Justicia y Paz, San Salvador, El Salvador, C.A.

45. Price Waterhouse, *Update of Baseline Study,* 50.

46. National Labor Committee, *Paying to Lose Our Jobs,* 24–25.

47. Estimates are that Mexico spent some $30 million lobbying for the passage of NAFTA, more than twice the previous record of foreign lobbying, which was Kuwait's spending of $10 to $12 million before and during the Persian Gulf War. See "Trading Game," by the Center for Public Integrity, May 27, 1993, and "Mexico Buys Free Trade," by Don Hazen, in *Facts and Fictions About "Free Trade"* (New York: Institute for Alternative Journalism, 1993), 89–92.

48. "NAFTA Trade-off: Some jobs lost, others gained," *New York Times,* October 9, 1995.

49. Author's interview with Othal Brand, mayor of McAllen, Texas.

50. Nancy J. Perry's "What's Powering Mexico's Success," *Fortune,* February 10, 1992, 109–115.

51. Jorge G. Castañeda, *The Mexican Shock: Its Meaning for the U.S.* (New York: The New Press, 1995,), 36.

52. "School of Real Life Results: NAFTA at 5," by Public Citizen Global Trade Watch, January 1999; also "NAFTA Index: Three Years of NAFTA Facts," Public Citizen Global Trade Watch, 1998.

53. Thomas Black, "A Milestone for Maquiladoras: with Their Millionth Worker, Mexico's Plants Key to Exports," *Miami Herald, International Satellite Edition,* January 26, 1998. Also *NAFTA'S Broken Promises,* iii.

54. The reason for the growth in the hazardous waste problem is simple. Half of the 125 manufacturing plants that relocated south of the border in NAFTA's first two years were either plastics or electronics firms. Both of these industries routinely rank among the American industrial sectors that produce the most toxic waste. See *NAFTA's Broken Promises: The Border Betrayed,* iv; also *No Laughter in NAFTA: Mexico and the United States Two Years After,* a joint report by the Institute for Policy Studies, the Development GAP, and Equipo PUEBLO (Washington, D.C.: December 1995): 3–4.

55. "School of Real Life, NAFTA at 5," 10.

56. *No Laughter in NAFTA: Mexico and the United States Two Years After,* 5.

57. "New Dangers Make Way to U.S. Tables," *Boston Globe,* September 20, 1998.

## CHAPTER 14: PUERTO RICO, U.S.A.

1. Héctor Cordero Guzmán, "Some Contradictions of Dependent Development in Puerto Rico in the Context of the Global Economy," Centro de Estudios Puertorriqueños, September 19, 1996; also Gino Ponti, "Puerto Rico Crime Wave Reaches Tidal Proportions," *San Juan Star,* November 30, 1992. The *Star* reported that in 1991 Puerto Rico's homicide rate was 23.2 per 100,000, compared to Louisiana, the worst state, where the rate was 16.9.

2. Pérez, "From Assimilation to Annihilation," 8–27.

3. Lewis portrayed the Rios family, an intergenerational dysfunctional group with a history of prostitution and other social problems. He popularized the term "culture of poverty" to describe individuals who became accustomed to living at the margins of society. See Oscar Lewis, *La Vida: A Puerto Rican Family in the Culture of Poverty, San Juan and New York* (New York: Random House, 1966).

4. Chavez, *Out of the Barrio,* 140.

5. During a May 6,1999, U.S. Senate hearing on Puerto Rico's status, for instance, Senator Mary Landrieu (Dem.-La.) said Puerto Ricans would rather have a "free lunch" than join the union and pay taxes. See Kenneth R. Bazinet, "Senate Furor on Puerto Rico," *New York Daily News,* May 7, 1999.

6. Héctor Cordero Guzmán, "Lessons from Operation Bootstrap," in Rosen, *Free Trade and Economic Restructuring in Latin America,* 79; also Dietz and Pantojas-García, "Puerto Rico's New Role in the Caribbean: The High-Finance/Maquiladora Strategy," in *Colonial Dilemma: Critical Perspectives on Contemporary Puerto Rico,* ed. Edwin Meléndez and Edgardo Meléndez (Boston: South End Press, 1993,) 108.

7. According to a 1964 report to Congress by the Commonwealth of Puerto Rico, over 40 percent of companies that started with local tax exemptions closed their doors when those exemptions expired. See Fernández, *The Disenchanted Island: Puerto Rico and the United States in the Twentieth Century* (New York: Praeger, 1992), 208.

8. U.S. General Accounting Office, *Tax Policy: Puerto Rico and the Section 936 Tax Credit* (Washington, D.C.: June 1993), 3.

9. Ibid., 9; also Congressional Budget Office, "Potential Economic Impacts of Changes in Puerto Rico's Status Under S. 712," April 1990, 7; also Emilio Pantojas-García, *Development Strategies as Ideology: Puerto Rico's Export-Led Industrialization Experience* (London: Lynne Rienner Publishers, 1990), 117–18.

10. Those 110 firms had 300 factories operating then. See Pantojas-García, *Development Strategies,* 114.

11. Ibid., 115–16.

12. Ibid., 153. According to Pantojas-García, Abbott Laboratories listed 71 percent of worldwide profits from Puerto Rico; Digital Equipment, 57 percent; Union Carbide, 25 percent; Pepsi-Cola, 21 percent; and Motorola, 23 percent.

13. The twenty-two drug company subsidiaries in Puerto Rico averaged 77.5 percent return on operating income in 1983, compared to the mainland average of 18.7 percent for pharmaceuticals. See GAO, *Tax Policy,* 52–53.

14. Kelly Richmond, "Drug Companies Fear Loss of Tax Exemption," *New Jersey Record,* November 8, 1993.

15. This compared to $5.1 billion in Canada and $4.6 billion in Germany. While the size of U.S. investment in Canada was twice that of Puerto Rico's, the island's rate of return on investment is more than twice Canada's—a phenomenal 23.7 percent. See Pantojas-García, *Development Strategies,* 167; for lost federal revenues, see U.S. General Accounting Office, "Pharmaceutical Industry Tax Benefits of Operating in Puerto Rico" (Washington, D.C.: May 1992), 14.

16. Puerto Rico Planning Board, *Economic Report to the Governor 1995* (San Juan: March 1996), chap. 5, 11.

17. Ibid., chap. 5, p. 13.

18. Ibid., chap. 9, p. 2. Also GAO, *Tax Policy,* 25.

19. Jaime Bofill Valdés, "Comportamiento de Diversas Variables Macro-Económicas de Puerto Rico . . . ," *in Boletín de Economía,* no. 1, 4.

20. In 1989, for instance, pharmaceutical companies gave a mere $1 million in charitable contributions in Puerto Rico while earning more than $3 billion in profits from their operations there. See GAO, *Tax Policy,* 64.

21. U.S. Maritime Administration, "United States Oceanborne Foreign Trade Routes" (October 1992); also U.S. Census Bureau, "U.S. Trade with Puerto Rico and U.S. Possessions," 1992.
22. Angel L. Ruiz and Fernando Zalacain, "The Economic Relation of the United States and the Puerto Rican Economies: An Interregional Input-Output Approach," in *Boletín de Economía* 3, no. 1., Unidad de Investigaciones Económicas, Universidad de Puerto Rico.
23. Torruella, *The Supreme Court in Puerto Rico,* 257–59.
24. In April 1999, one Puerto Rican civilian was killed and four people wounded when an F-18 jet on a practice run mistakenly dropped two five-hundred-pound bombs on an observation post in Vieques.
25. Luis R. Dávila Colón, "The Blood Tax: The Puerto Rican Contribution to the United States War Effort," *Review of Colegio de Abogados de Puerto Rico* (November 1979). Also W. W. Harris, *Puerto Rico's Fighting 65th U.S. Infantry, from San Juan to Corwan* (San Rafael: Presidio Press, 1980); also Nicolás Santiago Ortíz, *Korea 1951, La Guerra Olvidada: El Orgullo de Haber Sobrevivido* (Río Piedras: Esmaco Printers, 1991).
26. Richard Goldstein, "The Big Mango," *New York,* August 7, 1972, 24, quoted in Manuel Maldonado-Denis, *The Emigration Dialectic: Puerto Rico and the USA* (New York: International Publishers, 1980), 76–77.
27. Raymond Carr, *Puerto Rico: A Colonial Experiment* (New York: Vintage Books, 1984), 294, 297.
28. Chavez, *Out of the Barrio,* 159.
29. Frantz Fanon, *The Wretched of the Earth* (New York: Grove Press, 1963), 210–11.
30. Quoted in Torruella, *Puerto Rico and the Supreme Court,* 223.
31. Arturo Morales Carrión, *Puerto Rico: A Political and Cultural History,* 326–30.
32. Chavez, *Out of the Barrio,* 159.
33. Palmira Ríos, "Export-Oriented Industrialization and the Demand for Female Labor: Puerto Rican Women in the Manufacturing Sector, 1952–1980," in Meléndez, *Colonial Dilemma,* 89–92.
34. Clara E. Rodríguez, *Puerto Ricans Born in the U.S.A.* (Boston: 1989), 86.
35. Ivonne Acosta, *La Mordaza: Puerto Rico, 1948–1957* (Río Piedras: Editorial Edil., 1989). Gives the best account of the gag law and persecution of *independentistas.*
36. For an account of the FBI subversion campaign against the independence movement during the 1967 referendum, see Ronald Fernández, *The Disenchanted Island: Puerto Rico and the United States in the Twentieth Century,* 214–19. Also Juan Manuel García-Passalacqua, "The 1993 Plebiscite in Puerto Rico: A First Step to Decolonization," *Current History* 93, no. 581 (March 1994): 78.
37. For a thorough discussion of the Carter administration debate, see Beatriz de la Torre, "El Plebiscito Nació en la Era de Carter," in *Puerto Rico y los Estados Unidos: El Proceso de Consulta y Negociación de 1989 y 1990,* vol. 2: *1990,* ed. Juan Manuel García Passalacqua y Carlos Rivera Lugo (Río Piedras: Editorial de la Universidad de Puerto Rico, 1991), 10–21.
38. Edgardo Meléndez, "Colonialism, Citizenship and Contemporary Statehood," in Meléndez, *Colonial Dilemma,* 41–52.
39. Pedro Caban, "Redefining Puerto Rico's Political Status," in Meléndez, *Colonial Dilemma,* 24–27.

40. Congressional Budget Office, "Potential Economic Impacts . . . ," 26–27.

41. García-Passalacqua, "The 1993 Plebiscite," 103–7.

42. José Trías Monge, *Puerto Rico: The Trials of the Oldest Colony in the World* (New Haven: Yale University Press, 1998), 64. For a full discussion of early colonial policy, see 36–76.

43. Roger Bell, *Last Among Equals: Hawaiian Statehood and American Politics* (Honolulu: University of Hawaii Press, 1984), 1–5; also Lawrence H. Fuchs, *Hawaii Pono: A Social History* (New York: Harcourt, Brace & World, 1961), 406–14.

44. From "Testimony Before the Co-Coordinators of the Interagency Working Group on Puerto Rico on the Future of Puerto Rico," June 22, 1995, at the White House, in *Cambio xxi,* Washington, D.C., 11–25.

## EPILOGUE

1. U.S. Census Bureau, *Statistical Abstract of the United States: 1997* (Washington, D.C.: U.S. Government Printing Office, 1997), table 12.

# Glossary

**Balsero.** Ferryman. Often applied to Cubans entering the United States illegally on boats.

**Barrio.** A neighborhood or district.

**Bongó.** Small drum played by hand in African and Caribbean music.

**Bufo.** A theatrical farce.

**Cabildo.** Town council in Latin America.

**Casa real.** The king's building in Spanish colonial towns, where representatives of the Crown met and where government funds and the stores of traders and merchants were kept.

**Chino.** The child of an Indian and a salta-atrás (a white person with Negroid features).

**Comedia.** A theatrical play, usually with a cheerful ending.

**Compadrazgo.** The relationship between the father and the godfather of a child; in general, family-like ties between neighbors not connected by bloodlines.

**Corregidor.** A magistrate in colonial Spanish America.

**Coyote.** The child of a mestizo and an Indian; also, a person who leads people illegally into the United States for a fee.

**Criollo.** Someone born of Spanish parents in Spain's Latin American colonies.

**Danza.** A formal style of music and dance characteristic of Puerto Rico's upper classes.

**El jefe.** Chief. In some countries, the term applies to a dictator or strongman.

**Encomiendas.** Trusteeships granted to Spanish settlers in Latin America during the early colonial era, whereby Indians were turned into feudal serfs in return for their protection.

**Guaracha.** Cuban music with roots in the eighteenth century; usually a song with racy lyrics for chorus and a solo voice that lends to improvisation.

**Güiro.** A musical instrument made from the shell of a fruit, similar to a gourd, derived from the Taino Indians of the Caribbean.

**Hijo natural.** Child born out of wedlock in Latin America.

*La Matanza.* The slaughter; in El Salvador, the name given to the massacre of thirty thousand Pipil Indians by dictator Hernández in the 1930s.

*Latifundio.* A large landed estate.

*La Violencia.* The violence; in Colombia, the name given to the mid-twentieth-century civil war that claimed several hundred thousand lives.

*Maracas.* A musical instrument in a dry gourd in which some pebbles are placed. Usually played two at a time.

*Mayorazgo.* An entailed estate that remains in the family and is passed on to the firstborn son. The system of primogeniture.

*Merengue.* Typical dance of the Dominican Republic with a rapid 2/4 rhythm.

*Mestizaje.* The mixing of races.

*Mestizo.* The child of an Indian and a Spaniard.

*Mexicanos.* Mexicans; as used here, those who were in the Southwest when the Anglos came.

*Mozárabe.* Spanish Christian living in Muslim Spain.

*Mudéjar.* Muslim who remained in Christian Spain after the Reconquest.

*Mulato.* The child of a Negro and a Spaniard.

*Padrino.* Godfather.

*Pájaro.* Bird. In Colombia: a hired killer during La Violencia.

*Pandereta.* Tambourine.

*Peninsular.* Spaniard living in colonial Latin America.

*Plena.* A Puerto Rican dance with roots in African music, developed in the island's coastal areas around World War I, mostly in the city of Ponce, marked by satirical four- or six-line verses and a refrain.

*Querida/corteja.* A lover or mistress.

*Quincenario.* The fifteenth-birthday celebration for a girl that symbolizes her becoming a young woman; a more elaborate version in Latin America of the Anglo sweet sixteen.

*Repartimiento.* The system of drafting Indians for labor permitted by the king to Spanish settlers after the abolition of outright Indian slavery.

*Revista.* A play or skit.

*Salsa.* Hot, up-tempo, big-band Caribbean music as it developed in New York City in the late twentieth century.

*Salta-atrás.* A white person with Negroid features.

*Son.* The oldest and most classic Afro-Cuban musical form with a strong syncopated rhythm.

*Tejano.* Mexicans born and raised in Texas.

*Vaqueros.* Cowboys.

*Yola.* A small boat.

*Zarzuela.* A Spanish operetta which includes dialogue, usually with a comic or satirical theme.

# Bibliography

Abramson, Michael. *Palante: Young Lords Party*. New York: McGraw-Hill, 1971.

Acosta, Ivonne. *La Mordaza: Puerto Rico, 1948–1957*. Río Piedras: Editorial Edil, Inc., 1989.

Acosta-Belén, Edna, and Barbara R. Sjostrom. *The Hispanic Experience in the United States*. New York: Praeger, 1988.

Acuña, Rodolfo. *Occupied America: A History of Chicanos*. New York: Harper-Collins, 1988.

Adams, John Quincy. *The Writings of John Quincy Adams, vol. 7*. Edited by Worthington C. Ford. New York: Macmillan, 1913–17.

Alvarez, Jr., Roberto R. *Familia: Migration and Adaptation in Baja and Alta California, 1800–1975*. Berkeley: University of California Press, 1991.

American Friends Service Committee, Mexico–U.S. Border Program. *Sealing Our Borders: The Human Toll*. Philadelphia, February 1992.

American Rivers. *Endangered Rivers of America: The Nation's Ten Endangered Rivers and Fifteen Most Threatened Rivers for 1993*. Washington, D.C., April 20, 1993.

Aptheker, Herbert. *The Colonial Era*. New York: International Publishers, 1959.

Arrigoitia, Delma S. *José De Diego, El Legislador: Su visión de Puerto Rico en la Historia, 1903–1918*. San Juan: Instituto de Cultura Puertorriqueña, 1991.

Auster, Laurence. "The Forbidden Topic." *National Review*, April 27, 1992.

Azicri, Max. "The Politics of Exile: Trends and Dynamics of Political Change Among Cuban-Americans." *Cuban Studies 11*. Pittsburgh: University of Pittsburgh Press, 1981.

Bailyn, Bernard. *The Peopling of British North America*. New York: Vintage Books, 1988.

Balderrama, Francisco E., and Raymond Rodríguez. *Decade of Betrayal: Mexican Repatriation in the 1930s*. Albuquerque: University of New Mexico Press, 1995.

Bannon, John Francis. *The Spanish Borderlands Frontier 1513–1821*. Albuquerque: University of New Mexico Press, 1974.

Barber, Willard F., and Neale Ronning. *Internal Security and Military Power: Counterinsurgency and Civic Action in Latin America.* Columbus: Ohio State University Press, 1966.

Barbier, Jacques, and Allan J. Kuethe, eds. *The North American Role in the Spanish Imperial Economy, 1760–1819.* Manchester: Manchester University Press, 1984.

Barry, Tom, and Deb Preusch. *The Central America Fact Book.* New York: Grove Press, 1986.

Belanger, Maurice. "A Chronology of the Treatment of Central American War Refugees in the U.S." Washington, D.C.: National Immigration Forum, 1997.

Bell, Roger. *Last Among Equals: Hawaiian Statehood and American Politics.* Honolulu: University of Hawaii Press, 1984.

Bermann, Karl. *Under the Big Stick: Nicaragua and the United States Since 1848.* Boston: South End Press, 1986.

Bethell, Leslie, ed. *Colonial Spanish America.* New York: Cambridge University Press, 1987.

Bofill Valdés, Jaime. "Comportamiento de Diversas Variables Macro-Económicas de Puerto Rico . . ." *Boletín de Economía,* vol. 1, no. 1, julio–septiembre 1995.

Bolívar, Simón. *Selected Writings of Bolívar,* vol. 1: *1810–1822.* Edited by Harold A. Bierck Jr., New York: The Colonial Press, Inc., 1951.

Booth, John A., and Thomas Walker. *Understanding Central America.* Boulder: Westview Press, 1993.

Boswell, Thomas D., and James R. Curtis. *The Cuban American Experience: Culture, Images and Perspectives.* Totowa, N.J.: Rowman & Allanheld Publishers, 1984.

Brackenridge, Henry Marie. "South America: A Letter on Present State of That Country to James Monroe." Washington: Office of the National Register, October 15, 1817.

Bradford, William. *Of Plymouth Plantation, 1620–1647.* Edited by Samuel E. Morrison. New York: Random House, 1952.

Brimelow, Peter. *Alien Nation: Common Sense About America's Immigration Disaster.* New York: Random House, 1995.

Brown, Charles H. *Agent of Manifest Destiny: The Lives and Times of the Filibusters.* Chapel Hill: University of North Carolina Press, 1980.

Bush, Rod. *The New Black Vote: Politics and Power in Four American Cities.* San Francisco: Synthesis, 1984.

Cabeza de Vaca, Alvar Núñez. *Adventures in the Unknown Interior of America.* Translated and edited by Cyclone Convey. Albuquerque: University of New Mexico, 1990.

Calder, Bruce J. *The Impact of Intervention: The Dominican Republic During the U.S. Occupation of 1916–1924.* Austin: University of Texas Press, 1984.

Canales, Judge J. T. "Juan N. Cortina Presents His Motion for a New Trial." *Collected Papers of the Lower Rio Grande Valley Historical Society.* Vol. 1. Harlingen, Texas: 1949–1979.

Carr, Albert Z. *The World and William Walker.* New York: Harper & Row, 1963.

Carr, Norma. "The Puerto Ricans in Hawaii: 1900–1958." University of Michigan, doctoral dissertation, 1989.

Carr, Raymond. *Puerto Rico: A Colonial Experiment.* New York: Vintage Books, 1984.

Castañeda, Carlos. *The Mexican Side of the Texas Revolution*. Washington, D.C.: Documentary Publications, 1971.

———. *Our Heritage in Texas, 1519–1933*. Vol. 6. New York: Arno Press, 1976.

Castañeda, Jorge G. *The Mexican Shock: Its Meaning for the U.S.* New York: The New Press, 1995.

Castro Caycedo, Germán. *El Hueco: La entrada ilegal de colombianos a Estados Unidos por México, Bahamas y Haití*. Bogotá: Planeta Colombiana Editorial S.A., 1989.

Cavazo Garza, Israel. *Diccionario Biográfico de Nuevo León*. Tomo 1. Monterrey: Universidad Autónoma de Nuevo León, 1984.

Centro de Estudios Fronterizos y de Promoción de los Derechos Humanos. *La Industria Maquiladora en Reynosa y Matamoros*. Tamaulipas, Mexico, 1992.

Centro de Estudios Puertorriqueños. *Documents of the Puerto Rican Migration*. Research Foundation of the City University of New York, 1977.

———. *Extended Roots: From Hawaii to New York, Migraciones Puertorriqueñas*. New York: CUNY, 1988.

Chavez, John. *The Lost Land: The Chicano Image of the Southwest*. Albuquerque: University of New Mexico Press, 1984.

Chavez, Linda. *Out of the Barrio: Toward a New Politics of Hispanic Assimilation*. New York: Basic Books, 1991.

Chomsky, Aviva. *West Indian Workers and the United Fruit Company in Costa Rica, 1870–1940*. Baton Rouge: Louisiana State University Press, 1996.

Cloward, Richard A., and Frances Fox Piven. *Why Americans Don't Vote*. New York: Pantheon Books, 1988.

Cockcroft, James D. *Outlaws in the Promised Land: Mexican Immigrant Workers and America's Future*. New York: Grove Press, 1986.

Cohen, Felix. "Americanizing the White Man." *America Scholar* 21, no. 2 (1952).

Collier, Simon, Thomas E. Skidmore, and Harold Blakemore, eds. *The Cambridge Encyclopedia of Latin America*. New York: Cambridge University Press, 1992.

Colón, Jesús. *A Puerto Rican in New York and other Sketches*. New York: Mainstream Publishers, 1961.

Commager, Henry Steele. *The Empire of Reason: How Europe Imagined and America Realized the Enlightenment*. New York: Doubleday/Anchor, 1977.

———. *Documents of American History*. Vol.1: *To 1899*. Englewood Cliffs, N.J.: Prentice-Hall, 1988.

Conniff, Michael L. *Black Labor on a White Canal: Panama, 1904–1981*. Pittsburgh: University of Pittsburgh Press, 1985.

Corbett, Theodore G. "Migration to a Spanish Imperial Frontier in the Seventeenth and Eighteenth Centuries: St. Augustine." *Hispanic American Historical Review* 54, no. 3 (August 1974).

Cordero Guzmán, Héctor. "Some Contradictions of Dependent Development in Puerto Rico in the Context of Global Economy." Centro de Estudios Puertorriqueños, September 19, 1996.

Crawford, James. *Hold Your Tongue: Bilingualism and the Politics of "English Only."* Reading: Addison-Wesley Publishing Company, 1992.

Crow, John A. *The Epic of Latin America*. Berkeley: University of California Press, 1992.

Cruse, Harold. *Plural But Equal: Blacks and Minorities in America's Plural Society.* New York: William Morrow, 1987.

Davidson, Chandler. *Race and Class in Texas Politics.* Princeton: Princeton University Press, 1990.

Dávila Colón, Luis R. "The Blood Tax: The Puerto Rican Contribution to the United States War Effort." *Review of the Colegio de Abogados de Puerto Rico,* November 1979.

De la Garza, Rodolfo, Manuel Orozco, and Miguel Baraona. *The BiNational Impact of Latino Remittances."* Report of the Tomas Rivera Policy Institute. Claremont, Calif: March 1997.

De la Garza Treviño, Ciro. *Historia de Tamaulipas: Anales y Efemérides.* Mexico City: Princeton University Press, 1956.

De las Casas, Bartolomé. *A Short Account of the Destruction of the Indies.* London: Penguin Classics, 1992.

De León, Arnoldo. *Tejanos and the Numbers Game: A Socio-Historical Interpretation from the Federal Censuses, 1850–1900.* Albuquerque: University of New Mexico Press, 1989.

Deive, Carlos Esteban. *Las Emigraciones Dominicanas a Cuba (1795–1808).* Santo Domingo: Fundación Cultural Dominicana, 1989.

Del Valle, Manuel. "Developing a Language-Based National Origin Discrimination Modality." *Journal of Hispanic Policy* (1989–1990). John F. Kennedy School of Government, Harvard University.

Denevan, William M. *The Native Population of the Americas in 1492.* Madison: University of Wisconsin Press, 1992.

Díaz del Castillo, Bernal. *The Conquest of New Spain.* London: Penguin Books, 1963.

Díaz-Callejas, Apolinar. *Colombia–Estados Unidos: Entre La Autonomía y la Subordinación de la Independencia a Panamá.* Bogotá: Planeta Colombiana Editorial S.A., 1997.

Dietz, James L. *Economic History of Puerto Rico: Institutional Change and Capitalist Development.* Princeton: Princeton University Press, 1986.

Diez Castillo, Luis A. *El Canal de Panamá y Su Gente.* Panamá: L. A. Diez Castillo, 1990.

Drake, Paul W., ed. *Money Doctors, Foreign Debts, and Economic Reforms in Latin America from the 1890s to the Present.* Wilmington, Delaware: Scholarly Resources, 1994.

Duany, Jorge. *Los Dominicanos en Puerto Rico: Migración en la Semi-Periferia.* Río Piedras: Ediciones Huracán, 1990.

Durham, George. *Taming the Nueces Strip: The Story of McNelly's Rangers.* Austin: University of Texas Press, 1962.

Dwyer, Augusta. *On the Line: Life on the US-Mexican Border.* London: Latin American Bureau, 1994.

Eckes, Jr., Alfred E. *Opening America's Market: U.S. Foreign Trade Policy Since 1776.* Chapel Hill: University of North Carolina Press, 1995.

Eisenhower, John S. D. *So Far from God: The U.S. War with Mexico, 1846–1848.* New York: Doubleday, 1989.

Elliot, J. H. *The Old World and The New.* New York: Cambridge University Press, 1970.

Elton, Geoffrey. *The English.* Cambridge, Massachusetts: Blackwell Publishers, 1995.

Ericson Eblen, Jack. *The First and Second United States Empires: Governors and Territorial Government, 1784–1912.* Pittsburgh: University of Pittsburgh Press, 1968.

Esquenazi-Mayo, Roberto, ed. *El Padre Valera: Pensador, Sacerdote, Patriota.* Washington: Georgetown University Press, 1990.

Esteva-Fabregat, Claudio. *Mestizaje in Ibero-America.* Translated by John Wheat. Tucson: University of Arizona Press, 1995.

Fagen, Richard R., Richard A. Brody, and Thomas J. O'Leary. *Cubans in Exile: Disaffection and Revolution.* Palo Alto: Stanford University Press, 1968.

Falcon, Angelo. "Beyond La Macarena: The New City Latino Vote." *Hispanic Link Weekly Report* 25 (November 1996).

Fanon, Frantz. *The Wretched of the Earth.* New York: Grove Press, 1963.

Faulk, Odie B. *The Last Years of Spanish Texas, 1778–1821.* London: Mouton, 1964.

Fernández, Ronald. *The Disenchanted Island: Puerto Rico and the United States in the Twentieth Century.* New York: Praeger, 1992.

———. *Prisoner of Colonialism: The Struggle for Justice in Puerto Rico.* Monroe: Common Courage Press, 1994.

———. *Cruising the Caribbean: U.S. Influence and Intervention in the Twentieth Century.* Monroe: Common Courage Press, 1994.

Fernández Retamar, Roberto. *Caliban and Other Essays.* Translated by Edward Baker. Minneapolis: University of Minnesota Press, 1989.

Ferreras, Ramón Alberto. *Trujillo y sus Mujeres.* Santo Domingo: Editorial del Nordeste, 1982.

Figueroa, Loida. *Tres Puntos Claves: Lares, Idioma y Soberanía.* San Juan: Editorial Edil, 1972.

Fisher, John. *Commercial Relations Between Spain and Spanish America in the Era of Free Trade, 1778–1796.* Liverpool: Centre for Latin American Studies, University of Liverpool, 1985.

Fitzpatrick, Joseph P. *Puerto Rican Americans: The Meaning of the Migration to the Mainland.* Englewood Cliffs, N.J.: Prentice-Hall, 1987.

———. *The Stranger Is Our Own: Reflections on the Journey of Puerto Rican Migrants.* Kansas City: Sheed & Ward, 1996.

Folkman, David, Jr. *The Nicaragua Route.* Salt Lake City: University of Utah Press, 1972.

Foner, Laura, and Eugene D. Genovese, eds. *Slavery in the New World.* Englewood Cliffs, N.J.: Prentice-Hall, 1969.

Foner, Philip S. *The Spanish-Cuban-American War and the Birth of American Imperialism.* 2 vols. New York: Monthly Review Press, 1972.

———. *Labor and the American Revolution.* Westport, Conn.: Greenwood Press, 1976.

Free, Lloyd. "Attitudes of the Cuban People Toward the Castro Regime." Princeton: Institute for International Social Research, 1960.

Frost, Elsa Cecilia, et al. *Labor and Laborers Through Mexican History.* Tucson: University of Arizona Press, 1979.

Fuchs, Lawrence H. *Hawaii Pono: A Social History.* New York: Harcourt, Brace & World, 1996.

Galeano, Eduardo. *Open Veins of Latin America: Five Centuries of the Pillage of a Continent.* New York: Monthly Review Press, 1973.

García, Ignacio M. *United We Win: The Rise and Fall of La Raza Unida Party.* Tucson: Masrc, 1989.

García, María Cristina. *Havana USA: Cuban Exiles and Cuban Americans in South Florida, 1959–1994.* Berkeley: University of California Press, 1996.

García-Passalacqua, Juan Manuel. "The 1993 Plebiscite in Puerto Rico: A First Step to Decolonization." *Current History* 93, no. 581 (March 1994).

García-Passalacqua, Juan Manuel, and Carlos Rivera Lugo, eds. *Puerto Rico y los Estado Unidos: El Proceso de Consulta y Negociación de 1989 y 1990.* Vol. 2. Río Piedras: Editorial de la Universidad de Puerto Rico, 1991.

Gilbert, Alan. *The Latin American City.* London: Latin American Bureau, 1994.

Glasser, Ruth. *My Music Is My Flag: Puerto Rican Musicians and Their New York Communities, 1917–1940.* Berkeley: University of California Press, 1995.

Gleijeses, Piero. *Shattered Hope: The Guatemalan Revolution and the United States, 1944–1954.* Princeton, N.J.: Princeton University Press, 1991.

Goldfinch, Charles W. "Juan N. Cortina, 1824–1892: A Re-Appraisal." University of Chicago, master's thesis, 1949.

Goldstein, Richard. "The Big Mango." *New York,* August 7, 1972.

Gómez Quiñones, Juan. *Chicano Politics: Reality and Promise, 1940–1990.* Albuquerque: University of New Mexico Press, 1990.

González, Juan. "The Turbulent Progress of Puerto Ricans in Philadelphia." *Bulletin of the Center for Puerto Rican Studies* 2, no. 2 (Winter 1987–1988).

Gottfried, Robert S. *The Black Death.* New York: The Free Press, 1993.

Grant, Charles. *Democracy in the Connecticut Frontier Town of Kent.* New York: Columbia University Press, 1961.

Grant, Ulysses S. *Personal Memoirs of U.S. Grant.* Vol. 1. New York: Charles A. Webster & Co., 1885.

Grasmuck, Sherri, and Patricia R. Pessar. *Between Two Islands: Dominican International Migration.* Berkeley: University of California Press, 1991.

Gregory, Desmond. *Brute New World: The Rediscovery of Latin America in the Early Nineteenth Century.* London: British Academic Press, 1992.

Grimaldi, Victor. *El Diario Secreto de la Intervención Norteamericana de 1965.* Santo Domingo: Amigo del Hogar, 1989.

Guerra y Sánchez, Ramiro. *La Expansión Territorial de los Estados Unidos: A Expensas de España y de los Países Hispanoamericanos.* La Habana: Editorial del Consejo Nacional de Universidades, 1964.

Gugliotta, Guy, and Jeff Leen. *Kings of Cocaine.* New York: Harper Paperbacks, 1990.

Hagan, Jacqueline Maria. *Deciding to Be Legal: A Maya Community in Houston.* Philadelphia: Temple University Press, 1994.

Halperin-Donghi, Tulio. *The Contemporary History of Latin America.* Durham: Duke University Press, 1993.

Harris, William Warner. *Puerto Rico's Fighting 65th U.S. Infantry: From San Juan to Chorwan.* San Rafael: Presidio Press, 1980.

Hazen, Don. *Facts and Fictions About "Free Trade."* New York: Institute for Alternative Journalism, 1993.

Herman, Edward S., and Frank Brodhead. *Demonstration Elections: U.S.-Staged Elections in the Dominican Republic, Vietnam, and El Salvador.* Boston: South End Press, 1984.

Hermann, Hamlet. *Francis Caamaño.* Santo Domingo: Editorial Alfa y Omega, 1983.

Hernández, Ramona, Francisco Rivera-Batiz, and Roberto Agodini. "Dominican New Yorkers: A Socioeconomic Profile." *Dominican Research Monographs.* New York: CUNY Dominican Studies Institute, 1995.

Horsman, Reginald. *Race and Manifest Destiny: The Origins of American Racial Anglo-Saxonism.* Cambridge: Harvard University Press, 1981.

Human Rights Watch. *Mexico, No Guarantees: Sex Discrimination in Mexico's Maquiladora Sector.* New York, August 1996.

———. *War Without Quarter: Colombia and International Humanitarian Law.* New York, 1998.

Humboldt, Alexander von. *Political Essay on the Kingdom of New Spain.* Norman: University of Oklahoma Press, 1988.

Immerman, Richard H. *The CIA in Guatemala: The Foreign Policy of Intervention.* Austin: University of Texas Press, 1982.

Institute for Puerto Rican Policy. *The Puerto Rican and Latino Vote in the 1984 NYS Democratic Presidential Primary.* New York, April 5, 1984.

———. *Puerto Ricans and the 1988 Presidential Elections: Results from the National Puerto Rican Opinion Survey.* New York, November 7, 1988.

———. *The 1989 Mayoral Election and Charter Revision Vote in New York City: The Role of the Puerto Rican/Latino Voter.* New York, November, 1989.

———. *The Dinkins Administration and the Puerto Rican Community: Lessons From the Puerto Rican Experience with African-American Mayors in Chicago and Philadelphia.* New York: February 1990.

Inter-American Development Bank. *Annual Report 1986.* Washington, D.C., 1987.

———. *Annual Report 1994.* Washington, D.C., 1995.

———. *Annual Report 1996.* Washington, D.C., 1997.

Jefferson, Thomas. "Notes on the State of Virginia." Boston: H. Sprague, 1802.

Jennings, Francis. *The Invasion of America: Indians, Colonialism and the Cant of Conquest.* New York: W. W. Norton, 1976.

Jennings, James, and Monte Rivera. *Puerto Rican Politics in Urban America.* Westport, Conn.: Greenwood Press, 1984.

Johansen, Bruce E. *Forgotten Founders: How the American Indians Helped Shape Democracy.* Boston: Harvard Common Press, 1982.

Jones, Anson. *Memoranda and Official Correspondence Relating to the Republic of Texas, Its History and Annexation.* New York: Arno Press, 1973.

Josephy, Alvin, Jr. *The Indian Heritage of America.* Boston: Houghton Mifflin, 1991.

Kahn, Robert S. *Other People's Blood: U.S. Immigration Prisons in the Reagan Decade.* Boulder: Westview Press, 1996.

Kanellos, Nicolas. *A History of Hispanic Theater in the U.S.: Origins to 1940.* Austin: University of Texas Press, 1990.

Karns, Thomas. *Tropical Enterprise: The Standard Fruit and Steamship Company in Latin America.* Baton Rouge: Louisiana State University Press, 1978.

Kearney, Milo. *More Studies in Brownsville History.* Brownsville: Pan American University, 1989.

Kehoe, Alice B. *North American Indians: A Comprehensive Account.* Englewood Cliffs, N.J.: Prentice-Hall, 1992.

Keller, William F. *The Nation's Advocate: Henry Marie Brackenridge and Young America.* Pittsburgh: University of Pittsburgh, 1956.

Kelley, Pat. *River of Lost Dreams.* Lincoln: University of Nebraska Press, 1986.

Klein, Herbert S. *African Slavery in Latin America and the Caribbean.* Oxford, U.K.: Oxford University Press, 1986.

LaFeber, Walter. *Inevitable Revolutions: The United States in Central America.* New York: W. W. Norton, 1993.

———. *The Panama Canal: The Crisis in Historical Perspective.* New York: Oxford University Press, 1978.

Lamm, Richard D., and Gary Imhoff. *The Immigration Time Bomb: The Fragmenting of America.* New York: Truman Talley Books, 1985.

Lane, Wheaton J. *Commodore Vanderbilt: An Epic of the Steam Age.* New York: Alfred A. Knopf, 1942.

Langer, Erick, and Robert H. Jackson. *The New Latin American Mission in History.* Lincoln: University of Nebraska Press, 1995.

Langley, Lester D. *The United States and the Caribbean in the Twentieth Century.* Athens: University of Georgia Press, 1989.

———. *The Americas in the Age of Revolution, 1750–1850.* New Haven: Yale University Press, 1996.

Latorre Cabal, Hugo. *The Revolution of the Latin American Church.* Translated by Frances K. Hendricks and Beatrice Berler. Norman: University of Oklahoma Press, 1978.

León-Portilla, Miguel. *The Broken Spears: The Aztec Account of the Conquest of Mexico.* Boston: Beacon Press, 1992, n. 17, chap. 1.

Lewis, Oscar. *La Vida: A Puerto Rican Family in the Culture of Poverty, San Juan and New York.* New York: Random House, 1966.

Lewis, Sanford J. *Border Trouble: Rivers in Peril, A Report of Water Pollution Due to Industrial Development in Northern Mexico.* Boston: National Toxic Campgain Fund, 1991.

Lidin, Harold J. *History of the Puerto Rican Independence Movement.* Vol. 1: *19th Century.* Hato Rey: Master Typesetting of Puerto Rico, 1981.

Liebman, Lance, ed. *Ethnic Relations in America: Immigration, the Cities, Lingualism, Ethnic Politics, Group Rights.* Englewood Cliffs, N.J.: Prentice-Hall, 1982.

Lockward, Alfonso, Dr. *Documentos para la Historia de las Relaciones Dominico-Americanas.* Vol. 1: *1837–1860.* Santo Domingo: Editorial Corripio, 1987.

López, Alfredo. *The Puerto Rican Papers: Notes on the Re-Emergence of a Nation.* New York: Bobbs-Merrill, 1973.

Lungo Uclés, Mario. *El Salvador in the Eighties: Counterinsurgency and Revolution.* Philadelphia: Temple University Press, 1996.

Luque de Sánchez, Maria Dolores. *La Ocupación Norteamericana y la Ley Foraker: La Opinión Pública Puertorriqueña, 1898–1904.* Río Piedras: Editorial de la Universidad de Puerto Rico, 1986.

Lutz, Ellen L. *Human Rights in Mexico: A Policy of Impunity.* New York: America's Watch, June 1990.

Lynch, John, ed. *Latin American Revolutions, 1808–1826.* Norman: University of Oklahoma Press, 1994.

Mahler, Sarah J. *American Dreaming: Immigrant Life on the Margins.* Princeton: Princeton University Press, 1995.

Maldonado-Denis, Manuel. *The Emigration Dialectic: Puerto Rico and the USA.* New York: International Publisher, 1980.

Malavet Vega, Pedro. *La vellonera está directa: Felipe Rodríguez (La Voz) y los años '50.* Republica Dominicana: Editorial Corripio, 1984.

Marte, Roberto. *Cuba y La República Dominicana: Transición Económica en el Caribe del Siglo XIX.* Santo Domingo: Editorial CENAPEC, 1988.

Martin, John Bartlow. *Overtaken by Events: The Dominican Crisis from the Fall of Trujillo to the Civil War.* New York: Doubleday, 1966.

Martínez-Alier, Verena. *Marriage, Class and Colour in Nineteenth Century Cuba: A Study of Racial Attitudes and Sexual Values in a Slave Society.* Ann Arbor: University of Michigan Press, 1989.

Mataloni, Jr., Raymond J. "U.S. Multinational Companies: Operations in 1995." *Survey of Current Business,* October 1995.

McCullough, David. *The Path Between the Seas: The Creation of the Panama Canal, 1870–1914.* New York: Simon & Schuster, 1977.

McEwan, Bonnie G., ed. *The Spanish Missions of Florida.* Gainesville: University Press of Florida, 1993.

McFeely, William S. *Grant, a Biography.* New York: W. W. Norton, 1981.

McWilliams, Carey. *North from Mexico: The Spanish-Speaking People of the United States.* Edition updated by Matt S. Meier. New York: Praeger, 1990.

Meléndez, Edwin, and Edgardo Meléndez, eds. *Colonial Dilemma: Critical Perspectives on Contemporary Puerto Rico.* Boston: South End Press, 1993.

Merk, Frederick. *Slavery and the Annexation of Texas.* New York: Alfred A. Knopf, 1972.

Meyer, Gerald. *Vito Marcantonio: Radical Politician, 1902–1954.* Albany: State University of New York, 1989.

Minge, Ward Alan. *Acoma: Pueblo in the Sky.* Albuquerque: University of New Mexico Press, 1991.

Montejano, David. *Anglos and Mexicans in the Making of Texas, 1836–1986.* Austin: University of Texas Press, 1987.

Moody, Kim. *Workers in a Lean World: Unions in the International Economy.* New York: Verso, 1997.

Morales Carrión, Arturo. *Puerto Rico: A Political and Cultural History.* New York: W. W. Norton, 1983.

Mormino, Gary R., and George E. Pozzetta. *The Immigrant World of Ybor City: Italians and Their Latin Neighbors in Tampa, 1885–1985.* Urbana: University of Illinois Press, 1987.

Morrison, Toni. "On the Backs of Blacks." *Time* 142, no. 21 (Fall 1993).

Moya Pons, Frank. *The Dominican Republic: A National History.* New York: Hispaniola Books, 1995.

Munro, Dana. *Intervention and Dollar Diplomacy in the Caribbean, 1900–1921.* Princeton: Princeton University Press, 1964.

Myers, Gustavus. *History of the Great American Fortunes.* Vol. 2. Chicago: C. H. Kerr, 1910.

NAFTA. *Broken Promises: The Border Betrayed*. Washington D.C.: Public Citizen Publications, 1996.

National Association of Latino Elected Officials. *1994 National Roster of Hispanic Elected Officials*. Los Angeles, 1995.

———. *1996 Latino Election Handbook*. Los Angeles, 1996.

National Labor Committee Education Fund. *Paying to Lose Our Jobs*. New York, September 1992.

———. *Free Trade's Hidden Secrets: Why We Are Losing Our Shirts*. New York, November 1993.

Neal, Larry. *The Rise of Financial Capitalism: International Capital Markets in the Age of Reason*. Cambridge: Cambridge University Press, 1990.

Nearing, Scott, and Joseph Freeman. *Dollar Diplomacy: A Study in American Imperialism*. New York: B. W. Huebsch, 1925.

Nelson Limerick, Patricia. *The Legacy of Conquest: The Unbroken Past of the American West*. New York: W. W. Norton, 1987.

Nerval, Gaston. *Autopsy of the Monroe Doctrine*. New York: Macmillan, 1934.

Novak, Michael. *The Rise of the Unmeltable Ethnics: Politics and Culture in the Seventies*. New York: Macmillan, 1972.

Ortega Frier, José. *Memorandum Relativo a la Intervención de Sumner en la República Dominicana*. Santo Domingo: Ediciones de Taller, 1975.

Ortego y Gasca, Phillip, and Arnoldo De León, eds. *The Tejano Yearbook: 1519–1978: A Selective Chronicle of the Hispanic Presence in Texas*. San Antonio: Caravel Press, 1978.

Ortiz Angleró, David. *Testimony Before the Co-Coordinators of the Interagency Working Group on Puerto Rico on the Future of Puerto Rico*. Washington, D.C.: Cambio XXI, 1995.

Pantojas-García, Emilio. *Development Strategies as Ideology: Puerto Rico's Export-Led Industrialization Experience*. London: Lynne Rienner Publishers, 1990.

Parker Hanson, Earl. *Puerto Rico: Land of Wonders*. New York: Alfred A. Knopf, 1960.

Passel, Jeffrey S., and Rebecca L. Clark. *Immigrants in New York: Their Legal Status, Incomes, and Taxes, Executive Summary*. Washington: Urban Institute, April 1998.

Pedraza Bailey, Silvia. "Cubans and Mexicans in the United States: The Functions of Political and Economic Migration." *Cuban Studies* 11. Pittsburgh: University of Pittsburgh Press, 1981.

Peña, Manuel H. *The Texas-Mexican Conjunto: History of a Working Class Music*. Austin: University of Texas Press, 1985.

Pérez, Louis A. *Cuba Under the Platt Amendment, 1902–1934*. Pittsburgh: University of Pittsburgh Press, 1986.

———. *Cuba and the United States: Ties of Singular Intimacy*. Athens: University of Georgia Press, 1990.

———. *Cuba Between Reform and Revolution*. New York: Oxford University Press, 1995.

Pérez, Richie. "From Assimilation to Annihilation: Puerto Rican Images in U.S. Films." *Center for Puerto Rican Studies Bulletin* 2, no. 8 (Spring, 1990).

Perry, Nancy J. "What's Powering Mexico's Success." *Fortune,* February 10, 1992.

Petras, James, and Morris Morley. *Latin America in the Time of Cholera: Electoral Politics, Market Economics, and Permanent Crisis.* New York: Routledge, 1992.

Plant, Roger. *Sugar and Modern Slavery: A Tale of Two Countries.* London: Zed Books, 1987.

Portes, Alejandro. "The Rise of Ethnicity: Determinants of Ethnic Perceptions Among Cuban Exiles in Miami."*American Sociological Review* 49, no. 3 (June 1984).

Portes, Alejandro, and Alex Stepick. *City on the Edge: The Transformation of Miami.* Berkeley: University of California Press, 1993.

Portes, Alejandro, Juan M. Clark, and Manuel M. López. "Six Years Later, the Process of Incorporation of Cuban Exiles in the United States: 1973–1979." *Cuban Studies,* July 1981–January 1982.

Portes, Alejandro, and Rubén G. Rumbaut. *Immigrant America: A Portrait.* Berkeley: University of California Press, 1996.

Pratt, Julius W. *Expansionists of 1898: The Acquisition of Hawaii and the Spanish Islands.* Chicago: Quadrangle Paperbacks, 1964.

Price Waterhouse. *Update of Baseline Study of Honduran Export Processing Zones.* Report to United States Agency for International Development. Washington, D.C., 1993.

Puerto Rico Planning Board. *Economic Report to the Governor 1995.* San Juan, March 1996.

Quintanilla, Luis. *A Latin American Speaks.* New York: Macmillan, 1943.

Rama, Carlos M. *La Idea de la Federación Antillana en los Independentistas Puertorriqueños del Siglo XIX.* Río Piedras: Librería Internacional, 1971.

Rayburn, John C., and Virginia Kemp Rayburn. *Century of Conflict, 1821–1913: Incidents in the Lives of Willian Neale and William A. Neale, Early Settlers in South Texas.* Waco: Texian Press, 1966.

Research Institute for Cuba and the Caribbean Center for Advanced International Studies. "The Cuban Immigration 1959–1966 and Its Impact on Miami–Dade County, Florida." University of Miami, July 10, 1967.

Reyes, Belinda I. "Dynamics of Immigration: Return Migration to Western Mexico." Public Policy Institute of California, January 28, 1997.

Ríos, Palmira N. "Acercamiento al Conflicto Dominico-Boricua." *Center for Puerto Rican Studies Bulletin* 4 no. 2 (Spring 1992).

Rivera, Eugene. "The Puerto Rican Colony of Lorain, Ohio." *Center for Puerto Rican Studies Bulletin* 2, no.1 (Spring 1987).

Rivero, Angel. *Crónica de la Guerra Hispano Americana en Puerto Rico.* New York: Plus Ultra Educational Publishers, 1973.

Rivlin, Gary. *Fire on the Prairie: Chicago's Harold Washington and the Politics of Race.* New York: Henry Holt, 1992.

Roa, Jorge. *Los Estados Unidos y Europa en Hispano America: Interpretación Política y Económica de la Doctrina Monroe, 1823–1933.* Havana: Carasa, 1933.

Roberts, John Storm. *The Latin Tinge: The Impact of Latin American Music on the United States.* New York: Oxford University Press, 1999.

Roddick, Jackie. *The Dance of Millions: Latin America and the Debt Crisis.* London: Latin America Research Bureau, 1988.

Rodríguez, Clara. *Puerto Ricans Born in the U.S.A.* Boston: Unwin Hyman, 1989.

————. *Latin Looks: Images of Latinas and Latinos in the U.S. Media.* Boulder: Westview Press, 1997.

Rodríguez, Clara, and Héctor Cordero-Guzmán. "Placing Race in Context." *Ethnic and Racial Studies* 15, no. 4 (October 1992).

Rodríguez Demorizi, Emilio. *Luperón y Hostos.* Santo Domingo: Editorial Taller, 1975.

Rodríguez, Richard. *Hunger of Memory: The Education of Richard Rodriguez.* Toronto: Bantam Books, 1982.

Rogin, Michael Paul. *Fathers and Children: Andrew Jackson and the Subjugation of the American Indian.* New York: Alfred A. Knopf, 1975.

Rohrbough, Malcolm. *The Land Office Business: The Settlement and Administration of American Public Lands, 1789–1837.* New York: Oxford University Press, 1968.

Rosen, Fred, and Deidre McFadyen, eds. *Free Trade and Economic Restructuring in Latin America.* New York: Monthly Review Press, 1995.

Rubin, Nancy. *Isabella of Castile: The First Renaissance Queen.* New York: St. Martin's Press, 1991.

Ruiz, Angel L., and Fernando Zalacain. "The Economic Relation of the United States and the Puerto Rican Economies: An International Input-Output Approach." *Boletín de Economía* 3, no. 1. Unidad de Investigaciones Económicas: Universidad de Puerto Rico.

Said, Edward W. *Culture and Imperialism.* New York: Alfred A. Knopf, 1993.

Salazaar, Alonso. *Born to Die in Medellín.* New York: Monthly Review Press, 1990.

Saldivar, Gabriel. *Historia Compendida de Tamaulipas.* Mexico: Academia Nacional de Historia y Geografía, 1945.

Sanchez Korrol, Virginia. *From Colonia to Community: The History of Puerto Ricans in New York City, 1917–1948.* Westport, Conn.: Greenwood Press, 1983.

Santiago Ortíz, Nicolás. *Korea 1951, La Guerra Olvidada: El Orgullo de Haber Sobrevivido.* Río Piedras: Emaco Printers, 1991.

Scheips, Paul, ed. *The Panama Canal: Readings on Its History.* Wilmington, Del.: Michael Glazier, 1979.

Schlesinger, Arthur M. *The Disuniting of America: Reflections on a Multicultural Society.* New York: W. W. Norton, 1992.

Schlesinger, Stephen, and Stephen Kinzer. *Bitter Fruit: The Untold Story of the American Coup in Guatemala.* New York: Doubleday, 1983.

Scott, Florence Johnson. *Historical Heritage of Lower Rio Grande.* San Antonio: Naylor, 1937.

————. *Royal Land Grants North of the Rio Grande, 1777–1821.* Rio Grande City, Tex.: La Retana Press, 1969.

Scott, Peter Dale, and Jonathan Marshall. *Cocaine Politics: Drugs, Armies, and the CIA in Central America.* Berkeley: University of California Press, 1991.

Seguín, Juan N. *A Revolution Remembered: The Memoirs and Selected Correspondence of Juan N. Seguín.* Edited by Jesús De la Teja. Austin: State House Press, 1991.

Seijo Bruno, Mini. *La Insurrección Nacionalista en Puerto Rico, 1950.* Río Piedras: Editorial Edil, 1989.

Selser, Gregorio. *Sandino: General of the Free.* New York: Monthly Review Press, 1981.

————. *Cronología de las intervenciones extranjeras en América Latina.* Vol. 2, *1776–1848.* Mexico City: UNAM, 1994.

Smith, Adam. *The Wealth of Nations (1776)*. Vol. 2. Edited by Edwin Cannan. London: University Paperbacks, 1996.

Smith, Carol, ed. *Guatemalan Indians and the State: 1540–1988*. Austin: University of Texas Press, 1992.

Stack, John F., and Christopher L. Warren. "Ethnicity and the Politics of Symbolism in Miami's Cuban Community." *Cuban Studies* 20. Pittsburgh: University of Pittsburgh Press, 1990.

Stallings, Barbara. *Banker to the Third World: U.S. Portfolio Investment in Latin America, 1900–1986*. Berkeley: University of California Press, 1987.

Stillman, Chauncey Devereux. *Charles Stillman, 1810–1875*. New York: C. D. Stillman, 1956.

Stockwell, John. *In Search of Enemies: A CIA Story*. New York: W. W. Norton, 1978.

Suro, Roberto. *Strangers Among Us: How Latino Immigration Is Transforming America*. New York: Alfred A. Knopf, 1998.

Tansil, Charles C. *The United States and Santo Domingo, 1798–1873: A Chapter on Caribbean Diplomacy*. Baltimore: Johns Hopkins University Press, 1983.

Teitelbaum, Michael. "Right Versus Right: Immigration and Refugee Policy in the United States." *Foreign Affairs* 59, no. 1 (Fall 1980).

Teitelbaum, Michael S., and Myron Weiner, eds. *Threatened Peoples, Threatened Borders: World Migration and U.S. Policy*. New York: W. W. Norton, 1995.

Texas Department of Health. "An Investigation of Neural Tube Defects in Cameron County, Texas," July 1, 1992.

Thomas, Hugh. *Conquest: Montezuma, Cortés, and the Fall of the Old Mexico*. New York: Simon & Schuster, 1993.

Torruella, Juan R. *The Supreme Court and Puerto Rico: The Doctrine of Separate and Equal*. Río Piedras: Editorial de la Universidad de Puerto Rico, 1988.

Trías Monge, José. *Puerto Rico: The Trials of the Oldest Colony in the World*. New Haven: Yale University Press, 1998.

Turner, John Kenneth. *Barbarous Mexico*. Chicago: C. H. Kerr, 1910.

Tzvetan, Todorov. *The Conquest of America*. New York: HarperCollins, 1984.

United Nations Conference on Trade and Development. *TNC's and World Development*. London, 1996.

United Nations Development Programme. *Human Development Report 1998*. New York: Oxford University Press, 1998.

U.S. Census Bureau. *Hispanic Americans Today: Current Population Reports, P23-183*. Washington, D.C.: U.S. Government Printing Office, 1993.

U.S. Census Bureau. *Statistical Abstract of the United States: 1997*. Washington, D.C.: U.S. Government Printing Office, 1997.

U.S. Congressional Budget Office. "Potential Economic Impacts of Changes in Puerto Rico Status Under S. 712." April 1990.

U.S. Department of Justice. *1996 Statistical Yearbook of the Immigration and Naturalization Service,*. Washington, D.C.: U.S. Government Printing Office, 1997.

U.S. General Accounting Office. *Pharmaceutical Industry Tax Benefits of Operating in Puerto Rico*. Washington, D.C.: May 1992.

———. *Tax Policy: Puerto Rico and the Section 936 Tax Credit*. Washington, D.C.: June 1993.

United States Hispanic Leadership Institute. *Latino Electoral Potential 2000–2025, Report No. 312*. Chicago, 1998.

Valle Ferrer, Norma. *Luisa Capetillo: Historia de una Mujer Proscrita.* San Juan: Editorial Cultura, 1990.

Van Alstyne, R. W. *The Rising American Empire.* Chicago: Quadrangle Books, 1965.

Vargas, Zaragosa. *Proletarians of the North: A History of Mexican Industrial Workers in Detroit and Midwest, 1917–1933.* Berkeley: University of California Press, 1993.

Vega, Bernardo. *Control y Represión en la Dictadora Trujillista.* Santo Domingo: Fundación Cultural Dominicana, 1986.

———. *Trujillo y el Control Financiereo Norteamericano.* Santo Domingo: Fundación Cultural Dominicana, 1990.

Villagrá, Gaspar Pérez de. *Historia de la Nueva México, 1610.* Translated and edited by Miguel Encinias, Alfred Rodríguez, and Joseph P. Sánchez. Albuquerque: University of New Mexico Press, 1992.

Wagenheim, Kal, and Olga Jiménez de Wagenheim. *The Puerto Ricans: A Documentary History.* Maplewood, N.J.: Waterfront Press, 1998.

Weatherford, Jack. *Indian Givers: How the Indians of the Americas Transformed the World.* New York: Fawcett Columbine, 1988.

Weber, David J. *The Mexican Frontier, 1821–1846: The American Southwest Under Mexico.* Albuquerque: University of New Mexico Press, 1982.

———. *The Spanish Frontier in North America.* New Haven: Yale University Press, 1992.

Welles, Sumner. *The Time for Decision.* New York: Harper, 1944.

Weyr, Thomas. *Hispanic U.S.A.: Breaking the Melting Pot.* New York: Harper & Row, 1988.

Whitaker, Arthur Preston. *The Spanish-American Frontier: 1783–1795.* Lincoln: University of Nebraska Press, 1927.

Wilkins, Mira. *The Emergence of Multinational Enterprise: American Business Abroad from the Colonial Era to 1914.* Cambridge, Mass.: Harvard University Press, 1970.

Wilkinson, J. B. *Laredo and the Rio Bravo Frontier.* Austin, Tex.: Jenkins Publishing Company, 1975.

Williams, Eric. *From Columbus to Castro: The History of the Caribbean, 1492–1969.* New York: Vintage Books, 1984.

Williams, John Hoyt. *Sam Houston: A Biography of the Father of Texas.* New York: Simon & Schuster, 1993.

Wilson, Samuel. *Hispaniola: Caribbean Chiefdoms in the Age of Columbus.* Alabama: University of Alabama Press, 1990.

Wissler, Clark. *Indians of the United States: Four Centuries of Their History and Culture.* New York: Doubleday Doran, 1940.

Wittke, Carl. *Refugees of Revolution: The German Forty-eighters in America.* Philadelphia: University of Pennsylvania Press, 1952.

Wood, Conan T. "Cerralvo as the Mother City of the Lower Rio Bravo Valley." *Selected documents of the Lower Rio Grande Historical Society: 1949–1979.* Vol. 1. Harlingen, Tex., 1980.

Zeitlin, Maurice. "Economic Insecurity and Political Attitudes of Cuban Workers." *American Sociological Review* 31 (February 1996).

Zorrilla, Luis G. *Historia de las Relaciones entre Mexico y los Estados Unidos de América 1800–1958.* Mexico: Editorial Porrua, 1995.

# Interviews

The list below represents a small portion of the hundreds of interviews I have conducted in the United States, Mexico, Central America, and the Caribbean during the past decade that touched on the subject of this book.

William Acosta, New York City police officer, March, May, December 1992; November 1995.
Victor Alfaro Clark, attorney, Tijuana, Mexico, May 1992.
Beatrice Beaumont, Puerto Cortés, Honduras, March 1990.
Lalyce Beaumont, Puerto Cortés, Honduras, January 8, 1995.
Aquilino Boyd, Panama City, Panama, December 1989.
Rev. Greg Boyle, Los Angeles, April 1992.
Othal Brand, mayor of McAllen, Texas, June 1995.
Sila Calderón, mayor of San Juan, Puerto Rico, March 1999.
Rafael Callejas, president of Honduras, San Pedro Sula, Honduras, April 1990.
Gerónimo Campo Seco, former leader, Atanasio Tzul, August 1998.
Eduardo Canales, Canales family descendant, San Antonio, Texas, January 20, 1992.
Gil Cedillo, Los Angeles labor leader, April 1993.
Rafael Chinea, Korean War veteran, Guaynabo, Puerto Rico, August 22, 1992.
Daniel Dacreas, Panamanian pioneer, Brooklyn, New York, February 19, 1993.
Erna Dacreas, Brooklyn, New York, February 6, 1995.
Manuel de Dios Unanue, member of the Committee of Seventy-Five, New York City, May 1990.
Luis Del Rosario, Cuban refugee, Miami, Florida, August 1994, May 1996.
Dorca Noemi Díaz, Honduran *maquila* worker, June 1994.
Carlos Julio Gaitan, consul of Colombia, November 1992.
José and Henrietta García, son killed in Los Angeles riot, April 1992.
Diane Garza, school administrator, Brownsville, Texas, January 19, 1992.
Imelda Garza, Canales family descendant, Kingsville, Texas, April 28, 1992.
Paula Gómez, Brownsville Community Health Center, Texas, June 1993.

Agapito González, Jr., labor leader, Matamoros, Mexico, June 1993.
Antonio González, Southwest Voter Registration and Education Project, San Antonio, Texas, May 11, 1992.
Domingo González, Coalition for Justice for the Maquiladora Workers, Brownsville, Texas, May 1992, June 1995.
Mario González, Kobler Center, Chicago, Illinois, August 1998.
Sergio González, González family, Cayey, Puerto Rico, August 14, 1992.
Eva Guadrón, Potrerillos, Honduras, April 1990.
Juan Guerra, district attorney, Raymondville, Texas, June 1995.
Ana Sol Gutiérrez, Montgomery County School Board member, August 18, 1998.
Juan Gutiérrez, Matamoros, Mexico, June 1993.
Jorge Hinojosa, U.S.–Mexico Border Program, American Friends Service Committee, San Diego, California, May 1992.
Carlos Ixuuiac, Guatemalan Support Center of Los Angeles, August 20, 1998.
Mayra Jiménez, *maquila* worker, San Pedro de Macorís, Dominican Republic, August 1991.
Benito Juárez, Guatemalan Support Network, Houston, Texas, August 1998.
Rafael Lantigua, Dominican pioneer, New York City, May 1994.
Guillermo Linares, New York City councilman, April 1996.
Rev. Héctor López Sierra, Santurce, Puerto Rico, August 28, 1992.
Jorge Giovanni López, San Pedro Sula, Honduras, April 1990.
Ana María Luciano, Luciano family, May 29, 1992.
Carlos Malagón, Colombian pioneer, Queens, New York, January 27, 1995.
Monica Manderson, Panamanian pioneer, Brooklyn, New York, January 21, 1995.
Roberto Martínez, U.S.–Mexico Border Program, American Friends Service Committee, San Diego, California, May 1992.
Patricia Maza-Pittsford, consul of Honduras, New York City, September 8, 1997.
Ana Meléndez and Charlie Meléndez, June 1993.
Héctor Méndez, Colombian pioneer, Queens, New York, January 20, 1995.
Luis Mojica, Federation of Provincial Workers of San Pedro de Macorís, San Pedro, Dominican Republic, August 1991.
Claudia Leticia Molina, Honduran *maquila* worker, New York City, July 1995.
Santos Molina, Canales family descendant, Brownsville, Texas, May 9, 1992.
Eugenio Morales, New York City, June 1992.
Pura Morrone, González family descendant, Bronx, New York, August 11, 1992.
Cecelia Muñoz, National Council of La Raza, Washington, D.C., July 1997.
Edward James Olmos, actor, Los Angeles, April 1993.
Eddie Palmieri, musician, New York City, May 12, 1990.
Mario Paredes, Catholic Archdiocese of New York, December 1997.
José Francisco Peña Gómez, Dominican Republic, September 2, 1992.
Tito Puente, musician, March 1998.
Graciela Ramos, González family descendant, New York City, August 8, 1992.
Dr. Arnulfo Reyes, victim of Trujillo dictatorship, Dominican Republic, September 5, 1992.
Silvestre Reyes, Border Patrol chief, McAllen Sector, June 1995.
Palmira Ríos, New York City, June 1994.
Heraclio "Pancho" Rivera, Santo Domingo, Dominican Republic, September 4, 1992.

Matias Rodríguez, Sixty-fifth Infantry veteran, Puerto Rico, August 20, 1992.

Carlos Romero Barceló, resident commissioner of Puerto Rico, March 1996.

Israel Roque Borrero, political dissident, Cojimar, Cuba, September 1994.

Albor Ruiz, member of Committee of Seventy-five, January 1998.

Alfonso Ruiz Fernández, director, Quimica Flour factory in *maquiladora* zone of Matamoros, Mexico, June 1991.

Emilio Ruiz, editor of *La Tribuna,* Long Island, New York, July 26, 1998.

Emilio Sagardía, Sixty-fifth Infantry veteran, Puerto Rico, August 20, 1992.

Fiacro Salazaar, San Antonio, Texas, Canales family descendant, January 20, 1992.

Angela Sambrano, CARECEN, Los Angeles, August 1998.

Gil Sánchez, labor leader, Los Angeles, October 1991.

David Sandoval, educator, Los Angeles, April 1992, June 1995.

Amparo Sención, Luciano family member, Dominican Republic, September 3, 1992.

Tony Sención, Luciano family member, Dominican Republic, September 2, 1992.

José Serrano, U.S. House of Representatives from New York City.

Harley Shaiken, professor of education, University of California, Berkeley.

Ignacio Soto, labor leader, Dominican Republic, August 1991.

Carlos Spector, immigration attorney, El Paso, Texas, May 1992.

Sandra Spector Garza, Canales family descendant, El Paso, Texas, May 6, 1992, June 1995.

Julio Sterling, legislator, Dominican Republic, September 5, 1992.

Esteban Torres, U.S. representative from Los Angeles, November 1996.

Beatrice Uribe, Queens, New York, February 4, 6, 1995.

Gloria Uribe, Queens, New York, August 1992.

Virtudes Uribe, Dominican Republic, August 1991.

Carlos Vaquerano, Los Angeles, August 1998.

Estela Vázquez, Luciano family descendant, New York City, April 10, April 18, August 7, October 24, 1992.

Mary Velásquez, mother of Willie Velásquez, San Antonio, Texas, May 12, 1992.

Nydia Velázquez, U.S. Representative from New York City.

Vicente White, New York City, February 10, 1993, December 29, 1994, April 16, 1994, January 15, 1995.

Judith Yanira, Salvadoran *maquila* worker, New York City, July 1995.

Pedro Zamón Rodríguez, Cuban refugee, Key West, Florida, August 1994.

# Index